The Great
Rapprochement

By Bradford Perkins

*The Great Rapprochement: England and the United
States, 1895–1914*   (1968)
*Castlereagh and Adams: England and the United States,
1812–1823*   (1964)
*The Causes of the War of 1812: National Honor or
National Interest? (editor)*   (1962)
*Prologue to War: England and the United States,
1805–1812*   (1961)
*Youthful America: Selections from Henry Unwin Addington's
Residence in the United States of America (editor)*   (1960)
*The First Rapprochement: England and the United
States, 1795–1805*   (1955)

BRADFORD PERKINS

The Great Rapprochement

England and the United States, 1895-1914

NEW YORK

ATHENEUM

1968

FOR

Deck, Matt, and Martha

The character of the present American is not one to be lightly lost from the world. His worst fault is that he dislikes us. But that—though it sound a paradox—is because he respects us. Entirely free from personal self-consciousness, the Americans are nationally most self-conscious; they resent the existence of a nation they are bound to respect. But that will go with time. Meanwhile the American may make his mind easy about his country. It is a credit to him, and he is a credit to it. You may differ from him, you may laugh at him; but neither of these is the predominant emotion he inspires. Even while you differ or laugh, he is essentially the man with whom you are always wanting to shake hands.

George W. Steevens, THE LAND OF THE DOLLAR (1897)

Preface

This book describes Anglo-American relations in the two decades before World War I. Much of this story, particularly for the early years, has been told before, as the bibliographical note at the end of this volume shows. Building on the work of able scholars who have preceded me and extending the coverage to 1914, I have sought to give a rounded treatment of the great transformation—particularly the shift in American sentiment which was to be so important after Europe went to war—and to explain whence it came. The years of settlement prior to 1903 and the years of consolidation thereafter really are parts of the same whole, although the first is of course essential to the second, and neither part fully makes sense without some understanding of the other. Together they comprise one of the most important revolutions in the drama of American diplomacy.

The main themes of this book were presented as the Commonwealth Fund Lectures in American History for 1965, and I am deeply indebted to Vice-Chancellor Sir Ifor Jennings and Professor H. C. Allen of University College, London, for the opportunity to give those lectures. I am also very grateful to the members of the colloquium which accompanied them, particularly to Alexander E. Campbell and John A. S. Grenville, for their comment and friendly criticism.

Grants from the Horace H. Rackham School of Graduate Studies speeded the completion of this book by making it possible for me to engage the services of Daniel Brown and Thomas

Maddux, two young scholars whose assistance in research was invaluable, and Dorothy Foster, who typed the manuscript with the efficiency and aplomb members of my department have come to expect.

I also owe thanks to colleagues at the University of Michigan. Albert Feuerwerker, who read Chapter IX, and Sidney Fine and John Higham, who reviewed the entire manuscript, suggested many important improvements. Above all, my wife and my father, who have lived with this project since its inception, are responsible for whatever merits this volume may have, since they provided in marvelous balance a combination of encouragement, criticism, and stimulus.

Bradford Perkins

ANN ARBOR, MICHIGAN

Contents

The Great
Rapprochement

CHAPTER ONE

Themes

FOUR GERMAN ARMIES swept across the Belgian frontier on
August 3, 1914. The next afternoon George V left Buckingham Palace to address Parliament. As everyone knew, his ministers had decided on war after, as most suspected, hard examination of their Liberal consciences. Along the King's route, crowds
lined the streets, cheering and waving in happy ignorance of
what the war would cost in British blood and ultimately in British power. As the royal carriage passed the Carlton Hotel, a
group of American tourists on the steps joined in the applause. A
booming Yankee voice cut through the noise of the crowd:
"New York is with you!" [1] Bowing, smiling, George V acknowledged this salute to England.

A noisy tourist speaks only for himself. And New York is
not South Boston or Milwaukee. Very few Americans really
wished to be "with" England in the great war then commencing,
if this meant joining the struggle on the plains of Flanders and
the approaches to Paris. Public-opinion polls did not then exist
to influence the executive and aid the historian, but the *Literary
Digest's* poll of newspaper editors provides a rough substitute.
Three months after the war began—and, the *Digest* reported,
after an increase in pro-German sentiment—the magazine asked
367 editors to assess public feeling in their areas. One hundred
and eighty-nine, a clear majority, reported sentiment favoring the
Allies, 140 found opinion neutral or divided, and only thirty-

[1] Walter Millis, *The Road to War, 1914–1917* (Cambridge, 1935), p. 45.

eight believed that local opinion favored Germany. (The editors themselves professed greater neutrality.) The *Digest* noted that sentiment varied from section to section, that in large cities heavily populated by immigrants and persons of foreign descent it was very mixed, and above all that "the sympathy on either side is that of the distant observer. No belligerency is evident anywhere." [2] Clinging to an isolationist tradition, aware that war guilt was not the simple thing that Article 235 of the Treaty of Versailles later pronounced it, hopeful that their country would not be drawn into the vortex, most Americans nevertheless hoped the Allies would hold off their enemies.

An Englishman who had lived for some years in the United States alleged in 1914 that until recently the average American had quite contrary feelings toward England: "He saw her hand in nearly every disaster, domestic and foreign; he suspected her interference in every election that ran counter to his wishes; . . . and he rejoiced over her misfortunes, crowed over her mistakes, and thanked God he was not an Englishman." [3] Jeffersonians, Jacksonians, expansionists of the 'forties and 'fifties—all had appealed to this sentiment. Since the Civil War, Anglophobia had declined, but it was still a far from negligible force. Republicans made effective use of an indiscretion by the British minister in Washington, Sir Lionel Sackville-West, who endorsed the candidacy of the Democrat, Grover Cleveland, in 1888 and by doing so helped cost him reelection. When the Democrats sought to turn the cards eight years later, charging the Republicans with friendship with England, their opponents commissioned a pamphlet entitled "How McKinley is Hated in England." The tactic made sense.

Despite placid and even friendly periods, generation after generation had learned to look upon England as an enemy. John Adams and his contemporaries absorbed this lesson from events surrounding the American Revolution. John Quincy Adams and

---

[2] *Literary Digest* (New York), vol. XLIX (1914), p. 939.
[3] Frederick C. DeSumichrast, *Americans and Britons* (New York, 1914), p. 277.

his generation learned it in the early years of the nineteenth century. John Quincy's grandson merely conformed to a pattern when he wrote, recalling his experiences in London during the Civil War, "It was the hostility of the middle-class"—Henry Adams simply assumed aristocratic hostility—"which broke our hearts, and turned me into a life-long enemy of everything British." [4] Squabbling over control of a still-to-be-built isthmian canal, resumption of the ancient dispute over fishing rights off the coasts of British North America and a quarrel over the Pacific seal fishery followed, but after the treaty of Washington settled issues arising from the Civil War in 1871 no confrontations as serious as those of the past troubled the two countries. A brief storm in 1895, provoked by a Democratic President and joined by Adams and his Republican friends Henry Cabot Lodge and Theodore Roosevelt, showed that the old spirit still lived. The Republican pamphlet the next year understandably appealed to it.

Between that time and 1914 the almost instinctive American dislike of England lost much of its force, a generally favorable inclination developing to replace it. This change had roots in the past and severe limits even in 1914. American hostility toward Britain had become more ritualistic and less a reflection of actual tensions than in the days of Lord North, the *Chesapeake*, Oregon, or the *Trent* affair, although very few Americans had thought their way through to this conclusion before the difficulty of 1895 forced them to assess their position.

Once, while traveling in America, Rudyard Kipling attended a banquet in San Francisco. The principal entertainment was a patriotic address, most notable for its denunciations of England, "our natural enemy." With more than his usual philosophy and less than his usual spleen, the Englishman noted that his country was the only one "for the American public speaker to trample upon. France has Germany; we have Russia; for Italy, Austria is provided; and the humblest Pathan possesses an ancestral enemy. Only America stands out of the racket; and

---

[4] Adams to Charles Francis Adams, February 21, 1896, Worthington C. Ford, ed., *Letters of Henry Adams, 1892–1918* (Boston, 1938), p. 102.

therefore, to be in fashion, makes a sand-bag of the mother-country, and bangs her when occasion requires." [5] No challenger stepping forward to displace England, she occupied a place of dishonor in American thoughts long after the last serious quarrels.

Yet, as Cushing Strout has observed, "The role of England in American demonology has been a special one. As America's most ancient enemy she has been the prime villain of the Old World. As the 'mother country' she had been a favored exception to the general rule." [6] From Tom Paine's time to William Jennings Bryan and beyond, Americans declared their republic a standing challenge to European forms, a matrix of virtues heralding a better day for mankind. England, target of the American Revolution and subsequently the republic's most frequent foreign antagonist, drew abuse directed at antique, aristocratic systems generally. At the same time Americans knew they owed much to their English background and found British institutions more praiseworthy than those of France, Russia, or Germany. Textbooks denounced English perfidy toward America and yet favorably contrasted her system with the rest of Europe.

The great rapprochement thus had historical underpinnings. It also had boundaries within its own setting. In the United States, particularly, the new spirit most affected the political elite, those groups from which were recruited the officers of government. As always in the republic, their freedom of action was restricted by the attitudes of their constituents. Henry Cabot Lodge might shuck off inherited Anglophobia, as he did between 1895 and 1903, but his Irish constituents would not, so it behooved Lodge to move cautiously. Nor would the great mass of Americans, even those who became more friendly toward England, even dream of abandoning the hallowed policy of isolation. For most, world politics were not only sinful but also far less important than domestic issues—imperialism, the gold standard,

---

[5] Rudyard Kipling, *American Notes* (Boston, 1899), pp. 66–67.
[6] Cushing Strout, *The American Image of the Old World* (New York, 1963), p. 134.

the trusts, party conflict. One day in 1912 the Presidential campaign drove all foreign news from Henry Adams' morning newspaper.

German Ambassador Bernstorff, a shrewd observer, reported in 1911, "The British efforts [to cultivate America] are meeting with a certain return of platonic affection. The old rooted dislike to England is gradually vanishing. . . . But it is not accompanied by any wish to offer anything in return." [7] In hard diplomatic coin, the Americans took but they did not give. British ministries from Salisbury to Asquith made important concessions of substance and form to the United States. These statesmen gained not alliance nor even true reciprocity, but the elimination of grounds of conflict, occasional and essentially "platonic" or negative support in world politics, and above all a transformation of American attitudes which would pay immense dividends after 1914. While other factors propelled America in the same direction, British policy from 1895 to 1914 was the indispensable element.

The most important formal agreements between the two countries were made between 1901 and 1903. These agreements, liquidating American fears that Britain might resist her hegemony in the Western Hemisphere, would probably have been impossible without developments surrounding the Spanish-American War a few years earlier. In their turn, these settlements opened the way to steady, almost silent improvement in relations from 1903 until Sarajevo. The man who directed British foreign policy after 1905 wrote in his memoirs that for the first six years of his tenure "there was not much in the handling of public affairs between the Government of the United States and ourselves that retains sufficient interest to be described here." [8] This laconic statement, reflecting Grey's harrowing European responsibilities, fails to draw the proper implication: the two

[7] Bernstorff to Bethmann-Hollweg, July 21, 1911, E. T. S. Dugdale, ed., *German Diplomatic Documents, 1871–1914* (4 vols.; London, 1928–1931), vol. IV, p. 30.
[8] Viscount Grey of Fallodon, *Twenty-Five Years, 1892–1916* (2 vols.; London, 1928), vol. II, p. 85.

nations found nothing to justify a real quarrel. When, just before the war, new issues arose—out of revolution in Mexico and the proposed preferential treatment for American ships using the Panama Canal—they were settled in a new way, by reciprocal if not connected concession, and accompanied by far less than the usual quota of hostile ranting in the United States.

Toward Great Britain, alone of major powers, the United States became more friendly in the two decades before Sarajevo. Such a striking change, a contrast to feeling toward Germany or Russia or Japan or even France, naturally sprang from many causes. Anglo-Saxonism was one, a combination of corrupted Darwinian ideology and faith in limited government which suggested both superiority and, as challenges arose from St. Petersburg or Berlin or backward peoples, a vaguely shared angle of vision. (Especially after the Liberals came to power in Britain in 1905, the two nations seemed bastions of parliamentarianism in a world troubled by autocracy.) Springing from the racist side of Anglo-Saxonism came imperialism, and once the Americans acquired an overseas empire they became more tolerant of British imperialism and, like many *arrivistes*, concerned to preserve the new status quo. Finally, the shadow of Wilhelms and Holsteins and Bernhardis seemed threatening, ominously so in London and troublesome in Washington. When British statesmen began to feel that "glorious isolation" did not ensure security, they sought alliances where they could be found—in Tokyo, then Paris, finally St. Petersburg—and the eradication of quarrels elsewhere, most notably with the sole important power in the Western Hemisphere. On both sides of the Atlantic Ocean most leading figures and much of the multitude came to feel Anglo-American discord undesirable, unnatural, perhaps unthinkable.

A major stimulus to the rapprochement was the sheer growth of American power, in relation to Britain and in relation to the world. Henry Adams later wrote, "one held one's breath [in 1892] at the nearness of what one had never expected to see, the crossing of courses, and the lead of American energies." More brutally, his younger brother wrote at century's end that he

considered the British Isles no more than "a fortified outpost of
the Anglo-Saxon race." By almost any standard one might
choose, America had passed Britain. Her population, which
topped that of England some time in the 1850's, by 1900 was
more than twice as large. She produced a million more tons of
iron and steel than Great Britain in 1890, mined and consumed
more coal in 1895, wove more cotton in 1900—and what was
more symbolic of British strength than iron and coal and textiles?
Only in disposable military might did the republic lag. In 1895
the Royal Navy possessed forty-four battleships, the United
States Navy only two. Still, as a First Lord of the Admiralty observed, "If the Americans choose to pay for what they can easily
afford, they can gradually build up a navy, fully as large and then
larger than ours." [9]

The mushrooming of American power, making quarrels
with the United States so risky as to be almost unthinkable, encouraged Salisbury and his successors to follow conciliatory policies. In addition, America's power made her sympathy critically
important in a world where Russia and then Germany—the latter growing in some ways even more spectacularly than the
United States—cast shadows over British security. The growth
of power altered American views as well. "The sensitiveness and
uneasy self-assertiveness of the Americans, as a mass, has virtually
passed away," one of them assured British readers, thus eliminating ("moderating" would have been a more accurate word) an
unpleasant characteristic of past relations.[10]

Scarcely less important than the growth of American puis-
sance, and very closely connected, was the development of trans-
Atlantic similarities. "Wherever the American has gone in Europe," said the reporter just cited, "he has seen clearly that it is
with Britain alone that his own country has much in common,
whether in social or moral sentiments, political principles, or

[9] Henry Adams, *The Education of Henry Adams* (Modern Library ed.; New
York, 1931), p. 330; Brooks Adams, *America's Economic Supremacy* (New York,
1900), p. 10; Selborne to Curzon, April 19, 1901, quoted in George Monger,
The End of Isolation: British Foreign Policy, 1900–1907 (London, 1963), p. 72n.

[10] Philip A. Bruce, "American Feeling Toward England," *Westminster Review*
(London), vol. CLIV (1900), pp. 457–458.

fundamental laws." [11] Both countries now faced the problems, first visible in Britain, posed by an industrial proletariat. Both now faced the challenge to Smithian economics created by oligopoly and monopoly, first important on the other side of the Atlantic. Pittsburgh and Pullman inhibited criticism of Lancashire; the agglomeration of British industrial groups gave a hollower sound to strictures on Yerkes and Rockefeller. Reform groups in the two countries—in politics, the social gospel, evangelism, social work—shared common outlooks and borrowed unabashedly from one another. At the same time the two countries shared a general conviction that industrialism rather than a land-centered economy, capitalism rather than state control, offered the best hope for the future. When concern for the health of the industrial order helped to create imperialism in the United States and to revive it in England, the two nations found a further element of similarity.

While the American economy rushed in a British direction, the political forms of England sidled toward those of the United States. Queen Victoria, American obituaries noted in 1901, had presided over the transformation of her nation from an aristocratic monarchy to a democratic empire. England no longer symbolized monarchical opposition to the ideals of the American republic. Extension of the franchise and its increasingly voluble use by the nonaristocratic classes; penetration of the highest levels of government by men like Joseph Chamberlain, a Birmingham industrialist, and David Lloyd George, a Welshman of modest antecedents; and the parallel decline of the nobility symbolized by the retirement of Lord Salisbury in 1902 and later by the battle over the powers of the House of Lords—all these made British politics more like those of the United States. Particularly did this seem true when one contrasted England with Continental states. Americans never took French republicanism seriously, bewailing the evident lack of cohesion and balance. Russian czarism alienated them. Toward Wilhelmian Germany, despite fears of her ambitions around the turn of the

[11] *Ibid.*, p. 459.

century, the Americans adopted a more ambivalent stance, sometimes anticipating the gradual evolution of parliamentarianism there, but Germany never seemed nearly as convinced of the wisdom of the American lesson as England.

In the military sense, American power remained merely potential or at most partial. Not all Americans lost their touchiness, whatever optimists might say, nor did Englishmen cease to criticize American materialism. British government, admittedly much more closely akin to American than in the days of Pitt and Palmerston, still bore heavy encrustations of the past in manner and personnel, as it would continue to do long after 1914, and Americans never ceased to feel their own system far preferable. Yet, despite all qualifications, the two nations seemed more than ever before to be moving along parallel courses with neither a mere cockboat in the other's wake. When Henry Adams returned to Washington after a European visit disrupted by the outbreak of the World War, he found his old friends in the German embassy "half-mad with solitude and desolation," for the industrial weight of America and most of her sympathies had begun to be thrown into the balance with England and her allies.[12] This much had things changed since 1895.

[12] Ernest Samuels, *Henry Adams: The Major Phase* (Cambridge, 1964), p. 555.

CHAPTER TWO

Lord Salisbury's Difficulties

THE BRITISH ELECTION of June 1895 ended one era and began another. A year before, the "Grand Old Man" retired from politics, taking with him for a time the Irish issue. By a narrow margin in votes but a decisive one in parliamentary seats, voters repudiated Gladstone's heir and returned to power the Conservatives, or Unionists as they preferred to call themselves in deference to Liberal supporters like Joseph Chamberlain who opposed home rule for Ireland. Despite a change at the top, the new ministry continued in power until 1905, presiding reluctantly over the end of British isolation, not the least manifestation of which was the cultivation of American friendship. At first, the task proved difficult.

The Marquis of Salisbury, already sixty-five when the Unionists came to power, presided over fractious colleagues, colleagues impatient with a man so set in his ways he even refused to move into 10 Downing Street upon becoming premier. While none doubted Salisbury's astuteness, many considered him indecisive and too cynical to support any positive course. During his ministry, ended by retirement in favor of his nephew, Arthur Balfour, in 1902, Salisbury found himself overruled by more aggressive cabinet members, notably Balfour and Joseph Chamberlain and Lord Lansdowne. Opposed to alliances, he allowed his lieutenants to force through a Far Eastern agreement with Germany in 1900 and the first major breach in British isolation, the Japanese alliance of 1902. Salisbury viewed the

United States with disdain, though not hostility; even when he combined the premiership with command of the Foreign Office, as he did until 1900, the initiatives in American relations usually came from subordinates.

During an earlier ministry, in 1888, Salisbury appointed Sir Julian Pauncefote envoy to the United States. Washington was then considered a diplomat's graveyard, no place to win distinction. Still Pauncefote abandoned his under-secretaryship to take the post, and in 1893, when the major legations in Washington were upgraded to embassies, he became *doyen* of the diplomatic corps. Sir Julian, a neat, slightly stooped little man with whiskers and cool blue eyes, was no master of small talk and made little effort to improve American opinion, even senatorial opinion. Although American politicians often irritated him and he cocked a skeptical eye at sentimental effusions of Anglo-Saxonism, he kept these feelings well hidden, reserving them for private letters to his superiors. Pauncefote was a capable, cautious diplomatic technician, and he managed to conceal his one real indiscretion —a false step just before the opening of the Spanish-American War—even from his own government. He gained the respect of official Washington and of informed Americans generally. In 1900 he received honorary degrees from both Harvard and Yale, and the year before, in recognition of his success, Queen Victoria created him Baron Pauncefote of Preston, the first time an envoy to the United States was thus rewarded. Salisbury, then, had a capable representative in Washington, but in 1895 and 1896, when a squall unsettled Anglo-American relations, London made far less use than it should have of his shrewdness and understanding.

The trouble arose out of a boundary dispute between British Guiana and Venezuela. For years the Venezuelans had sought American support without success. Then William L. Scruggs, a former minister at Caracas discharged for bribing a Venezuelan president and now a purveyor of Venezuelan propaganda, published a screed entitled *British Aggressions in Venezuela, the Monroe Doctrine on Trial,* and early in 1895 both houses of Congress unanimously passed a resolution calling for arbitration, obviously to challenge British claims. Senator Lodge published an error-studded article in the *North American Review*, declaring that British pretensions threatened the Monroe Doctrine. "A worse case of land-grabbing from an inoffensive and weak state it would be hard to find," Lodge wrote a friend, although the real merits of the dispute lay hidden in historical mist. "I wanted first to call attention to the facts but little known here, and second, to pave the way for a stiff declaration of the Monroe Doctrine by the next Congress." [1]

President Cleveland joined the hue-and-cry. Failure to do so might have cost his party heavily, given the extent of public feeling. In addition, Scruggs and others had convinced him Britain was the guilty party, and a brief British landing in Nicaragua early in 1895 may have led him to believe the time had come to emphasize American predominance in the hemisphere. Although there is no evidence the President himself felt this way, Lodge and others thought the British threat to Venezuela had to be checked in order to give warning to other European nations, particularly Germany. The President's annual message in December 1894 suggested arbitration, and when Britain ignored the suggestion Cleveland decided to act more forcefully.

Cleveland's new secretary of state, Richard Olney, who took office on the death of Walter Q. Gresham in the spring of 1895, willingly joined his chief's campaign. An able lawyer and a good hater—after a quarrel he banished a daughter from his home for thirty years—Olney was an advocate rather than an appeaser. Basically friendly to England, he considered her territorial claims grossly inflated and moreover believed that Anglo-American cordiality depended upon the elimination of just such irritants. During a vacation on peaceful Cape Cod, Olney drafted a belligerent note to England, a contrast to his usual practice of outlining notes and leaving the actual composition to underlings. The President softened the language in minor ways but let the sub-

---

[1] Lodge to White, June 5, 1895, quoted in Allan Nevins, *Henry White: Thirty Years of American Diplomacy* (New York, 1930), p. 108.

stance go forward as instructions to Ambassador Bayard at London on July 20, 1895. In a torrent of ten thousand words, Olney argued that the Monroe Doctrine extended to such matters as the boundary dispute and demanded that London agree to arbitration. In a piece of gratuitous bravado, a passage making clear that the note was intended for ultimate communication to the public, Olney added a famous statement: "To-day the United States is practically sovereign on this continent, and its fiat is law upon the subjects to which it confines its interposition." The note resounded, the President later observed complacently, like a shot from a twenty-inch gun.

It seemed at first more like a small boy's popgun to Lord Salisbury and to Joseph Chamberlain, the Colonial Secretary who took over management of the affair. Beset with the problems of establishing a new ministry, they did not even bother to make sure that Queen Victoria received copies of the correspondence, and for four months they withheld an answer while Cleveland's temper mounted. The ministry refused to believe the dispute was really serious, partly because Ambassador Bayard failed to underscore his superiors' determination. At the same time British leaders, particularly Joseph Chamberlain, felt it necessary to stand the small boy on his head. "The Americans are not people to run away from," he wrote, and a bit earlier he advised his chief, "it is essential that the reply should emphatically repudiate this attempt to apply the Monroe Doctrine to the question of the Venezuela boundary, and should place in strong relief the fact that Great Britain is an American Power with a territorial area greater than the United States themselves." [2]

The cabinet finally approved a two-part answer to the Americans dated November 26. In condescending language, with perhaps excessive attention to shortcomings in Olney's logic although without his inflammatory perorations, the reply denied

---

[2] Chamberlain to Selborne, December 24, 1895, quoted in Joseph L. Garvin and Julian S. Amery, *The Life of Joseph Chamberlain* (4 vols.; London, 1932–1951), vol. III, p. 67; Chamberlain to Salisbury, September 11, 1895, quoted in Ernest R. May, *Imperial Democracy: The Emergence of America as a Great Power* (New York, 1961), pp. 44–45.

the applicability and, even more challenging, the legal validity of the Monroe Doctrine. It absolutely refused to arbitrate the boundary of a territory established before Venezuela even existed as a nation. Still seeing no reason for speed, Salisbury failed to cable the reply to Pauncefote and, if Foreign Office legend is believed, the first copy found its way into the Tokyo bag by mistake.[3] Not until December 7 did Sir Julian deliver the reply to Olney's Washington home. In Pauncefote's opinion the British challenge shocked the President, who learned for the first time how deep were the waters into which he had ventured.

Cleveland's annual message, delivered before Pauncefote called on Olney, asked no action despite four months of haughty British silence. Salisbury's *non possumus* changed things; no President could have accepted such a rebuke by turning the other cheek. Olney drafted a message to Congress; Cleveland and an old crony, Secretary of War Lamont, spent a long night revising it; and on December 17 the message was submitted to Congress along with copies of the notes by Olney and Salisbury. Asserting the right to intervene in defense of Monroe's principles and rejecting as unsatisfactory England's refusal to arbitrate, the President went on, "The course to be pursued by this Government . . . does not appear to admit of serious doubt." He sought (and soon received) funds to establish an investigatory commission to determine a just boundary, after which the United States would use "every means in its power" to prevent English domination of lands properly belonging to Venezuela.

Bravo, cried Theodore Roosevelt, who set his eye on the conquest of Canada and sent an hyperpatriotic letter to the *Harvard Crimson* which brought down on his head the wrath of Professor Albert B. Hart. Hooray, cried Senator Lodge, who was reported by the London *Times* to be alive with delight. And the message struck like a thunderclap in London, where, James Bryce complained to Roosevelt, not one tenth of the House of Commons "even knew there was such a thing as a Venezuela

[3] Sir John Tilley and Stephen Gaselee, *The Foreign Office* (London, 1933), pp. 133–134.

question pending." A few set down the effrontery of Cleveland and Olney to bad manners, the *New Review* observing, "The United States stands so much apart from the society of civilised Powers that they are hardly to be judged by its laws." [4] Most Englishmen, on the other hand, considered the crisis serious.

Two students have recently noted that Cleveland's message "was a most skillful piece of work; it satisfied even the wildest jingoes without, in fact, involving the United States in any real danger of conflict." Both points are important. The Presidential message did appeal to nationalistic sentiment. At the same time, while the President increased the explosive charge of Olney's note by threatening to enforce American views he also lengthened the fuse by suggesting no action until the commission completed its investigation. Pauncefote considered the message "very pale and washy," and Joseph Chamberlain concluded, "the American affair cannot become serious for some time." [5] When Joseph Pulitzer, the energetic press lord, cabled the Prince of Wales for a statement, the Prince replied that he trusted peace would be maintained.

In Britain, despite grumbling about Cleveland's brusqueness, most public men urged a compromise which would preserve peace. Three hundred and fifty M.P.'s signed a petition urging arbitration, Salisbury and Chamberlain received sharp criticism from colleagues who had once approved the reply to Olney, and the Liberal leader in the House of Commons threatened to make trouble. The first American reaction was quite different, Cleveland winning applause for his message. Most Americans considered Britain wrong or, like Andrew Carnegie, unreasonably greedy not to leave the United States one continent to manage. The public cooled off very quickly. To twist

[4] Bryce to Roosevelt, January 1, 1896, quoted in Howard K. Beale, *Theodore Roosevelt and the Rise of America to World Power* (Baltimore, 1956), p. 84; "Z," "The Monroe Doctrine," *New Review* (London), vol. XIV (1896), p. 47.

[5] John A. S. Grenville and George B. Young, *Politics, Strategy, and American Diplomacy: Studies in Foreign Policy, 1873–1917* (New Haven, 1966), p. 167; Pauncefote to Barrington, December 17, 1895, quoted in John A. S. Grenville, *Lord Salisbury and Foreign Policy: The Close of the Nineteenth Century* (London, 1964), p. 67; Chamberlain to Meade, December 18, 1895, quoted in Garvin and Amery, *Chamberlain*, vol. III, p. 72.

the lion's tail was one thing, a pleasant tradition of American politics; to face the possibility of an English war was quite another. "The clamor of the peace faction has convinced me that this country needs a war," Theodore Roosevelt commented disgustedly,[6] and the President himself later complained that the cowardly business classes let him down. The American people wanted to assert themselves at British expense, and they hoped London would let them do so.

The tangled negotiations which lasted until September 1896, when Great Britain and Venezuela signed an arbitration agreement, saw compromise on both sides. First Britain receded, spurred by the crisis surrounding Dr. Jameson's raid on the Transvaal and the Kaiser's telegram of support to President Kruger. At the first cabinet meeting after Cleveland's message, ministers shrugged off Salisbury's grumbling resignation threat and agreed to approach Ambassador Bayard through Lord Playfair, a Liberal married to an American. From these conversations the Americans learned that the ministry was prepared to arbitrate on unsettled territory and even to consider any alternative Washington might suggest. Britain broke off the talks when it became apparent the crisis had eased but also that Cleveland and Olney wanted unconditional arbitration of all disputed territory, whether occupied or not. However, Salisbury's government had retreated from its insistence that a dispute with Venezuela was no concern of the United States. This retreat was made even clearer at the end of February when the cabinet accepted Olney's request that negotiations go forward at Washington, where the Secretary of State could keep an eye on Venezuelan interests. Henry Cabot Lodge claimed a victory for his country and for the cause of friendship based upon mutual respect.

Sir Julian Pauncefote, only now consulted and informed by Lord Salisbury, could not budge Olney from his insistence on unconditional arbitration. That two visiting Republicans, John

[6] Roosevelt to Lodge, December 27, 1895, Henry Cabot Lodge, ed., *Selections from the Correspondence of Theodore Roosevelt and Henry Cabot Lodge, 1884–1918* (2 vols.; New York, 1925), vol. I, p. 205.

Hay and Henry White, assured them the American people were behind the administration failed to shake Downing Street. Finally Joseph Chamberlain, as energetic in seeking compromise as he once had been in resisting American pretensions, took a hand. He visited the United States in September and, at the Massachusetts home of his American wife, had several conversations with the Secretary of State, while two guards provided by Olney prowled in the shrubbery to protect the English Minister from Irish-Americans. At first Olney seemed stiff. Then he offered a compromise by which areas settled for more than fifty years would be excluded from arbitration, while less lengthy occupations would be taken into account by the arbitrators. Chamberlain accepted and returned home, leaving final details to Pauncefote. In Caracas, crowds rioted when they learned that arbitration would take place under conditions fatal to Venezuela's extreme claims. Well they might have. The award, handed down in the autumn of 1899 by the chairman, the famed Russian jurist Frederic Martens, upheld most British contentions. England had won in substance, but at the cost of recognizing the breadth of American interest in affairs of the hemisphere.

In the controversy thus ended, both governments at first reacted as history had taught, assuming a conflict of interest and indulging historical sentiments of bellicosity on one side and disdain on the other. If Cleveland left himself an escape hatch, much as Polk had done during the Oregon dispute fifty years earlier, he also found it comfortable to pose as an extreme nationalist. A cooler assessment of realities plus public pressure forced the administrations in both countries to revise their positions. "Sensations of horror . . . passed over both countries," the *Westminster Review* recalled in 1900, "at the mere thought of . . . fratricidal war." [7] Responding, the governments settled by compromise an inflated but nevertheless dangerous controversy. But the quarrel had been created by American opinion in the first place. Scruggs and other propagandists, Republicans eager to embarrass the administration and Democrats unwilling

[7] *Westminster Review* (London), vol. CLIV (1900), p. 460.

to seem less patriotic than their opponents all accepted Anglophobia as a fact of American political life.

The Venezuelan crisis, if it ever really deserved such a term,
lasted only a few days, from Cleveland's special message until
the British cabinet approved approaches through Lord Playfair.
Long before Olney and Chamberlain reached agreement on the
Endicott veranda, the affair drifted from the front pages. A Presidential campaign of unusual ferocity, "the Battle of the Standards," monopolized American attention, and in England people
were more frightened by William Jennings Bryan than by Richard Olney, now the mouthpiece of an administration repudiated
by its own party. The cabinet probably settled with Olney in 1896
partly to avoid having to negotiate with Bryan, should he win the
election. In any case, Republican visitors had assured every influential person they met that the G.O.P., too, insisted upon arbitration. There seemed little point, and much risk, in further
delay.

Britain's shuddering distaste for Bryanism, sometimes combined with sneaking admiration for the candidate's personal
courage and sincerity, did not differ much from that of American
conservatives. Like Keir Hardie and later Mrs. Pankhurst, the
feminist, Bryan upset comfortable patterns. In sharp contrast to
British views before the Civil War, on those rare occasions when
English leaders judged American parties after 1865 they had
tended to favor the Democrats, whose views on the tariff best
suited a free-trade nation. When Pauncefote's predecessor so in-
discreetly and harmfully endorsed the Democrats in 1888, he did
so partly with the tariff issue in mind. The Republican nomination of William McKinley placed at the head of the ticket "a
bigoted Protectionist," as Joseph Chamberlain called him.[8] Still,
even a protectionist was better than a revolutionary. When the
Democrats selected William Jennings Bryan, British political
leaders of all parties swung into the Republican camp, there to

[8] Chamberlain to Victoria, September 10, 1896, George E. Buckle, ed., *The Letters of Queen Victoria, Third Series* (3 vols.; London, 1930–1932), vol. III, p. 76.

remain until the campaign of 1912.

Bryan Democracy and its Populist allies revolted against the thrust of American life, particularly the challenge to rural well-being. Although they sought other reforms, they emphasized free silver, a broad program of inflation which would ease the pressure upon debtors and, presumably, the less fortunate generally. When Cleveland set his face against silverite pressure, his party repudiated him. The campaign of 1896 became a contest between Bryan and free silver and McKinley and the gold standard, gestures in the direction of a bimetallic standard being virtually ignored. England had been on the gold standard since 1821, and in 1893 she partially extended it to India, hitherto exempt. British governments refused consideration to proposals for an international system to relieve the deflationary impress of the gold standard, and of all major British figures only Arthur J. Balfour was even tempted. Henry Cabot Lodge, an extremely partisan New Englander but also a bimetallist, chastised Britain for her obstructive attitude, and Democrats surpassed him. As the center of the restrictive gold system, as the close ally of eastern financial interests against which the Bryanites rebelled, Britain naturally became a target of their jibes.

In 1893, unsuccessfully seeking to prevent repeal of the mildly inflationary Sherman Silver Purchase Act, William Jennings Bryan staked out his position. "Let me appeal to your patriotism," he said to fellow congressmen. "Shall we make our laws dependent upon England's action and thus allow her to legislate for us upon the most important of all questions? . . . Are we an English colony or an independent people?" The next year William H. Harvey put into the mouth of the English villain of *A Tale of Two Nations* the sneering declaration, "I am here to destroy the United States—Cornwallis could not have done more." In his *Coin's Financial School* (1894), a diffuse but immensely powerful tract, Harvey declared that war with England would be not only popular but just; he hoped to wipe her name from the earth. "To John Bull," huffed a member of Parliament, "such language and such a menace is so strange as to be almost inexplicable." [9] Mary Elizabeth Lease, another silver propagandist, accused Cleveland of being the agent of Jews and Englishmen.

At Omaha, in the famous speech that won him the Democratic nomination, Bryan argued the parallel between 1776 and 1896. Drafters of the platform agreed. "Gold monometallism," they said, "is a British policy and its adoption has brought other nations into financial servitude to London. . . . It can be fastened on the United States only by the stifling of that spirit and love of liberty which proclaimed our political independence." The young campaigner and his supporters, notably John P. Altgeld, repeatedly inserted the theme in their speeches. The correspondent of the London *Daily Mail*, George Warrington Steevens, a brilliant young journalist who died while reporting the Boer War four years later, pointed out that this was a subsidiary rather than a major theme, that Democrats after all hated Republicans more than Englishmen. Few Britons made the distinction, and they found enough in American oratory to disturb them.

Since many Americans considered the fate of the nation threatened by Bryan, it is perhaps unfair to chastise Englishmen for viewing the campaign in such gloomy colors. They were woefully badly informed, for almost no newspapers or journals had regular American correspondents. William T. Stead's *Review of Reviews* simply drew its information from an American counterpart of the same name, firmly allied with McKinley. The *Nineteenth Century* accepted the views of the American consul at Birmingham. The *Mail* did not send Steevens across the Atlantic until midsummer. Perhaps ninety percent of the information published in England came directly or indirectly from George W. Smalley, New York correspondent of the London *Times*. A Yale man married to Wendell Phillips' daughter, Smalley spent a quarter of a century as a newspaperman abroad, chiefly in London, before he returned to the United States at sixty-two to write

[9] William Jennings Bryan, *The First Battle: A Story of the Campaign of 1896* (Chicago, 1896), p. 93; Richard Hofstadter, *The Age of Reform: From Bryan to F.D.R.* (New York, 1955), p. 77; Arthur George Peel, "The American Crisis," *National Review* (London), vol. XXVIII (1896), p. 65.

for the *Times*. He had lost touch with his native land and, hardly venturing outside the stuffiest circles in New York, never regained it. He deplored every threat to Anglo-American friendship, and his conservative outlook made him dislike winds of change. During the Venezuelan affair he steadily pooh-poohed the American position as inconsequential jingoism, and later on he interpreted Theodore Roosevelt's policy in much the same light. Roosevelt once denounced Smalley as "a copper-riveted idiot." In 1896 he more reasonably described the journalist as "a pleasant, cultivated, gentlemanly man, well-read and interesting; but he is an ingrained snob and hasn't a particle of understanding of America." [10] Smalley covered the 1896 campaign from an easy chair in New York, except for one occasion when he traveled with Chauncey DePew by private Pullman to visit McKinley in Ohio. His prejudiced, oversimplified reports became even more crude when adapted by other English papers. A few editors recognized the dangers in the situation, but none did anything about it until the *Mail* belatedly sent Steevens to the United States.

In addition to Anglophobia, examples of which Smalley excerpted from the torrent of words, three things worried Englishmen. The election seemed to show what conservatives had always feared, the danger of democracy run rampant. Instead of arguing rationally, American politicians blatantly appealed to prejudices and class hatreds. Moreover, the American system, with a very broad franchise and no tradition of deference to experts and the informed, meant that the most ignorant citizens decided complicated, important questions by their votes. How could an illiterate Tennessee farmer or an uneducated Italo-American understand arguments which proved the gold standard essential to economic stability? Such complaints about the American system, a time-honored feature of British observation, had

[10] Roosevelt to Lodge, June 19, 1901, Elting E. Morison, ed., *The Letters of Theodore Roosevelt* (8 vols.; Cambridge, 1951–1954), vol. III, p. 97; Roosevelt to Anna R. Cowles, January 19, 1896, *ibid.*, vol. I, p. 510. In 1901, when he met the editor of the *Times*, Roosevelt explained his differences with Smalley and candidly recounted that conversation to the newspaperman.

their last real run in 1896. By 1900, although the parties fought
heatedly over imperialism and again over silver, the doubts were
muted.

Secondly, English observers emphasized Bryan's radicalism.
"Communism," "socialism," and "anarchism" were words employed to describe the Democratic program. Other editors saw a
parallel between developments in the United States and those in
France one hundred and twenty years earlier, with Bryan cast as
a Robespierre or a St. Just. Against this exaggeration of the Democratic program, some voices entered dissents. The *Economist*
observed, "It is not, of course, Socialism to support an income-
tax, to condemn monopolies, or to demand tariff for revenue
purposes only." [11] However, with the exception of Steevens, who
doubted the practicality rather than the justice of free silver, and
of a handful of bimetallist journals, no one raised his voice to
challenge the third and overriding theme of British journals, the
danger posed by the demand for free silver. Inflation through the
coinage of silver was nothing more than barefaced robbery, would
certainly deprive Englishmen with investments in the United
States of a portion of their capital, and might break down the
entire economic structure of the United States and seriously
affect that of the world.

Based as they were upon a tiny spectrum of knowledge, English views were not profound. Most sound rather like encapsu-
lated versions of the arguments of McKinley's supporters and
Smalley's friends. Their importance is their virtual unanimity.
Not even those who found redeeming personal qualities in Bryan
or criticized distortions of his political program hoped he would
gain the White House. Except for Moreton Frewen, a leader
who formerly lived in the American West and was proud to be
"a devoted henchman of Bryan," [12] even the tiny fraction of
bimetallists opposed the Democrats. Labour and Fabian voices
were thin, muted, and contradictory. The voices of authority all
agreed that success for Bryan would be a disaster, although poli-

[11] *Economist* (London), vol. LIV (1896), p. 890.
[12] Shane Leslie, *Studies in Sublime Failure* (London, 1932), p. 272.

ticians, remembering Sackville-West's gaffe and knowing that the Democrats would love to turn the tables on their opponents, kept silent until the election was over.

Then they heaved a collective sigh of relief. The royal capitalist of Balmoral gave thanks, in her journal, in the name of those with investments in the United States. Lord Playfair rejoiced at the defeat of principles which threatened to bring about "the breakdown of constitutional government and the loss of faith in democracy everywhere," a sentiment shared by his fellow Liberal, John Morley, who congratulated the American workingman for his devotion to sound, deferential principles. The party leader, Sir William Harcourt, who was married to the daughter of the American historian John Lothrop Motley, wrote to Chamberlain, "We semi-Americans have much reason to rejoice over the defeat of Bryan, and your 'sound money' democrat wife and my republican wife may embrace one another like Mercy and Truth." Even the Marquis of Salisbury, usually the very soul of discretion, could not contain his satisfaction. Speaking at a Guildhall banquet, he allowed himself a passage praising the American people for their wisdom in electing McKinley and their sturdy defense of "the principles which lie at the base of all human society." [13] Americans complained, and some Britons thought the Prime Minister's statement ill-advised, but there is no evidence that Salisbury regretted it.

Even at the distance of seventy years it is difficult to estimate the consequences of a Bryan victory. Domestic issues, the Cuban question, the uses of victory if war with Spain had come —these the Nebraskan might have managed differently from McKinley. Would President Bryan have continued the anti-British stance he showed in the campaign of 1896? Perhaps not, but a Bryan victory would have increased the chances of friction. Because Bryan gathered beneath his banner so many who pronounced themselves enemies of England, Salisbury and his

[13] *Nineteenth Century* (London), vol. XLI (1897), p. 2; Harcourt to Chamberlain, November 17, 1896, quoted in A. G. Gardiner, *The Life of Sir William Harcourt* (2 vols.; London, 1923), vol. II, p. 403; *Nineteenth Century*, vol. XLI, p. 1.

colleagues would inevitably have looked with disfavor on American policies, like that toward Spain, which they tolerated when performed by Republicans. The election of 1896, so important in American political history, was also important for diplomacy and even for relations with England. It ushered in sixteen years during which British governments, thankful of their narrow escape, did their best to eliminate tension between the two countries.

Bryan's political crusade and the Venezuelan imbroglio not only overshadowed all other issues during Cleveland's last year in the White House; they also influenced lesser matters, including an effort to carry through an Anglo-American arbitration treaty. During the last two decades of the nineteenth century, and indeed until the guns began in 1914, the world peace movement mushroomed. Most advocates of peace considered arbitration a panacea and sought to arrange it either through a general international system or, less grandiosely, through bilateral treaties. While none of those actually charged with governmental responsibilities shared the agitators' enthusiasms, even such bellicose men as Theodore Roosevelt and such cynical ones as Lord Salisbury considered bilateral agreements, properly limited in scope, potentially useful and certainly politic. The Anglo-American treaty of 1897, signed by the outgoing Democratic administration, compromised the hopes of peace enthusiasts and the negotiators' greater realism.

Pacifists found it easy to mobilize legislative opinion in both countries, for who, after all, could oppose peace? Congressional resolutions endorsed the principle of arbitration, usually, in deference to American prejudices, avoiding mention of the particular desirability of an agreement with England. Less inhibited than their American counterparts, members of the House of Commons—232 in 1887 and 354 in 1894—signed memorials calling for an Anglo-American treaty, and in 1893 they formally resolved in favor of such an understanding. In 1895 Secretary of State Gresham opened conversations with Pauncefote. The talks died with Gresham in June, and soon the Venezuelan controversy arose to cast a pall over the project.

Once that controversy had begun to cool, it actually stimulated a new effort. The English publicist William T. Stead argued that Venezuela proved the danger of "rub[bing] along,
taking no thought as to the morrow, but trusting that whenever a
difficulty or a hitch arose, the two nations would be able to im-
provise a way out." [14] He urged permanent machinery to defuse
controversy, and college presidents, the American Bar Association and others, even the Irish- and German-infested New York
state legislature, joined the call. To Britain it seemed prudent to
conclude an agreement freeing statesmen for the Old World's
more important problems. In addition, Joseph Chamberlain saw
advantage in diverting America from contentious Venezuela negotiations to a more positive theme. He talked Salisbury into
agreement.

At British initiative, then, negotiations recommenced. Although Olney welcomed the general idea, as always he had a me-
ticulous eye for detail, a lawyer's suspicion of proposals by an
adversary. American pettifoggery annoyed Pauncefote, although
he tended to blame the President rather than the Secretary of
State. Forwarding home one American note he found particularly irritating, he wrote, "I doubt whether Mr. Olney is responsible for more than the first and last pages. It was probably
written by the President sitting in his shirt sleeves, between two
bottles of whisky, under which conditions he is reported to have
penned his previous message about Venezuela." [15] Pauncefote
concealed his feelings from the Americans, however, and after
months of discussion he and Olney put their signatures to a
treaty on January 11, 1897.

The agreement made arbitration compulsory in all disputes
not settled by negotiations, but it so arranged things that, except
in minor cases, the decisions would have to be unanimous or at
worst with the approval of five of six arbitrators.[16] The negoti-

[14] Stead, *Always Arbitrate Before You Fight*, quoted in Frederick Whyte, *The
Life of William T. Stead* (2 vols.; New York, 1925), vol. II, p. 85.
[15] Pauncefote to Salisbury, June 26, 1896, quoted in R. G. Neale, *Great Britain
and United States Expansion: 1898–1900* (Lansing, 1966), pp. 40n–41n.
[16] More precisely, the treaty provided that pecuniary claims of less than

ators congratulated themselves on their fine work. Pauncefote forgot his anger and, in florid overconfidence, wrote to Salisbury, "The great Arbitration Treaty will take the wind out of the sails of the Jingoes as regards Great Britain, & the Eagle will have to screech at the other Powers, & let the British Lion nurse his tail." [17] Richard Olney, whose true feelings toward England are sometimes forgotten because of the violence of his "twenty-inch gun" note, later wrote that he considered the treaty more important than negotiations over Venezuela.

The Olney-Pauncefote treaty soon ran into trouble. Probably a great majority of those Americans with opinions approved it; certainly a deluge of favorable memorials, some stimulated by Olney, descended upon the Senate. That body refused to be stampeded, and the Fifty-fourth Congress died without action taken. In his inaugural address the new President urged "the early action of the Senate thereon, not merely as a matter of policy, but as a duty to mankind." Neither speedy nor favorable action followed. The Senate first eviscerated the treaty by amendment, particularly by exempting the most important types of disputes from its operation and by requiring that every agreement to arbitrate be submitted to the Senate for approval. This done, on May 5 the legislators disapproved even the bobtailed treaty by a vote of forty-three to twenty-six, three short of the required two thirds. Opposition was bipartisan, with Democrats mildly preponderating.

Probably, as the two authors of the treaty and other observers believed, the Senate's jealousy for its prerogatives was the most important factor in its action. Even after amendment, the treaty threatened to deprive that body of a portion of its role in foreign affairs. Still, the Senate was able to indulge itself only because the American public did not insist that it do otherwise.

£100,000 would be decided by one English, one American, and one outside arbitrator; claims above £100,000 and all others not involving territorial claims would be settled by a similar board, but the decision must be unanimous; disputes over territory would be adjudged by three leading jurists from each country, only one of whom could dissent if the verdict were to be effective.

[17] Pauncefote to Salisbury, January 1, 1897, quoted in Charles S. Campbell, *Anglo-American Understanding, 1898–1903* (Baltimore, 1957), p. 6.

The peace factions, at this time as during the discussion of other treaties later on, had too little political punch to affect many senators; they were probably discounted as visionary cranks. Others who supported the treaty did so in a forceless fashion. With the Venezuelan affair out of the way it seemed less important to accept Stead's advice, easier to "rub along." Certainly no one dared defend the treaty for its chief value, the mild improvement it might bring to Anglo-American relations. Support, though broad, was more passive than intense, whereas on the other side prejudices were deep. In a letter written for British eyes, Richard Olney estimated that, the question of senatorial prerogatives aside, the silver issue contributed most to the defeat of his treaty. Silverite senators opposed a treaty, any treaty, with "the most conspicuous and efficient supporter of the gold standard." [18] Olney did not mention the efforts of Irish-Americans, leaving Hibernian spokesmen to claim that they too played a major part in the battle.

Olney insisted that defeat of the treaty was a ghastly mistake. In another indirect communication to the British cabinet, he asserted, "the American people . . . feel themselves to be not merely in name but in fact, part of one great English-speaking family whose proud destiny it is to lead and control the world." [19] Olney may have been prescient; he certainly was premature. That the arbitration treaty came close to ratification, unmatched as it was by treaties with other powers and thus a sort of negative alliance ensuring against American cooperation with her enemies, hinted that the force of Anglophobia was declining. The Venezuela affair more forcefully demonstrated the contrary, even though the American people had no desire to carry their feelings as far as war, and the Bryanite campaign also shows the inaccuracy of Olney's assessment. The sense of kinship he proclaimed existed in only limited circles. Its growth awaited the thrust of new forces during and after McKinley's administration.

[18] Olney to White, May 14, 1897, quoted in W. Stull Holt, *Treaties Defeated by the Senate* (Baltimore, 1933), pp. 159–160.
[19] Olney to White, May 8, 1897, quoted in Nevins, *White*, p. 125.

Grover Cleveland and Richard Olney passed into the political wings in 1897. William Jennings Bryan withdrew *pour mieux sauter* in 1900, when his supporters, but not the candidate himself, again attempted to exploit the British bogey. Thomas F. Bayard, the ambassador at London who undermined his superiors during the Venezuelan disagreement and helped to inflame English officials against Bryan, returned to the United States after the change in administrations. Bayard bore in his luggage a precious document, the manuscript of William Bradford's history of Plymouth Plantation. The seventeenth-century treasure, filched from the Old South Church in Boston during the American Revolution, turned up in the Bishop of London's library at Fulham Palace, and as early as 1855 agitation for its return to Massachusetts began. Inertia and ecclesiastical red tape foiled these efforts until Bishop Mandell Creighton, a Harvard LL.D., arranged release of the manuscript early in 1897. Bayard stayed in London until formalities were completed and then carried Bradford's history to the United States. Although this episode showed that the England of Lord Salisbury understood the advantages of improving American opinion, less symbolic and more substantial concessions would be required to make firm friends of England and the United States.

CHAPTER THREE

England Welcomes an Imperial Partner

S IDNEY AND BEATRICE WEBB visited the United States in the spring of 1898 to investigate American government. To their irritation, Washington politicians refused to give Fabian researches the attention they deserved. Henry Cabot Lodge scarcely concealed his boredom when summoned from the Senate floor for an interview, and he fled back to a debate on foreign policy at the first opportunity. With no one to cross-examine on American shortcomings, the Webbs found themselves in the gallery of the House of Representatives on April 11, 1898. Shortly after noon "a seedy looking old gentleman appears in one of the gangways with a large folio of paper under his arm." Handed to a clerk who read it to the legislators and galleryites in a dull monotone, the paper proved to be a "long-winded epistle" from President McKinley requesting authority to use military force to end the civil war in Cuba.[1] Only half realizing it, the Webbs had seen the United States take a major step toward world power. The President's resistance to intervention having ended, war with Spain soon followed, then empire and involvement.

However disreputable the activities of yellow journalists, however much underlings like Assistant Secretary of the Navy

[1] David A. Shannon, ed., *Beatrice Webb's American Diary*, 1898 (Madison, 1963), pp. 26–27.

Roosevelt thirsted for war, no clique of intriguers provoked the conflict. Few who became imperialists foresaw that war with Spain would open the way; in fact, many who later resisted imperialism demanded war to free the Cubans in the winter of 1898. Since 1895 Americans had watched with horror, and with sympathy for a crusade for freedom, the bloodshed on that island. It soon became apparent that neither patriots nor colonialists could hope for victory, but the contenders showed little inclination to compromise. Humanitarian revulsion swept the United States, and President Cleveland had all he could do to prevent jingoes from using this noble sentiment, admittedly magnified by yearnings for prestige and adventure, to bring about a confrontation with Spain.

Cleveland's successor, William McKinley, continued the fight for more than a year. Early in February 1898 the *insurrectos* released through William Randolph Hearst, who characteristically tried to monopolize the scoop, an intercepted letter in which the Spanish ambassador at Washington described the President in very unflattering terms. An anti-Spanish uproar followed. (In England, officials and editorialists pleased the Americans by joining in the pursuit of Ambassador de Lome's scalp, perhaps because his letter alleged that Great Britain desired a war between Spain and the United States, a slander which infuriated Downing Street.) One evening less than a week later an explosion sank the battleship *Maine* in Havana harbor, killing two hundred and sixty of the crew. Americans leaped to the conclusion that colonial officials or Spanish sympathizers were to blame. (Sir Julian Pauncefote rushed to the White House early the next day to express his country's sympathy, scoring points on diplomats who arrived later or did not bother to come at all.) Prodded by fellow Republicans weary of seeing Democrats wrap themselves in the flag, convinced Spain was hopelessly miscast as an imperial power, seeing no other way out of the Cuban impasse, President McKinley reversed course. The Webbs saw the result.

Thousands of miles away rather than on the doorstep, Cuba never deeply penetrated the English conscience. Moreover, as holders of empire, British leaders did not, like so many Americans, instinctively side with an anticolonial revolt. As time passed, reports of the sanguinary struggle, whether directly from British journalists on the spot or copied from New York papers, brought the English to a conclusion very much like the American. First, Liberal organs began to argue that Spain had shown her incapacity as an imperial power, that the insurrection was a noble struggle for self-determination, and that the United States, commercially oriented and essentially peaceful, deserved far more sympathy than militaristic Spain. The Liberal line coincided with the thrust of public opinion, and soon almost all leading ministerial journals began to take up the refrain, either as a matter of political prudence or because they too were converted. Early in 1898 the new view melded with a surge of friendly emotion for the United States, now safely in the hands of Republicans rather than Bryanites, to produce a feeling that Americans should do something to help Cuba. The de Lome and *Maine* incidents strengthened this view.

Shortly after these two dramatic events, Ambassador Hay returned to London from a winter vacation on the Nile with Henry James and Henry Adams. The wave of sentiment warmed his heart. Even official reports reflected his exhilaration; his private correspondence bubbled over with excitement. One English peer, unburdened by the cares of office, suggested that the United States borrow the Royal Navy for use against Spain, repaying the favor later, an idea which led Hay to write, "If we wanted it—which, of course, we do not—we could have the practical assistance of the British Navy." (The ministry did expedite the sale to the United States, in March, of two cruisers being built in British yards for Brazil.) Joseph Chamberlain talked earnestly with the Ambassador about an alliance and delivered speeches scarcely more circumspect, while Liberals hailed American friendship in what became a party contest in hyperbole. Time and again, Hay reported, someone said to him, "I wish you would take Cuba at once. We would n't have stood it this long." [2] He urged his friend Lodge to procure

---

[2] Hay to Lodge, April 5, 1898, quoted in William R. Thayer, *The Life and Letters of John Hay* (2 vols.; Boston, 1915), vol. II, pp. 165–166.

an appropriation of $473,000 to pay an arbitrators' award to Great Britain for American seizures of sealing vessels in the Pacific. The Senator quickly obliged, though the appropriation had been held up by a feeling the award was unfairly high. Thus a minor irritant disappeared beneath the wave of good feeling.

The Marquis of Salisbury watched these developments with his usual coolness. Like his sovereign's, his sympathies went out to the Queen Regent of Spain, Victoria's niece, a woman vexed by internal politics as she sought to save the throne for her young son, born in 1886 after his father's death. Having a true conservative's dislike of revolutions, Salisbury deplored the Cuban uprising and worried that the revolt or conflict with the United States might bring down the Spanish morarchy. Moreover, the first phase of American agitation coincided with the last acts of the Venezuelan affair, when Salisbury was still angry but had seen the Americans back off quickly from the brink of crisis. To the Queen he airily predicted in the spring of 1896, "The United States will do all the mischief they can without going to war." [3] Perhaps because he knew it would warm Victoria's heart, he even talked of extending cautious aid to Spain in her quarrel with the United States.

Yet the crafty old statesman never had the slightest intention of running risks for Spain, and he became increasingly cautious in the face of rising evidence of American seriousness. Only a month after reassuring Victoria, he wrote in quite a different vein to Henry White, the wealthy, bland, and very Anglophile first secretary of the American embassy. Cuba, he commented, "is no affair of ours, we are friendly to Spain and should be sorry to see her humiliated, but we do not consider that we have anything to say in the matter whatever may be the course the United States may decide to pursue." Before Hay left for Egypt, Salisbury told the Ambassador that British interest in the island was purely commercial, not at all political, and would therefore be best served by restored tranquillity. He seemed almost to in-

[3] Salisbury to Victoria, May 25, 1896, George E. Buckle, ed., *The Letters of Queen Victoria, Third Series* (3 vols.; London, 1930–1932), vol. III, p. 45.

vite positive American action when he added that America need not fear British interference if she "adopt[ed] energetic measures." [4] During most of the critical weeks just before the war, Salisbury was away from London, seeking a better climate in which to fight a bad case of flu. His nephew, left to mind the store, scrupulously followed the Premier's policy of avoiding even the appearance of a challenge to the Americans, while his colleague Chamberlain favored a still more forward course.

Salisbury's views roughly coincided with those of Continental statesmen. Official Europe, in some cases (particularly at Vienna) more sympathetic to Spain, was equally unwilling to run risks for Queen Maria Christina. "You are isolated," Germany's Foreign Minister, Prince Bernhard von Bülow, told the Spanish ambassador, "because everybody wants to be pleasant to the United States, or, at any rate, nobody wants to arouse America's anger." If Downing Street resisted pleas from Sir Henry Drummond Wolff, the irritatingly insistent ambassador at Madrid, so too did the Wilhelmstrasse, the Quai d'Orsay, and even the Ballplatz refuse to consider seriously any plans for action forceful enough to influence the Americans. Rumors sweeping through the Continent and England, speeches by British politicians and the vociferous pro-Americanism of almost all English newspapers led the American public and even official Washington to give the cabinet undeserved credit for preventing a European *démarche.* "It has been said," commented a Pennsylvania congressman on the eve of war with Spain, "that our intervention [in Cuba] may cause foreign complications. . . . There is no such danger; any foreign interference would be met by the two great English-speaking people of the world." [5] This belief was more important than the facts.

[4] White to Olney, June 17, 1896, quoted in Henry James, *Richard Olney and His Public Service* (Boston, 1923), p. 244; Hay to McKinley, October 6, 1897, quoted in Charles S. Olcott, *The Life of William McKinley* (2 vols.; Boston, 1916), vol. II, p. 129.

[5] Bülow to ———, n.d. [April, 1898], quoted in Orestes Ferrara, *The Last Spanish War: Revelations in Diplomacy* (William F. Shea, trans.; New York, 1937), p. 127; Rep. William C. Arnold, *Congressional Record*, 55th Congress, 2nd Session, p. 3193.

After months of gingerly maneuvering productive of nothing save a papal appeal for peace, Britain and Europe did make a very timid effort—too little and too late—to influence events. Spain, growing desperate as affairs neared a climax, stepped up her efforts to secure support. Maria Christina sent a tearful appeal to her aunt, Victoria, in the middle of March, and on the twenty-sixth and again on April 2 her government requested European powers to use their good offices in Washington. The Austrians endorsed the idea, and France cautiously approved. Prince von Bülow surrounded German approval with unfavorable comments on Spanish rule in Cuba, but at least he did approve, provided no one asked his government to take a lead.

Thus London held the key. Although well aware of the slipperiness of the situation, Salisbury decided to proceed. He still sympathized with Spain at heart, he believed quite wrongly that a European declaration in favor of peace might help President McKinley in a battle against congressional jingoes, and he planned to arrange things so as to minimize his risks. He asked Pauncefote to find out whether the United States would be affronted by a European declaration. Pauncefote replied that Assistant Secretary of State William R. Day, the effective head of the department who had earlier let it be known that the administration would resent interference, now said that his government would not object to an appeal for peace impartially directed to both Spain and the United States. On April 4 the cabinet agreed to permit Pauncefote to join other ambassadors in presenting an appeal to President McKinley, provided however—for ministers wished to be absolutely sure of their ground—that the President himself first assured Pauncefote such a declaration would not be unwelcome.

Pauncefote, who deeply wanted peace and had really inspired London's misconception that the President and Congress were at odds, took over from there. He talked with McKinley and then drafted a statement which was approved by the Department of State and presumably the President. On April 6, he and five ambassadorial colleagues presented themselves at the

Presidential office. As *doyen*, Pauncefote delivered what was now a forceless call for peace and continued negotiations. The President solemnly read a reply, prepared to dovetail with the appeal, stating that, while his country also cherished peace, "a duty to humanity" made it imperative to end "a situation the indefinite prolongation of which has become insufferable." [6] With this the farce of "intervention" ended.

And yet not quite. The elephantine minuet in McKinley's study had a more effective counterpart in Madrid. A parallel statement by European ambassadors tipped the scales, causing Spain to order what she had long withheld, an armistice in Cuba. Although historians still debate whether or not this concession might have been exploited by the President to avert war, at the time many Europeans and even the American ambassador at Madrid believed the door to peace had opened. The Spaniards not unnaturally sought aid to secure reciprocal concession, and Continental chancelleries, seeing logic in this request and instinctively siding with Spain, were disappointed to discover that the President paid scarcely more attention to the armistice than did the jingoes against whom he presumably fought. There was talk of a second appeal for peace, directed this time solely at the United States.

The actual initiative came from the European ambassadors at Washington. Which one took the first step is still uncertain, although the closest student of the episode, R. G. Neale, suspects the Austrian, Baron von Hengelmüller. Sir Julian Pauncefote, horrified at the President's call for intervention in Cuba, enthusiastically supported a plan "to give the United States a lecture in international morality," as Balfour later described it. Taking advantage of discretionary authority, given him after Spain's retreat, to urge the United States to consider it a basis for settlement, Pauncefote convened the ambassadors at his home to discuss a joint *démarche*. Although the envoy concealed his leadership from Downing Street, he left a clear impression in

---

[6] Quoted in Ernest R. May, *Imperial Democracy: The Emergence of America as a Great Power* (New York, 1961), p. 156.

the mind of the German ambassador, who deplored the whole
scheme, that the idea was his. The evening meeting in Pauncefote's study demonstrated that, while most of those present
deplored America's attitude, they had no power and in some
cases no desire to act. After discussion they agreed to pass the
responsibility to their superiors. They jointly recommended that
each foreign ministry present to the American ambassador an
identic note emphasizing European displeasure at the course
being followed by the United States. At the very least, Pauncefote wrote, such a note would disabuse Americans of "the erroneous impression which prevails that the armed interference of
the U.S. in Cuba for the purpose of effecting the independence
of the island commands, in the words of the Message, 'the support and approval of the civilized world.' " [7] This was a rather
feeble reason to risk American anger, and the course proposed
was most unlikely to prevent intervention in Cuba, already approved by the House of Representatives. Pauncefote had temporarily lost his usually impeccable sense of balance.

Berlin shot down the proposal without hesitation, partly because Ambassador Holleben made clear his lack of enthusiasm.
On the margin of Holleben's report on the plan, the Kaiser
scratched angrily, "I consider it perfectly futile, pointless, and
therefore harmful! We should put ourselves in wrong with the
Americans!" [8]

At first, Britain responded less decisively. When Pauncefote's dispatch arrived, Lord Salisbury was on the Continent and
Balfour, his *locum tenens*, at his home in Wiltshire. Very aware
of the dangers but unable to consult his colleagues, Balfour
equivocated. "If Pauncefote had not associated himself with this
policy," he wired the Foreign Office, "I should have rejected it at
once, but . . . he is on the spot, and he is a man of solid judgment. It seems a strong order to reject his advice." He cabled

[7] Balfour to Sanderson, April 5, 1898, quoted in R. G. Neale, *Great Britain
and United States Expansion: 1898–1900* (Lansing, 1966), p. 21; Pauncefote to
Salisbury, April 14, 1898, quoted in Alexander E. Campbell, *Great Britain and
the United States, 1895–1903* (Glasgow, 1960), p. 142.

[8] Johannes Lepsius, ed., *Die Grosse Politik der Europäischen Kabinette* (40
vols.; Berlin, 1922–1927), vol. XV, p. 24n.

Pauncefote that England would join other powers in a declaration not much more forceful than the first appeal to McKinley. As for going further, he said, "it seems very doubtful whether we ought to commit ourselves to a judgment adverse to the United States" or even whether such a course would improve the chances of peace.[9] This reply chilled Pauncefote's ardor, but it fell short of a refusal to act if Europe agreed to the course proposed by the ambassadors.

Balfour did not sleep soundly that night. Upon arising, he wrote his colleague Joseph Chamberlain that, because he had been forced to make up his mind in fifteen or twenty minutes, he had perhaps given too weak a reply. Chamberlain shot back a telegram, "Am convinced message will do no good and will be bitterly resented," and followed this up with a letter. The acting Foreign Secretary cabled Pauncefote again: because of "the extreme improbability that unsought advice will do any good and the inexpediency of . . . [taking] sides . . . , we shall at least for the moment, do nothing." [10] Pauncefote did not protest. Since Berlin and then Paris also refused to act, the fantastic scheme collapsed.

The episode remained secret until 1902. Then Salisbury's son, Lord Cranborne, speaking for the Foreign Office in the House of Commons, told a questioner that Britain had joined the first appeal to McKinley only after receiving assurances it would not offend and that she had set her face against a second effort because it gave the appearance of putting pressure on the United States. British and American newspapers built a campaign on Cranborne's statement, alleging that Britain alone prevented a European challenge in 1898. Not surprisingly, the Germans, then actively wooing the United States, reacted violently. The Kaiser himself invaded the British embassy one night to shake his finger at a sleepy ambassador and demand fair share of

[9] Balfour to Sanderson, April 15, 1898, quoted in Neale, *Britain and Expansion*, p. 21.

[10] Chamberlain to Balfour, telegram, April 16, 1898, quoted in Blanche E. C. Dugdale, *Arthur James Balfour* (2 vols.; New York, 1937), vol. I, p. 263; Balfour to Pauncefote, April 17, 1898, quoted in Neale, *Britain and Expansion*, p. 24.

the credit. His government followed up with more formal action, releasing Holleben's dispatch, with its description of Pauncefote's prominent role and the Kaiser's decisive marginal comments. The Foreign Office then sought the Ambassador's comments, perhaps with the thought of publishing a counterrebuttal as Chamberlain desired, but when Pauncefote produced a series of intricate, embarrassed letters filling in some of the gaps in his four-year-old reports, Lord Lansdowne, then Foreign Secretary, decided to leave well enough alone.

Had the Spanish-American War occurred before 1895, the Americans would probably have accepted the German version. In 1902 they simply laughed at it as a clumsy forgery, "very maladroit and blundering and German," as Henry Adams described it. President Roosevelt called at the British embassy to demonstrate his faith in Pauncefote and permitted George W. Smalley, still the London *Times* correspondent, to report that the President did not believe German allegations. Smalley later wrote in his memoirs, "a high personage in Washington"—probably a Smalley-ism for Roosevelt—"said: 'I do not believe the Imperial ink on the margin of Holleben's four-year-old dispatch was dry when the press telegram was sent from Berlin.'" To cap the Germans' discomfiture, Pauncefote soon had the ill grace to die, permitting imaginative journalists to charge that slanderers hounded him to his grave, although if anything troubled the Ambassador's last days it must have been the difficulty of explaining history to the Foreign Office. Roosevelt lowered the White House flag, not "because he was the British Ambassador, but because he was a damn good fellow," [11] and ordered the battleship *Brooklyn* to carry the corpse home to England, where the gesture received proper recognition. In death as in life, a rare indiscretion aside, Pauncefote served the cause of friendship.

Wilhelm had a point when he sought credit for scotching

[11] Adams to Elizabeth Cameron, February 16, 1902, Worthington C. Ford, ed., *Letters of Henry Adams, 1892–1918* (Boston, 1938), p. 372; George W. Smalley, *Anglo-American Memories, Second Series* (London, 1912), p. 182; Beckles Wilson, *Friendly Relations: A Narrative of Britain's Ministers and Ambassadors to America, 1791–1930* (Boston, 1934), p. 280.

the second appeal to President McKinley. Still, Pauncefote's misstep should not have exposed Salisbury, Balfour, and their colleagues to special criticism. Almost all European and English statesmen deplored the aggressive manners of republicans across the Atlantic but agreed they had no interest in the Spanish-American quarrel sufficient to justify intervention. Downing Street's policy nevertheless differed from that of Europe in three important respects which help to explain the American belief, then and later, that England was her truest friend. From the onset of the Cuban revolution, Salisbury, Balfour, and their colleagues made it clear to the American government, in as many as a dozen statements, that England would take no action the United States opposed. No other power took such pains, and the Continental powers, even Germany, reserved the right to judge every project in terms of its practicality. Furthermore, because Britain controlled the seas in 1898, she bore far more responsibility, and was seen to bear it, than Austria or France or Germany. They could propose, but she would always dispose, and the Americans knew it. On the other hand, Britain herself could have organized an anti-American front for the simple reason that Europe knew she would bear the chief burden of making it effective, and the Americans saw that she did not choose to do so. Finally, British policy differed from that of Europe in being superimposed upon the only public opinion favorable to the United States. This gave official attitudes a firmness lacking on the Continent. While Wilhelm might justifiably protest that his role was underestimated, clearly British policy was the most important in Europe. In a negative sense, if not the positive one legend-makers concocted, Salisbury's ministry permitted America to press Spain to the wall.

On April 20, with none of that reluctance Pauncefote expected, William McKinley signed a congressional resolution authorizing the use of force to free Cuba. Two days later an American ship fired the first shots of the war at a Spanish merchantman, and formal declarations soon followed. The contest, if such it can be called, lasted less than four months. Although, contrary to pre-war fears in Europe, the dynasty survived, in all other ways the war was a disaster for Spain. By the time she secured an armistice her naval strength had been destroyed in battles off Manila and Santiago de Cuba, an invading army in Cuba had so nearly completed its task that evacuation of the disease-ridden island had already begun, and American troops were mopping up Puerto Rico and preparing major moves in the Philippines. Only 385 Americans had died in battle, six times that many from disease. Never has a nation so inexpensively established itself as a major power.

Unlike Europe, where most people hoped against hope that Spain would fight off her assailant, England resounded with applause for the Americans. As Harry Thurston Peck, describing Britain's reaction in a very popular history written less than a decade later, wrote, "Within six hours after the cable had told the story, all London burst out into the rainbow hues of the American national colours. Thousands of American flags . . . [and] streamers of red, white and blue effected a brilliant contrast with the smoky walls of the metropolis. A great multitude of people assembled before the American Embassy, cheering heartily for the United States. . . . [The demonstration] banished from the hearts of all Americans who witnessed it the memory of other days, when the ties of blood and language had been nearly sundered." If Peck exaggerated, he did not do so by much. Washington Gladden, the great reform clergyman, toured England that summer giving a lecture entitled "Causes of the War, and the Reasons for Friendship Between England and America." His hearers heartily sang "The Star-Spangled Banner" —better than most Americans, Gladden observed—and applauded his speech vigorously: "I have never spoken to audiences, in which the signs of enthusiasm were so marked."[12] George III's ghost remained silent when English celebrations marked the Fourth of July for the first time in history, and shortly after the

---

[12] Harry Thurston Peck, *Twenty Years of the Republic, 1885–1905* (New York, 1906), pp. 557–558; Washington Gladden, *Recollections* (New York, 1909), pp. 357–358.

armistice the American flag, but no other foreign ensign, flew among a forest of British standards at the army's annual "march past" on Salisbury Plain.

An English journalist, Sidney Low, made the most serious of numerous attempts to explain the enthusiasm for the American cause and for Anglo-American friendship. Low discovered four basic sources: international challenges that left his country feeling isolated from all other powers and even in rivalry with them; satisfaction in the gallantry and success of another branch of the Anglo-Saxon race at a time when all races seemed likely to be tested in the crucible of world politics; America's "moderation and good temper in the hour of victory"; and the welcome Americans gave to the first signs of British sympathy.[13] Of these, the second was most important, and Low inadequately stressed it. Looking upon conflict as part of the evolutionary process by which a race won its way toward a deserved position atop the pyramid of power, Britons were exhilarated by evidence that the Anglo-Saxons had the stuff of victory within them; the American success gave them greater confidence in their own future.

What of official policy, as opposed to public sentiment? Ostensibly, Britain observed strict neutrality, and at the opening of the war the Foreign Office issued a neutrality proclamation prudently prepared just after McKinley recommended intervention in Cuba. Yet, primarily to avoid affronting the power everyone expected to win the war, a consideration particularly important to the Prime Minister, Britain so managed her policy as to benefit the Americans. Positive decisions in London and a refusal to overrule pro-American policies adopted by colonial authorities worked to the same end. Years later the *Saturday Review*, hostile to a supposed friendship which it alleged had produced only insults, claimed, "we in effect lent America the use of our Navy to prevent a European combination against America."[14] Less ridiculous is Queen Maria Christina's complaint to

[13] Sidney Low, "The Change in English Sentiment Toward the United States," *Forum* (New York), vol. XXVI (1898), pp. 369–370.
[14] *Saturday Review* (London), vol. CXV (1913), p. 639.

Victoria after the armistice that Great Britain let the Americans use facilities in ports and colonies that she denied to the Spaniards. The Marquis of Salisbury contradicted the charge, and Victoria passed on the denial to her niece, but the facts were against them.

Separate but parallel episodes in Canada and Gibraltar justify the Queen Regent's complaint. American agents in Montreal rifled the correspondence of a Spaniard, removing a letter which spoke of organizing an espionage ring. The State Department asked his expulsion from Canada. Because the evidence was tainted, Britain could have declined to act. Instead, she induced Canadian authorities to oust the man involved and other Spaniards as well. At Gibraltar the shoe was on the other foot. When war began, two American consuls in Spain withdrew to that British outpost, whence they sent to Washington a stream of coded messages, presumably containing military intelligence. The governor of Gibraltar, armed with reports from the local telegraph office, proposed to oust at least one of the Americans. Joseph Chamberlain, his direct superior, overruled the governor, and Salisbury minuted, "an awkward case but concur." "It is a very awkward case indeed," the Foreign Office's legal adviser added, pointing out that if Spain contrasted this decision with the Canadian expulsion order, "it would be not too easy to show that we have been entirely consistent." [15] The Americans continued their activities.

Among other things, these agents were watching Spanish naval movements. Late in June a Spanish squadron under Admiral Cámara, as strong as or stronger than the American force in the Far East, weighed anchor for the Philippines by way of Suez. In Egypt, Cámara sought permission to coal, and, since Egypt was still technically a Turkish possession and the Porte had not issued a proclamation of neutrality, there seemed good reason to permit Cámara to do so. However, after consulting with London,

[15] Salisbury endorsement on Colonial Office to Foreign Office, July 22, 1898, quoted in Neale, *Britain and Expansion*, p. 53; W. E. Davidson minute attached to preceding, *ibid.*, pp. 53–54.

Lord Cromer, the British voice at Cairo, induced Egyptian authorities to prevent coaling, even if carried on from lighters beyond the three-mile limit, and to order the Spanish ships to leave. They returned to Spain.

In the Caribbean, British officials consistently showed their partiality. Consul Ramsden at Santiago distinguished himself in American eyes. When, just after the armistice, he succumbed to the same noisome conditions plaguing the invaders, a delegation of American officers attended his funeral and the State Department offered official condolences to Pauncefote.

The United States also benefited from the bias of British neutrality in the Far East. American agents, planning to make use of the exiled Filipino insurrectionist Emilio Aguinaldo, made contact with him at Singapore and carried him first to Hong Kong in the revenue cutter *McCulloch* and then, after further negotiations, to Manila in the transport *Naushan*. Spain protested and sought to prevent Aguinaldo's return to his homeland, but law officers in the colonies replied that there was no evidence which would justify action, thus permitting the Americans to mount a threat to Spain from English soil. London tolerated this decision, only complaining to Washington in a forceless way long after the whole affair had come to an end.

Authorities at Hong Kong of course asked Commodore George Dewey, whose squadron had been concentrated there since February on the orders of Assistant Secretary of the Navy Theodore Roosevelt, to leave British waters when war came. Before sailing off to fame in Manila Bay, Dewey shifted his advanced base to Mirs Bay, off the mainland. British tars on ships in Hong Kong harbor, thinking him bound directly for battle, cheered the Americans as they sailed away. Mirs Bay lay in an area the British had long sought to lease from China, and in June Peking at last agreed to the request. Since Dewey's supply vessels would have been forced to leave Mirs Bay just as they had had to leave Hong Kong harbor if the British took possession, Lord Salisbury suggested that execution of the lease be delayed. The Americans used Mirs Bay for the rest of the war. In another demonstration of friendship, local authorities allowed Commodore Dewey to maintain communications with Washington through the Hong Kong cable, the only trans-Pacific link. Messages concerning military operations, they said, would not be allowed since that would violate neutrality, but Dewey was permitted to decide which of his ciphered messages fell into the prohibited category. Cable traffic did not markedly diminish.

When Dewey's cruisers sailed southeastward from Mirs Bay at the end of April, Hong Kong's best wishes followed them. The Commodore had little need of this moral support, for the Spanish force in Manila Bay was so weak that its commander, anticipating destruction, anchored his ships in shallow water to minimize the loss of life. In a seven-hour bombardment of the sitting ducks, Dewey wiped out Spanish naval power in the Pacific. Washington learned of his success from Joseph Chamberlain, who received the word from Singapore before Dewey could cable through Hong Kong. Congratulations poured in upon him, the London *Spectator* observing, "We rejoice in the efficiency of the American representative of our race, because we believe that, failing the Anglo-Saxon, the wronged of the world will find no defender." [16] After his victory the agent of Anglo-Saxon beneficence blockaded Luzon, sought to use Aguinaldo to beat the Spaniards on land, and sat back to read messages of praise, await American troops which began to arrive at the end of June, and worry a bit about Cámara until Curzon stopped him.

What followed soon became tangled in legend, thanks in large part to an erroneous account published the next year in Henry Cabot Lodge's *Our War with Spain*. Neutral naval detachments, Germany's the largest, arrived at Manila Bay to observe events and, in the German case, to support a claim to the Philippines should the Americans decide not to take them. Dewey became involved in quarrels with Vice-Admiral von Diederichs, who challenged his rules of blockade and seemed willing to put obstacles in Aguinaldo's way. By contrast the Brit-

[16] *Spectator*, May 7, 1898, quoted in Campbell, *Britain and the United States*, p. 152.

ish commander, Captain Edward Chichester, and the consul at Manila, E. H. Rawson-Walker, sided with the Americans. When, like his opposite number at Santiago, Rawson-Walker died, his funeral also received the honor of the attendance of American officers; Dewey himself was among the mourners.

When Dewey bombarded Manila to soften up the city for a ground assault, Chichester moved two ships nearby to observe the effect of American fire. In so doing, he appeared to place himself deliberately between the American and German ships. Although none on the scene so reported at the time, there soon developed a tale that Chichester saved Dewey from a stab in the back at a critical time. Nothing von Diederichs or his superiors could say was able to check the legend's growth, and many still believe it despite the refutation by Thomas A. Bailey as long ago as 1939. More than any real episode, this imaginary one contributed to the belief that England was the only friend America had during the war with Spain. The tale grew in fertile ground prepared by the contrasting attitudes of von Diederichs and Chichester before and after the attack on Manila. Only Chichester fired a twenty-one-gun salute when the Stars and Stripes rose over the city, whereas a German cruiser departing a few days later churlishly did not even offer to carry dispatches for the American commander, a common courtesy when communication was difficult.

Only a few days after Dewey sent Spain's Far Eastern squadron to the bottom, Lord Salisbury concluded that the United States would keep the Philippines. This was either a very shrewd or a very lucky guess, for the President left the issue open at the time of the armistice two months later and only at the end of October did he finally instruct his representatives at the peace negotiations to demand the entire archipelago. Perhaps Salisbury engaged in wishful thinking, for once it became apparent that Spain no longer had the strength to hold the Philippines, various considerations suggested that American ownership would best serve British interests.

Sentimental racism, particularly the concept of "the white

man's burden," almost never affected Salisbury's judgment. But the Prime Minister could not ignore the hardship British firms, which controlled seventy percent of the Philippines' import trade, might suffer should another European power take over the islands. He might even be forced, against his wishes, to take the islands for Britain if the Americans withdrew; trading interests urged this course whenever news reports suggested the Americans did not intend to stay in the Philippines. Moreover, while other great powers might accept transfer of the islands to a nation not deeply involved in international rivalries, they would raise difficulties if one of their own number moved into Manila, thus adding to the already unsettling scramble in the Far East. Britain had little hope that anything, even the possession of Far Eastern colonies, would induce the Americans to cooperate actively with her against other imperialists, but she did feel that American acquisition of the Philippines would least disturb the shaky status quo.

Strong as this feeling was, wisdom suggested that it would be best served by a policy of silent restraint. Drummond Wolff, who wanted his country to offer her services as mediator, received only rebuffs from superiors who understood that neither Spain nor America was likely to be grateful to whoever suggested a compromise peace. Downing Street contented itself with a careful sounding of American intentions, at the same time making clear that if the United States did not take the islands Great Britain might wish to do so. The British government almost never sought to influence either Madrid or Washington, although on one occasion Salisbury passed on to Vienna a report of American demands, then not including cession of the entire Philippine group, in the hope that Austria would urge Spain to accept them as a basis for peace. When Frederick W. Holls, a confidant of McKinley, visited Balfour for a wide-ranging discussion of world politics, the English statesman cautiously refrained from making known his government's views on the Philippine question. A visit to the United States by Joseph Chamberlain led to rumors that he had gone there to influence the Americans in an imperialistic direction. Apparently some colleagues entertained this suspicion, for upon his return the Colonial Secretary felt constrained to reassure them, "I did not see nor did I have any communication direct or indirect with any member of the United States Government, and I declined to the reporters to offer any advice as to the way in which the United States Government should deal with the Philippines." [17] It had been simply a summer visit to Democratic in-laws. Even the impulsive Chamberlain recognized that anti-imperialists would exploit the slightest British effort to influence McKinley if it became known. Nor did it seem necessary to act since the ministry believed what proved to be the case: that in the end McKinley would demand the Philippines.

The British government adopted much the same posture toward two lesser bits of American imperialism. After the Americans signed a treaty of annexation with Hawaii in June 1897, Germany approached England to suggest a joint protest or common action to procure compensation in the form of American withdrawal from Samoa. Salisbury declined, and, except to show mild interest in gaining a cable station by lease, preserved a granitic silence until annexation was finally completed in July 1898. In Samoa, where an Anglo-German-American protectorate of 1889 failed to bring stability, trouble broke out in the spring of 1898. British and American officials on the spot cooperated against the Germans, but neither London nor Washington sought to coordinate policy at a higher level. After long discussions, the islands were divided by an agreement in December 1899, the best share falling to the United States as the result of a German proposal designed to impress American opinion.

Once the United States chose an imperialistic course the British showed their benevolence. Although traders with the Philippines and Puerto Rico expressed concern at the prospect of seeing markets disappear behind tariff walls, Salisbury raised the matter with Washington in only the most perfunctory fashion.

[17] Chamberlain memorandum, October 11, 1898, quoted in Neale, *Britain and Expansion*, p. 146.

Actually, British exports to the Philippines, which declined drastically between 1889 and 1898, recovered even more spectacularly after the United States took the islands. American regulations stimulated the growth of her own trade with the Philippines without, thanks to a steady increase in the market, causing harm to British traders.

In the Philippines, Aguinaldo, who considered American rule just as unpalatable as Spanish, raised a new standard of revolt early in 1899. British consular and naval officials instinctively supported the Americans as the latter fanned out over the archipelago. English assistance, including the loan of what then passed for landing craft, made much easier a landing at Iloilo harbor which established American power on the island of Panay, and a British gunboat intervened at Cebu to bring about the peaceful surrender of that strategic city in the central Philippines. American naval officers repeatedly praised English representatives for the help they gave, whereas the Germans, seeking to remove the bad impression left by events at Manila Bay, gained no credit when they too offered assistance. The war against Filipino insurrection took a good deal of the bloom off American imperialism, and many Englishmen and Americans deplored the way in which the campaign of repression developed. "Since our own Crimean muddle," commented the *Economist* after viewing bushwhacking for several months, "there has been no worse instance of military mismanagement than that displayed by the American War Department in Cuba and the Philippines." [18] Bedeviled by a quarrel and soon by a war with the Boers which suggested obvious parallels to the American experience, Salisbury's government never withdrew its sympathy from the United States. The two conflicts ended almost simultaneously in 1902.

Not all British opinion was sympathetic. Those who opposed imperialism for their own country, notably James Bryce,

---

[18] *Economist*, June 24, 1899, quoted in H. C. Allen, *Great Britain and the United States: A History of Anglo-American Relations, 1783–1952* (New York, 1955), p. 43.

deplored the American decision to go down the same road. Professor Goldwin Smith, an indefatigable advocate of Anglo-American understanding who taught both at Oxford and Cornell during a long career, believed that friendship purchased at the price of parallel imperialisms was not worth it. Like counterparts in the United States who feared for the militarization of life, the *Manchester Guardian* asked, "What is to become of the root ideas of the American Republic?" In addition, conservatives to the right of the ministry itself often suggested that McKinley's decision for empire heralded American efforts to displace England as the world's paramount power. More moderately, Frederick Greenwood, a contributor to the *Nineteenth Century*, suggested that, while American imperialism might temporarily benefit England, "a wise man will say that the appearance of another competitor for empire by no means lightens the obligation to go well armed." [19]

Such comment was greatly overshadowed by favorable judgments. While the *Guardian* might worry about the fate of American democracy, others felt that the new policy would confer stability—"a stability which it at present lacks," said the *Saturday Review*—upon the United States. This was standard imperialistic doctrine, as applicable to another country as to Britain herself. Additionally, Englishmen welcomed the American departure because it reflected favorably upon their own exertions. "After a nation has pursued certain paths alone in the face of some slight misrepresentations," Kipling said without mentioning that much of this "misrepresentation" had been American, "it is consoling to find another nation (which one can address without a dictionary) preparing to walk along the same lines to, I doubt not, the same ends." [20]

Finally, English commentators played upon the racial theme. Racist concepts, says Geoffrey Seed, a British historian,

[19] *Guardian*, quoted in Richard H. Heindel, *The American Impact on Great Britain, 1898–1914* (Philadelphia, 1940), p. 85; Frederick Greenwood, "The Anglo-American Future," *Nineteenth Century* (London), vol. XLIV (1898), p. 11.
[20] *Saturday Review*, quoted in Heindel, *American Impact*, p. 85; Kipling, quoted in *ibid.*, p. 88.

"received the most ardent attention, and inspired the most fluent rhetoric." By imperialism, as by victory in war, the Americans showed themselves part of a superior race. They had emerged from one phase of the evolutionary struggle into another, less dramatic, perhaps, and more demanding. Professor Edward Dicey, a tub-thumper for empire, welcomed evidence that "they, as well as we, are prepared to carry out that manifold destiny which is the birthright of the Anglo-Saxon race." After all, the Professor observed, Anglo-Saxon expansion had "done more than any other cause to promote civilization and progress," [21] as it would inevitably continue to do. For Dicey and many compatriots, racial disparities justified American rule over the Filipinos and Puerto Ricans, while the benevolent Anglo-Saxon outlook assured that the new dominions would not be cruelly exploited like other imperial possessions.

Many Englishmen expected the new imperialism to bring about diplomatic involvements which would throw America into British arms. What easier way could there be to improve security in a hostile world—a world of alliances in which Britain had no allies—than to link up with the one great power which carried no costly baggage of commitments to others, required no surrender of substantial British interests as the price of friendship? Early in 1898, before the war, the McKinley administration rebuffed a British attempt to forge an agreement on Far Eastern questions. Nevertheless, what Kaiser Wilhelm in 1897 called "the American-British Society for International Theft and Warmongering" [22] now seemed a real possibility to him, and indeed to most European statesmen, for they could not believe that where there was a great deal of smoke there were not at least many eager arsonists. In the United States, talk of an alliance became so common, even before the war, that Irishmen in New York organized an Anti-British Alliance Society as early as February

[21] Geoffrey Seed, "British Reactions to American Imperialism Reflected in Journals of Opinion, 1898–1900," *Political Science Quarterly* (New York), vol. LXXIII (1958), p. 257; Edward Dicey, "The New American Imperialism," *Nineteenth Century*, vol. XLIV, p. 501.

[22] Ray Ginger, *The Age of Excess: The United States from 1877 to 1914* (New York, 1965), p. 197.

1898. Anti-imperialists, particularly Carl Schurz, considered it an effective tactic to declare that overseas expansion was the result of or would lead to entangling commitments with England.

Actually no one in authority, and very few without it, seriously proposed political ties. Any rational man knew that, however American sentiment had changed, alliance was a political impossibility. The implications of empire were too new, the advantages of isolation too apparent, the legacy of Anglophobia too strong. Moreover, most of those, whether British or American, who supported closer ties expected their own country to dominate the partnership, and serious negotiations would have led to immense difficulties. Few Englishmen were prepared to accept Brooks Adams' description of their island as a mere "fortified outpost of the Anglo-Saxon race," [23] while Americans felt that they could take a back seat to no one.

There was, on the British side, one notable exception: William T. Stead, an enthusiast, a preacher, a reformer. In 1890 Stead had founded the English *Review of Reviews*, which quickly developed an American offshoot of the same name, with a view of bringing the two people closer together, and the prospect of American leadership did not faze him. In *The Americanization of the World*, published in 1901, he wrote, "The Briton instead of chafing against this inevitable supersession, should cheerfully acquiesce in the decree of Destiny, and stand in betimes with the conquering American. . . . Is there no Morgan who will undertake to bring about the greatest combination of all—a combination of the whole English-speaking race?" Among all the other enthusiasms of his career, as diverse as spiritualism and disarmament, Stead never lost sight of Anglo-American union. After he died in the sinking of the *Titanic* an obituarist wrote, "His grave is where he might have chosen it, midway between England and America, under the full stream of their intercourse." [24] Even Stead did not speak as he did in *The Americani-*

[23] Brooks Adams, *America's Economic Supremacy* (New York, 1900), p. 10.
[24] William T. Stead, *The Americanization of the World, or the Trend of the*

zation of the World until the Boer War lowered British self-confidence, and most Englishmen doubtless considered his views there as nonsensical as others he was then propounding about spiritualism.

Many writers simply expected, or hoped, that each nation would naturally tend to support the other's policies, as England had done during the Spanish-American War. Some thought both peoples had already learned this lesson; others saw the need for time and education—education they sought to provide. Whenever accomplished, this community of outlook promised great things. " 'Continental Europe' is not even now a match for the combined strength of the English-speaking peoples," asserted Sir George Clarke, "and a permanent *rapprochement* between them would be the best guarantee of the world." [25]

Even the Anglo-American League, the most prestigious propagandist for friendship, which had Bryce as chairman and wealthy men like Andrew Carnegie and Albert Harmsworth on its executive committee, asked no more than that "every effort should be made in the interest of civilization and peace to secure the most cordial and constant co-operation between the two nations." [26] Formed in London (and soon copied in New York) with great pomp in the summer of 1898, supported by peers, politicians, and celebrities, including Asquith, Balfour and Haldane, Conan Doyle, Rider Haggard and Tennyson, the League did its best to influence opinion, but by 1903, because it had no real program, it was moribund.

Some who, for reasons of conviction or tactics, did not recommend an alliance in 1898 hoped to see one develop at a later date. Bryce, Dicey, Mahan, and the aspiring political apprentice Albert J. Beveridge all spoke that way. Aside from Beveridge, the most eloquent advocate was Lyman Abbott, preacher and editor of the *Outlook*, who considered alliance talk premature but

---

Twentieth Century (London, 1901), pp. 5, 12; J. L. Garvin, quoted in Frederic Whyte, *The Life of William T. Stead* (2 vols.; London, 1925), vol. II, p. 315.

[25] Sir George Sydenham Clarke, "England and America," *Nineteenth Century*, vol. XLIV, p. 195.

[26] Sir Frederick Pollock, *The Monroe Doctrine* (London, 1902), p. 6.

asked, "Who can measure the advantage to liberty, to democracy, to popular rights and popular intelligence, to human progress, to a free and practical Christianity, which such an alliance
would bring with it?" In similar vein an English journal commented, "They can make right triumph over mere might; they
can render wars impossible without their permission; they can
introduce an era of peace and prosperity such as had been unknown in history." [27] But this happy day lay still a good way in
the future.

Alliances, said the *Edinburgh Review,* were "naturally dis-
tasteful to the robust independence of the Anglo-Saxon race."
The few who favored immediate political ties either had no influence or, like Professor George Burton Adams of Yale, hedged
their bets by advocating an alliance as the first step toward a
"united commonwealth of all nations." [28] In any case an alliance,
rigorously defined, had very little appeal in either country, no
matter how often writers hailed Anglo-American understanding,
no matter how much they dreamed of the Stars and Stripes and
the Union Jack marching in step at the head of the world parade.

True of mere journalists and abstract observers, this was even
more true of those directing events. John Hay is the American official most often considered to have favored an alliance. An
Anglo-Saxon from the tip of polished London shoes to the point
of his neat gray beard, Hay had long since shucked off anti-British feeling absorbed while serving as President Lincoln's secretary during the Civil War. Diplomatic service in Europe at the
end of the 'sixties left him cynical about Continental monarch-
ies. At the same time Hay deplored the erosion of deferential
politics in the United States and the displacement of Anglo-
Saxon leadership. His novel *The Breadwinners,* published in
1884, described the losing fight waged by a retired soldier of English descent against immigrant strikers and political bosses. Eng-

---

[27] Lyman Abbott, "The Basis of an Anglo-American Understanding," *North
American Review* (New York), vol. CLXVI (1898), p. 521; *Fortnightly Review,*
quoted in Seed, "British Reactions," p. 262.

[28] *Edinburgh Review,* quoted in *ibid.,* p. 270; George Burton Adams, "A Century of Anglo-Saxon Expansion," *Atlantic Monthly* (Boston), vol. LXXIX
(1897), p. 538.

land seemed the perfect middle ground between autocracy and undisciplined democracy. When McKinley defeated Bryan, Hay wanted to become ambassador to Great Britain. He presented McKinley with a gold ring containing a lock of George Washington's hair to wear at the inauguration and, more important, gained the support of Henry Cabot Lodge. Just before the inauguration, McKinley let Hay know that he would gain his object.

Hay sailed happily for England in April 1897. A large crowd met his ship at Southampton, horrifying Hay's friends Henry James and Henry Adams. Adams, Hay commented in typical style, "fled to the innermost recesses of the ship—some authorities say to the coal-bunkers—out of sight and sound of the whole revolving exchange of compliments." Once Adams had been recovered, Hay proceeded to London, where, with the aid of his wife's fortune, he quickly established himself in the social world. Hay had the good luck to arrive in Britain just as the wave of friendship began to rise, and he gloried in his English experiences. His seventeen months there were, his biographer observes, "the happiest months of his life." [29] The Ambassador was called upon to negotiate very few issues, although the sealing question did occupy him for a while. For the most part, he simply reported happily on both the official and the public reactions to events in Cuba and the United States.

Hay's two most noted speeches in Britain, the "partnership in beneficence" speech in April 1898 and a Fourth of July oration three months later, contained rococo imagery. In the former, he described a nighttime naval review when the U.S.S. *Brooklyn's* searchlights suddenly broke the darkness to illuminate the mast where "those friendly banners fluttered, proclaiming to the navies of the world their message of good will. . . . May we not hope," he asked his audience, "that the lesson and inspiration of that spectacle may last as long as those banners shall float over the seven seas, carrying always in their shadow freedom and civilization?" This led him to the main theme of his speech, the com-

[29] Hay to Lodge, May 6, 1897, quoted in Thayer, *Hay*, vol. II, p. 159; Tyler Dennett, *John Hay: From Poetry to Politics* (New York, 1933), p. 181.

mon responsibility to bear imperial burdens, but not to any suggestions that the colors be nailed side by side on the mast. On
the Fourth of July the flag metaphor shifted. This time Hay described Carnegie's solution to the vexing problem of how to fly
the Stars and Stripes and the British standard over his castle,
Skibo, without giving precedence to one or the other: "he had
the two flags sewed together. . . . The combination was rather
—I will not say heavy, but weighty, and in the still days of midsummer it drooped upon the staff. But when a breeze came the
twin flags unfolded the splendor of their colors, and when a gale
blew they stood stiffly out to the air, proclaiming their attach-
ment to every quarter of the sky." [30] The speaker intended to
suggest that England and the United States would rally together
in international storms, but once again he contented himself
with simile. Neither Hay's speeches nor his correspondence suggested any political connection.

In August 1898, President McKinley recalled Hay to become secretary of state. Hay delayed his departure as long as he
could, and when he left England he carried friendly letters from
leading statesmen and the plaudits of the political world. Perhaps this provided consolation; it did not make him happy. "All
the fun of my life ended on the platform at Euston," he wailed
to his wife, who had the good fortune to stay a little longer in the
mother country.[31]

Everyone expected Hay to use his new office to further
Anglo-American understanding. "Day's leaving the Department,
means a great loss to us," the German ambassador at Washington commented, "the more so because his . . . successor, Col.
John Hay, belongs wholly to the British direction." "As long as I
stay here," Hay wrote to his old subordinate Henry White, "no
action shall be taken contrary to my conviction that the one indispensable feature of our foreign policy should be a friendly understanding with England. But an alliance must remain, in the

---

[30] Quoted in *ibid.*, pp. 218–219; *The Addresses of John Hay* (New York,
1906), p. 71.
[31] Hay to Clara Hay, October 19, 1898, quoted in Dennett, *Hay*, p. 196.

present state of things, an unattainable dream." Hay never changed his position. He sought to improve relations, always used courteous language, and deplored appeals to Anglophobia, but he made no gratuitous concessions and, if anything, let fear of criticism overrestrain him. He once expostulated, "All I have ever done with England is to have wrung great concessions out of her with no compensation. And yet, these idiots say I'm not an American because I don't say, 'To hell with the Queen,' at every breath." [32] Hay never learned to live with criticism, and it galled him to be accused of doing things which he might have wished to do but which common sense prevented him from considering, either at London or Washington.

Joseph Chamberlain, the most phil-American member of Salisbury's cabinet, occupied a position very similar to Hay's. The Colonial Secretary, who had taken as his third wife the daughter of Cleveland's Secretary of War, a woman nearly thirty years his junior whom he met while in Washington on a diplomatic mission in 1888, frequently visited the United States and always cherished its friendship. Chamberlain was far less set in his ways than the aging Prime Minister and other Unionists who had inherited rather than hammered out their principles. Devoted above all to the idea of empire, he willingly adopted radical tactics to further it, at one time or another leaving the party of his youth, engaging in devious and politically risky machinations in South Africa, urging alliances almost indiscriminately, and throwing overboard the time-honored ballast of free trade to crusade for imperial preference. Chamberlain moved jauntily through the political world, monocle on a black ribbon, orchid in the buttonhole of a somewhat foppish frock coat, but his jauntiness concealed deep concern over British isolation.

These factors made Chamberlain more willing than his colleagues to consider a close connection with the United States, and contemporaries fastened upon him a lasting reputation as

[32] Holleben to Foreign Office, August 16, 1898, quoted in *ibid.*, p. 385; Hay to White, September 24, 1899, quoted in Thayer, *Hay*, vol. II, p. 221; Hay to John W. Foster, June 23, 1900, quoted in *ibid.*, pp. 233–234.

the chief apostle of alliance. In several famous speeches the Colonial Secretary used that very word, rousing storms in both countries. Yet Chamberlain, sometimes indiscreet and impulsive but rarely a fool, clearly had little hope of any binding, immediate commitment for reciprocal aid, and his use of the word "alliance" was perhaps deliberately imprecise and certainly often tangled in qualifications. "Brummagem Joe" spoke his hopes rather than his plans, failing only to see that his speeches might rebound against an Anglo-American connection rather than ease the path.

On the eve of America's war with Spain, Chamberlain had a long conversation with Ambassador Hay. The British leader, Hay reported, desired an alliance but, accepting the barrier of American tradition, really hoped only for "an assurance of common action on important questions." United in outlook, he went on, the two nations could enforce peace all over the world. Then, in a less irenic vein, he added, "I should rejoice in an occasion in which we could fight side by side. The good effect of it would last for generations." [33] Chamberlain did not suggest negotiations for an alliance, did not even press Hay to seek instructions looking to the establishment of a common outlook, and implied that dramatic events—a war—would have to precede close union.

Hay pointed out to Chamberlain that the Liberals had so far had "a monopoly on expressions of goodwill to America." Hay thought this observation at least partially explained the speech Chamberlain gave at Birmingham on May 13, just three weeks after the Spanish-American War began. In this famous address Chamberlain told his constituents it was Britain's duty "to establish and maintain bonds of amity with our kinsmen across the Atlantic." Race, custom, and ideals drew the nations together. "I do not know what the future has in store for us, I don't know what arrangements may be possible with the United States, but this I know and feel—that the closer, the more cordial, the fuller and the more definite, these arrangements are with the consent of both people, the better it will be for both

[33] Hay to McKinley, April 4, 1898, quoted in Olcott, *McKinley*, vol. II, p. 130.

and for the world." An effective challenge to the Liberals' monopoly and, because of the speaker's office, an apparent indication of ministerial plans, this speech really only expressed a fervent hope. In the quoted passage the Colonial Secretary indicated his understanding of the realities, including the importance of American opinion, and in a peroration he returned to a theme expressed to Hay, that the price of alliance might be common action in time of war. "Terrible as war may be," he declared, "even war itself would be cheaply purchased if in a great and noble cause the Stars and Stripes and the Union Jack should wave together over an Anglo-Saxon alliance." [34]

In the heat of the moment, amidst all sorts of rumors of secret agreements, Chamberlain's apostolic vision was taken as an indication of immediate intentions. The uproar led to questions in the House of Commons. Chamberlain, who proudly affirmed at this time and in other speeches throughout the year that he desired "a cordial and intimate connection," assured the members that he did not want and was sure the Americans did not want an alliance. [35]

Visiting the United States that summer, Chamberlain may well have seen the way in which Americans misinterpreted, or overinterpreted, his original speech. In any case, he elaborated upon his views in an article published in an American magazine, *Scribner's*, in December. By the use of the word "alliance" in the title, he once again left himself open to misconstruction. However, the body of the article, while it waxed rhapsodic on the growth of American friendship, explicitly advised both countries to heed the counsel of Washington's Farewell Address. Time, he seemed to imply, would lead to a recognition of mutual interests in many areas, not to an agreement which pledged one state to come to the aid of the other.

For nearly a year thereafter Chamberlain remained not silent, for he was incapable of that, but at least discreet. Then, for

[34] Hay to Lodge, May 25, 1898, quoted in Thayer, *Hay*, vol. II, p. 169; Chamberlain, quoted in Joseph L. Garvin and Julian S. Amery, *The Life of Joseph Chamberlain* (4 vols.; London, 1932–1951), vol. III, pp. 301–302.
[35] Quoted in *ibid.*, p. 303.

reasons having very little to do with the United States, he once more raised the subject of an alliance, although with a strange twist. In November 1899, Kaiser Wilhelm paid a visit to his grandmother, Victoria. Chamberlain and Balfour talked with Prince von Bülow, who accompanied his master, about Anglo-German disputes; though they reached no agreements, the climate seemed promising. Once more Chamberlain burst forth at a public gathering, this time at Leicester. "If the union between England and America is a powerful factor in the cause of peace," he said, seeming to assume, incidentally, that union existed, "a new Triple Alliance between the Teutonic race and the two great branches of the Anglo-Saxon race will be a still more potent influence in the future of the world." Once again the full text made it clear that Chamberlain was at most floating a trial balloon and that when he used the dread word he had in mind an entente, not a formal pledge. This did not save him from condemnation in all three countries. Americans felt as before about involvement abroad, Germans interpreted the speech as a reflection of British weakness caused by the Boer War, and many Englishmen considered a departure from isolation unthinkable, particularly if it meant connection with Germany. Chamberlain "really must be kept out of foreign politics or he will make everything impossible, even friendship with America," complained Sir Edward Grey, the Liberal spokesman on foreign policy.[36]

Although grateful for real and imagined British support during the Spanish war, the American people were, as Sir Edward knew, in no mood to abandon nonentanglement. Chamberlain's talk roused suspicions which Democrats found it good politics to exploit and which perhaps caused the McKinley administration to proceed with more circumspection than would otherwise have been the case. Chamberlain's error was that he never made clear, on the one hand, that he did not speak for his colleagues and, on the other, that while he dreamed of an American connection,

[36] Chamberlain, quoted in Lionel M. Gelber, *The Rise of Anglo-American Friendship: A Study in World Politics, 1898–1906* (London, 1938), p. 70; Grey to Haldane, December 4, 1899, quoted in George M. Trevelyan, *Grey of Fallodon* (London, 1937), p. 77.

undefined but close, he knew the ground was not yet ripe.

"No British Minister . . . would be such a fool as to embark on anything so absurd as alliance negotiations with the United States," the *National Review* confidently asserted in 1900, commenting on rumors seeping through the American campaign. Chamberlain's oratory led to no approaches to Washington. On the other hand, his suggestion about Germany received cautious support. Discussions with Berlin continued sporadically until the autumn of 1901. (When negotiations finally collapsed, the then Foreign Secretary, Lord Lansdowne, gave as one reason for avoiding a commitment "the risk of entangling ourselves in a policy which might be hostile to America. With our knowledge of the German Emperor's views in regard to the United States, this is to my mind a formidable obstacle." His under-secretary went further, declaring that he considered the Kaiser's anti-Americanism alone "sufficient to condemn the policy as far as we are concerned." [37]) The long Anglo-German negotiations demonstrate many things, among them that the British government had written off an approach to the United States as a means of meeting the problems caused by British isolation.

Nevertheless, as we have seen, Salisbury and his countrymen welcomed America's new departure of 1898. An alliance might for the present remain, to use Hay's phrase, "an unattainable dream," but the new American posture was likely to prove useful to Great Britain. Although even Salisbury hoped for too much too soon, the events of 1898 had developed in a fashion extremely helpful to his country. They had, as Theodore Roosevelt observed, drawn the two nations closer together than at any time since the end of the Seven Years' War in 1763.

Above all, 1898 had seen a great change in American sentiment. Even Beatrice Webb, singlemindedly pursuing her inves-

[37] *National Review* (London), vol. XXXV (1900), p. 191; Lansdowne memorandum, November —, 1901, George P. Gooch and Harold Temperley, eds., *British Documents on the Origin of the War, 1898–1914* (11 vols.; London, 1926–1938), vol. II, p. 92; Cranborne memorandum, November 18, 1901, quoted in George Monger, *The End of Isolation: British Foreign Policy, 1900–1907* (London, 1963), p. 66n.

tigations, recorded that the new spirit of "mutual admiration" lent "a pleasant flavour to our intercourse with this emotional people." [38] Other factors, especially the racist emphasis which came with imperialism, helped to transform American feelings, but the change was produced above all by British sympathy during the war with Spain. The historian can show that official policy was calculated rather than instinctive, that legend often exaggerated both its depth and importance. Contemporary Americans only saw, or thought they saw, that the government and people of England sided with the United States when the rest of the world was unfriendly. They warmly reciprocated, even those who, like Carl Schurz, deplored the drift to imperialism and were horrified by talk of a close political connection between the two countries.

While the greatest outpourings of sentiment, both in England and America, occurred during the war, the new spirit lived on. A year later one of the heroes of the war, Theodore Roosevelt, attended a great Methodist meeting of thirteen thousand people. Two little girls marched onto the stage bearing the national flags of England and the United States; one sang "Columbia" and the other "Rule Britannia," after which they crossed flags. "The taste of the manifestation might possibly be criticised," wrote Roosevelt, "but the sentiment it stood for was excellent, and the audience boiled with enthusiasm and demanded two encores. This could not have occurred a couple of years ago. . . . Now, all of this may not last, and it probably won't last quite in its present good shape, but I am greatly mistaken if we ever slide back into the old condition of bickering and angry distrust." [39]

[38] Shannon, ed., *Webb Diary*, p. 94.
[39] Roosevelt to Spring Rice, August 11, 1899, Elting E. Morison, ed., *The Letters of Theodore Roosevelt* (8 vols.; Cambridge, 1951–1954), vol. II, p. 1051.

CHAPTER FOUR

The Imperial Impulse

IMPERIALISM TRAVELS in a multitude of guises. From direct
control over subject peoples it shades off into political influence or economic exploitation or even cultural domination, to
say nothing of the ideological and emotional underpinning of
policy, and the imaginative critic can find it in the presence of
Coca-Cola in Afghanistan or chewing-gum in Tuscany. If one
focuses only on territorial acquisition, the vastness and subtlety
of the imperial drive is missed, but if the track of influence is
followed to its farthest tendons—to the green bottles and the
tinfoil wrappers—the concept becomes unmanageably diffuse. In
a study of Anglo-American relations rather than of the imperial
phenomenon itself, one may simply pursue the most relevant
manifestations of the various forms of imperialism.

Imperialism played a major role in the great rapprochement. Imperialism narrowly defined—American conquests in
1898, England's war with the Boers—had a great impact. So too
did certain developments which fit only within the broader conceptions of imperialism—for example, the economic penetration
of China by both countries and the establishment of American
predominance in Latin America. Looming over all these things
lay doctrines which very often suggested the superior virtue of
the Anglo-Saxon and in other ways indicated the similarity and
common interests of the two peoples. The Anglo-American relationship is best illustrated by focusing on these areas, areas where
their imperialisms came into contact or resulted from the flow of
similar ideals.

The world over, imperialism came into fashion toward the end of the nineteenth century. The very word, smacking of Caesarism and evoking unpleasant memories of two Napoleons, had been in disrepute. Sir Charles Dilke's *Greater Britain* (1866–1867), in some ways almost an imperialistic tract, nevertheless denounced "a mere imperialism, where one man rules and the rest are slaves," [1] and Disraeli's campaign to make Victoria an empress roused protest because of the term's unfortunate connotations. While Americans less frequently employed the word, they considered themselves sworn enemies of colonial exploitation. The doctrine of President Monroe summed up their feeling, statesmen appealed to it in their quarrels with England and Spain over territory on the North American continent, and most Americans refused to see any similarity between their own expansion and foreign patterns they denounced.

And yet there were stirrings as the century moved on. The great English historian James A. Froude propagated the imperial idea in the 1870's. Victorian statesmen, devoted to what has been called "the imperialism of free trade," drifted reluctantly or unwittingly into expansion into African areas which themselves had little value as markets in order to protect those already under the Union Jack. In the United States, the Pan-American policy begun by James G. Blaine and widely supported, the pressure to annex Hawaii following the revolution which deposed Queen Liliuokalani in 1893, concern over faraway Samoa, and even Cleveland's interference in Britain's dispute with Venezuela all forecast the coming of a new spirit.

When imperialism burst into the open in the later 'nineties, both in England and the United States it no longer had the militaristic, despotic aura of the past, nor was it ever really to regain that aura despite water cures in the Philippine Islands and concentration camps in South Africa. Like so much else in the two countries, imperialism had become democratized, its appeal broadened and its justifications sentimentalized. American expansionism, once primarily the expression of agricultural inter-

[1] Quoted in Archibald P. Thornton, *Doctrines of Imperialism* (New York, 1965), p. 23.

ests, and British imperialism, formerly the province of small political and economic cliques, now commanded far wider support. Conservatives in England were joined, in this instance, by Liberal Imperialists and even Fabians like George Bernard Shaw and the Webbs. In the United States the drive for territory was largely a Republican doctrine, although some Democrats like Walter Hines Page, editor of the *Atlantic,* supported it. Most Democrats, rallying behind William Jennings Bryan once again, condemned the policy of acquisition. As in Great Britain, the force of this narrow form of imperialism soon spent itself. By 1900 even Republicans sought no more and in some cases regretted what had already been obtained. They and the Democrats, like all parties in Great Britain, agreed on a broader imperialism, an imperialism of economic penetration, political influence, and moral leadership. The advent of Liberals in 1905 and Democrats in 1913 changed rhetoric more than policy. Woodrow Wilson deployed more force against Latin Americans than his favorite enemy, Theodore Roosevelt, and in 1916 he approved legislation which, while promising Filipino independence, postponed it to an indefinite date. Imperialism, and particularly imperialist doctrine, had done its work.

American entry into the elite company of empires, coinciding with renewed imperial interest in Britain, demolished many irritants between the nations. Only two weeks after the Senate approved the treaty by which the United States annexed the Philippines, Puerto Rico, and Guam, the most famous Anglo-American of his day wrote, "To live in England, is, inevitably, to feel the 'imperial' question in a different way and take it at a different angle from what one might . . . do in America." In quick time, many stay-at-homes absorbed Henry James' angle of vision. The exhilaration of empire, when felt, was now common to both countries; the burdens of empire, when imposed, were also like British burdens. In 1900, when anti-imperialism crested in American politics, an English journal of impeccable conservatism observed that if any other power had taken the Philippines "American sympathy would have been enlisted actively on behalf of the natives. Circumstances alter cases." The writer continued, "They can [now] believe that others than themselves may unwillingly annex and assume the government of territory which they do not covet." [2] America's imperial career partially disarmed criticism of England, converting some to the cause and giving others, if they would avoid obvious hypocrisy, a primary target nearer to hand.

English opinion drew comfort from the new American course. Although a few reactionaries grumbled at republican aggressiveness, most Britons found pleasure in "an assumed, vicarious motherhood of an imperial youngster." Moreover, that the Americans found it proper to ape the imperialism of the mother country, to establish institutions against which they had so long inveighed, made British policy seem even more just or inevitable. At the same time the American advance assured that the burdens of empire—and almost all but the most unreasonably sanguine assumed the burdens would be heavy—would to some degree be shared. Two nations with similar ideals would spread them to the benighted heathen in far away lands. Professor Edward Dicey "deem[ed] it matter for congratulation that our American fellow-townsmen . . . have shown that they have preserved the ideal of an Imperial mission," and the *Fortnightly Review* suggested that Englishmen "not look upon them as rivals, but welcome them as fellow labourers in the work of the better ordering of the world." [3]

From the very outset of the American adventure Englishmen realized what Americans were more reluctant to learn, that in addition to the burdens of internal regulation the possession of an empire necessarily involved the owner in world politics. They hoped this involvement would mean quarrels with other

[2] James to Henry James, Jr., February 24, 1899, Percy Lubbock, ed., *The Letters of Henry James* (2 vols.; New York, 1920), vol. I, p. 318; "The Coming Presidential Election," *Quarterly Review* (London), vol. CXCII (1900), p. 492.
[3] Richard H. Heindel, *The American Impact on Great Britain, 1898–1914* (Philadelphia, 1940), p. 51; Edward Dicey, "The New American Imperialism," *Nineteenth Century* (London), vol. XLIV (1898), p. 501; J. Lowry Whittle, "Bryan and McKinley: The Parting of the Ways," *Fortnightly Review* (London), vol. LXXIV (1898), p. 789.

powers rather than Britain, who would thereby benefit. The Prime Minister himself, commenting at the end of 1898 on the new power of the United States, declared, "no one can deny that their appearance among the factors at all events of Asiatic, and possibly of European diplomacy is not a grave and serious event, which may not conduce to the interests of peace, though," he added, "I think in any event they are likely to conduce to the interests of Great Britain."[4] Speakers, writers, and journalists, more perhaps in England than the United States, stressed the two empires' community of interest in a world otherwise dominated by predatory if civilized vultures and backward, recalcitrant savages.

None of these strands—declining American criticism of British imperialism, the erosion of British defensiveness, an awareness of similar interests—would have become so strong had not the two imperialisms shared a virtually identical ideology. While late-nineteenth-century imperialism was a worldwide phenomenon and many nations reacted to very much the same stimuli, the tone and style and motives of British and American imperialism were particularly close. They had far more in common with one another than with those of Germany, France, Russia, or Japan. To an unusual degree the English-speaking powers shared a feeling of uncomfortableness with the drift of contemporary life which they hoped to exorcise by vigorous action at home and abroad; neither the Japanese nor the Germans shared this feeling. The Anglo-Americans viewed in nearly identical ways the economic problem posed, as they saw it, by overproduction at home and the closing of markets abroad; the economic arguments for imperialism in less industrialized countries were rather different. All imperial powers assumed themselves to be superior to those they subdued, and all in one way or another considered themselves to be bestowing important benefits—security, prosperity, spiritual vigor—upon those they ruled. Still, the concept of "the white man's burden," as Westerners called it, particu-

---

[4] Quoted in Ernest R. May, *Imperial Democracy: The Emergence of America as a Great Power* (New York, 1961), p. 225.

larly infested the United States and England. In addition, the racist sentiments underlying imperialism suggested a closer relationship between those two than between any other major powers. The British and American peoples were drawn together by their rationalizations for imperialism just as they were by the policy itself.

Thus leaders in both countries suffered the sense of malaise that Richard Hofstadter has christened, with reference to the United States alone, the "psychic crisis of the 1890's." They worried when they saw the comfortable stability of society upset by new forces, most of them the product of industrialization. In America the growth of uncontrolled agglomerations of capital, immense faceless cities, and labor violence challenged the country's traditional optimism. Alienation of the farmer, the Populist challenge, and even the much ballyhooed end of the frontier worked the same way, and there seemed to be some force in Professor Dicey's argument that democratic panaceas had lost their usefulness. The depression of 1893 and the painful process of recovery gathered together and stimulated the elements of pessimism. In England a similar situation existed, exacerbated by the fact that living generations had seen Britain at the zenith of her power. "The fall of foreign investment in the 1870's, the intermittent depression of the 1880's, the passing of industrial leadership to the United States and Germany, had made Englishmen conscious," A. P. Thornton observes, ". . . that their lead was after all not secure." [5]

Brooks Adams' mordant tract *The Law of Civilization and Decay*, a *succès de scandale* among the elites of both countries in 1895, rather impartially warned them that their vigor was being sapped. Adams' silverite quirks and wild generalizations, included despite cautions from his brother, irritated many readers who nevertheless saw merit in his general thesis. Theodore Roosevelt, for example, rejected Adams' apocalyptic predictions

[5] Richard Hofstadter, "Manifest Destiny in the Philippines," Daniel Aaron, ed., *America in Crisis* (New York, 1952), p. 173; Archibald P. Thornton, *The Imperial Idea and Its Enemies: A Study in British Power* (London, 1959), p. 67.

but did not, like his less sophisticated English friend Sir Cecil
Spring Rice, deny the indictment entirely. Only a few years later,
after British defeats by the Boers, Roosevelt wrote, "There are
grave signs of deterioration in the English speaking peoples here
and there, not merely in the evident lack of fighting edge in the
British soldier, but in the diminishing birth rate . . . ; in the
excessive urban growth; in the love of luxury, and the turning of
sport into a craze of the upper classes." [6] British developments,
in other words, reinforced American malaise, and vice versa.

To meet the psychic crisis, several routes were open. One
might initiate social reform to dampen working-class discontent, one of the most frightening challenges in the view of those
who governed. American progressives, notable both as reformers and imperialists, followed this path. If Conservatives in Great
Britain showed limited interest in social legislation, the same was
not true of Liberal Imperialists, who quickly gained predominance in the party and founded the Liberal League in 1902 to
propagate imperialism and reform. In addition, following a second path, one might attempt to convince workers that imperialism would improve conditions at home, an argument employed with particular success in England and endorsed even by
Fabians. Alternatively, following a well-worn path, one might divert attention from problems at home by embarking upon foreign adventure, as indeed the Russians also did. In the United
States the Spanish-American War, the overture to imperialism,
justified itself for many because it promised, in the words of one
newspaper, to "clear the atmosphere, and stamp out the growth
of socialism and anarchy, discontent and sectional prejudice that
is gaining a foothold in this nation." In Britain, Elie Halévy suggests, imperialism and foreign crises may help to explain the falling off of strikes after 1895 and the failure of labor, which first
gained important electoral success only in 1906, to command
public sympathy. "If you want to avoid civil war," the great

---

[6] Roosevelt to Anna R. Cowles, December 17, 1899, quoted in Howard K.
Beale, *Theodore Roosevelt and the Rise of America to World Power* (Baltimore,
1956), p. 79.

builder Cecil Rhodes is supposed to have said in 1895, "you must become imperialists." [7] Finally, those in doubt about the national future could choose another road, a rugged one which would not bemuse discontent but instead put the state to a test of discipline and service. Men like Joseph Chamberlain and Theodore Roosevelt explicitly welcomed imperialism for this reason. By trial, a nation could prove it had not lost its fiber, gather trophies the world could not ignore, eradicate doubts of its future, and perhaps strengthen its own sense of purpose.

In both countries the moral crisis had roots in concern over the vitality of the industrial economy. Those who worried about the national future in mystical, psychological terms usually shared as well the more down-to-earth view that imperialism would reinvigorate economic life. The two countries' emphasis differed somewhat, American imperialists developing one idea which did not catch hold in England. At least since the appearance in 1890 of Alfred T. Mahan's collection of essays *The United States Looking Outward*, educated Americans had been familiar with the view that the output of factories might outrun the absorptive capacities of the domestic market. After the depression of 1893, with steel mills running at half capacity and tens of thousands of industrial workers unemployed, the gloomy view gained wide circulation. After a later, even deeper depression, Franklin D. Roosevelt concentrated on expanding the domestic market; in the 'nineties, his type of program was not even considered. Instead, voices cried for the aggressive development of foreign markets, sometimes, like Mahan, arguing for colonies as *points d'appui* for commerce generally and sometimes asserting that great markets could be found in colonies themselves. America, Brooks Adams intoned, "must protect the outlets of her trade, or run the risk of suffocation." [8]

If Englishmen, no longer challenged by an explosive, unset-

[7] *Linn County Republic*, October —, 1895, quoted in Ray Ginger, *The Age of Excess: The United States from 1877 to 1914* (New York, 1965), p. 188; Bernard Semmel, *Imperialism and Social Reform: English Social-Imperial Thought, 1895–1914* (Cambridge, 1960), p. 16.

[8] Brooks Adams, *America's Economic Supremacy* (New York, 1900), p. 19.

tling rise in national output, failed to share American fears of a glut, they did agree that foreign markets were essential. Events were to show that hopes for great economic benefits from the expansion of empire were unreal, that by far the largest proportion of international trade would continue to flow between already industrialized nations. In the last decade of the nineteenth century this was not the accepted view.[9] A desire for markets stimulated English imperialism, and the search became feverish as rivals threatened to gather in underdeveloped portions of the world. In the United States the National Association of Manufacturers, founded in 1895, devoted half its first manifesto to a call for greater overseas trade. Like most businessmen, members of the association were wary of territorial expansion in 1895; they simply called for economic imperialism based upon reciprocal trade agreements which would tie other countries to the United States. In 1898, on the wings of victory, many business groups joined the call for colonies alongside those who argued that, whether Wall Street or Pittsburgh knew what was good for them or not, a forthright policy of annexation was essential to economic well-being.

The quest for markets is, almost by definition, a system of rivalries, and the imperialistic drive brought with it all sorts of international complications. Both Britain and the United States considered themselves engaged in competition with Russia and Germany. Until around 1898 they also felt themselves rivals, and the uproar over the Venezuelan boundary sprang partly from this. Then came an abrupt change, and until 1914, whatever the actual fact may have been in Latin America or Asia or elsewhere, the two countries seldom viewed themselves as competitors for specific colonial or underdeveloped markets. Instead, they considered themselves allies. Before a wildly cheering audience in Boston in April 1898, a young and ambitious Republican orator declared, "American factories are making more than the American people can use; American soil is producing more than they

[9] For the realities of international trade insofar as they affected Anglo-American relations, see below, pp. 121–130.

can consume. Fate has written our policy for us; the trade of the world must and shall be ours. And we will get it as our mother has told us how. . . . If it means Anglo-Saxon solidarity; if it means an English-American understanding upon the basis of a division of the world's markets . . . the stars in their courses will fight for us and countless centuries will applaud." [10] Economic appetites drew Englishmen and Americans to the same table, not to quarrel over choice servings but to share them and protect them from less polite diners.

Markets—this was the steady theme. Imperialists seldom employed other economic arguments for expansion. Almost no one in Great Britain or the United States maintained that dominion was necessary over areas which provided essential raw materials, although on the eve of the Great War both countries showed an increasing interest in petroleum-producing areas. The Anglo-Americans left this argument to the Japanese, Russians, and Germans. Nor did the drive for capital export play a major role, despite the prominence given it in John A. Hobson's famous diatribe, *Imperialism*, published in 1902. A few capitalists —Cecil Rhodes, for example—sought areas of investment, but even for Rhodes it is a good question whether an interest in imperialism preceded or followed the success of his overseas ventures. (Even in a discussion of motives rather than results, one may note that the facts are against Hobson, for little English or American investment actually flowed to the colonies and little but trading capital to other areas.) Contemporary literature is almost barren of this theme. Charles A. Conant, an American with a particular interest in China, did argue that markets were less important for England and America than opportunities for investment. "How necessary to the salvation of these countries," he wrote, "is an outlet for their surplus savings, if the entire fabric . . . is not to be shaken by a social revolution. The law of self-preservation, as well as that of the survival of the fittest, is

[10] Claude G. Bowers, *Beveridge and the Progressive Era* (Cambridge, 1932), p. 69. In a passage omitted in the text, Beveridge genuflected in the direction of fair play for Ireland, perhaps because of Hibernian importance in the city where he spoke.

urging our people on." [11] Other writers touched upon investment opportunities in passing, but none adopted Conant's tone of urgency.

Like most historical movements, Anglo-American imperialism cannot be explained solely in terms of material calculation. Capitalists are usually by nature peaceful and anti-imperialist, as Joseph Schumpeter has argued, and business leaders, slow to see the pot of gold at the end of the imperial rainbow, were converted as individuals by very much the same concerns as other men. A desire to increase national prestige—foreshadowed in the United States by the upgrading of diplomatic posts from legations to embassies in 1893 and the initiation of a naval building program before either an enemy or a doctrine of naval power had been found—helps to explain American imperialism but played a small role in Great Britain. The same is true of the interest in overseas naval bases, a matter of some concern in the United States but far less so in England, whose holdings already sprinkled the globe. Nor did the psychic crisis in both countries make an imperialistic response inevitable. The keystone of the structure, particularly for the Americans but for Englishmen as well, was the concept of race. Racist ideas and the ancillary belief in national struggle and "the white man's burden" drove the Anglo-Americans toward a new course and, while doing so, drove them toward one another.

Contemporaries agreed that life was a struggle in which only the fittest survived. Charles Darwin had told them so, and philosopher-sociologists like Herbert Spencer and his American disciple William Graham Sumner had adapted Darwin's concept of a struggle between species or types to one which explained—and excused—a ruthless competition between individuals. This Social Darwinism, however useful in easing the consciences of the successful, really distorted the implications of evolutionary theory. The full title of Darwin's seminal work, *On the Origin of Species*, included a phrase, *the Preservation of Favoured Races in*

[11] Charles A. Conant, *The United States in the Orient: The Nature of the Economic Problem* (Cambridge, 1900), p. 3.

the Struggle for Life, which made his emphasis clear. Upon occasion he applied his concept to nations, among other things predicting American success. Thus it was in a sense a return to first principles when a new wave of interpreters began to stress competition between peoples and to apply Darwinian concepts to international relations. Just as Sumner pictured life as an inevitable competition which brought Rockefellers and Morgans to the top, so the new Darwinists considered world developments a process by which favored races reached a commanding position. Darwin himself emphasized natural selection and environmental adjustment, not violence; and some, including Sumner and Bryan and William James, denied that physical strife—war and colonialism—was an inevitable concomitant of race struggle without, however, challenging the underlying concept. Many others, including Roosevelt, Mahan, Rhodes, and the English eugenicist Karl Pearson, believed Darwinism meant violent racial conflict. "It is the fiery crucible out of which comes the finer metal," Pearson proclaimed, and he predicted that progress would cease when wars ceased.[12] Dinosaurs must die at the hands of *homo sapiens*—it was inevitable and desirable.

Darwinists welcomed the idea of conflict between backward peoples—Negroes, Malays, and others—and advanced races. A war with savages, Theodore Roosevelt and others believed, was by its very nature a righteous war. Contemporaries did not proceed beyond this point to a conviction that all wars were righteous or that only war forwarded the evolutionary process. They hoped the advanced races would stand together against the backward at least until evolution was much further advanced, reserving the competition between themselves to peaceful rivalry. At the same time English and Americans believed the racial differences between various advanced peoples were sharp. In time, one particular race must dominate the globe. Perhaps one aspirant would attempt to force the pace of evolution by the use of force. One hoped for peace but kept an eye cocked for danger.

Racist concepts pervaded Anglo-American life, though less

[12] Quoted in Semmel, *Imperialism and Reform,* p. 41.

malevolently than the France of Captain Dreyfus and the Russia of Kishinev. The American Negro suffered more blows than at any time since Appomattox. The movement for immigration restriction gained strength, with Henry Cabot Lodge arguing, on the basis of a study of sketches of distinguished Americans in *Appleton's Encyclopedia* (some of them biographies of imaginary characters submitted by contributors who were paid by the inch), that those of British descent contributed three times as much to American abilities as all others combined. Except for limitations on Chinese immigration, no discriminatory legislation survived a Presidential veto until 1917, but one branch of Congress thirty-two times and both branches four times passed a bill incorporating a literacy test, a device clearly aimed at reducing immigration from eastern and southern Europe.

At the same time anti-Semitism became more important or at least more visible than before, just as it did in France and Russia. Anglo-American anti-Semitism was comparatively mild, and the word "Jew" often became, as it did for American Populists, a shorthand term used to describe anyone who profited without labor, who manipulated money and symbolized the great financial octopus that oppressed honest men. Englishmen worried because collapse of the house of Baring in 1890 left control of all the great banking houses in the hands of Jews and foreigners; they let anti-Semitism help to stimulate an anti-usury law in 1900 and learned from J. A. Hobson and others that the Boer War had been provoked by Jewish exploitation of the Rand. In America, progressives and Populists, including the drawing-room variety like the Adams brothers, sprinkled their correspondence and speech with anti-Jewish epithets. Rather illogically, since they considered Jews in their own countries cowardly and often unpatriotic, both Englishmen and Americans tended to blame Russian imperialism in the Far East, presumably a major threat to Anglo-American interests, upon Jews who maneuvered the czar. Once again the two nations viewed a portion of the contemporary world from the same angle of vision.

The root problem, however, was what constituted a race,

particularly a race with superior natural characteristics. It was easy enough to write off the Jews as failures at everything except making money. It was easy enough to agree that white men differed from Negroes and Orientals, although even this caused difficulty when the Japanese showed their virtue, in Anglo-American eyes, by driving back Russian incursions into Korea and Manchuria. "The Japs have played our game because they have played the game of civilized mankind," Theodore Roosevelt told his secretary of state,[13] who really needed no convincing. Contemporary wits observed that the President had conferred honorary membership in the Anglo-Saxon race upon the Japanese in recognition of their contribution to the highly competitive "game."

Observers also found it easy to distinguish between Saxon, Slav, and Latin, assigning stereotypical traits to each. Commenting upon the French, an eminent professor at Columbia University declared, "A people that idly sips its cognac on the boulevards as it lightly takes a trifling part in the *comédie humaine* can only go down in the struggle for existence," and most writers tended to dismiss other Latin peoples as easily. The Slavs were another matter. An American magazine, *Outlook*, predicted in 1900 that, "as the issue of the past was between Anglo-Saxon and Latin civilization, so the issue of the future is between Anglo-Saxon and Slavic civilization." This theme, a well-known aspect of American thought, thanks to the writings of Brooks Adams and others, also appeared in English commentaries on world affairs. Even Lord Salisbury, who temperamentally mistrusted sweeping predictions, embraced this one. It remained a habit of thought at least until the Russo-Japanese War. Roosevelt's correspondent Cecil Spring Rice, observing Russia from the St. Petersburg embassy or from the Anglo-Russian battlefield in Persia, deluged his friend with warnings describing the Russians as strong, docile brutes who would follow their leaders into battle against superior races. "I look upon them," Roosevelt replied in

---

[13] Roosevelt to Hay, July 26, 1904, Elting E. Morison, ed., *The Letters of Theodore Roosevelt* (8 vols.; Cambridge, 1951–1954), vol. IV, p. 865.

1897, attempting to dissipate Spring Rice's gloom, "as people to whom we can give points, and a beating. . . . It may be that we [the United States and England] are going the way of France, but just at present I doubt it, and I still think that though . . . the English-speaking races may have to divide the future with the Slav, yet they will get rather more than their fair share." [14] Roosevelt's tone, concerned but not desperate, is far more characteristic of the day than the gloom of Adams or Spring Rice, but both are the product of Darwinian calculations.

Nonwhites, Jews, Latins, Slavs—the process of distillation continued. Could the Saxon race, sometimes called "Teutonic," be further broken down? In particular, where did the Germans stand? This was a difficult problem, especially in the United States, where for nearly a generation scholars had taught that America's origins lay in ancient German forests, whence institutions and traits passed through England to the New World. (Frederick Jackson Turner's purer Americanism, ideological and economic rather than racial, reflected adversely on Europeanist theories by stressing frontier origins. Turner promulgated his doctrine at the Columbian Exposition in 1893, and the antiforeign implications seem to have been ignored for some years.) As the century came to a close, historians began to modify the prevailing theory. Professor Wilson of Princeton, for example, wrote of a Germanic race which spawned the Anglo-Saxons, but when he dealt with political institutions he stressed American obligations to England. The trend continued throughout the first decade of the new century. In 1908 one of Roosevelt's teachers, John W. Burgess of Columbia, a man who deplored the drift, said, "when the Americans consent to dwell under the same diplomatic roof with the mother who has chastised them, they are not going to allow the grandmother, who has always taken their part to be left out in the cold." [15] Burgess spoke these words to a German-American audience. Most others

[14] Franklin M. Giddings, quoted in Thomas F. Gossett, *Race: The History of an Idea in America* (Dallas, 1963), pp. 312–313; *Outlook* (New York), vol. LXVI (1900), pp. 968–969; Roosevelt to Spring Rice, August 13, 1897, Morison, ed., *Letters of Roosevelt*, vol. I, pp. 646–649.

[15] Quoted in Edward N. Saveth, *American Historians and European Immigrants, 1875–1925* (New York, 1948), pp. 43–44.

would have considered the proposition out of date. The Germans, too, had lost their claim to membership in the small college of superior races.

The Anglo-Americans were speaking of race and employing Darwinian metaphors in a very special sense. When they accepted Japanese superiority over a people more closely related to their own, the Russian, their science was suspect. When they shunted Germans aside the same was true. Moreover, as any reasonable man had to admit, neither the American people, swelled by immigration from many countries, nor even the British could claim to be pure Anglo-Saxons. Were the Irish, an inferior people at home, magically transformed when they crossed the Irish Sea or the Atlantic Ocean? Did Germans in St. Louis differ racially from those in Berlin? Few dared make the assertion. "Anglo-Saxon is of course an utterly unscientific word," observed Theodore Roosevelt.[16]

What, then, was the essence of Anglo-American superiority? In 1897 Edmond Demolins, a French sociologist who wished to stimulate reform in his own country, asked precisely this question. In À *Quoi Tient la Supériorité des Anglo-Saxons?* he answered that the lazy, sociable Celtic people and the Normans, addicted to "Lordolatry, Patronage, and Snobbery," both of them types unfortunately strong in France, failed to undermine Britain's strength because that society was dominated by a belief in individualism, "the real foundation of Anglo-Saxon superiority" and a concept spread to the entire population by the schools.[17] French jingoes fulminated against Demolins, but the professor found honor, acceptance, and a translator abroad. The English and Americans welcomed this foreign demonstration of their merit. The ground shifted from biological tests to cultural ones, from Darwinian fact to Darwinian metaphor. As many came to realize, those who spoke of Anglo-Saxon superiority really meant that the English and American peoples had developed the best governments and societies in the world. By cling-

[16] Roosevelt to Robert J. Thomson, April 30, 1900, Morison, ed., *Letters of Roosevelt*, vol. II, p. 1274.

[17] Edmond Demolins, *Anglo-Saxon Superiority: To What It Is Due* (Louis B. Lavigne, trans.; New York, 1898), pp. vi, viii.

ing to concepts of evolution and competitive struggle, Anglo-Saxonists merely gave an aura of scientism and inevitability to what was essentially a political claim.

Demolins stressed education. This might mean, although the Frenchman did not so argue, the inculcation of Protestant virtues. American clergyman had argued that individualism and "a pure *spiritual* Christianity," presumably meaning non-Catholic Christianity, were essential attributes of race at least since the Reverend Josiah Strong published *Our Country* in 1885. Or education might be secular, an efficient means of spreading that outlook Demolins envied. Toward the end of the pre-war period, Admiral Lord Fisher visited the United States. Almost everything in America impressed this apostle of bigness, but especially the schools. "The most miraculous engine of power in America is their school system," he wrote. "Nationalities of every species pour in their thousands into the United States. . . . But in the second generation they are *all pure Americans*—their language English, their literature English, their traditions English, and, quite unconsciously to themselves, their *aspirations* are English! What d——d fools we shall be if we don't exploit this into a huge Federation of the English-speaking peoples!" [18]

The idea of federation through education had long since attracted the attention of Cecil John Rhodes, the great imperialist, and the scholarships at Oxford provided by his will began to be filled in 1904. As a young man Rhodes dreamed of political reunification, and he always considered the American Revolution a tragic, stupid accident which set back the race's domination of the world. Amassing a tremendous fortune in southern Africa, Rhodes devoted a good deal of attention to testamentary problems during his declining years. His first will talked of political reabsorption of the United States, but later versions merely suggested some vague form of union and specifically approved national as well as racial patriotism. To further the spread of

[18] Josiah Strong, *Our Country*, quoted in Louis L. Snyder, ed., *The Dynamics of Nationalism* (Princeton, 1964), p. 274; Fisher to Lionel Yexley, December 8, 1910, Arthur J. Marder, ed., *Fear God and Dread Nought: The Correspondence of Admiral of the Fleet Lord Fisher of Kilverstone* (3 vols.; London, 1952–1959), vol. II, p. 343.

common beliefs among potential leaders, Rhodes devised the Oxford scholarships which still bear his name. A will drawn in 1893 provided for colonial scholarships only, but a new one signed in 1899, at the crescendo of Anglo-Saxonism, added thirty-two American scholarships a year along with only sixty for the entire empire. (In 1901, dreaming of an even larger partnership, Rhodes added a codicil bestowing five German scholarships annually, a provision revoked by act of Parliament during the First World War.) When Rhodes died in the spring of 1902, his gesture gained applause in both countries, although at Oxford some grumbled at the prospect of an invasion by uncultured students who might not wish to study Greek. The will was printed with solemn diplomatic documents in the Department of State's annual volume, *Foreign Relations of the United States.* Despite some vacancies in the early years, Rhodes' trustees managed to appoint nearly four hundred and fifty Americans to the scholarships by 1917. The plan, even the far smaller quota granted to Germany as an afterthought, reflected Darwinian conceptions.

Finley Peter Dunne's fictional barroom philosopher, Mr. Dooley, poked fun at the theory that, by education or osmosis, all Americans became Anglo-Saxons. "An Anglo-Saxon," he told a barkeep, ". . . is a German that's forgot who was his parents. . . . Mack is an Anglo-Saxon. His folks come fr'm th' County Armagh, an' their naytional Anglo-Saxon hymn is 'O'Donnell Aboo.' Teddy Rosenfelt is another Anglo-Saxon. An' I'm an Anglo-Saxon. I'm wan iv th' hottest Anglo-Saxons that iver come in Anglo-Saxony. . . . I tell ye, whin th' Clan an' th' Sons iv Sweden an' th' Banana Club an' th' Circle Francaize an' th' Pollacky Benivolent Society an' th' Rooshian Sons of Dinnymite an' th' Benny Brith . . . an' th' other Anglo-Saxons begin f'r to raise their Anglo-Saxon battlecry, it'll be all day with th' eight or nine people in th' wurruld that has th' misfortune iv not bein' brought up Anglo-Saxons." [19] Like all good satire, this had the bite of truth.

Race thus gained a different meaning, implying simply a

[19] Finley Peter Dunne, *Mr. Dooley: Now and Forever* (Louis Filler, ed.; Stanford, 1954), pp. 42–44.

community of outlook, as it often had for those who employed
the concept earlier in the century before scientism thrust its way
forward. Individualism, political liberties, perhaps peace and
Protestantism—these characteristics gave Anglo-Saxons their
uniqueness, their superiority—and their bond. As acquired characteristics rather than genetic ones gained emphasis and the
phrase "Anglo-Saxon" hardened into a biological mold, it gave
way to a new one, "the English-speaking peoples," which admitted the nonbiological emphasis. "Your Continent is making a
new race and a new type," the British Foreign Secretary wrote
President Roosevelt, ". . . just as in old times the race in these
Islands was evolved from many sources." This did not mean an
absence of kinship, far from it, for "some generations of freedom
on both sides have evolved a type of man and mind that looks
at things from a kindred point of view." [20] Roosevelt agreed. By
1914, when the centennial of peace stimulated more oratory and
writing on Anglo-American ties than most people were prepared
to absorb, the new phrase had won the day.

The Anglo-Saxon, English-speaking theme was not invented
in the 1890's, although it then reached a crescendo. Americans
even of the Revolutionary generation considered themselves sons
of England. British premiers since Pitt and Liverpool referred
from time to time to the blood relationship. Still, the century
after independence was much more often marked by events
demonstrating differences than similarities, the understratum of
connection being taken for granted. The new emphasis exploded
out of Darwinism, and the concept of conflict between unlike
peoples remained central to all discussion of Anglo-American
ties, the corollary being that they stood together against the
world. The Darwinian, more truly racial theme was strengthened
and then supplanted by the institutional, cultural one which
leaped over obvious fallacies in the original theory. Each contributed powerfully to the outpouring of Anglo-Saxonism that began
shortly after the Venezuelan controversy and continued, with di-

[20] Grey to Roosevelt, December [2], 1906, quoted in George M. Trevelyan,
Grey of Fallodon (London, 1937), p. 116.

minishing intensity after 1900, when its major work was done, until 1914. Where ideology had once driven monarchy and republic apart, the new racist form drew them together.

Scores of commentators agreed it would be deplorable if some less worthy people—Russian, German, perhaps Japanese— carried off the Olympian laurel. Protected by the Atlantic moat, Americans almost unanimously refused even to consider an Anglo-American military league, and most Englishmen were realists enough to see that such a connection was beyond Antaeus' reach. Men in both countries counted instead on their combined moral force to prevent disaster, urged policies to prevent enervating intraracial strife, or simply gave their sympathies to the racial relative when trials arose. "The two countries which stand best for a free civilization have all their interests in common," the *Independent* observed, ". . . and each should rejoice in the other's welfare. Together they can do much for the world." [21] Their hearts, still not joined, were linked as never before.

The spirit of race, when tempered by moral sentiment, had a further consequence, the myth of "the white man's burden." Darwinian theory cast a cloak of inevitability over racial conflict, sanctifying conquest as the triumph of greater over lesser breeds. Applied harshly, Darwinism might even suggest the losers' literal obliteration, or at least their enslavement. Imperialists in all countries, with no Hitler to guide them, refused to follow the implications of Darwin to this brutal end. They developed a nobler view. Imperialism was progress. Lesser peoples must learn to accept control, and rulers had a duty, an obligation precisely because they were superior, to bring as much of their civilization as possible to their subjects.

Imperialists must not expect thanks nor might they anticipate speedy success. The economic, social, and especially political backwardness of the Negroes, Malays, and others which justified imperialism meant that the process would be resisted and time-consuming. Some anti-imperialists even maintained, with

[21] *Independent* (New York), vol. LII (1900), p. 389.

James Bryce, that "Polynesians and Asiatics, Creole Spaniards and mulattoes are not fit to receive those [Anglo-American] principles," to say nothing of even more inferior Negroes. Imperialists accepted the admittedly difficult challenge partly as a means of showing the moral fiber of the nation. In his best-selling novel *The Weavers,* an imperialistic tract, Sir Gilbert Parker had one of the characters deliver a speech condemning interference in Egyptian affairs simply in order to be able to repudiate the speaker's views: "There was at bottom a spirit of anti-expansionism, of reaction against England's world-wide responsibilities. He had no largeness of heart or view concerning humanity. . . . With less responsibility taken, there would be less trouble, national and international—that was his point of view." [22]

The concept of duty, at least as old as imperial Rome, sprang forth again in the 1890's. Even those who opposed political imperialism believed superior races ought to lead the less successful. Newspapers, magazines, and speeches, both English and American, frequently referred to torches illuminating the wilderness, preachers of the Anglo-Saxon gospel converting the heathen, and so on. The London *Spectator* declared, "our race is meant to do in the world the work of foreman and ganger," surely a more apposite metaphor than most, and went on to say that no one in England would complain if Americans became "fellow-labourers in the work of the better ordering of the world." [23] There was more than enough work for both branches of the race in a world largely in darkness, too often threatened by non-Anglo-Saxon and thus less benevolent imperialists.

Rudyard Kipling, the crotchety little prophet of empire, a virtual recluse dominated by an American wife—Henry James gave away the bride when they were married—bestowed upon the concept its popular name with a poem, "The White Man's

[22] Bryce, "The Policy of Annexation for America," *Forum* (New York), vol. XXIV (1897), p. 394; Gilbert Parker, *The Weavers* (London, 1907), p. 452.
[23] *Spectator,* quoted in Geoffrey Seed, "British Reactions to American Imperialism Reflected in Journals of Opinion, 1898–1900," *Political Science Quarterly* (New York), vol. LXXIII (1958), pp. 259–260.

Burden," published in an American magazine, *McClure's,* in February 1899. At first sight his willingness to see the Americans join England as an imperial partner seems surprising, for Kipling deplored many things about America, and he made his views known. "There is no earthly reason he should not call New York a pig trough, but there is also no reason why he should be allowed to associate with the pigs," commented Theodore Roosevelt in 1892,[24] responding to a rumor that Kipling had been turned down for membership in a New York club. (Later they became friends, although they never ceased to spar over some of Kipling's views, and the Englishman conferred the title "Great-Heart" upon Roosevelt in an obituary poem.) Despite this, the author basked in the popularity he had gained in America. His long residence in India had left him with a conviction that backward races needed many years of tutelage. He considered the British and American people basically similar in their ideals and aspirations, and he welcomed the American decision, approved by the Senate the same month in which his poem appeared, to join England in a task beyond the resources of any single country. Thus Rudyard Kipling quite sincerely penned a plea to the Americans to:

> Take up the White Man's burden—
>   Send forth the best ye breed—
> Go bind your sons to exile
>   To serve your captives' need;
> To wait, in heavy harness,
>   On fluttered folk and wild—
> Your new-caught, sullen peoples,
>   Half-devil and half-child.

This stern call to duty gave a moral tone to the imperialistic crusade. "Rather poor poetry, but good sense from the expansion standpoint," commented Roosevelt. "I like it," responded

[24] Roosevelt to J. Brander Matthews, May 31, 1892, quoted in Beale, *Roosevelt,* p. 21.

Lodge; "I think it is better poetry than you say, apart from the sense of the verses." [25] Publication in *McClure's,* one of the most popular magazines of the day, assured the poem a wide audience. The title phrase instantly became an integral part of expansionist oratory. In England, too, the verses became a marching song of imperialism. Kipling soon visited the grateful Rhodes' African domain, where for several years he wintered as a guest of the great imperialist.

Today imperialism is out of favor, along with the racist arrogance beneath it, and even at the time many people considered Kipling and his allies hypocritical. "I think most of the current jingoism on both sides of the water is due to him," Edwin L. Godkin wrote. "He is the poet of the barracks room cads." [26] Yet the poet deeply believed what he wrote. To him and to many others, imperialism was a challenge and a duty, not merely an opportunity for profit or exploitation. Many contemporaries held the same views, although some Americans showed a willingness to throw off the burden when Aguinaldo's revolt in the Philippines made it more onerous than even Kipling's lines led them to expect. By service, by a demonstration of vigor, by devotion to an ideal, it was hoped, a nation might justify its favored position in the world. The most striking speech given by Theodore Roosevelt during a visit to England in 1910 was an almost Kiplingesque challenge to his hosts, a warning that the duties of empire should not be lost sight of through sloth or selfishness. "The white man's burden" was no knapsack of feathers.

Even the most predatory imperialists, like Leopold II of the Belgians, whose rule of the Congo caused an international scandal before he was forced to surrender it in 1908, have believed they served their charges' need. The English and Americans simply conformed to a type. Equally common is a refusal to admit that other powers are similarly motivated or equally well prepared to rule. It came as a shock to Winston Churchill to dis-

[25] Roosevelt to Lodge, January 12, 1899, Henry Cabot Lodge, ed., *Selections from the Correspondence of Theodore Roosevelt and Henry Cabot Lodge, 1884–1918* (2 vols.; New York, 1925), vol. I, p. 384; Lodge to Roosevelt, January 14, 1889, *ibid.,* vol. I, p. 385.

[26] Godkin to Louise Dowson, December 23, 1899, Rollo Ogden, *Life and Letters of Edwin Lawrence Godkin* (2 vols.; New York, 1907), vol. II, pp. 30–31.

cover, when visiting Cuba in 1895, that Spaniards took pride in their mission. "I thought it rather cheek," he later recalled with amusement, "that these foreigners should take just the same views and use the same sort of language about their country and their colonies as if they were British." In 1898 the *Spectator* observed, "The Frenchman is too fickle, the Russian too full of guile, and the German too harsh" to manage an empire properly.[27] Such feelings, generally shared, also conformed to a common pattern.

Yet England and America largely exempted the imperialism of the other from criticism. England welcomed the United States to the company of empires, confident the newcomer would assume the same burden in the same spirit as she had done. Americans could not forget their anti-imperialist heritage, but most of them firmly believed Britons were far better qualified to direct colonies than any other nation. This is one more evidence of the strength of the Anglo-Saxon, English-speaking sentiment. Poured from a common mold, cherishing similar values, the two peoples were assumed to have the same noble conception of the duties of empire.

The theme found its most florid expression in a speech delivered by John Hay, then ambassador at the Court of St. James, before the Lord Mayor's banquet in April 1898. As a matter of prudence, Hay consulted the Foreign Office, where only the most timid officials may have dreamed of protest, before delivering a famous peroration on Anglo-American friendship: "All of us who think cannot but see that there is a sanction like that of religion which binds us to a sort of partnership in the beneficent work of the world. . . . We are bound by a tie which we did not forge and which we cannot break; we are joint ministers of the same sacred mission of liberty and progress, charged with duties which we cannot evade by the imposition of irresistible hands." [28] Hay's speech, preceding as it did a Presidential decision to accept

---

[27] Winston L. S. Churchill, *A Roving Commission: My Early Life* (New York, 1930), p. 82; *Spectator*, May 7, 1898, quoted in Alexander E. Campbell, *Great Britain and the United States, 1895–1903* (Glasgow, 1960), p. 152.

[28] Quoted in Charles S. Campbell, *Anglo-American Understanding, 1898–1903* (Baltimore, 1957), p. 125.

the burdens of empire, brought down some unfavorable comment at home. The Ambassador should have shown more restraint. Still, the complaints were relatively mild, and Hay's theme gained added meaning when McKinley decided to keep the Philippines and Puerto Rico. The two nations were, in the minds of leading citizens, partners sharing the burden of leadership and tutelage, partners in a compact forged by their racial affinity.

The major influences propelling England and the United States in the direction of imperialism, including the concept of an Anglo-Saxonized "white man's burden," dovetailed nicely with one another. In 1908, Lord Curzon, former governor-general of India and husband of a wealthy American bride, summed it all up, saying, "In Empire, we have found not merely a key to glory and wealth, but the call to duty, and the means of service to mankind." [29] By that time Americans had long since lost the flush of enthusiasm for political empire. They had begun to follow less ambitious but more secure paths to power and profit, eschewing for the moment responsibilities the *fin de siècle* years cast upon them as full partners in the fate of the English-speaking race. But they could never shuck off the sense of partnership that developed between 1895 and 1900, the feeling that the two nations shared a common outlook. Doctrines of imperialism, particularly pseudoscientific Darwinism, irrevocably influenced their outlook far into the future.

[29] Quoted in Thornton, *Imperial Idea*, p. 72.

CHAPTER FIVE

A New Century

I FIND AMERICA so cheerful, and so full of swagger and self-satisfaction, that I hardly know it," Henry Adams complained in 1900, when victory over Spain and "McKinley prosperity" had done their work. "The change since 1893 is startling. . . . Grumblers now have to scold in private, for they get nothing but chaff in reply." [1] Toward Asia and particularly Latin America, new policies emerged, policies most significant in fixing the pattern of relations with England during the later Roosevelt era. Other manifestations of the new spirit, visible only in the years surrounding the turn of the century, showed how national egotism could actually mean greater friendship with England. The raucous Anglo-Saxonism of 1898 quickly passed away, but the new confidence—and the new responsibilities of empire—encouraged less touchy, less truculent views of Great Britain. During the Boer War, Americans for the first time did not unite behind a people resisting the British yoke, and at the time of Victoria's death there was an outpouring of sentiment in the United States such as no other monarch had ever received. Finally, the new American mood found its symbol and expression in Theodore Roosevelt, who entered the White House after McKinley's murder in September 1901. A whole new age had begun.

Britain's quarrel with the Boers dated back many years, to the 1870's and the battle of Majuba Hill in 1881. The spearhead

[1] Adams to Sir Robert Cunliffe, January 25, 1900, Worthington C. Ford, ed., *Letters of Henry Adams, 1892–1918* (Boston, 1938), pp. 254–255.

of the campaign to bring the Boer republics into the British Empire came to be Cecil Rhodes, gold and diamond king, statesman and intriguer. Rhodes' enterprises in South Africa employed many American mining engineers, and most shared his conviction that the Dutch farmers stood in the way of progress and civilization. In 1895, when Rhodes organized a comic-opera plot against the Transvaal that went astray in the fiasco of the Jameson raid, one of the Americans, John Hays Hammond, was Rhodes' undercover representative in Johannesburg. The American consular agent at Kimberley, Gardner Williams, also a mining engineer, smuggled arms in Standard Oil drums with false bottoms, and a "George Washington corps" planned to join Dr. Jameson when he penetrated the Transvaal. The plot collapsed. Hammond and seven other Americans were arrested, jailed for a time (during which a visit from Mark Twain eased the monotony), and released after paying fines. Agent Williams remained in office until 1906, and John Hays Hammond went on to become a millionaire and official American representative at the coronation of George V in 1911. Rhodes lost his privy-councilorship but continued his agitation to bring the Boer republics into the empire.

Open war between Britons and Boers finally came in October 1899. Although the Transvaal and the Orange Free State declared war, everyone knew British pressure had provoked their decision. Similarly, although the stated cause of British anger was the undoubted Boer discrimination against English residents, everyone suspected that the gold and diamonds of Rhodes and other capitalists lay in the background. Taking up arms like the Minute Men of 1775, Boers fought gallantly and maintained the fight until 1902, although never able to put as many as fifty thousand men into the field. The war, and particularly General Kitchener's harsh pacification program—concentration camps, destruction of food and water supplies—caused worldwide protest. In England the government faced powerful attacks, although half the Liberal opposition supported it, and Sir Cecil Spring Rice admitted, "If I were not an Englishman I should certainly sympathize with the Boers—and we can't possibly complain of people doing it." [2]

In America, Carl Schurz summed up one strain of thought when, after praising the new cordiality between England and the United States, he went on to declare that he viewed "with shame and abhorrence this spectacle of a great Power . . . slaughtering a little people, men, women and children, because they do what the best in the history of the world have done: hold fast with indomitable spirit to their national independence, and struggle on for the free possession of their homes." Ex-President Benjamin Harrison summed up another strain, the distrust of British motives dating back to the Jameson raid, when he wrote Secretary of State Hay, "gold in South Africa seems to have submerged the British sense of justice. I think the fact that the British wash gold, and not the rather inconsequential fact that the Boers do not wash themselves, has brought on the war." [3] Some Americans, including the maverick Democrat and professional Irish-American Bourke Cockran, considered the war a plot by aristocrats to halt England's trend toward democracy.

The anti-British reaction took several forms, most of them ludicrous or ineffectual. Resolutions were noisily introduced in both houses of Congress and then buried in committee. At Harvard, Franklin Delano Roosevelt collected a small relief fund from fellow undergraduates. His uncle, then governor of New York, claimed to have scotched a planned filibustering expedition against Canada. One leading Irish-American offered to recruit five thousand men to serve in the Transvaal, but nothing came of the scheme. Instead, the Ancient Order of Hibernians created a so-called Red Cross unit of fifty men under Dr. John R. McNamara, and as soon as McNamara's band reached Africa

[2] Spring Rice to Roosevelt, October 17, 1899, quoted in Howard K. Beale, *Theodore Roosevelt and the Rise of America to World Power* (Baltimore, 1956), p. 97.

[3] Schurz to William Vocke, December 5, 1901, Frederic Bancroft, ed., *Speeches, Correspondence and Political Papers of Carl Schurz* (6 vols.; New York, 1913), vol. VI, p. 280; Harrison to Hay, January 22, 1900, quoted in John H. Ferguson, *American Diplomacy and the Boer War* (Philadelphia, 1939), pp. 182–183.

most of its members threw away their medicines and bandages to pick up rifles.

Politicians in both parties were tempted to exploit the issue in the campaign of 1900, but only the Democrats actually did so. To speak to their convention at Kansas City they invited Webster Davis, a veteran Republican who renounced his party after a visit to Africa because he objected to the McKinley administration's favorable attitude toward England. The platform hailed the Boers' courage in defense of their homes and excoriated England, and from time to time the candidate, William Jennings Bryan once more, touched upon this theme. Englishmen tended to discount these shenanigans as crude political appeals to "Irish Papists, who take their cue from Dublin and Rome, and . . . German Jews, who look to Berlin for their political orders." At the Republican convention, the platform chairman, Senator Joseph Foraker, dealt roughly with pro-Boer maneuvers, although for a time the issue was doubtful enough to frighten Secretary of State Hay. The plank that emerged dealt only in generalities, except to praise the President for his refusal to become involved in schemes for diplomatic intervention. "We may be thankful," a London magazine commented, "that while the platitudes of the Republican platform must make foreigners smile, they do not infringe the ordinary decencies of international intercourse." [4]

Britain's tolerant reaction made good sense since, except among those like the Irish who had other reasons to dislike England, pro-Boer sentiment was fairly flaccid. Henry Adams, who viewed the war as a sort of second American Revolution, was shocked that so few countrymen shared his view: "their hostility to England seemed mere temper; but to Adams the war became almost a personal outrage." [5] In 1900, of the fourteen men up for reelection who had supported a pro-Boer resolution in the Senate, nine met defeat, an indication of the weakness of this issue. Asked which side they favored, a majority of Americans would have supported the Boers, but passion was lacking. No

[4] *National Review* (London), vol. XXXV (1900), pp. 26–27; *Saturday Review* (London), vol. LXXXIX (1900), p. 801.

[5] Henry Adams, *The Education of Henry Adams* (Modern Library ed.; New York, 1931), p. 372.

previous struggle in the name of republicanism and self-determination had received less vociferous American support.

How is this feebleness to be explained? Although the Boers were not so inferior in contemporary racial terms as to justify their rule by others, they were generally considered a backward-looking people who stood in the way of progress. Moreover, the Filipino revolt undermined pro-Boer activism. It showed imperialists that this sort of unpleasantness might arise in even the most benevolent empires, and it tended to disarm anti-imperialists, as Bryan acknowledged, by exposing them to charges of hypocrisy if they did not concentrate their fire upon American sins rather than British ones. Finally, the new friendliness with Britain, the apparent similarity of views particularly in the Far East, and even the existence of Liberal opposition to the war in England all meant that, however she might have sinned in Africa, Britain no longer seemed the very symbol of evil European *machtpolitik*.

A substantial number of Americans, particularly Republicans, even hoped for British victory. Among them was Theodore Roosevelt, who sympathized with the Boers and believed England largely responsible for the war, yet was certain "It is the interest of the English-speaking peoples, and therefore"—this was self-evident to Roosevelt—"of civilization, that English should be the tongue South of the Zambesi." He saw Britain playing a role in Africa like that of the United States in the Western Hemisphere, a benevolent policeman bringing order and progress at the same time that it kept predatory, non-Anglo-Saxon powers from interfering. Even broader was Mark Twain's argument: "England must not fail; it would mean an inundation of Russian and German political degradations . . . a sort of Middle-Age night and slavery which would last till Christ comes again. Even wrong—and she is wrong—England must be upheld." [6] When the German ambassador cheekily suggested to Hay that too great sympathy for England might spoil the Presi-

[6] Roosevelt to J. St. Loe Strachey, January 27, 1900, Elting E. Morison, ed., *The Letters of Theodore Roosevelt* (8 vols.; Cambridge, 1951–1954), vol. II, p. 1144; Twain to William D. Howells, January 25, 1900, Albert Bigelow Paine, ed., *Mark Twain's Letters* (2 vols.; New York, 1917), vol. II, p. 693.

dent's chances for reelection, the Secretary of State replied that
all reasonable men would consider England's downfall a great
misfortune.

People who thought this way were appalled by British defeats early in the war. Lodge thought the English had been fighting savages so long they had forgotten how to handle white opponents. Hay, the two Adamses, Roosevelt—all in one way or
another reached the same conclusion. Although the victories of
Lord Roberts and Kitchener destroyed the worst pessimism,
doubt about Britain's martial vigor never died.

Since England never sought American help, her friends usually remained inactive. The one major exception was really only
half American. Just after the war began, a number of American
women married to Englishmen decided to outfit a hospital ship.
Lord Randolph Churchill's widow headed the group, which also
included the Duchess of Marlborough and Mrs. Joseph Chamberlain. They raised more than £40,000 despite some reluctance
on the part of Americans they approached; Andrew Carnegie declined to write a check, although his employees subscribed
£500. Having obtained the promise of a flag from Queen
Victoria, Lady Randolph, a great believer in Anglo-Saxonism and
founder of the short-lived *Anglo-Saxon Review,* requested a
standard from President McKinley so that the Stars and Stripes
and Union Jack could fly side by side on the hospital ship. The
President prudently declined to risk a public outcry, so an unan-
nointed flag flew from the mast when Lady Randolph and a
complement of medical men sailed for Africa. (During the voyage Lady Randolph met a man her son Winston's age whom she
subsequently married.) Englishmen did not learn of the various
contretemps, and the "American" hospital ship strengthened
their opinion that respectability was on their side.

The existence of pro-British sentiment and the forceless
character of that which supported the Boers allowed President
McKinley and Secretary of State Hay to proceed as they chose,
provided they engaged in no openly non-neutral maneuvers. The
closest student of their policy, John H. Ferguson, has gone as far
as to declare, "the American government acted throughout the

war as if in friendly alliance with England, and by doing so did much to prevent intervention by European powers, thus assuring the annihilation of the Boer republics." [7] American authorities, unlike their counterparts in 1914, made not even the briefest effort to cut off the flow of credit to the belligerents. Lacking security of any kind, the Boers were able to borrow only tiny sums in the United States. On the other hand, Britain floated roughly twenty percent of her war costs in American security markets, primarily through the house of Morgan. Similarly, Washington let all but the most obviously military goods be exported, and, thanks to Britain's control of the sea, she benefited immensely more than the Transvaal and the Free State. American exports to the British Empire rose by more than $100 million over annual pre-war averages, and hundreds of thousands of pairs of military boots and nearly two hundred thousand mules and donkeys, shipped largely through New Orleans, eased British logistical problems. Washington protested a few British violations of American rights on the high seas, but all of these protests were delivered in a forceless fashion.

American diplomats handled British interests in the enemy countries, Germany having declined the responsibility. Adelbert Hay, a twenty-two-year-old, was appointed consul at Pretoria in December 1899, without his father's knowledge. Del Hay visited London on his way to Africa and again when he returned after the fall of Pretoria, and between times he corresponded with his father's friend Henry White, who was in London and passed his views on to British officials. Because of his father's reputation as an Anglophile, the Boers watched young Hay like a hawk, although he acted circumspectly in all his official doings. His performance pleased both his father and the President, and upon his return he was scheduled to become McKinley's secretary, only to die when he fell from a third-story window at a class reunion at Yale in 1901. To most of the world his appointment to Pretoria had seemed a symbol of administration sympathies for Great Britain.

Better evidence of those sympathies was provided by the

[7] Ferguson, *American Diplomacy*, p. ix.

government's handling of Boer efforts, sometimes supported by European powers desiring to drive a wedge between England and the United States, to secure American mediation or political intervention. Efforts in this direction started even before the declaration of war, and the day after the conflict began, the President issued a statement saying that intervention could not then be considered because neither side had requested it, an assertion only technically true since several informal feelers had been received. In March 1900 the Boers formally asked Washington to offer mediation. With an election in the offing and Congress stirring, they clearly could not simply be rebuffed. Hay quickly transmitted the proposal to London, garnished not with a request for British acceptance but merely with conventional remarks in favor of peace. Within three days Salisbury replied that mediation was not desired. Although some English reactionaries grumbled, Hay had actually served British interests by omitting to act in conjunction with other, anti-British powers and by permitting London to get a negative reply on the record before those powers could coordinate an approach.

A few months later, in May, a three-man Boer mission arrived in the United States. Warmly received at New York, largely by Democrats, they found the climate in official Washington much chillier. Hay received them coolly, turned down their request for mediation by reading a reply already on his desk when they entered the room, and ushered Sir Julian Pauncefote into his office as they were leaving. Hay had moved so rapidly that the unfortunate envoys never even had a chance to present their official credentials. A visit to the White House the next day was hardly more consoling, for the President merely repeated his lieutenant's observations and then conducted the visitors on a tour of the south lawn. Although they had announced that they did not intend to become involved in American politics, the angry ministers toured the United States denouncing the administration until they left the country in July.

The Boers and their friends hoped American policy would change when Theodore Roosevelt, Dutch by descent rather than

English, entered the White House. The new President disappointed them. He would not receive any Boer representatives until March 1902, when the war was almost over, and even then he insisted upon ostentatiously unofficial visits. Roosevelt, while admitting that public sentiment overwhelmingly favored the Boers, declared official action unthinkable and brusquely rejected complaints against the unequal effect of American neutrality policies.

Throughout the war, then, the American government showed that it had no sympathy for the Boer cause. With Hay, McKinley, and Roosevelt running the show, this is not astonishing. What is surprising is that the administration found it so easy to maintain this posture. Knowledgeable observers recognized that, a few exceptions aside, "The sympathy expressed by American politicians for the Transvaal Boers was never more than Platonic," [8] as the London *Times* put it. After the Presidential election, denunciations dwindled to almost nothing. As a result of the war, American affection for Britain slackened, but events of the recent past made it impossible for really serious criticism to arise, criticism deep enough to drive a government before it.

Because the Boer War never stirred American consciences as deeply as earlier struggles for liberty, the state of relations with England was only a secondary issue in the election of 1900. Thanks to Senator Foraker's strong gavel, the Republicans failed to endorse the Boer cause. They also considered but rejected a plank calling for the acquisition of Canada, an aspiration which had made part of their program in 1896 and which some thought it would be good politics to include again. During the campaign itself Republican orators rather self-consciously took a high-minded line. Just before rushing off for a post-election vacation during which he shot eight cougars and killed four more with a knife, the successful Vice-Presidential candidate wrote, "In the campaign that has just closed the victorious side has never for a moment appealed to any anti-English feeling, or disclaimed its own self-respecting friendliness for England—the first time I

[8] *Times* (London), September 11, 1900.

think that such an attitude has been taken. Of course," continued Roosevelt, "we with entire truthfulness disclaimed any alliance with England." [9]

Before the outbreak of war in South Africa, during a gubernatorial campaign in Ohio, Democrats spread rumors that the administration had concluded a secret alliance with Great Britain. Hay dignified the allegation with an elaborate response. After the war began, many people, among them Webster Davis and also Charles Macrum, Adelbert Hay's predecessor at Pretoria who was summarily dismissed for pro-Boer activity, thought they saw evidence to support the charge in the policies of the American government. Democrats in Congress frequently noised their suspicions, sometimes generously admitting that there might be nothing more formal than a verbal understanding "to render aid, if occasion requires"; they often pointed to Hay's sabotage of mediation plans as evidence. Therefore the Democratic platform, in addition to praising the Boers, denounced the "ill-concealed Republican alliance with England." [10] Campaign orators and some newspapers, particularly within the German-American press, developed this theme. The campaign differed subtly from the anti-British innuendos of 1896, for this time the emphasis was upon treasonable Americans rather than malevolent British plotters, and it was less vehemently if equally frequently put forward. There is no evidence the charge measurably aided the Democrats. Republicans often amused themselves with sarcastic descriptions of the private wire connecting McKinley with Downing Street or of a coup d'état to establish a regency under Sir Julian Pauncefote, and British commentators commonly discounted the charge as a rather ludicrous gesture to Anglophobes in the United States.

As this reaction suggests, Britons took a much more relaxed view of the second McKinley-Bryan bout than the first. War in

[9] Roosevelt to White, November 23, 1900, Morison, ed., *Letters of Roosevelt*, vol. II, p. 1436.

[10] Sen. Richard F. Pettigrew, *Congressional Record*, 56th Congress, 1st Session, p. 4166; Kirk H. Porter and Donald Bruce Johnson, eds., *National Party Platforms, 1840–1960* (2nd ed.; Urbana, 1961), p. 115.

Africa, the Boxer uprising in China and an election of their own in which the Unionists gained a five-year lease on life diverted their attention. Moreover, a surprisingly large number of British critics believed that it made little real difference which party won the election. Some, including the *Times*, reacted in typical style, predicting serious discord if Bryan and, even worse, his disreputable supporters gained positions of authority. However, in marked contrast to 1896, when most Englishmen expected dire things from Democrats, in 1900 many declared that Bryan could not reverse the direction of American policy, a course imposed by destiny. St. Loe Strachey's *Spectator* spoke for this group when it declared, "If Mr. Bryan wins, the United States, in spite of the clatter, will neither attack or be unfriendly to England, nor reverse the policy of taking up her share of the 'white man's burden' which Mr. McKinley has begun. The United States of America will, in a word, be run on Anglo-Saxon lines whether Mr. Bryan or Mr. McKinley wins." [11] Finally, almost all Englishmen who cast an American political horoscope expected McKinley to win handily; this permitted them to speculate more philosophically on the campaign in 1900, whereas in 1896 they feared a Bryan victory which might upset social stability and exacerbate Anglo-American relations.

These views produced two strikingly new attitudes in Great Britain. More often than ever before, journalists cautioned their countrymen not to take sides in the American contest. A pro-Republican press like that four years earlier, they suggested, would probably aid the Democrats and certainly stiffen anti-British forces within that party. Even in the face of Democratic criticism it behooved Englishmen, as the *Spectator* put it, to "possess our souls in patience, and receive American censure with the dogged stolidity with which we receive censure from the remainder of the world." Someday, if not in 1900, the Democrats would come to power, and it would be very unfortunate if Britain had nailed her emotional colors to the Republican mast. British officialdom understood this argument and ac-

[11] *Spectator* (London), vol. LXXXV (1900), p. 39.

cepted it, though desiring McKinley's reelection. "They are deeply interested in it here, and quite understand that they must not let this feeling be known," Henry White reported.[12] Probably not by coincidence, it was decided to refurbish the British embassy on Connecticut Avenue in Washington during the summer of 1900, providing a plausible reason for Pauncefote to absent himself from the American capital until after the election. Newspapers and magazines found it more difficult to heed their own counsel, but in general the tone of the British press was much less strident than before.

A second departure, reflecting somewhat the same spirit as the first, was the far more balanced treatment of Bryan. The *Times* denounced him as a "quick-change artist" appealing to one nostrum after another, and one frenzied conversative compared him with Savonarola, violent, threatening, and ineffective. On the other hand, a number of journals, even some which admitted that a Democratic administration might temporarily impair good relations with England, found favorable things to say about the candidate. In praising his vigor and honesty, they pointed out that only a courageous, principled man would insist upon reasserting the free-silver argument when more effective issues lay at hand. By contrast, McKinley was universally considered to be dull, opportunistic, unprincipled, and weak. If some of the challenger's ideas were impractical, as many believed them to be, the responsibilities of office would alter them. Some Liberals even denied that Bryan was particularly radical, although of course they had no sympathy for his "economic heresies." Sydney Brooks, a frequent commentator on America, wrote, "There is . . . little in the Bryanite programme that is not in line with Liberal principles as we knew them here up to 1880" and that Bryanism merely aimed "at making America almost as democratic as we are ourselves." [13] His battle against entrenched interests,

---

[12] *Ibid.*, vol. LXXXIV (1900), p. 511; White to Hay, May 26, 1900, quoted in Alexander E. Campbell, *Great Britain and the United States, 1895–1903* (Glasgow, 1960), p. 198.

[13] *Times*, October 5, 1900; Sydney Brooks, "Bryanism," *Contemporary Review* (London), vol. LXXVIII (1900), pp. 638, 642.

materialism, and plutocracy commanded sympathy in England.

All of this is not to say that most Britons wished success to Bryan and his campaign against imperialism, but only that they took a more dispassionate and sophisticated view of American politics. They had learned to see mixed hues among the blacks and whites of American campaigns. Neither of the two succeeding elections aroused deep concern in England, although a preponderance of comment favored the Republicans. In 1912 all observers agreed that American friendship did not depend upon the success of one party or the other, and the rivals were judged solely in terms of their domestic programs.

Less than a year after his reelection William McKinley was assassinated. A shock of horror spread through Europe, at least official Europe, but was nowhere as strong as in England. The court went into mourning, and there were special services at Westminster Abbey and St. Paul's. The American ambassador to Germany, happening at the time to be en route from London to Scotland, was gratified to see black bunting not only on public buildings but also on country churches and even, he said, humble cottages.

The mourning was a gesture of sympathy to a friendly nation and a reaction to a dastardly crime rather than a mark of respect for the dead President. Most British obituaries were labored, particularly the *Times'*, and a few were frankly critical. They stressed McKinley's devotion to a high tariff, noting however that his last speech suggested he had finally learned better, and sometimes suggested, as well, that he was responsible for the rise of monopolies in the United States. Above all, they pictured him as a weak man, though honest and well-meaning. "He has originated no national movement," one paper asserted, "he has counseled no particular domestic policy, he has conceived no plans. He is the honest and laborious servant of one political force." [14] This skepticism is understandable, since only in recent years have historians begun to disturb the image of McKinley as a handsome figurehead.

[14] *Speaker*, quoted in *Literary Digest* (New York), vol. XXIII (1901), p. 410.

Even these revisionists have turned up no important instances of Presidential involvement in relations with England. In
1901 the *Times* thought McKinley had been an active friend of
Britain but could point to no evidence. Far more common was
the view expressed by another London paper: "it will be forever
remembered of President McKinley that in his time Great Britain ceased to be thought of and spoken of as the secular foe of
the United States." [15] McKinley, in other words, had reigned but
had not ruled during a very happy period in Anglo-American relations, and Britons paid tribute to the fortunate changes of his
administration rather than to the President himself when they
poured forth their condolences.

McKinley's successor awakened contemporaries and still in-
trigues historians. Roosevelt's order changing the official designa-
tion from "Executive Mansion" to "White House" accurately
reflects the new tone of informality and vigor. The most indefatigable of Presidents, both intellectually and physically, Theodore Roosevelt read and did almost anything, tangled with professional wrestler Oscar Hackenschmidt in the White House
gymnasium, and converted an arriving British diplomat's protocol visit into a probing discussion of recent excavations at Knos-
sos. About wrestling, archaeology, and other things, Roosevelt
was sometimes more energetic than knowledgeable, but he almost always made his views known. Shortly after he became
President, Henry Adams dined at the White House for the first
time since he had been bored half to death by Rutherford B.
Hayes. The old egotist complained, "what annoys me is his
childlike and infantile superficiality with his boyish dogmatism
of assertion. He lectures me on history," the great historian expostulated, "as though he were a high-school pedagogue." [16]

As President, Roosevelt well understood the political advantages of a bold stance toward foreign powers, and his nationalism, along with a highly developed streak of self-righteousness,

---

[15] *St. James Gazette,* quoted in *ibid.,* p. 473.
[16] Adams to Elizabeth Cameron, January 12, 1902, Ford, ed., *Adams Letters,*
p. 366.

also often counseled him to fight hard in disputes with other countries. Sometimes Roosevelt ran risks, yet he was no posturing adventurer. He dealt forcefully, even brutally, with Latin American states, since they were weak and lay within a sphere in which the American people expected the nation to be dominant. He sometimes treated Great Britain brusquely, for reasons which included a conviction that English concessions were needed to clear the air between the two countries. On the other hand, he moved very cautiously in the Far East, more cautiously than he sometimes liked to admit, and his rare interventions in European politics were, in deference to the isolationist spirit, concealed from public gaze.

Roosevelt gained a reputation for indiscretion, and sometimes he was indiscreet, particularly in conversations with friends, including foreign ambassadors. Yet he never claimed to have delivered a famous ultimatum to Germany nor boasted of having suborned a Panamanian revolution until he left the Presidency. Except in private correspondence with the British foreign secretary, who had every reason to keep the secret, he kept silent about the aid he claimed to have given Britain and France during the Moroccan crisis of 1905–1906, and it took historians twenty years to uncover an important informal agreement with Japan in 1904. He used flamboyant language, and he tailored his foreign correspondence to the nationality of the recipient, using it either to instruct or to flatter. He was, however, well aware of the danger of seeming too partial, and once, after writing an English friend, "I am sorry to learn that Chamberlain is not in good health," he hypercautiously added, "By the way, I have also really regretted the Kaiser's sickness." [17] In short, while the President showed more interest in foreign affairs than any chief executive since James Madison, he usually proceeded with caution and circumspection, except, at least, when he knew that God—and American opinion—was on the side of his battalions. By his visible concern rather than any risky or indiscreet actions he led the

[17] Roosevelt to Lee, December 7, 1903, Morison, ed., *Letters of Roosevelt*, vol. III, p. 665.

United States down the road toward world participation.

The President shared the Darwinian, racist views of the day. He considered international affairs a competitive game in which the weak suffered at the hands of the strong and in which the strong proved their virtue by accomplishment. Even war, he thought, often served a eugenic purpose, although he deplored military conflict between advanced races. Above all, he feared that a nation would decay if it allowed materialism and money-grubbing to sap its martial fiber, and at times he gloomily commented upon American and British tendencies in this direction. Like most imperialists, he viewed empire as both challenge and reward. Although it did not take him long to decide that the Philippine acquisition he so strenuously urged in 1898 had led to excessive responsibilities, he always considered it America's duty to discipline and to protect backward nations in her own hemisphere. He approved of British imperialism, whether in South Africa or Egypt or India. He only feared that Englishmen would deal too weakly with their subjects, either from misplaced humanitarianism or from a declining sense of obligation.

Until the Russo-Japanese War, Roosevelt sometimes talked in a sweeping way about the conflict of Saxon and Slav, although with far more optimism and far less frequency than his friends Spring Rice and Brooks Adams. More often, in the early years, he worried about Germany. "Germany's attitude toward us makes her the only power with which there is any reasonable likelihood . . . of our clashing within the future," he wrote while Vice President; ". . . Germany is the great growing power, . . . and her ambitions in extra-European matters are so great, that she may clash with us." [18] In particular, he feared German ambitions in America's hemisphere.

As time passed, Roosevelt's emphases changed. In the Far East the Russian threat lost force. The President never ceased to consider Japan a progressive factor in Asia, but he did fall into conflict with her, which embarrassed the British government since it had to juggle American friendship and the Anglo-Japanese

[18] Roosevelt to George von L. Meyer, April 12, 1901, *ibid.*, p. 152.

alliance. Roosevelt's fear of German penetration of the hemisphere diminished. By letter, he developed a friendship with the Kaiser and made good use of it during the Russo-Japanese War and the Moroccan crisis. By 1905 suspicious minds even concluded that Wilhelm unduly influenced the President, and Roosevelt felt it politic to explain the true situation to the British foreign secretary in confidence. While he respected some of the Kaiser's qualities, the President considered him erratic, egotistical, and too stupid to see through even the most blatant flattery.

From 1905 until about 1910, when he stressed the theme during a post-Presidential jaunt to Europe, Roosevelt sought to meliorate the growing hostility between England and Germany. He did not blame Germany alone—"Each Nation is working itself up to a condition of desperate hatred of each other from sheer fear," he wrote at the time of the Morocco crisis—[19] but did hold that country more responsible. The prospect of a European war horrified him as no war between or with inferior peoples could have done, the danger of a German victory he frequently mentioned in private, and he chafed at restraints which prevented a President from effective interference in the interest of peace.

Before Roosevelt entered the White House he often used shrilly nationalistic language, at least twice making Anglo-American settlements more difficult, and Henry James was not alone in deploring the rise to power of "a dangerous and ominous Jingo." Interestingly, the British press did not view him in the same light. The reactionary *Saturday Review* hopefully predicted that he would be led by moneyed and aristocratic forces, and a number of editorialists specifically denied that he could be considered a jingo—that he could, for example, be compared with that horrid man Grover Cleveland, who had stirred up the Venezuelan affair for political purposes. A few commentators considered Roosevelt overimpulsive; the *Times*, after listing his valuable qualities—character, intelligence, literary power, and will—observed cautiously, "It is too soon to conjecture whether Presi-

[19] Roosevelt to Taft, April 20, 1905, *ibid.*, vol. IV, p. 1162.

dent Roosevelt will add to these advantages the saving leaven of a wise and far-seeing prudence." [20] The *Times* and almost all other commentators expected the new President to be a vigorous nationalist, but they quite rightly did not expect him to let domestic political considerations control his diplomacy or to show an Anglophobe streak.

As President, Roosevelt pressed Great Britain very hard in a dispute over the boundary between Canada and Alaska, the most important disagreement with Britain during his administration. He deplored the fawning attitude of many Americans, socialites and expatriates like Henry James, who in his view were disloyal to their country. Yet he considered himself a realistic and hardheaded friend of England, a friend who did not engage in "gush." "I am sure you will agree with me," he wrote Finley Peter Dunne, the satirist, in 1904, "that in our political life, very unlike what is the case in our social life, the temptation is toward Anglophobia, not toward Anglomania. The cheapest thing for any politician to do . . . is to make some yell about England." Roosevelt proudly claimed he had never done so. "I feel," he went on, "a sincere friendliness for England; but you may notice that I do not slop over about it." [21] This is a fair description, even granted that the President was seeking to disarm Dunne's criticism of his allegedly pro-British policies. Roosevelt's Anglo-Saxonism, the events of 1898, and his view of world politics all led him—at least after Britian visibly accepted American hegemony in the New World—to follow policies of friendship.

Roosevelt clearly believed England and the United States were on parallel tracks. After the Alaskan boundary settlement, and probably before, he concluded that a collision between them was unthinkable. "You need not ever be troubled by the nightmare of a possible contest between the two great English-speaking peoples," he wrote a British junior minister in 1905. "In

[20] James to Jessie Allen, September 19, 1901, Percy Lubbock, ed., *The Letters of Henry James* (2 vols.; New York, 1920), vol. I, p. 379; *Times*, September 17, 1901.

[21] Roosevelt to Dunne, November 23, 1904, Morison, ed., *Letters of Roosevelt*, vol. IV, p. 1042.

keeping ready for possible war I never even take into account a war with England. I treat it as out of the question." As early as 1901 he wrote, "I do not at all believe in being over-effusive or in forgetting that fundamentally we are two different nations; but yet the fact remains, in the first place, that we are closer in feeling to her than to any other nation; and in the second place, that probably her interest and ours will run on parallel lines in the future." When, over the protest of cautious advisers, Edward VII wrote to congratulate "the elected chief of the republican branch of the English-speaking people" (a phrase deleted from the royal draft by the Foreign Office) on his success in the campaign of 1904, Roosevelt replied, "The larger interests of the two nations are the same; and the fundamental underlying traits of their characters are also the same." [22] The President pointed to the unity of interest in Latin America and the Far East. His respect and affection for England blinded him, as it did many Americans, to the very real but shadowy differences between British and American policy in the Orient. This in itself is evidence of the extent of his friendly feelings.

No world statesmen with whom Roosevelt dealt ever completely escaped his criticism, so British leaders were not exempt. As a group he considered them stodgy, less imaginative than the Kaiser, although he sometimes objected to Chamberlain's eccentricities and, like most American observers, had contempt for the young radical Winston Churchill. At first he preferred Conservatives, friends of 1898, to the Liberals, who gained power in 1905, primarily because he distrusted the Liberal party's peace-minded strain. However, he had mixed feelings about Arthur Balfour (and, like most readers, was baffled by the strange book, *Decadence*, Balfour published after leaving office). Moreover he positively hated the Marquis of Lansdowne, who became foreign secretary in 1900, while, after a suspicious beginning, he developed

[22] Roosevelt to Lee, June 6, 1905, *ibid.*, p. 1207; Roosevelt to Lodge, June 19, 1901, Henry Cabot Lodge, ed., *Selections from the Correspondence of Theodore Roosevelt and Henry Cabot Lodge, 1884–1918* (2 vols.; New York, 1925), vol. I, pp. 493–494; Edward VII to Roosevelt, February 20, 1905, and draft, quoted in Sir Sidney Lee, *King Edward VII* (2 vols.; London, 1925–1927), vol. II, pp. 429–431; Roosevelt to Edward VII, March —, 1905, quoted in *ibid.*, p. 432.

very warm relations with Sir Edward Grey, Lansdowne's Liberal successor. The President exchanged views with a number of British politicians of the second rank, most notably a Conservative, Arthur Hamilton Lee, once a military observer attached to the Rough Riders, who was promoted from "Dear Lee" to "Dear Arthur" after he sent a picture appropriately titled, without apologies to Gilbert Parker's novel, "The Seats of the Mighty," to grace the White House.

At least until the end of Roosevelt's first administration in 1905, his closest British friend was Sir Cecil Spring Rice. The two men met during an Atlantic crossing in 1886, and they became friends so quickly that Spring Rice served as best man at Roosevelt's second marriage in London a few weeks later. Spring Rice, a spade-bearded little man, a bachelor until he safely married the daughter of England's ambassador to Germany in 1904 ("Can't you both take in the White House on your bridal trip?" Roosevelt asked),[23] served in Washington on and off in the 1890's. He shared the Lodges' vacant house with Roosevelt one summer while the owners were away and Mrs. Roosevelt enceinte in New York. He visited Oyster Bay several times and only once suffered the indignity of having an active Rooseveltian horse bolt with him. Combining cynical wit and tact, Spring Rice cultivated social Washington so well that even "Uncle Henry" Adams accepted him. In 1901, when Roosevelt succeeded McKinley, Spring Rice had long since departed for dreary stations in the Middle East and Egypt, but he deluged the new President with correspondence.

Far more than Roosevelt, Spring Rice was the creature of his prejudices. In the early 1890's he hated Americans, his friends aside, and opposed concession to them: "You might as well conciliate a jackal or, let us say, a tiger." [24] This passed in 1898, and Spring Rice devoted much of his correspondence with the new President to a fashionable prejudice against the Russians, Brit-

[23] Roosevelt to Spring Rice, February 2, 1904, quoted in Stephen Gwynn, *The Letters and Friendships of Sir Cecil Spring Rice* (2 vols.; Cambridge, 1929), vol. I, p. 377.
[24] Spring Rice to Francis Villiers, April 12, 1895, quoted in *ibid.*, p. 175.

ain's chief rival and one which could be denigrated in racist terms. As Germany, too, rose to challenge England, Spring Rice developed an additional hatred. Spicing his apocalyptic fears and predictions about these two rivals with inside information, particularly that which he gathered after becoming first secretary at the St. Petersburg embassy in 1904, Spring Rice tried to use his correspondence with Roosevelt to lead the United States in directions desired by his government.

While Spring Rice probably had genuine affection for Roosevelt, he underestimated his friend's good qualities and cynically sought to exploit his bad ones. His reports helped lead the Foreign Office to a temporary conclusion that Roosevelt was under the Kaiser's influence. He recommended the appointment of a battle-scarred veteran as military attaché at Washington solely because he expected the President to unburden himself to a war hero, and the appointment deservedly proved a failure. When asked by a *Times* correspondent to explain Roosevelt's inconsistencies, Spring Rice compared his friend to a six-year-old boy who discovers a number of attractive pebbles on a beach and picks up and drops one after another.

Roosevelt, who of course did not know of these backstairs judgments, welcomed the correspondence with Spring Rice. He always cherished old friendships, and he was so sure that Spring Rice understood him—the Englishman could be a good listener —that he several times sought his appointment as British ambassador at Washington. Furthermore, Roosevelt considered Spring Rice a first-class political reporter, better than all but Henry White in the American service; he enjoyed the gossip; he valued an indirect channel to the Foreign Office; and he knew how to take Spring Rice's sentiments with a grain of salt. He good-humoredly dissected his correspondent's most savage predictions about Russia, and when told that Britain's honor prevented her from using her influence with her ally Japan as Roosevelt desired, he asked, "Don't you think you go a little needlessly into heroics . . . ?" [25] Early in 1905, at Roosevelt's request, Spring Rice

[25] Roosevelt to Spring Rice, July 24, 1905, quoted in *ibid.*, p. 478.

made a flying visit to Washington to be filled in on American views toward the Russo-Japanese War. He returned to London with much valuable information but without having shaken the President an iota.

In sum, Spring Rice never had the influence on Roosevelt that he and even some historians thought he had. The President made his own judgments, and they were usually less extreme and wiser than Spring Rice's. The far more subtle propagandist Lee displaced Spring Rice as the President's favorite British correspondent after 1906, partly because Spring Rice left St. Petersburg for less exciting posts and partly, perhaps, because the President had tired of the correspondence.

While Spring Rice tried to influence things from afar, more effective work was done by Sir Michael Herbert, the young British ambassador at Washington. Herbert, younger son of the Earl of Pembroke, married a wealthy American in 1888, creating a happy household but winning less money than relatives who married an Astor and a Vanderbilt. The next year Herbert came to the United States, where he served four years. He quickly became Roosevelt's friend and was converted by him into that exotic type, an Englishman who is also a baseball fan. When Pauncefote died, Herbert, whose greater talents and more influential family enabled him to rise far more rapidly in the diplomatic service than Spring Rice, was number-two man at the Paris embassy. Lansdowne wished to appoint Sir Mortimer Durand, an old protégé, but at Henry White's suggestion he selected Roosevelt's friend instead.

Although Sir Michael served at Washington during the climax of the dispute over Alaska, the most difficult part of Roosevelt's administration, he was more successful with the President than any other British ambassador. He never toadied to the President, but he listened well. His reports to London were very perceptive, loyal both to his country and to the American leader with whom he sometimes strongly disagreed. Although Herbert often dined at the White House and took part in the almost obligatory rock-climbing expeditions in Rock Creek Park, he never became as intimate with Roosevelt as the German ambassador, Speck von Sternburg, another old friend, or the Frenchman, Jules Jusserand, a wit and an appreciative student of English literature who most perfectly complemented the President's personality and, more than the others, shared his catholic interests. (Like Herbert, Sternburg and Jusserand married Americans who adopted much of their husbands' patriotism. When Roosevelt praised the German *Niebelungenlied,* Mme. Jusserand protested. Her husband soon presented a copy of the *Chanson de Roland* to Roosevelt, who praised it but objected that the heroes wept and swooned too much for his taste.) A lack of real intimacy did not prevent Roosevelt from developing great respect for a man he later described as "one of the sweetest and most attractive men I have ever met." [26] Unfortunately, Herbert died in September 1903, still only forty-six. His loss proved unfortunate.

Of American diplomats, Roosevelt most trusted Henry White, first secretary at London until 1905. White, a wealthy Maryland Republican with a vivacious wife who enchanted British leaders, first served in London in 1884 and spent most of the next twenty years there. McKinley offered to send him to Madrid, the critical point in American diplomacy, in 1897, but White preferred to stay among his London friends. From the British capital, he deluged Roosevelt and Hay with reports of his conversations with members of the government, and the Americans found him an extremely useful channel of communication. At the beginning of Roosevelt's second term, White moved on to Rome as ambassador and then to Algeciras for the Moroccan conference.

White was a great snob whose contacts were almost entirely confined to the well-to-do and conventional. In England, he saw most of Conservatives but kept out a sheet anchor to chosen Liberals, among them Sir William Harcourt, Richard Haldane, and H. H. Asquith. He thought nothing of inviting himself to Hat-

[26] Roosevelt to George Otto Trevelyan, February 4, 1907, Morison, ed., *Letters of Roosevelt,* vol. V, p. 579.

field or some other estate owned by a friend to discuss Anglo-American affairs, and in such surroundings he excelled. In large gatherings, official and unofficial, White was very bland. Spring Rice cattily commented, "He is good nature itself and agrees with everyone in turn without irritating them as much as one would expect from the habit," and Sir Harold Nicolson, whose father encountered White at Algeciras, sneered, "Mr. Henry White . . . was conciliatory, ignorant, and charming; Mr. White was so full of charm that there was room for little else." [27]

Still, as a reporter rather than a policy-maker, White was an effective diplomat. His wide circle of influential acquaintances, relaxed and evocative style of conversation, obvious affection for England, and well-deserved reputation for discretion enabled him to pump vast amounts of information across the Atlantic. He had a good eye for detail, shrewd political judgment, and healthy skepticism about some of the things he was told. On only rare occasions did he permit himself the backbiting which Spring Rice made into a habit. In 1896, when, as a Republican, he was out of office, the Democrats had to use him as a channel of communication with the Salisbury ministry, and under McKinley and especially Roosevelt, restored to office, he played the same role. White sometimes overstated the vigor with which he transmitted the President's views to British statesmen, but he never left them in doubt about Roosevelt's meaning. Similarly, while he often excused British views with which he disagreed, he left Washington in no doubt about their substance. Roosevelt had every right to trust White, a more loyal and valuable friend than Spring Rice.

Roosevelt's two ambassadors to London were very much alike, what a cartoonist might imagine ambassadors to be. Both were famous, wealthy, and old, so old that both celebrated a seventieth birthday in London. Both were deserving Republicans. Both were unabashed Anglophiles, the type of man the President

---

[27] Spring Rice to Agnes Spring Rice, April 1, 1895, quoted in Gwynn, *Spring Rice*, vol. I, p. 169; Harold Nicolson, *Portrait of a Diplomatist* (Cambridge, 1930), p. 127.

often criticized, and both eagerly sought appointment to London, where they distinguished themselves by lavish entertainment and cloying speeches in favor of Anglo-American friendship. Neither did anything to distinguish himself as a diplomat.

Joseph Choate, a legacy from McKinley, was sent to London in 1899. Perhaps the most famous and certainly one of the most prosperous lawyers of his generation, he had a reputation for courtroom skill rather than penetrating ideas or solid preparation, and Roosevelt passed Choate off as "not really a worker at all, but a brilliant advocate." The spirit of Choate's embassy is suggested by a passage from a speech he gave just before his departure, when he said, "I am running a great risk, if I stay here much longer, of contracting a . . . serious disease . . . —I mean Anglomania, which many of my countrymen regard as more dangerous and fatal than even cerebro-spinal meningitis. To a young man it is absolutely fatal, but to one who has well-nigh exhausted his future, the consequences are not quite so serious." [28] During a reorganization of the diplomatic corps after his reelection, Roosevelt let Choate resign, sending him a suspiciously fulsome letter of regret.

Choate's successor, Whitelaw Reid, was particularly close to John Hay, who stood in as editor of the New York *Tribune* for him while Reid was on his honeymoon in 1881. Reid failed of appointment to London in 1897, his old lieutenant getting the nod, but in 1905 he received it and sailed for England so precipitately that his ship passed Choate's in mid-Atlantic. If anything, Reid was more of an Anglophile than Choate, and for a while he even swallowed the foolish rumor that Kaiser Wilhelm had converted Roosevelt into an enemy of England. Thanks to intervention by his friend Edward VII, Reid survived the shift from Roosevelt to Taft, and he died in London in December 1912. "We regard him as a kinsman," the Prime Minister declaimed in the House of Commons.[29] After a memorial service at Westminster

[28] Quoted in Edward S. Martin, *The Life of Joseph Hodges Choate* (2 vols.; New York, 1920), vol. II, p. 297.
[29] Asquith, quoted in Royal Cortissoz, *The Life of Whitelaw Reid* (2 vols.; New York, 1921), vol. II, p. 451.

Abbey, the Scots Guards and Household Cavalry escorted his coffin to the railroad station, and H.M.S. *Natal* returned it to the United States.

During his first term, and indeed until Hay died in July 1905, Roosevelt continued him in office, pleasing those who shudderingly predicted that the new President would install Henry Cabot Lodge at the Department of State. At the outset Roosevelt needed Hay, if only to show that he did not intend a dramatic break with McKinley policies, but their relationship was never really an easy one. Roosevelt, Hay wrote to Henry Adams just after the assassination, "came down from Buffalo Monday night—and in the station, without waiting an instant, told me I must stay with him—that I could not decline nor even consider. I saw, of course, it was best for him to start off that way, and so I said I would stay. . . . I can still go at any moment he gets tired of me, or when I collapse." [30] In a way, the two men loved each other, although Hay let his cynicism color his judgments of the President while Roosevelt, particularly after the posthumous publication, under Henry Adams' editorship, of Hay's sometimes irreverent correspondence, described his colleague as superannuated and too much under Adams' baleful influence. But the new President's determination to run diplomacy himself and the reversal of their respective positions of influence, the experienced and elderly Hay being passed by the young and inexperienced Roosevelt, were too much for them. Hay several times talked of resigning, Roosevelt took management of the most important issues out of his hands, and Hay's death in 1905 no doubt brought relief to both of them. Hay's successor, Elihu Root, was clearly Roosevelt's man, though by no means a sycophant, and he served capably and self-effacingly during the second administration.

Until the autumn of 1905 Hay and Roosevelt dealt with a Unionist ministry, a comfortably predictable quantity. Salisbury shucked off the Foreign Office in 1900 and retired entirely in July

[30] Hay to Adams, September 19, 1901, quoted in William R. Thayer, *The Life and Letters of John Hay* (2 vols.; Boston, 1915), vol. II, pp. 267–268.

1902 without visibly affecting relations with the United States, although in other fields his successors, the sober Lord Lansdowne at the Foreign Office and his nephew, Balfour, a languid statesman and ardent golfer, as Prime Minister, showed themselves much more willing to experiment. Both men considered American friendship indispensable. Balfour "has always been 'an American,'" a friend said, continuing, ". . . he never allows the expression 'foreigner' or 'foreign State' to be used in speaking of America or Americans." The Prime Minister even dreamed of a loose political union at some future time; after both he and Roosevelt had left office, he prepared for the American a long memorandum arguing for "a confederation [which] would be practically unassailable and would dominate the world." [31]

Seven months before Roosevelt became President, and while Balfour's uncle still clung to the levers of power, there occurred what contemporaries considered a far more dramatic change of cast than the resignation of Salisbury or even the murder of McKinley. The death of Queen Victoria in February 1901, all observers agreed, marked the end of an era. Englishmen welcomed the world's sympathies. Even the Kaiser, who rushed from Germany to keep a death watch at his grandmother's home, earned British praise. But of all condolences the most gratefully received were those from America, and indeed the obituaries for McKinley a few months later were sometimes a half-conscious effort to repay the United States.

During her long reign, Queen Victoria saw American attitudes toward herself transformed. In the 1840's she was the symbol of that tyranny, in Oregon and elsewhere, so roundly denounced by spokesmen for Manifest Destiny. As late as 1887, when Britons the world over celebrated Victoria's diamond jubilee, the Foreign Office dared not order its representatives in the United States to erect special decorations or fancy lighting in honor of the event, and when an imprudent group engaged Fan-

---

[31] John S. Sanders, quoted in Kenneth Young, *Arthur James Balfour* (London, 1963), p. 279; Balfour, "The Possibility of an Anglo-Saxon Confederation," quoted in *ibid.*, p. 283.

euil Hall in Boston for a dinner in the Queen's honor a Catholic clergyman of Irish descent protested this desecration of the cradle of liberty, with the result that fifteen thousand people milled around the hall, yelling imprecations at diners within. A decade later the situation had changed, at least if the politically astute McKinley's assessment was correct. For celebrations of Victoria's sixty years on the throne, the President sent a special ambassador, Whitelaw Reid, to England as well as the cruiser whose floodlights provided Ambassador Hay with his oratorical inspiration.

When Victoria died, a wave of sentiment swept the United States. The Irish-American press denounced her as the enslaver of Erin, and Mayor Van Wyck of New York City declined to lower city flags even on the day of her funeral, a piece of *lèse majesté* which irritated respectables, although not so seriously that a writer to the *Times* missed a chance for a pun when he denounced Van Wyck as a man "who is akin to the Boers, if not a boor himself." [32] On the other hand, McKinley lowered the White House flag to half-mast, the first time this had ever been done for a foreign sovereign. Five state legislatures and both houses of Congress passed resolutions of regret, and sober statements were issued by prominent citizens like Andrew Carnegie, ex-President Harrison, and, with the proper garnish of historical allusion, ex-Professor Lodge.

In London, Ambassador Choate and Henry White struggled over the choice of flowers. They did not wish to seem *outré* like the Portuguese, whose wreath was so heavy it taxed five bearers, nor did they want their country to seem stingy; in the end they settled on a fifty-guinea display, neither unrepublican nor ostentatious. Other Americans also became involved. A visitor from Kalamazoo volunteered his services as embalmer, an offer Choate did not pass on to British authorities. Ella Wheeler Wilcox, a very popular, very conventional poet, did better. When Victoria became ill, Miss Wilcox's publishers rushed her to England to cover the death and funeral. Inspiration eluded the poet

---

[32] "Potomac," letter to the editor, *New York Times*, January 24, 1901.

for some time, but finally, as she leafed through an old newspaper, her eye caught a court circular which began, "The Queen is taking a drive to-day." [33] This she used as a recurring line in a poem describing the funeral procession, a treacly product which became an instantaneous success in both countries.

Irish-American boors and some others aside, American editors pulled out all the stops in their praise of Victoria. They lauded her as a wise and gracious sovereign who had presided over an age of British greatness, differing only as to whether this marked the apogee of her nation's power or the prelude to an even more golden age. They especially praised her as "a most noble and faithful mother" (the New York *Herald*) who had (the St. Paul *Dispatch*) "shown how eminent and how beautiful are the old-fashioned virtues," [34] for at least in the eyes of middle-aged men who directed most American newspapers Victoria had become the Plimsoll mark which showed Anglo-Saxons everywhere what were and what were not the proper standards. On the basis of fairly recent revelations they usually cited her role and that of her husband, Prince Albert, during the *Trent* affair of 1861, when a British war was nearly added to the civil contest in the United States. Like English commentators on McKinley's death a few months later, American newspapermen pointed out that the Queen had presided over a transformation. She died at a time when the two countries had learned, after nearly a century and a half of discord, to respect each other. For these reasons, Americans joined their British cousins in the often maudlin mourning which followed Victoria's death. Most dissenters considered it good taste and good tactics to remain silent.

Even leaving aside for the moment those developments which cast deep shadows for the future in Latin America and Asia, the developments which followed close on the heels of the Spanish-American War indicated how profoundly things had changed. The heady months of 1898 led some to hope for too

[33] Quoted in Amy Cruse, *After the Victorians* (London, 1938), p. 153.
[34] *Herald* (New York), January 24, 1901; St. Paul *Dispatch*, quoted in *Literary Digest*, vol. XXII (1901), p. 122.

much too soon. In the United States, Anglophobia had not been exorcised, but it had been so weakened or transformed that, as in the case of the Boer War, it had become a lesser factor for policymakers to consider. Enduring friendship would require time and further work, primarily by McKinley's successor and the servants of the new monarch, but by any reasonable standards of comparison the transformation had already been remarkable.

CHAPTER SIX

The Substructure of Diplomacy

"ENGLISH UNFAIR IN Olympic Games," read a *New York Times* headline on July 18, 1908. A story from London explained that Olympic officials—and in those days all officials came from the host country—had permitted a British tug-of-war team to wear hobnailed boots although Olympic rules required "ordinary shoes." Their American opponents had protested to no avail, officials explaining that such footwear was regular attire for the Liverpool bobbies who made up the team. To emphasize their anger, when the contest began the Americans let the rope slip through their hands. The policemen fell over backward in a heap—but they also advanced to the next round. A few days later, in the final of the 400 meters, three Americans faced the English favorite. As they swept down the back stretch, British officials began to wave their arms, and before the runners reached the finish line, a Yank in the lead, the judges cast the tape to the ground. They declared the contest "no race," alleging that one American had unfairly interfered with the Englishman to ensure victory for a countryman, and ordered a rerun the next day. The Americans declined to appear, the English runner waltzed around the track alone, and no silver or bronze medals were given. At the close of the marathon, an Italian entered the stadium well in the lead but in a state of near collapse. When he turned the wrong direction on the track, officials rushed onto the cinders to steer him correctly. Four times, when he fell, they helped him regain his feet. As the Italian wobbled toward the finish an American chugged into the stadium and began his last lap. The Italian collapsed just short of the line, but willing hands dragged him across a few feet ahead of his pursuer. The Italian flag rose on the winner's pole, though when the Americans lodged a formal protest it was hauled down and replaced by the Stars and Stripes.

The ugly cheers of the British crowd, chauvinistic responses by a bloc of two or three hundred American visitors, and the nationalistic reports of sportswriters inflated the importance of these episodes. The American commissioner complained to President Roosevelt, who let his anger be known and even wrote Ambassador Bryce, informally but strenuously protesting Bryce's defense of British officials. In London, many thoughtful people wondered if the Olympic Games should be discontinued.

The controversy showed that old prejudices had not disappeared, even in 1908, after a series of important settlements arranged by Roosevelt and his opposite numbers in London. Statesmen were ahead of opinion, particularly American opinion, for the enthusiasms of 1898 were not maintained. In the United States, recrudescences of Anglophobia emerged as early as the Boer War and reappeared during disputes with England over Canada's boundary with Alaska and over America's desire to monopolize control of a waterway linking the Atlantic and Pacific Oceans. Irish-Americans remained emerald green, and other citizens clung to traditional prejudices. In England it became fashionable in reactionary and radical circles to criticize the materialism of plutocracy-dominated America. For reasons peculiar to each case, these forces were not as potent as they might have been, but they did act as brakes upon the managers of diplomacy.

Other factors supported a rapprochement. An economic pattern developed which enabled Britain to accept American industrial leadership with little animosity. A somewhat similar pattern of accommodation emerged in the field of literature, where

Britain shucked off much of her condescension toward cultural upstarts, and members of the ruling consensus in both countries tended to draw together. Each of these themes, although complex and requiring frequent qualification, makes it crystal clear that the growth of understanding was not the creation of diplomacy alone. The limits upon restraining forces and the contributions of positive ones were both important parts of the Anglo-American equation.

For years after the Declaration of Independence the Americans remained, economically, semi-vassals of Great Britain, and the relationship often led to touchiness on one side and arrogance on the other. At the end of the nineteenth century, a different form of friction seemed possible. America had outstripped England in manufacturing output, and in the 1890's Britons began to worry about qualitative superiority as well. In 1900 Joseph Chamberlain and others established the University of Birmingham very largely to educate scientists and technologists who could help the country keep pace. The material for corrosive economic warfare lay at hand.

However, except just at the turn of the century, Englishmen accepted the growth of American economic power with relative equanimity. One recession aside, the years from 1900 to 1912 were prosperous, and with international trade increasing, the question of shares seemed fairly unimportant. Moreover, in a manner varying from area to area, and sometimes incompletely or with noisy dissent from losing parties, the two economies worked their way toward an implicit accommodation reflecting contemporary realities. This was easier because, despite the hullabaloo in 1898, Americans continued to devote most of their energies to domestic rather than foreign markets; the suffocating glut did not develop. Thus, to Britons the United States posed less of a challenge than Germany, which fought for trade all over the world. For example, the Americans exported only six percent of their steel output in 1904, whereas German firms sold thirty-five percent abroad, much of it in markets the British liked to think of as their own. Germany dramatically increased her share of international trade between 1900 and 1913 and on the eve of war was closing in on Britain; the United States remained well back in third place, with a share less than half those of her two rivals. In vain did John Hobson warn his countrymen, "We have reason to fear for the future, less perhaps of Germany, though her competition will be serious, than from America." [1]

New patterns developed in the direct trade between the two countries. Whereas America had once been England's biggest foreign market, in 1898 she purchased only a sixteenth of the goods Britain shipped abroad. Between 1900 and 1914 the monetary value increased sharply, but so much less rapidly than other branches of trade that in the last pre-war year only 5.6 percent of British exports went to the United States, the smallest percentage up to that time. Meanwhile, despite marked fluctuations, Britain continued to buy about one fifth of her imports in the United States. Penetration of the home market by American manufactures frightened Englishmen, although this was more important symbolically than economically; few of these imports were competitive, most filling demands met by no British suppliers. Raw materials and foodstuffs still predominated among imports, although England was decreasingly dependent upon the United States for such items as cotton, wheat, and frozen meat. The overriding theme of these years was the steady loosening of interdependence and the consequent destruction of remnants of the old client-patron relationship.

The new pattern aroused some concern in England, even fears that the old relationship would be reversed. Among other things, the new situation stimulated attacks upon the tradition of free trade. The American tariff wall, it was argued, harmed Britain in two ways, depriving her of markets and at the same time creating profit levels which allowed American firms to "dump" goods in foreign markets to the disadvantage of British competitors. The McKinley tariff of 1890 brought disaster to the

---

[1] "The Approaching Abandonment of Free Trade," *Fortnightly Review* (London), vol. LXXVII (1902), p. 435.

Welsh tin-plate industry, stimulating a rise in American production which helped to drive the Welsh output, heavily dependent upon exports, down from 327,000 tons in 1889 to a mere 64,000 tons in 1899. The Welsh also suffered in another case ferreted out by British investigators in 1905: protected by a tariff of about forty percent, steel bars sold at Pittsburgh for the equivalent of 117 shillings a ton, but the same bars were offered in Wales at 76 shillings, well under the price of 80 to 85 shillings for steel produced locally.

In response to this sort of thing, Joseph Chamberlain launched a campaign for tariff reform in May 1903. He wished to unite the empire behind walls of imperial preference, and obviously preference could not be effective in the absence of substantial tariffs upon nonimperial goods. During a struggle which continued until the war, supporters of imperial preference sometimes explicitly pointed to the American target, convinced that, in the words of the *National Review*, "until we have a serious tariff in this country enabling us to give tit-for-tat, no business worth speaking of can be transacted with the United States." Usually, however, tariff reformers directed their fire at Germany, apparently because the climate of opinion made it poor tactics to criticize the Americans. Opponents of reform, on the other hand, frequently argued that high tariffs had done more than anything else to turn the United States into a land of materialism. Lord Cromer declared, "The United States of America stand before us as an object-lesson of the demoralizing effect of protection on the political life of a country governed on democratic principles," and Winston Churchill, who bolted the Conservatives on the tariff issue, accused reformers of seeking to turn the party into a British counterpart of the Republicans, "rich, materialist, and secular." [2] This language was tough enough, but its effect was inconsequential compared with the potential effect of protec-

[2] *National Review* (London), vol. LX (1912), p. 547; Cromer, quoted in Richard H. Heindel, *The American Impact on Great Britain, 1898–1914* (Philadelphia, 1940), p. 159; Churchill, quoted in Bernard Semmel, *Imperialism and Social Reform: English Social-Imperial Thought, 1895–1914* (Cambridge, 1960), p. 100.

tionism itself. Moreover, the Americans faced already real challenges in German economic policies, policies which led to sharp
German-American exchanges in 1906–1907 and again in 1909–
1910, as well as the so-called "potash war" of 1909–1911, when
Berlin tried to force up the price of a fertilizer ingredient much
in demand in the United States. Such things diverted American
attention from the potential threat posed by Chamberlain and
his allies.

Early in the century British commentators bewailed "the
American invasion," the establishment of English subsidiaries or
the control of English firms by American companies. At least
since the Singer company built a sewing-machine factory near
Glasgow in 1867, this process had been going on. Often it had a
salutary effect. Thus techniques brought by Edison, General
Electric, and Westinghouse interests furthered the growth of an
important new industry in Britain, although the American invaders had mixed financial success. Thus, too, the Diamond
Match Company introduced automatic machinery in 1896, when
British firms still had each match dipped by hand, and captured
half the market in only five years before selling out to Bryant and
May, the largest English firm. Ford of England brought new production methods to the automotive industry in 1908 and by 1913
had captured almost one quarter of the British market. All in all,
success and failure were mixed, and there certainly was no tremendous flood of industrial investment prior to 1914. The totals
are elusive, but John H. Dunning, the closest student, estimates
that in 1914 Americans dominated or owned about seventy firms
with a total capital of only $75 or $100 million, employing
twelve or fifteen thousand men.

Long before even this total was reached, Englishmen worried about loss of control of important segments of their economy. Much of the investment was by large American trusts, in
most English eyes a vicious form of organization. In 1901 and
1902 two bold efforts to establish American-controlled monopolies aroused a furor. Purchasing a British firm in September
1901, the American Tobacco Company sought command of a

market previously divided between small firms. In retaliation, thirteen British cigarette-makers joined to form the Imperial Tobacco Company, fighting American price-cutting with price-cutting of their own as well as appeals to the patriotism of English smokers. After a year of heavy combat a compromise was arranged, but moral victory lay with the British. J. Pierpont Morgan's efforts to organize a trans-Atlantic shipping monopoly came closer to success. By April 1902 he had gained control of all but two of the largest British lines. Panic swept England; even on the ocean, Britons' second home, Americans sought to displace them. The *National Review* spoke of "an intolerable national humiliation" which threatened to make "Great Britain a mere annex of the United States,"[3] and angry questions were asked in Parliament. Once again the invader drew back. British firms remained technically British, and Morgan agreed that half the ships built in the future should fly the Union Jack. At the same time, the government granted one of the holdouts, Cunard, an annual subsidy of £150,000 in return for a promise never to sell out to non-British interests. Largely because of the repulse of these, the two most publicized American efforts, British complaints against the "American invasion" declined after 1902. Once again, a potentially troublesome issue fizzled out.

The highly visible "invasion" was of course not the only form of American investment in Britain. Between 1897 and 1914 English industrial securities worth nearly $200 million were purchased by Americans, and, particularly during the Boer War, the British government floated loans in the rapidly expanding American money market. Still, the totals were trivial compared with British investment in the United States. This probably topped $2.5 billion in 1900 and grew to $4.5 billion in 1914, at which time the Germans, who had passed the Dutch for second place since 1900, had only about $950 million invested in America. The British had capital in a wide range of businesses, and they even engaged in an "invasion" of their own, larger but less no-

---

[3] Quoted in Joseph L. Garvin and Julian S. Amery, *The Life of Joseph Chamberlain* (4 vols.; London, 1932–1951), vol. IV, p. 409.

ticed than the American. In 1914 they controlled firms—a Lever Brothers subsidiary, mortgage companies, mining firms, and others—worth about $600 million. By far the most British capital, more than three-fifths of the total, was in railroad securities, including a substantial bloc of New York Central bonds transferred to the Duke of Marlborough when he agreed to marry Consuelo Vanderbilt. In investments if not in commerce, Britain as yet had no need to worry about her position, which remained strong until World War I.

Trade rivalries never caused serious difficulty between the two countries. America's share of European trade rose while England's fell, but the renewed vigor of international trade meant that in absolute terms British volume increased. The same was true with respect to Japan, where a rapid American advance helped cut England's share of the market from two-fifths in the 1880's to one-fifth between 1896 and 1905. American exports to China, the pot of gold so often dreamed of in 1898, quintupled between 1898 and 1905. They remained tiny by comparison with British sales, and the greatest American effort went into trade with northern China, where the Japanese and Russians, not the British, had cause to fear American competition.

In 1897 Edwin Denby, the American minister to China, complained that "In spite of the immense amount of sentimentality that England and the U.S. have been engaged recently in expressing, the stern fact remains that in the Far East, and I believe elsewhere, England looks on all questions in the light of her own interest. Here in China her people are our rivals in every branch of trade and commerce and industry." With the arrival of new challengers, particularly Russia, this sort of sentiment became obsolete. In 1903 John W. Foster, a former secretary of state not uncritical of British policy, observed that England "has reserved to itself no selfish or exclusive privileges, but has extended to all other nations the right of trade and residence gained for its own subjects. . . . With a similarity of institutions, a common origin and language, and a community of trade interest in the East, the two governments are naturally inclined to cooperation." [4] This became the general view, and even in the heyday of dollar diplomacy under Taft little commercial friction developed in China.

In Latin America, by far the most competitive market, Germans and Frenchmen as well as Britons and Americans fought for sales. Here again circumstances muted the potential conflict between the English-speaking powers. The British steadily increased their sales, so much so that Latin America actually took a larger proportion of British exports than ever before. Moreover, except in the area north of Panama, the Germans acted as a sort of buffer between the British and Americans. Almost everywhere, notably in the great English markets of Argentina, Brazil, and Chile, they held second place; English traders defended themselves against a German challenge while the Americans sought to move up a rung at German expense. British and American officials and businessmen feared the Germans far more than they feared one another. In Mexico, the Caribbean, and Central America the picture was different, the result much the same. British sales to Cuba and Mexico, the two largest markets for American goods, never posed a serious challenge. In Mexico the very real rivalry was for investment opportunities rather than trading advantage, and at least by the time of the Mexican revolution Whitehall, recognizing the obvious, decided to withhold aggressive support from British firms. Germans, on the other hand, kept alive the feeling of rivalry by politico-economic machinations in Haiti on the eve of the World War.

A small amount of jealousy reached the surface in England, particularly when the Taft administration pressed for economic control of states to the southward. An unrepentent reactionary, John M. Kennedy, a critic of every aspect of American life, published a book, *Imperial America*, which emphasized the commercial rivalry in Latin America and even declared—this was written

[4] Denby to Sherman, April 2, 1897, quoted in A. Whitney Griswold, *The Far Eastern Policy of the United States* (New York, 1938), p. 53; John W. Foster, *American Diplomacy in the Orient* (Cambridge, 1903), pp. 436–437.

two months before the European conflict began—"we are just as likely to have a war with the United States as with Germany." Most observers disagreed. "At present," one magazine claimed, "we still have some of the best cards in our own hands, and by ordinary skill and care in playing them we might win the game." [5] Such commentators deplored British complacency more than they criticized American policy, and they worried more about the future than the present.

Americans traded four or five times as much with Canada as with all other British dominions combined. On the eve of World War I, Canadian purchases from the United States were, at over $400 million, triple those from the mother country, although ever since 1898, partly in reaction to American protectionism, Canada had granted preferential tariff treatment to British goods. Canadian exports showed a better balance, but here too the Americans led. Only in investments did Britain hold a top hand. She had about four times as much capital in Canada as the Americans, but the latter were closing the gap; during the Taft administration, American investments more than doubled, and by 1914 Canada had displaced Mexico as the leading field of investment. Moreover, whereas a large proportion of British investment was in government securities, an equally large proportion of American capital was in business and industry, which provided greater economic leverage.

In 1910 the Taft administration invited Canada to open negotiations for a reciprocal reduction of tariffs. After months of delay, the two parties agreed in January 1911 to an arrangement whereby the two legislatures would reduce or eliminate duties on specified goods, primarily raw materials entering the United States and manufactures shipped from the United States to Canada. Because it was alleged that the Taft administration had sacrificed farmers, miners, and lumbermen to benefit "big business," the enabling legislation had hard sledding in Congress. Taft had to call a special session before he secured passage in July 1911.

[5] John M. Kennedy, *Imperial America* (London, 1914), p. 10; *Saturday Review* (London), vol. CX (1910), p. 70.

The Canadian-American agreement provoked more controversy in Great Britain than any development involving the
United States, economic or political, since agitation over the
"American invasion." Conservatives and protectionists attacked
the agreement, and charged that the Liberals' ambassador at
Washington, James Bryce, had facilitated negotiations. They argued that the most-favored-nation clause might "become the key
to the disintegration and dissolution of the British Empire,"
since it would prevent imperial preference. On the basis of indiscreet talk in the United States, they maintained that the Taft
administration sought "the commercial and economic annexation of Canada" and probably political annexation as well.[6] Because Conservatives made far more noise than their opponents,
the American press considered their views almost national, and
newspapers denounced antique British concepts of empire, British lies and exaggerations.

During the controversy the Liberals played a very shrewd
hand, a role their low tariff views made easier. They maintained,
more emotionally than logically, that any agreement which promoted prosperity in Canada and the United States would "add a
new factor to the many other factors that are at work to harmo-
nize Anglo-American relations." They gave the silent treatment
to annexationist rumors; when asked in the House of Commons
if any of a whole string of such reports had been called to his
attention, the Foreign Secretary coolly replied, "The answer to
all the questions is in the negative."[7] Above all they stressed
that intervention to prevent the agreement would drive the Canadians into American arms.

How the British government would have reacted if the
agreement had gone into effect remains a moot point. In September 1911, in an election fought on the reciprocity issue, with
opponents arguing that the agreement would indeed sever ties
with Britain, the Canadian premier, Sir Wilfrid Laurier, went

[6] J. F. Remnant, quoted in *Parliamentary Debates*, Sixth Series, vol. XXIII,
p. 1038.
[7] *Daily Chronicle* (London), quoted in *Review of Reviews* (New York), vol.
XLIII (1911), p. 283; Grey, quoted in *Parliamentary Debates*, Sixth Series, vol.
XXV, p. 1815.

down to defeat after fifteen years in power. British Conservatives crowed, while the government kept an Oriental silence. In America the abortive agreement quickly disappeared as a political issue, Taft being vulnerable on so many other counts. The denouement served the cause of friendship, for reciprocity might well, in time, have driven the British government to counteraction.

In this episode, as in many other aspects of the economic relationship, the materials for controversy were present but one did not emerge. Because in economic power the United States pushed past England it would not have been surprising to see economic conflict or at least wide British resentment. The two economies were, after all, becoming steadily less complementary and more competitive. But competition grated less when the world was prosperous, the Germans acted as a buffer in areas of potential friction, and the Liberal government was devoted to free trade and aware of the necessity of serene relations with the United States. In the half century after the Civil War, especially in the two decades surrounding 1900, America displaced England as the world's greatest economic power without having to pay the price of acrimony. Britain's acceptance of her fate, so different from her concern about German economic power, was a vital factor in the great rapprochement. In America the new relationship, though imperfectly recognized at first, helped to undermine traditional feelings toward England.

On an ocean liner in 1892 Henry Adams met Rudyard Kipling, whose unthinking condescension galled him. Looking back years later, Adams commented, "All through life, one had seen the American on his literary knees to the European; and all through many lives back for some two centuries, one had seen the European snub or patronize the American; not always intentionally, but effectually. It was in the nature of things." [8] Adams' use of the past tense is significant; the truth of 1892 was less than accurate two decades later. All English condescension did not

[8] Henry Adams, *The Education of Henry Adams* (Modern Library ed.; New York, 1931), p. 319.

disappear, for some has lasted to this day. Nor had British critics denigrated and British readers ignored all American authors before the 1890's; at least since 1840 Englishmen read far more American books than any other foreign ones. Now, however, more American authors were read in England than ever before, and critics at least attempted to review their books on their literary merits, seldom dismissing them as the unsuccessful products of a cultural desert.

Beginning in the 1880's, a perfect flood of books by Americans inundated England. In the last two decades of the century British publishers, who did not have to worry about matters of copyright until 1891, published ninety individual volumes or collected works of Hawthorne, seventy of Holmes, sixty each of Twain and Irving, and many, many others. Interest continued into the new century. In 1909 ex-President Roosevelt, traveling in Kenya, an outpost of the British Empire, took pride in the number of American books he saw on the settlers' shelves. Every house, it seemed, had Edward Westcott's *David Harum* and Winston Churchill's books—"I mean, of course, our Winston Churchill, Winston Churchill the gentleman." [9] The *Times Literary Supplement* reviewed one hundred and twenty American books during its first decade, beginning in 1902, with three women, Gertrude Atherton, Edith Wharton, and Mary E. Wilkins Freeman, receiving most attention. Some writers, including Miss Atherton and the young poet Robert Frost, found success in England before they gained it in their own country.

British reviews, though by no means uncritical, were usually not unfriendly to American literature as a whole. There were exceptions, including the indefatigably hostile John M. Kennedy and a pretentious critic, John Alford, who wrote, "Mr. [Ezra] Pound is a unique phenomenon, for he has succeeded in being an American, a man of culture and a poet, all at the same time." The *Edinburgh Review* caught the prevailing tone when it said

[9] Roosevelt to Mr. and Mrs. Lodge, September 10, 1899, Henry Cabot Lodge, ed., *Selections from the Correspondence of Theodore Roosevelt and Henry Cabot Lodge, 1884–1918* (2 vols.; New York, 1925), vol. II, p. 349.

that America was producing "a body of literature which is not marked out by any commanding achievement, but which, by its high average of power and vitality, might do honour to any age and any country." The *Literary Supplement* smugly observed in 1910, "we are now pretty free from national prejudice in our estimates of American books. We take them on their merits; and when we find them uninteresting, it is either because they are so or because our taste is bad. It is not because we believe no American can write." [10] Americans noticed and welcomed the change.

Contemporary reviewers and readers often passed judgments which seem strange today. Some old demigods—Longfellow, Lowell, Emerson, and, a surprising British taste, Whitman—continued to be read, perhaps more than in America. Henry James stimulated a great deal of highbrow discussion and had a select clientele, probably somewhat smaller than in earlier years; a great fuss was made over his seventieth birthday in 1913, and two hundred and seventy English admirers banded together to commission a portrait by John Singer Sargent. But James' fiction overtaxed most readers; one reviewer stated, "the works of Mr. Henry James are a series of exquisite disappointments." [11] Howells' reputation ebbed rather than advanced as he grew older, but English commentators always considered him a grand old man of literature. The younger naturalists often received severe treatment in the press, but Theodore Dreiser's *Sister Carrie*, initially a failure in the United States, and Frank Norris' *The Octopus* and *The Pit* sold very well, probably because they explored aspects of American materialism many Englishmen deplored. Crane had immense public success with *The Red Badge of Courage*, but many reviewers described him as superficial and undisciplined. Most British critics did not like stylistic innovations, sordid or vulgar stories (a factor which undermined but did not destroy Twain's very high reputation), or unrelieved gloom. But on the

[10] Alford, quoted in Henry F. May, *The End of American Innocence: A Study in the First Years of Our Own Time, 1912–1917* (New York, 1959), p. 272; "Novels of American Life," *Edinburgh Review*, vol. CLXXXVII (1898), p. 414; *Times Literary Supplement* (London), July 21, 1910, p. 257.

[11] *Academy* (London), vol. LI (1897), p. 256.

whole contemporary Americans felt much the same way.

What British audiences really wanted—failing appearance of "the great American novel," an epic which would lay bare the entire life of the republic—was something which would explain a facet of that life, something which would educate and amuse at the same time. Those authors most popular in England, George W. Smalley observed, were those who were "American to the finger-tips, American in thought, in language, in method; nay, if you like, in accent." [12] This explains the popularity of dealers in dialect and local color, the appeal of Mary E. Wilkins Freeman, who sold well though her critical reputation was past its peak by 1910, and of Gertrude Atherton, whose stream of novels, many set in old California, romantic and strange, gained a wider sale than the writings of any other American author. The same desire to read about peculiarly American characters and events brought success to Bret Harte and Twain, both so appealing that John M. Kennedy exempted them from his worst strictures.

In addition, Englishmen acclaimed Harold Frederic's one great accomplishment, *The Damnation of Theron Ware*, published in Britain under the title *Illumination* in 1896, and the political novels of Winston Churchill, whose popularity and reputation were fully as great in England as America. Another critical spirit, Edith Wharton, was very popular—*Ethan Frome* created a sensation in 1911—although as much for novels set elsewhere as for those which pictured life in the United States. Her prose style and fastidious dislike of many aspects of modern life made her particularly attractive to the British middle class. Still, neither Frederic nor Churchill nor Wharton was half so somber as Norris and Dreiser, the only two uncompromising critics of contemporary American life who were widely read in England. While Englishmen did not read only pleasant things about American life, those who took time to peruse the most popular novels from across the sea gained a picture of a colorful society in which virtues outweighed evils, even the evils of industrialism.

[12] George W. Smalley, *Anglo-American Memories, Second Series* (London, 1912), p. 191.

The Britain which welcomed American books also provided a congenial home for some of their authors. Some poets who lived in England before the war, notably Ezra Pound and T. S. Eliot, developed their skills there, but many writers of fiction found their talent hard to sustain outside the land of their birth. Bret Harte, Harold Frederic, and Stephen Crane spent the last years of their lives in London. Gertrude Atherton frequently visited, and Edith Wharton, who lived in Paris for many years, was part of the English literary community. Quite probably the circle of acquaintances these authors developed in literary circles helped them to become popular with the reading public.

A far greater figure loomed over these author-visitors: the solitary, worrying, complicated craftsman and psychologist who lived in Britain for the last forty years of his life. Henry James is far too much an individual to make it possible to generalize about American attitudes on the basis of his novels and letters, and although he retained many American qualities throughout his years in Britain, he consciously repudiated or muted many others. Nevertheless, in certain ways his life and work, often considered to suggest the metaphorical width of the Atlantic, show this body of water to have been far less wide than the English Channel.

Free from financial or family cares, James had a choice of places to settle when he left the United States. His first choice, Paris, disappointed him although several of his literary masters were French, and in 1876 he moved to London. Perhaps James found England a useful point of vantage between the two poles of so many of his novels, America and Europe. In *The Portrait of a Lady* and *The Wings of the Dove*, published twenty years apart and otherwise quite different, James wove his story around American girls and English fortune-hunters. Although he knew less of Europe than of England, the other novels of confrontation usually placed Americans in counterpoise to Europeans, which suggests that he found Continental society much more useful for his literary purpose, the exploration of contrasts. (When, in the middle of his career, James turned to the conflict between portions of a society, particularly between the artistic spirit and worldly forces, he often employed an English setting, but not to point to any special national contrasts.) James shared the general feeling of his countrymen that England was both of and outside of Europe, more like the United States than other nations.

Moreover, James, at least the mature James, did not entirely turn his back upon America. Patriots often so believed, and James' flight and his finicky attitudes, as many considered them, provoked a shrill comment from Theodore Roosevelt: "What a miserable little snob Henry James is. His polished, pointless, uninteresting stories . . . make one blush to think that he was once an American. . . . I turned to a story of Kipling's with the feeling of getting into fresh, healthy, out-of-doors life." A snob Henry James perhaps was; a true-blue Briton he was not. He well knew he had paid a price when he cut himself off from his native country without joining the life of his adopted one. Particularly after he moved from London to Sussex in the 1890's he lived an almost solitary existence, observing with disapproval many developments around him. *The Spoils of Poynton*, although intended like his other novels to indicate larger truths, levied a sharp attack on English materialism, bringing down a spate of critical reviews when published in 1897. "England," he commented in 1904, pursuing the same theme, "never was the land of ideas, and . . . is now less so than ever." When war came in 1914 Henry James sided passionately with the English, but at the same time he feared his hosts might suffer retribution "for the exhibition that has gone on so long of their huge materialized stupidity and vulgarity." [13] On the other hand, he came away from visits to the United States in 1904, the first in over twenty years, and 1910–1911 with greater appreciation for the direction America was taking—and with a deep passion for motoring that never disappeared.

James was far too sensitive to accept Anglo-Saxon ideology,

[13] Roosevelt to Matthews, June 29, 1894, Elting E. Morison, ed., *The Letters of Theodore Roosevelt* (8 vols.; Cambridge, 1951–1954), vol. I, p. 390; James to Edward L. Childe, January 19, 1904, Percy Lubbock, ed., *The Letters of Henry James* (2 vols.; New York, 1920), vol. II, p. 11; James to Sir Claude Phillips, July 31, 1914, *ibid.*, p. 377.

but by 1900 he considered the two peoples kin. In 1903 he wrote
a warm letter of praise to Sir George Trevelyan for his recent
volumes on the American Revolution, welcoming them in part
because they promised to "help to build the bridge across the
Atlantic." [14] In 1915, only a year before he died, James became a
British citizen, the Prime Minister standing as one of the sponsors required by law. He would not have done so, he said, had his
country joined Britain in a war against a far grosser materialism
than those he deplored in England and the United States.

Since even those who found James' novels difficult respected the power of his intellect ("Mr. James thinks very hard
indeed," [15] one reviewer commented after reading *The Ambassadors*) and since Englishmen considered him more an American
than one of themselves, his writings contributed to the growing
recognition of American talents. Building upon the accomplishments of predecessors, he and Howells, lesser figures like Gertrude Atherton and Winston Churchill, and others firmly established a beachhead for their country that has never since been
liquidated. English critics and readers had come to appreciate
what they considered, without agreeing upon a definition, dis-
tinctively American literature.

Americans themselves found it more difficult to claim a national uniqueness, although a few critics did so, sometimes rather
self-defeatingly maintaining that this American literature was an
amalgam of regional ways. Most trail-blazing writers of the day
looked as much to Europe as to their own country for stimula-
tion. Most historians of American literature considered it, in the
words of one of their number, Henry S. Pancoast, "the continuation of English literature within the . . . United States, by
people English in their speech, English to a considerable extent
by inheritance, and English in the original character of their civilization." [16] Until the appearance of John Macy's *Spirit of Amer-*

---

[14] James to Trevelyan, November 25, 1903, *ibid.*, vol. I, p. 433.
[15] *Times Literary Supplement*, October 16, 1903, p. 296.
[16] Henry S. Pancoast, *An Introduction to American Literature* (1894), quoted
in Howard Mumford Jones, *The Theory of American Literature* (Ithaca, 1948),
p. 98.

ican Literature in 1913, Howard Mumford Jones tells us, all literary histories judged American authors by British standards and accepted the subordinate position of their culture.

American readers also accepted Britain's lead. A survey of loans from public libraries showed Scott, Dickens, Thackeray, Bulwer-Lytton, and George Eliot most in demand in 1893, along with only two Americans, Hawthorne and Cooper; and in 1901, when the College Entrance Board selected sixteen books as essential reading in preparation for examinations in literature, thirteen were the work of British authors. When an English author of only second-rate talent visited the United States, as did Arnold Bennett in 1911, he received adulation Americans withheld from their own literary figures. "In New York," Bennett's biographer writes, "in Chicago, where he was almost mobbed by women-admirers, in Indianapolis, in Philadelphia, he was haled from publishers' offices to dinner parties, from press banquets to literary clubs." [17]

When the first American best-seller list was compiled in 1895, five English writers and only two Americans made the top ten. Included were two volumes of sentimental tales of Scotland by John Watson, a Presbyterian minister who wrote under the nom de plume of Ian Maclaren; one of them, *Beside the Bonnie Briar Bush*, ultimately sold over half a million copies in the United States, more than any other piece of contemporary fiction except perhaps Frances Hodgson Burnett's *Little Lord Fauntleroy*, written in the United States by a woman of English birth. British predominance gradually declined, thanks in part to the delayed effect of the copyright law of 1891, which made it impossible to pirate the work of foreign authors. In 1906, for the first time, only American authors appeared on the list of best sellers, but Englishmen, particularly Sir Gilbert Parker, continued to find places on it after this temporary hiatus.

Like their British cousins, Americans did not necessarily import the best contemporary literature. They liked the Scottish tales and whimsy of J. M. Barrie, but even more the stories of

[17] Georges LaFourcade, *Arnold Bennett: A Study* (London, 1939), p. 50.

Ian Maclaren, a sort of British counterpart of Joel Chandler Harris or Thomas Nelson Page. The author thrice visited the United States, and he died in Iowa while so engaged in 1907. Americans also lapped up the stories of Rudyard Kipling. *The Day's Work,* which expressed his views about the demands of imperial rule in India, gained great popularity in 1898 and 1899, just when the United States was embarking upon an imperialistic course. Above all, readers sought romantic historical or political novels, novels which almost universally pictured England, or at least traditional English values, in a highly favorable light. Mrs. Humphry Ward, the epitome of Victorian novelists, did exceedingly well, particularly with *Lady Rose's Daughter,* which sold more than any other publication in 1903. Sir Gilbert Parker, Canadian born but now an ornament of the London scene, made the bestseller lists seven times between 1896 and 1913 with a clutch of novels, all of which in one way or another demonstrated the virtue of the English race, aristocratic rule, or imperialism.

What was preeminently true of Parker's books was generally so of all the British novels which sold best in the United States. A reviewer once suggested that Mrs. Ward's collected works "might not inappropriately be named 'The Stately Homes of England' Series." [18] The characters in Parker's novels, except those which dealt with old Canada in a fashion not unlike Cooper's, traveled in the same circles. All authors praised standard Victorian stereotypes, and many regretted the rising influence of the newly wealthy, never treating them with the subtle sympathy of *Silas Lapham.* Parker in particular praised imperialism—in Egypt in *The Weavers,* the Boer war in *The Judgment House.* All criticized foreigners, although not Americans; Parker permitted an American to join his hero in the task of forcing progress upon Egypt. Thus, even more clearly than in the United Kingdom, American reading preferences either showed a perhaps subconscious appreciation of the happy side of life in the other country or exposed people to pictures and images which left a generally favorable impression.

[18] *The Nation* (New York), vol. LXXX (1905), p. 336.

Themes which emerge in the reception of contemporary fiction—rising interest, declining xenophobia, emphasis on the pleasant—do not apply when one turns to written history, particularly American textbooks. British lack of interest in American history, even among those leaders who had to deal with the United States, was positively appalling. Sir George Otto Trevelyan's long history of the era of the American Revolution, so warmly received in the United States for its Whiggish interpretation, was hardly read in Great Britain. On the basis almost solely of information gleaned from James Bryce's *American Commonwealth*, which does seem to have been standard reading among the upper classes, politicians frequently drew shallow analogies to justify the course of action they desired for England. In 1906, in a book very similar in spirit to Herbert Croly's *The Promise of American Life*, a sensation in the United States three years later, F. S. Oliver used the career of Alexander Hamilton as an argument for stronger imperial ties, concluding, "The final question with us, as with Hamilton, is how we may convert a voluntary league of states . . . into a firm union." [19] On those rare occasions when Englishmen read the history of America more or less for is own sake, they usually turned to such savage works as Percy Greg's *History of the United States*, a reactionary tract which pictured Lincoln as an evil-minded yokel and made heroes of John Wilkes Booth and Ku Kluxers. Only slowly did more friendly works come into print, beginning perhaps with a history written in 1893 by Goldwin Smith, an Englishman then teaching in Canada. Whereas American history had little appeal in Great Britain, in the United States John R. Green's *Short History of the English People*, published as long ago as 1874, outsold all other history, American or not, in the closing years of the nineteenth century.

Americans could hardly ignore British history since it was an integral part of their own. When it became necessary to compare England and other foreign countries, the British came off well,

[19] Frederick Scott Oliver, *Alexander Hamilton: An Essay in American Union* (London, 1906), p. 486.

but these necessities were rare. Particularly because of their emphasis upon political and diplomatic currents, textbooks emphasized confrontations between the English-speaking countries. Almost always the British were harshly treated; praise of Britain's pre-1812 conduct in Woodrow Wilson's *History of the American People* is a striking exception. "Each popular history," George W. Steevens said in 1897, "is one long inculcation, if not of dislike, at least of distrust and profound suspicion." [20] During the Revolutionary epoch, the 1840's, and the Civil War, students learned, Great Britain stood athwart the legitimate and noble aspirations of the American people.

Current interpretations of the American Revolution and its roots make this crystal clear. The best professional historians, particularly those of the so-called "imperial school," were beginning to paint the period in mixed colors, showing how inevitable tendencies in both countries, rather than British malice, explained American's revolt. Such scholarship went over the head of other writers. Henry Cabot Lodge expressed the usual view when he wrote, "The American Revolution was wholly due . . . to the condition of England and of English politics, and to the gross and arrogant stupidity of the King and his ministers, supported by the mass of the people." A survey of forty textbooks used in 1897 showed, according to their examiner, Charles Altschul, that only four presented a balanced picture of the controversy. "One of the chief obstacles in the way of a better international understanding," a leading historian complained in 1911, "is the patriotic historian." (Could he have been thinking of Lodge?) Maintaining that "of all the nations in the world Great Britain is that one which is nearest to the United States in kinship, in institutions, and in aspirations," this scholar urged a reinterpretation of the American Revolution as an episode in the advance of Anglo-American democracy.[21] Such appeals appar-

---

[20] George W. Steevens, *The Land of the Dollar* (Edinburgh, 1897), p. 136.
[21] Henry Cabot Lodge, *A Short History of the English Colonies in America* (New York, 1881), p. 499; Albert Bushnell Hart, "School Books and International Prejudices," *International Conciliation* (New York), No. 38 (1911), pp. 4, 13.

ently did little good. In 1917, according to Altschul, only six of fifty-three texts presented a fair picture.

As this example suggests, more than a tiny residuum of anti-British feeling remained. The habits and attitudes of generations could not be wiped out overnight. Admiral Fisher might consider the American school system an engine to create Anglophilia; Theodore Roosevelt might claim that the prejudices immigrants carried in their baggage disappeared in their children. Yet Roosevelt and most other politicians often let the sentiments of racial groups influence them. They acted as if they more than half believed, not Fisher or Roosevelt, but George W. Steevens, who wrote, "As for the Germans, Irish, Scandinavians, Italians, Poles, and Bohemians, . . . they import the bitter Continental jealousy of us and here it finds a most congenial soil." [22] The American environment and, more narrowly, the educational system rather quickly converted most immigrants into American patriots. It did not demolish old habits of thought toward European powers, including England.

Although immigration from Germany had been declining since the 1880's, as late as 1910 approximately one out of every eleven Americans—over eight million in all—either had been born in Germany or had a German-born parent. The National German-American Alliance, founded in 1901, reached a membership of two million by 1914, and sometimes it took a stand on matters involving foreign policy, as for example when it sought to coordinate pro-Boer sentiment. In 1907 the Alliance entered into a formal compact with the Ancient Order of Hibernians, each party agreeing to oppose anything which might lead to a foreign alliance; the Irish, but not the Germans, later interpreted this to require opposition to an arbitration treaty with England. On the whole the national organization, the German-language press, and German-Americans as a group showed little interest in foreign affairs, much more in issues such as prohibition. (Their views won the Alliance and the press subsidies from the brewing industry.) Two German ambassadors, Sternburg and Bernstorff,

[22] Steevens, *Land of the Dollar*, p. 137.

warned the Wilhelmstrasse not to count upon German-American activism, and it did take a war in Europe to revitalize them. While many people of German descent regretted developments which converted England into America's closest friend, as a group they played an unimportant role.

Irish-Americans did not show the same passivity. In 1910 some four and a half million Americans claimed Irish birth or parentage, and many more were grandchildren of pre-Civil War immigrants or the offspring of men who came to the United States after first migrating to England. Most of these people hated the nation which still kept their blood brothers in subjugation. Some plotted in aid of Irish revolutionaries. Others, accepting the approach of John Redmond, the Irish leader in the House of Commons who sought home rule by bargaining with the Liberals, gave money to support him; a single meeting at Faneuil Hall in 1902 raised $100,000 for the cause. Whatever their tactical disagreements, most denounced England upon almost every possible occasion. The *Irish World* of New York, edited by Galway-born Patrick Ford, gave the lead, but the Clan-na-Gael, the Ancient Order of Hibernians, the United Irish League of America, and other groups required little stimulus.

The Anglo-American rapprochement outraged Irish-Americans. They often struck at the legend of 1898. Great Britain, claimed Representative Joseph F. O'Connell ten years later, "claims that she helped us to win the war with Spain. I am one of those who believe that we would have won that war if England had been allied with Spain. . . . The task would have been harder, . . . a more strenuous proposition, but . . . I am sure that we would have thrashed Britain the third time, as we have done it twice before." [23] With similar sentiments Irish-American politicians and publicists attacked American policy during the Boer War, made more difficult the settlement of Anglo-American disputes during Roosevelt's Presidency and fought against proposed arbitration treaties with England.

The Irish imposed restraints upon non-Irish politicians, particularly those like Henry Cabot Lodge who had heavily Celtic

[23] *Congressional Record*, 60th Congress, 1st Session, p. 4649.

constituencies. Sometimes they controlled state and city machines, as in New York, and elected men of the faith to carry forward the battle in Washington. The most notable was Bourke Cockran, who emigrated from Ireland because his parents proposed that he become a priest; first a henchman of Tammany and then a political maverick, he served five terms in the House of Representatives. Cockran attacked imperialism as a sinful policy of British origin, though he would have welcomed the acquisition of Canada, and also developed a warm and enduring friendship for a young English imperialist, Winston Churchill, who first visited him in 1895. Cockran also castigated the Boer War as an aristocratic plot to justify militarism in England, kept a wary eye open for signs of British influence in the United States, and of course repeatedly wept over the sorry plight of his homeland. However Irish-Americans functioned, they formed a far more effective force than the relatively apolitical Germans. They were the largest bloc to oppose England and, because most of them found a home in the Democratic Party, gave it an only partially earned reputation for Anglophobia in Great Britain.

Powerful and pervasive though Irish agitation was, it did not provoke effective counterorganization by Americans of British stock. "Most families of pure English descent," one explained to a visiting English reporter in 1896, "have been in this hemisphere so long that they have become Americans and nothing else." [24] This overstated the case but contained much truth. The British-American Association, founded in the 1880's precisely to face the Irish with a united front of English, Scots, and Welsh, died rather than grew during the new era. While some members drifted into the American Protective Association, an anti-Catholic movement, most apparently concluded that the need for a special organization had passed. For similar reasons, Englishmen showed little concern over Irish agitation in the United States. They often found it convenient, even consoling, to pass off all criticism of their country as simply the prejudiced effusions of hyphenates.

Granted the long tradition of Anglophobia in the United

[24] Steevens, *Land of the Dollar*, p. 137.

States, the nation's republican principles, and the political and psychological attractions of isolation, all opposition to the rapprochement cannot be ascribed to the Irish-Americans or other groups with a common national origin. Nevertheless, racism—a sort of anti-Anglo-Saxonism—was the most important ingredient keeping alive the sparks of Anglophobia and limiting the freedom of action of political leaders in Washington. In 1898 England's enemies were temporarily overwhelmed. Then they fought back, helping to destroy a compromise over isthmian control which was insufficiently humiliating to England. After complicating other diplomatic problems, Anglophobia declined as an effective force as the years moved toward 1914. Concord established by the diplomats and statesmen spread through American society, and the outbreak of war in Europe found Americans as little critical of England as at any previous time in their history.

British critics of the rapprochement were ineffective politically, partly because their country could not easily afford to indulge prejudices, partly because English practice gave the cabinet a relatively free hand in foreign affairs. Most of all, this criticism was ineffective because it came from groups on the fringes of British politics, from reactionaries out of touch with the mainstream of contemporary conservatism or from labor and radical groups still in the anterooms of power.

Whether from the right or the left, this criticism aimed at the same target. In the brutal jungle of American life, it was maintained, sympathy and honor and a sense of esthetics disappeared before the singleminded drive for profits. "Business governs America . . . ," asserted G. Lowes Dickinson, author of several books on the phenomenon. "In no civilised country . . . is capital so uncontrolled; in none is justice so openly prostituted to wealth. America is the paradise of plutocracy." [25] Materialism, such people argued, debased not only the economic but also the political life of the United States; the Webbs, finding what they came to see, confirmed this during their visit in 1898.

Of course critics of the right and the left attacked this mate-

[25] G. Lowes Dickinson, *Appearances* (London, 1914), p. 157.

rialism from different angles. Traditionalists objected to the lack of deference on the one hand and the decline of *noblesse oblige* on the other. They complained about the decline of religion in the United States, citing the rise of Christian Science as evidence. As one writer put it, employing a metaphor which occurred to several visitors who reached the United States by sailing past lower Manhattan, "The domes and spires of London, dedicated to God, overtop the towers of Mammon and ward off thunderbolts of wrath; but New York's towers of Mammon rise far above the scanty spires of her temples, dwarfing and crushing them into insignificance." [26] What was needed was not the false democracy of the United States, a mask for egotism destructive of the nation's fiber, but a sense of community and purpose, a devotion to ideals and order.

Except for Matthew Arnold, whose *Civilization in the United States* sold widely in Britain and was masochistically devoured by Americans in edition after edition for years after its appearance in 1888, the most prominent of these critics was Rudyard Kipling. Sometimes Kipling's criticism was sardonic. Sometimes it was brutal; of Chicago, he wrote, "Having seen it, I urgently desire never to see it again. It is inhabited by savages. Its water is the water of the Hugli, and its air is dirt." He described the American people as "bleeding-raw at the edges, almost more conceited than the English, vulgar with a massive vulgarity which is as though the Pyramids were coated with Christmas-cake sugar-works," and he blamed universal suffrage for the depravity of American politics. Yet Kipling had welcomed America's appearance as an imperial power, and he was a member of the governing body of the Anglo-American League, founded in 1898 to further the cause of cooperation. At another point in his book he described the Americans as "the biggest, finest, and best people on the surface of the globe" and said, "I love this People, and if any contemptuous criticism has to be done, I will do it myself. My heart has gone out to them beyond all peo-

[26] Charles R. Enock, *Farthest West: Life and Travel in the United States* (London, 1910), p. 122.

ples . . . ," although, he admitted, "for the life of me I cannot tell why." [27] Readers tended to overlook such passages, so both in Britain and America Rudyard Kipling was considered as uncompromising a foe of the United States as Matthew Arnold.

Far more original than criticism from the right, since reactionaries had played this game since 1776, was the new attitude of the left. From the time of Charles James Fox through the Chartists to John Bright, radicals hailed the American experiment as a beacon which might help England set her course. British acclaim for Henry George's *Progress and Poverty* (1879) marked the end of an era. As America became more and more the land of industrial success, as she combined the progress and the poverty that gave George his title, English reformers discarded the old idea. The image of America, land of immense wealth and industrial slavery, helped the rise of the Independent Labour Party, which gained its first parliamentary representation in the 1890's.

Intellectual supporters of the labor movement, and of radicalism and socialism, began to criticize the United States. They rejected what Sidney Webb, who hated the country, called "the quite unfounded belief that America is a Democratic country." Instead they believed, as many still do today, that she was, as Webb put it, a "peculiar copy of 18th century Toryism that Hamilton fastened on America 120 years ago." This view found its strongest expression in H. G. Wells' *The Future in America*, published in 1906. In one sentence Wells summed up his views, saying, "There seems to me an economic process going on that tends to concentrate first wealth and then power in the hands of a small number of adventurous individuals of no very high intellectual type, a huge importation of alien and unassimilable workers, and a sustained disorder of local and political administration." [28] At times Wells paid reluctant tribute to Ameri-

[27] Rudyard Kipling, *From Sea to Sea: Letters of Travel* (2 vols.; New York, 1899), vol. II, pp. 139, 120.
[28] Webb to Graham Wallas, October 20, 1898, quoted in David A. Shannon, ed., *Beatrice Webb's American Diary, 1898* (Madison, 1963), p. 152n; H. G. Wells, *The Future in America: A Search for Realities* (New York, 1906), p. 152.

can vigor and to stirrings of reform spirit, but on the whole *The Future in America* viciously attacked that society from the Fabian point of view.

As Wells' title indicates, American materialism came under heavy attack largely because critics feared it as the first wave of a future which threatened to inundate Britain and the rest of the world. Their concern was passionate and involved, not merely an exercise in academic distaste. "What America is, Europe is becoming," sighed a fictional character in G. Lowes Dickinson's *A Modern Symposium.*[29] Moreover, followers of Progressivism in the United States made many of the same criticisms of their society. In the most extreme version, President Hibben of Princeton even worried in 1914 that the post-war world would find Europe purged and purified while the United States, staying out, continued to welter in materialism. These two points add important shadows to the complaints of Arnold and Kipling, Webb and Wells, and in a sense draw some of their fangs.

While carpers made themselves heard and sometimes made themselves obnoxious to those in power, they obviously resisted the trend of the times. Favorable British commentators, for example, outweighed unfavorable ones, even if their approach was more restrained. James Bryce, the most respected authority, followed up his *American Commonwealth* with articles which, recognizing the warts in American society, on balance conveyed a very favorable impression. James F. Muirhead, author also of the Baedeker guide to the United States, published *America, the Land of Contrasts* in 1898. This widely read study, similar in spirit to Bryce's writings, was dedicated to "the land that has given me what makes life most worth living," specifically a wife.[30] The title of Stead's *The Americanization of the World* sufficiently indicates his sense of the nation's power, a theme which favorably impressed other authors.

Probably most popular of these observers was Arnold Ben-

[29] G. Lowes Dickinson, *A Modern Symposium* (New York, 1908), p. 105.
[30] James F. Muirhead, *America, the Land of Contrasts: A Briton's View of His American Kin* (London, 1898), p. v.

nett, the novelist, who visited the United States in 1911 to promote his books and promptly fell in love with the country and its
people. On his return home, Bennett wrote *Your United States:
Impressions of a First Visit,* a work which was, like almost everything he wrote, brisk rather than profound, sardonic rather than
deeply emotional. Sometimes haste or carelessness led him into
error, as when he stated that those who played professional baseball—"A beautiful game, superbly played"—returned to their
legal practices in the off season, or when, apparently on the basis
of President Lowell's gift of a lecture hall to Harvard, he wrote,
"it is etiquette for the president [of a university], during his
term of office, to make a present of a building or so to the university." Bennett loved the vitality, the sprouting growth, the application of mechanical power. Of American machines he wrote,
"For me they were the proudest material, and essentially the
most poetical achievements, of the United States." Chicago's
soot made him feel at home, and New York, especially its sky-
scrapers, enchanted him. When he felt moved to criticize he did
so in a way which would not wound. He described the Washington Monument as "one of those national calamities which ultimately happen in every country, and of which the supreme
example is, of course, the Albert Memorial in Kensington Gar-
dens." [31] No American save the most chauvinistic could object to
Bennett's sketch, and from it English readers received a lively an-
tidote to the vitriol of people like Wells.

Bennett and his school met head-on the charge that an
amoral, antisocial materialism, unique to the United States, undermined that nation's fiber. "The prevalent opinion that America has a double dose of the original sin of materialism," one
writer complained, ". . . is due, in large measure, to the falla-
cious theory that a people which has proved itself practical and
efficient in handling actualities must needs be devoid of spiritual
vision, energy and power." The American people, he went on,
"more completely, perhaps, than any other people, have faith in

[31] Arnold Bennett, *Your United States: Impressions of a First Visit* (London,
1912), pp. 126, 158, 83, 54.

humanity, passion for justice, and devotion to freedom; and enthusiasm, faith, generous instincts are neither the root nor the
fruit of materialism." Nor would America's friends admit that
those aspects of American life which some people found so objectionable were unique. Even though "Jonathan makes more
noise than John over his business," maintained one observer,
". . . I see no difference between the nations in their high estimate of the precious metals." [32] With such arguments and the
broader one that America and Britain now shared, more than at
any time since independence, a common set of values, phil-
Americans combatted their foes.

Since American visitors to the British Isles showed little
inclination to publish their views for the instruction of their
countrymen, the revealing British dialogue had no American
counterpart. Nor, by and large, did advocates of friendship seek
serious debate with Anglophobic groups in the United States.
Very often they were patricians, cultural and political aristocrats, at least in their own eyes, who did not deign to meet an
emotional rabble on equal terms. Instead, these Anglophiles
turned their energies to development of their own ties with welcoming Englishmen.

These ties took many forms. Sometimes they simply grew
out of individual travel abroad. Many Americans, Woodrow
Wilson among them, knew England well and the Continent almost not at all, and daughters of both Wilson and Theodore
Roosevelt were received in great style when they visited England
on their honeymoons. One hundred thousand Americans visited
Great Britain in 1913, and twenty-nine thousand Englishmen returned the compliment. Sometimes ties became more formal.
The Atlantic Union, founded in 1901 by Sir Walter Besant, advo-
cated a gigantic military combination of the English-speaking
peoples which could dominate the world, but perhaps for that
reason its appeal was limited, particularly in the United States.
More successful was the Pilgrim Society, founded in England in

[32] Alexander Francis, *Americans: An Impression* (New York, 1909), pp. 7, 9;
Samuel R. Hole, *A Little Tour in America* (London, 1895), p. 40.

1902 by a binational committee including Lord Roberts, hero of the Boer War; former General Joe Wheeler of the Confederate army; and industrialists including Charles Rolls of automobile fame and the unsavory traction magnate Charles T. Yerkes. Grover Cleveland, Thomas Nelson Page, and Mark Twain graced the membership of a branch established in New York in 1903. The Pilgrims quickly became a symbol, a rather haughty symbol, of Anglo-American ties, and arriving ambassadors considered it *de rigueur* to make their first public appearance at a dinner of this society in London or New York.

Other connections grew from common concern over social problems of the day, and interplay in this area was far greater than American exchanges with any other country despite the influence of some German reforms upon members of the Progressive movement. As an American historian, Arthur Mann, has observed, reform thought drew heavily upon English views and experience, partly because many American crusaders shared the *noblesse oblige* outlook of their trans-Atlantic counterparts and partly because British social criticism predated and certainly outweighed that which developed in the United States. Reformers of all sorts—settlement-house leaders, temperance crusaders, suffragettes—exchanged ideas and moral support, but most often Americans followed the British lead. The influence of London's Toynbee Hall upon Hull House and other settlement houses in the United States is a good example.

Respect for British efforts deeply marked the social-gospel movement in the United States. Frederick Denison Maurice, Charles Kingsley, John Ruskin, and other so-called "Christian socialists" influenced American figures like Walter Rauschenbusch and Washington Gladden. In a spectacular episode in 1893 William T. Stead stirred consciences and horrified the complacent with a speech and then a book entitled *If Christ Came to Chicago*, in which, after describing noisome conditions in that city, he urged a return to Christian principles. The first printing disappeared from booksellers almost overnight, either because, according to cynics, "the interests" bought it up or because a map

Stead included provided a guide to bars and houses of prostitution. In the end, hundreds of thousands of copies were sold in the United States and Britain.

Predictably, the Anglican Church and the Protestant Episcopal Church in the United States developed the closest ties. Their leaders met together at Lambeth conferences in 1897 and 1908, devoting attention to social and political issues as well as theological ones. Bishop William T. Manning of New York, born in Northamptonshire but a naturalized American citizen, personified the church connection and frequently spoke out in favor of close friendship between the two countries. William S. Rainsford, who came to the United States after doing social work in East London, made St. George's in New York the largest Episcopal congregation in the United States. His advanced views horrified many conservatives, and Rainsford sometimes had clashes with his own vestry, including J. P. Morgan, but his methods, outlook, and energy left a mark on the church that continued long past his own retirement after a breakdown from overwork in 1904.

A stream of marriages most visibly manifested the upper-class entente. Marrying the Yankee dollar was not unknown to other nationalities nor historically unprecedented; in 1906, six of the heads of diplomatic missions in Washington had American wives, and wealthy American girls had found British husbands at least since the 1790's. This period, however, marked the peak of the traffic. In 1895, a particularly popular year for benedicts, Consuelo Vanderbilt reluctantly espoused the Duke of Marlborough, Mary Leiter bestowed a fortune gained by her father as a Chicago merchant and real-estate speculator upon George Nathaniel Curzon, Pauline Whitney entered the peerage as Lady Queenborough, and Maud Burke, a California heiress, married Sir Bache Cunard. Some seventy such marriages took place before 1903, perhaps another sixty by 1914, almost all involving financial settlements. A few marriages, like the earlier ones of Chamberlain and Harcourt, united families of similar social position, but in most cases the American girls came from the

newly rich. Sometimes wealth joined to wealth, as in May
Goelet's marriage to the Duke of Roxburgh in 1903 or the Burke-
Cunard union, which led to creation of a famous London salon,
but more often the bride's money predominated. A sober econo-
mist concluded in 1901 that dowries and settlements drained the
United States of several millions of dollars a year.

While many of these marriages were happy or a least permanent, others were barbarous. The Duke of Manchester rather
openly shopped for a wealthy American, finally settling upon He-
lena Zimmerman, whose father had prospered in Standard Oil.
Although Mr. Zimmerman at first opposed the marriage, he soon
became reconciled and showed his good will by paying off $135,-
000 of the Duke's debts, fixing an income on the couple, and
tossing in an extra $150,000 so they could properly entertain
King Edward and Queen Alexandra for four days in 1904.
Consuelo Vanderbilt and Marlborough both abandoned other
loves to be married, Consuelo because her mother almost liter-
ally dragged her to the altar and the Duke because he reluctantly
concluded he could not maintain Blenheim Palace with his own
funds. The couple separated in 1906 and were divorced twelve
years later, the marriage having cost the Vanderbilts roughly ten
million dollars.

Such affairs opened the way to crude humor. When Tory
aristocrats attacked John Redmond for raising money in the
United States, the Irish leader's ally David Lloyd George sharply
riposted, "Since when have the British aristocracy started despis-
ing American dollars. (Laughter, and a voice, 'Marlborough.') I
see you understand me." On the other hand the marriages often
provided sentimental arguments for international friendship. "I
am not ashamed of the American blood in my veins," declared
the son of Sir William Harcourt. "I am proud to be the son of
the Englishman who led this House, and I am no less proud to
be the grandson of the American who wrote the 'Dutch Republic.' . . . There is talk," young Harcourt continued, perhaps al-
luding to Lloyd George's sally, "of American dollars. America is
not peopled only by those who buy the pictures and the first-born

of the British aristocracy at a price somewhat higher than the figure in the Home market. America is a sister whose pulse beats with our own." [33]

Americans observed the marriages with mixed feelings. President Roosevelt, and doubtless many others, considered those who whored after titles abroad "a mighty poor lot of shoats," traitors to republican principles. On the other hand, one writer maintained, "the average American citizen is [probably] . . . pleased when he hears that another American girl has entered the exclusive circle of the British aristocracy." In England, according to the autobiography of one who married happily into the Marlborough clan, American wives, once looked upon as "disagreeable and even dangerous persons" with an unfair advantage over British girls because of their bank accounts, had won acceptance.[34] The political importance of these marriages was not great, for in very few cases—Chamberlain, Harcourt, Randolph Churchill, and Curzon are the leading exceptions—did the husband gain a leading position. Still, they did foster contact between upper levels of society on both sides of the Atlantic and reaffirm the respect many Americans had for England.

Less than two months before Franz Ferdinand entrained for Bosnia, Walter Hines Page, Wilson's ambassador to London, wrote the new President that hostility toward the United States still existed in some aristocratic and business circles. "This old Tory notion of the corruption of the United States crops up oftener than you would think," he reported, "and there lurks in it a sort of aristocratic hope that it will yet fail." [35] But Page assured the President that this carping spirit was neither important nor organized. Much the same comment could have been made about radical hostility toward the United States. Englishmen

[33] Quoted in Heindel, *American Impact*, p. 245.

[34] Roosevelt to Alice R. Longworth, June 24, 1906, Morison, ed., *Letters of Roosevelt*, vol. V, pp. 312–313; Philip A. Bruce, "American Feeling toward England," *Westminster Review* (London), vol. CLIV (1900), p. 459; Mrs. George Cornwallis-West, *The Reminiscences of Lady Randolph Churchill* (New York, 1909), p. 60.

[35] Page to Wilson, May 1, 1914, quoted in Burton J. Hendrick, *The Life and Letters of Walter H. Page* (3 vols.; Garden City, 1922–1925), vol. III, p. 37.

had many other things to worry about in the years before Sarajevo—their own political battles, Ireland, Europe—and they could not easily afford the luxury of a quarrel with the United States. Without making much of a fuss about it, only half recognizing what they were doing, the British people accepted America as an equal partner in the Anglo-Saxon world. Their failure to resent or to resist the new state of things gave depth to the wise policy adopted by their government.

Progress in the United States was more eccentric. "There has undoubtedly been a recrudescence, although in a very much milder form, of the old anti-English spirit . . . ," Roosevelt wrote a British friend in 1901. "In '98 there was almost for the first time an attitude of real and practical friendliness, . . . but it would be a mistake not to realize that what I firmly believe will be the growth of good feeling between the countries must on the whole be a gradual growth." Good feeling did grow, gradually and silently, during the next decade. Henry Adams, the heir of three generations of foes of England, sighed as early as 1904, "I no longer feel the old acute pleasure in vilifying the British," [36] and more and more of his countrymen came to eschew this traditional pleasure. This change eased the path of diplomacy, but so too did diplomacy help to create the climate in which the change took place.

During the lifetime of Adams' grandfather, an obelisk was erected at Concord Bridge. The inscription read:

HERE
On the 19th of April
1775
was made
the first forcible resistance
to British aggression.
On the Opposite Bank
stood the American militia.

[36] Roosevelt to Lee, March 18, 1901, Morison, ed., *Letters of Roosevelt*, vol. III, p. 20; Adams to Cunliffe, July 4, 1904, Worthington C. Ford, ed., *Letters of Henry Adams, 1892–1918* (Boston, 1938), pp. 436–437.

Here stood the Invading Army.
And on this spot
the first of the Enemy fell
in the War of the Revolution
which gave
Independence
to these United States.

Early in the new century a simpler marker was placed across a path from the old one. After a dispassionate account of the engagement, the inscription ended, "The British fled, and here began the separation of two kindred nations, now happily long united in peace." Perhaps Charles Altschul's textbook writers were behind the times.

CHAPTER SEVEN

America's Hemisphere:
Alaska and Panama

H ENRY ADAMS, who loved John Hay, made Hay's death the closing episode of his famous *Education*. For many years Adams did not share his friend's feelings toward England; he urged Hay to elude what he considered Britain's fatal embrace. "The shadow from Germany and Russia has got there. They are clutching at us as their last hope," Adams warned in 1901. (Only three years later, in a sharp turn about, he admitted he had lost pleasure in "vilifying the British.") As the shadows formed, first in the closing decades of the nineteenth century and then more ominously in the new century, it became evident that Britain's responsibilities outstripped her resources for defense. "The truth is," wrote Sir Henry Campbell-Bannerman shortly before he became premier, "we cannot provide for a fighting Empire, and nothing will give us the power." [1]

If this were true, and more and more Englishmen came to believe it was, Britain could meet the situation by seeking to break out of her "melancholy isolation," [2] as a friendly American

[1] Adams to Hay, November 2, 1901, Worthington C. Ford, ed., *Letters of Henry Adams, 1892–1918* (Boston, 1938), p. 356; Campbell-Bannerman to Bryce, n.d. [1903], quoted in Archibald P. Thornton, *The Imperial Idea and Its Enemies: A Study in British Power* (London, 1959), p. 106.

[2] Springfield *Republican*, quoted in *Literary Digest* (New York), vol. XXII (1901), p. 122.

paper called it, by tailoring her responsibilities to her power or by a combination of the two courses. She opted for the third alternative. She sought alliances which would strengthen imperial defense and enable her to speak more confidently in European politics. At the same time, making a virtue of necessity, she abandoned the Western Hemisphere to the United States. This decision did more than anything else to further the great rapprochement, for it led to a series of Anglo-American settlements which were essential prerequisites to changes in the stance of the American government and to the tardier change in public attitudes toward England. Salisbury, Lansdowne, and Balfour sometimes stumbled, but they never lost sight of the path. Both Roosevelt and American opinion sometimes complicated the task, but the British government persevered, gaining great success before it handed over power to the Liberals in 1905.

The new British outlook led to major changes in defense policy. The Committee of Imperial Defence decided that the possibility of war with America could be ignored in determining the strength of West Indian garrisons in 1903 and the forces at Halifax in 1904. In 1906, thirty-five years after the departure of British troops from Quebec signified a reluctant acceptance of American predominance on land, the same concession was made to the naval power of the United States; English forces left the base at Halifax, a mote in America's eye at least since the time of Admiral Berkeley and the *Chesapeake* affair and a station essential to the effective prosecution of a naval war with the United States.

In 1902, Admiral Sir John Fisher, a smooth-faced, dictatorial, and energetic disciple of Alfred T. Mahan, began to prepare the Royal Navy to meet the German threat. Among his reforms, of which introduction of the dreadnought was most dramatic, a reallocation of naval strength was most important for Anglo-American relations. In keeping with Mahan's dictum, Fisher concentrated the main naval units in European waters. The Pacific squadron and its base at Esquimault virtually disappeared, and the North Atlantic station, based on Halifax, was abolished. To the Caribbean, formerly a subordinate command directed from Halifax, Fisher allotted only a cruiser squadron, and this force merely visited the area on annual trips from its base in England.

Not even Fisher, who never lacked for self-confidence, would have dreamed of denuding the American hemisphere if he had anticipated serious difficulties with the United States. In 1906 he described the United States as "a kindred state with whom we shall never have a parricidal war." At the same time he and his superiors recognized, as the secretary of the Committee of Imperial Defence put it, that "The U.S. Navy will soon be beyond rivalry *in its own waters* unless we are in a position to divide our battle fleet on this side, which we shall never be able to do." The parallel growth of American friendship and European threats led Britain to the conclusion that an Anglo-American war was "not merely the supreme limit of human folly, but also . . . so unlikely as to be a contingency against which it is unnecessary to make provision." [3] The American flag waved unchallenged over American waters for the first time in history.

Similar assumptions marked the running debate over the "two-nation standard." Since 1889, when France and her ally Russia seemed to pose a real threat, it had been a maxim of British policy that the Royal Navy should have a battleship strength equal to that of any two potential foes. By 1900, and particularly after the German naval law of 1901 calling for a massive building program, the two-nation standard had become obsolete, or at best a rationalization for naval forces substantially larger than the Kaiser's. Britain simply did not have the resources to build a fleet equal to the combined strength of Germany and the United States. Moreover, even the most alarmist Englishman could scarcely conceive of a German-American coalition against Britain, and if the unthinkable occurred the standard would be inad-

[3] Fisher memorandum, October —, 1906, quoted in Arthur J. Marder, *From the Dreadnought to Scapa Flow: The Royal Navy in the Fisher Era, 1904–1919*, vol. I (London, 1961), p. 125; Sir George Clarke memorandum, June 26, 1905, quoted in Kenneth Bourne, *Britain and the Balance of Power in North America, 1815–1908* (Berkeley and Los Angeles, 1967), p. 391; Committee of Imperial Defence memorandum, June —, 1907, quoted in Marder, *Dreadnought to Scapa Flow*, vol. I, p. 183.

equate to meet the need. "No one dreams of having to meet them [Germany and the United States] in combination," Admiral Jellicoe said. "But if we did so dream, the two-Power standard applied to that combination would not give us sufficient superiority in the near seas over Germany alone." [4]

Although those who wanted to keep a wide lead over Germany argued for the traditional yardstick, it was thrown away just before the war. Seeking a step-up in naval building in 1909, Conservatives urged application of the traditional standard. (Consulted in advance by his friend Lee, Theodore Roosevelt assured the Conservatives that no reasonable American would take it amiss if Britain affected to calculate upon potential American hostility.) Liberal spokesmen including Prime Minister Asquith and Reginald McKenna, First Lord of the Admiralty, replied that the government could not allow American naval strength to determine British policy, and the Prime Minister dismissed the standard as little more than a convenient rule of thumb. In 1911 McKenna, again under attack, declared it government policy to maintain a fleet "supreme as against any foreign navy, and as against any reasonable probable combination which we might have to meet single-handed." [5] Foreign Secretary Grey chimed in, reiterating that the United States Navy did not enter into the equation. Finally, in 1912, the new First Lord, Winston Churchill, declared that Great Britain needed a battleship fleet sixty percent larger than Germany's. All mention of the United States had ended.

Not only the imperatives of European politics forced Britain to forgo challenges to the United States in the Western Hemisphere. Although underlings in the Foreign Office, diplomats on the spot who resented the rise of American influence, and traditionalist journals all bewailed the new departure, the government and most informed Englishmen welcomed or at worst silently accepted the hegemony of the United States. Even

[4] Jellicoe memorandum, April —, 1909 [?], quoted in *ibid.*, pp. 184–185.
[5] Quoted in Elie Halévy, *The Rule of Democracy* (E. I. Watkin, trans.; *A History of the English People in the Nineteenth Century*, vol. VI; rev. ed., New York, 1961), p. 420.

without European distractions, it was obvious that the republic disposed, or could dispose, of sufficient power to make a contest over Latin America ruinous for Great Britain. As early as 1895, at the time of the Venezuelan crisis, glimmers of understanding began, and they grew stronger with time.

Satisfied with her own commercial position and reasonably confident the United States would not take unfair advantage, Britain asked only that the United States should prevent third powers from mounting challenges to the economic and political health of the empire in the Latin American arena. She ceased to contest the Monroe Doctrine, which statesmen from Canning to Salisbury had treated with jocose contempt, and indeed hugged it to her bosom. In 1903, after a misstep which gave a contrary impression, Arthur Balfour reassured the United States in a speech at Liverpool, saying, "We welcome any increase of the influence of the United States of America upon the great Western Hemisphere." [6] By this Balfour really meant that Great Britain expected the United States to block German penetration of the New World. Although American concern over this possibility antedated England's, and although the opening of archives has shown that both exaggerated the threat, Britons sometimes worried that the United States would not stand up to its responsibilities. The *Spectator*, in particular, asked Americans to heed the advice of Elihu Root and others who urged their countrymen to be prepared to fight in defense of the Doctrine. Neither country seems to have realized that with the Royal Navy athwart German lines of communication, political intervention was impossible. Both feared for the status quo, the situation which best served their interests in Latin America as in so many other parts of the world.

Besides welcoming a larger American role because it would inhibit European adventurism, Englishmen counted upon the United States to discipline Latin Americans. Even before the Roosevelt Corollary laid down the principle that the United

[6] Quoted in Richard H. Heindel, *The American Impact on Great Britain, 1898–1914* (Philadelphia, 1940), p. 100.

States must correct situations in Latin America which might invite European intervention, Britons urged the United States to play this role. The *Times* said, "Central and South American states may learn . . . that they have nothing to fear from the moral hegemony which the United States cannot but exercise over their destiny," and Prime Minister Balfour wrote, "These South American Republics are a great trouble, and I wish the U.S.A. would take them in hand." Such remained the British position down to World War I. Sir Edward Grey, pressed by subordinates to try to forestall American intervention in Mexico, responded, "These small Republics will never establish decent govt. themselves—they must succumb to some greater and better influence and it can only be that of the U.S.A.," and a public writer commenting on the same scene declared, "In the interests of civilisation the United States must keep order on the American continent not only for its own sake, but for that of all the rest of the world." [7] Both as defender and policeman of the New World, the United States served England's interests. At the same time, British withdrawal wiped away a long-standing area of controversy.

Withdrawal also marked British policy toward that portion of the hemisphere north of the United States. Since Benjamin Franklin's time, but with varying intensity, Americans had cast glances toward Canada, sometimes because they wished to add it to their country and sometimes simply because, at times of difficulty with England, it presented a tempting, almost undefended target. The Republican platform of 1896 called for annexation via negotiation, and in the new century such disparate political figures as Representative Claude Kitchin, a progressive Democrat; an indefatigable imperialist, Senator John T. Morgan of Alabama; and President Taft squinted in that direction. The British

[7] *Times* (London), August 23, 1901, quoted in *ibid.*, p. 97; Balfour to Carnegie, December 18, 1902, quoted in Howard K. Beale, *Theodore Roosevelt and the Rise of America to World Power* (Baltimore, 1956), p. 144; Grey minute on Reginald Tower to Grey, August 23, 1910, quoted in Peter A. R. Calvert, "The Mexican Revolution, 1910–1914: The Diplomacy of Anglo-American Conflict" (Cambridge University dissertation, 1964), p. 25; A. Maurice Low in *National Review* (London), vol. LVII (1911), p. 295.

connection continued to play its historic role in the salvation of
Canada from American clutches.

England had no desire to see Canada fall, nor did she wish
to become involved in quarrels with the United States over Canadian interests. Militarily, there could be no hope of defending
Canada. Madcap planners in the War Office once drew up a
scheme not merely for defense but for an offensive overland from
Montreal supported by landings at Boston and New York, all
hopefully in coordination with an Indian uprising in the American West. This plan understandably ran counter to thinking at
higher levels. Withdrawal of naval units made it even more difficult to imagine defending Canada, and in 1908 the Committee
of Imperial Defence admitted that Canada could not be held
against American attack. Thus military realities reinforced London's political outlook. Downing Street consistently and not always discreetly urged Canadians to compromise difficulties with
the United States. As so often in the past, Canadians, who sometimes tended to undervalue the British connection, objected that
the mother country sacrificed them for American friendship.

The greatest howls arose during a dispute over the boundary
between Canada and Alaska, when Canadians saw that Balfour's
government was more interested in drawing the venom of controversy than in pressing dominion interests. The trouble arose
out of ambiguous language in the Anglo-Russian treaty of 1825
purporting to fix a boundary line the Americans inherited when
they bought Alaska in 1867. In the Alaskan panhandle, this
agreement provided, the boundary should follow a mountain
range parallel to the sea or, if this fell too far inland, a curving
line ten marine leagues from the ocean. Unfortunately, no range
existed, only a jumble of unconnected peaks, leaving both sides
free to use their imagination or sometimes, in Canada's case, to
insist that only the maritime line made sense. In addition, the
negotiators of 1825 failed to indicate what they understood to be
the limits of the ocean; during the Canadian-American controversy the Americans usually held out for the head of tidewater,
the Canadians for a line of seacoast leaping over the mouths of
inlets running inland. The ambiguities are not surprising, for in

1825 the area was almost unknown. Not until 1892 did the two countries even order a survey, and when completed in 1895 it left many questions unanswered.

By and large, Canadian governments accepted and Canadian maps followed American interpretations of the boundary until the discovery of gold in the Klondike in 1896. Then Ottawa dusted off its claims. Canada principally sought some of the little ports which gave access to the gold fields, although, having little to lose and much to gain, she demanded a huge share of the panhandle and sought arbitration of the whole area in dispute. Canada expected England, then being asked by the United States to agree to revise a treaty which impeded construction of an isthmian canal, to use this as a lever to secure favorable terms for her south of the Klondike. Canada's position outraged Americans, and indeed Sir Wilfrid Laurier and Clifford Sifton, his minister of the interior, publicly admitted the strength of American claims to Dyea and Skagway, well beyond the maritime line.

In a talk with Ambassador Pauncefote in March 1898, McKinley suggested full-dress negotiations on all outstanding Canadian-American issues. A protocol signed at the end of May established a joint high commission, six from each side, and in August the commissioners met at Quebec. Although Sir Wilfrid Laurier and other Canadians sat on the imperial delegation, it was headed by Lord Herschell, Lord High Chancellor of Great Britain. Herschell, chosen by London to hold Canada in check, hoped to settle disputes by mutual concessions but was determined not to seem to betray the dominion. The Americans blamed him—"more cantankerous than any of the Canadians," said Hay[8]—for the deadlock which developed. After eighteen weeks of fruitless discussion the commission, then meeting at Washington, adjourned in February 1899. Lord Herschell, who proposed adjournment to let tempers cool and to explore informal channels of negotiation, died before the board could resume operations.

Although the commission and subcommittees through

---

[8] Hay to White, December 3, 1898, quoted in William R. Thayer, *The Life and Letters of John Hay* (2 vols.; Boston, 1915), vol. II, p. 204.

which it usually worked discussed several issues, the Alaskan boundary dominated proceedings. "Personally," wrote Joseph Chamberlain, who as colonial secretary oversaw things from London but dared not order Laurier or even Herschell into line, "I care very little for the points in dispute, but I care immensely for the consequential advantages of a thorough understanding between the two countries and the removal of these trumpery causes of irritation." [9] Neither set of negotiators shared Chamberlain's broad view. The imperial representatives held out for arbitration, with an outsider holding the decisive vote, a proceeding the Americans rejected on the plausible ground that arbitrators usually split the difference, even between just and artificial claims. They suggested that a six-man board of jurists, three from each side, should settle the dispute, a proposal which ensured that the United States would not lose unless betrayed by one of its own representatives. Canada declined to accept unless promised in advance that at least one port would fall to her.

Following the commission's collapse, Secretary of State Hay sought a stopgap settlement in areas nearest the Klondike, at the head of the Lynn Canal seventy-five miles or more north of the line claimed by Laurier's government. He wished to check the conflict already arising between Canadian and American authorities on the spot, and he well knew a temporary border might in time become permanent. Canadians recognized this, too, and they tried to extort from Hay a promise that if they agreed to his proposal the United States would accept arbitration of the whole claim. Hay held firm, London poured cold water on Canadian hopes, and in October 1899 three short stretches of boundary on the most convenient routes to the gold fields were fixed. In two areas Hay had his way, and even in the other the Canadians were driven back a few miles from navigable water. The Secretary of State considered the *modus vivendi* a victory, and he resented it when Democrats and Anglophobes, refurbishing the charge that he was under Britain's thumb, called it a sellout because Hay

[9] Chamberlain to White, December 27, 1898, quoted in Allan Nevins, *Henry White: Thirty Years of Diplomacy* (New York, 1930), p. 146.

gave up a few square miles of wilderness.

Canada accepted the *modus vivendi* largely because of pressure from London. At the outset of the Alaska dispute, Downing Street delayed action on an American request for abrogation of the Clayton-Bulwer Treaty, by which the United States agreed not to build an isthmian canal except in conjunction with England, in hopes that this would lead the United States to offer concessions to Canada. Canada's exaggerated claims and London's eagerness to strengthen relations with the United States caused reexamination of this strategy. In the summer of 1899 the Colonial Secretary told Canada that his colleagues considered America's case "unassailable" and that delay could only prove harmful to Canada. The *modus vivendi* soon followed. A few months later, reporting rising American indignation at British foot-dragging on the isthmian question, Sir Julian Pauncefote urged separation of the two issues. "America seems to be our only friend just now," he observed, thinking of Europe's attitude toward the Boer War, "and it would be unfortunate to quarrel with her." [10] Chamberlain cabled Ottawa a threat to proceed as Pauncefote suggested with or without Canadian approval, receiving in reply a grumpy acceptance of the inevitable. The Laurier government thereby lost its only effective weapon, while Britain became free to defuse the isthmian issue.

Negotiations for a permanent settlement overlapped those to establish a *modus vivendi*. In the spring of 1899 Pauncefote, in London en route to the Hague Conference, nearly settled the issue in discussions with Ambassador Choate. Speaking for Hay, Choate agreed to accept true arbitration, an outsider holding the balance. This departure from the established American position was less risky than it seemed, since Pauncefote agreed to exempt settled areas, a concession which meant the United States was bound to keep the vital ports. Everything seemed to be going well until Laurier decided that for reasons of domestic politics

[10] Chamberlain to Governor-General Lord Minto, July 21, 1899, quoted in Charles S. Campbell, *Anglo-American Understanding, 1898–1903* (Baltimore, 1957), p. 146; Pauncefote to Lansdowne, January 19, 1900, quoted in *ibid.*, p. 190.

he, too, must demand some exemptions. When Choate learned that the Canadian insisted upon Pyramid Harbor, negotiations came to a halt.

Nearly two years of silence followed. "An indefinite prolongation of the modus vivendi seems the probable result," a Foreign Office official predicted. However, with the election of 1900 safely out of the way, John Hay reopened the search for a solution. Britain received his offer to submit the rival claims to what he called arbitration but was in fact a binational commission in April 1901, and she besought Canada to accept it. The Canadians delayed six months, then again insisted upon the inclusion of neutral arbitrators. When Pauncefote finally passed this response to the Secretary of State in February, a more unyielding President had moved into the White House. Theodore Roosevelt, Hay uncomfortably told the Ambassador, disapproved of the offer sanctioned by his predecessor. The new President, Hay went on, "considers the claim of the United States is so manifestly clear and unanswerable that he is not disposed to run the risk of sacrificing American territory under a compromise which is the almost certain result of an arbitration." [11] The controversy was about to heat up again.

Roosevelt had been President for five months, since September. During that time he neither ordered Hay to withdraw his offer nor repudiated the modus vivendi to which he had objected when it was signed. He even gave it grudging approval, writing to Arthur Lee, "By this . . . we give you a bit of territory . . . to which . . . you have no more right than we have to take part of Cornwall or Kent. But so highly do I esteem the friendly relations with Great Britain that I should be willing to make the sacrifice by merely continuing the modus vivendi." [12] Roosevelt let the Boer War's closing months pass without pressing Britain, and probably, despite what Pauncefote reported, he

[11] Unsigned Foreign Office minute, August 1, 1900, quoted in Alexander E. Campbell, Great Britain and the United States, 1895–1903 (Glasgow, 1960), p. 104; Pauncefote to Lansdowne, March 28, 1902, quoted in ibid., pp. 105–106.
[12] Roosevelt to Lee, April 24, 1901, Elting E. Morison, ed., The Letters of Theodore Roosevelt (8 vols.; Cambridge, 1951–1954), vol. III, p. 66.

would have carried through Hay's scheme had Canada accepted it without change, for in essence this scheme conformed with the settlement he later approved.

However, he considered Canada's response provocative, even insulting. True arbitration he could not accept, for it seemed to put the two claims on a par. When Lee earlier had asked why, if the Americans were so convinced of the irrefutable rightness of their cause, they declined to arbitrate, the President responded, "there are cases where a nation has no business to arbitrate." Considering the Canadian claim "an outrage pure and simple," he refused to give it a day in court. Once aroused, the President determined to force matters to a finish. Recent events connected with the isthmian question made him wonder if England was really as friendly as she pretended to be; Alaska would provide a good test, since the right was so clearly on America's side. Moreover, he quickly convinced himself the last chance for settlement had come. Sooner or later, and more likely sooner if gold turned up in disputed territory, a clash would come. Britain and Canada must give way, the Canadians especially. "I feel a good deal like telling them that if trouble comes it will be purely because of their own fault," Roosevelt wrote, "and although it would not be pleasant for us it would be death for them." [13] Eight hundred cavalrymen sent to Alaska, although intended at least in part for police duties, convinced England he meant business, and a whole string of letters from the President, his friends, and those who interviewed him warned the British government this was so.

Because Roosevelt's gestures quickly found their mark, the crisis really lasted only a few months. In June 1902, when Sir Wilfrid and the Governor-General, Lord Minto, arrived in London for Edward VII's coronation, Lord Lansdowne implored them to open talks with Ambassador Choate and Henry White. The Americans quickly learned, first, that Lansdowne desperately wanted a settlement and, second, that Laurier had given up. Choate reported that the Premier now accepted the Ameri-

[13] Roosevelt to Lee, April 24, 1901, *ibid.*; Roosevelt to Hay, July 10, 1902, *ibid.*, p. 287; Roosevelt to Hay, July 16, 1902, *ibid.*, pp. 294–295.

can plan for an even-numbered commission including no third parties, expected the verdict to go against him but promised to surrender populated areas if any should fall on the Canadian side of the line, and only asked that the Americans agree to a settlement which would cause him the least possible political damage at home.

As promised at London, Sir Michael Herbert, who arrived at Washington to succeed Pauncefote in September, bore powers to negotiate. Adopting Roosevelt's posture, Hay proved difficult to deal with, and Laurier suffered second thoughts which roused concern in the British government, concurrently involved in difficulties with the United States over Venezuela. Finally, late in the afternoon on January 24, 1903, in Hay's library, the Secretary and the Ambassador signed a convention referring the boundary dispute to a commission of "six impartial jurists of repute," three from each side. The text of the convention carefully avoided the word "arbitration," which suggested compromise, although the dread syllables somehow slipped into the preamble and, after being submitted to the Senate, the convention had to be withdrawn so they could be exorcised. Even so, many senators objected to any discussion of a meritless Canadian claim. To procure approval, Roosevelt leaked the names of his intended appointees, and the spokesman of the Foreign Relations Committee, Henry Cabot Lodge, engaged in a bit of skullduggery, moving consideration at the end of a dreary session when many senators were absent and rushing the agreement through without a roll call after only forty minutes of debate.

Roosevelt's selection of commissioners aroused a furor. After two Supreme Court justices declined appointment and Lodge reported difficulty with the Senate, the President decided to appoint two senators, Lodge himself and George Turner of Washington, whose term was about to expire, along with Secretary of War Root, who very reluctantly agreed to serve. The selections may have eased the convention's path through the Senate, but they exposed the President to charges of bad faith, for although Root and Turner were lawyers by training—Turner began his career as a "carpetbagger" attorney in Alabama—none had any claim to judicial eminence or impartiality. Herbert, so outraged he wrote Lodge to ask if the Senator honestly thought he could hear the case fairly, was also wise enough to advise London that the risks of breaking up the settlement at this point were too great to be borne. Balfour and Lansdowne agreed. Britain ratified the convention without waiting to consult Canada, and her two leaders then bludgeoned the dominion, and the Colonial Office which inclined to support it, into acceptance of the American appointments. The Foreign Office agreed, as the Assistant Under-Secretary delicately phrased it, that the choice "fails to fulfil in their complete sense the conditions laid down in . . . the Convention" but nevertheless insisted that business proceed.[14] To their credit, Laurier and his colleagues then selected two leading Canadian jurists, resisting the temptation to answer Roosevelt in kind. Britain filled up the commission by selecting Lord Chief Justice Alverstone.

Roosevelt issued orders to his agents in the form of a "personal and confidential" letter. "You will of course impartially judge the questions that come before you for decision," he said, but he went on to state that the basic Canadian claim, for a maritime line leaving her some outlet to the sea, was not even a legitimate subject for discussion. "The treaty of 1825 between Russia and England was undoubtedly intended to cut off England, which owned the Hinterland, from access to the sea," and this principle must be observed. The letter, although undeniably strong, represented no new departure in Roosevelt's thought; it simply made explicit what everyone had assumed America expected of an evenly balanced commission.

When London asked more time to prepare the Canadian case, the hypersuspicious Lodge feared a sinister plot. On the basis of Lodge's reports, Roosevelt replied, "England must be kept right up to the mark," suggesting that he might simply run the line himself if settlement were delayed. "I don't intend that

[14] Francis Villiers to Colonial Office, February 25, 1903, quoted in Campbell, *Anglo-American Understanding*, p. 314.

they shall do any shuffling now." [15] Within a fortnight, armed with better information, Roosevelt sought to calm the Senator, arguing that a short delay was not only reasonable but acceptable. The President continued to worry that Alverstone and the two Canadians would refuse to back down and that the British government would not force them to do so, but he never again talked about a subtle plot by Balfour's ministry. As it turned out, the commission met at London on September 3, only two days late, although after selecting Alverstone president it adjourned twelve days to permit lawyers to complete their tasks.

As early as July, when Lodge reached London, Chamberlain and Balfour promised to urge moderation on the Canadians, but it soon became obvious that, although eminent jurists, the dominion representatives were by no means impartial and would refuse to budge. Alverstone held the key to success. He and Lodge, who dined together at Choate's the evening after the Senator arrived, hit it off well personally, but the Senator feared that Alverstone would refuse to separate from the Canadians. Partly at Lodge's urging, although he needed little prodding, Roosevelt bombarded London with warnings that he would establish a boundary himself if the commission did not do so. Henry White carried one particularly strong letter from Hay describing the President's intransigence to a weekend at Balfour's estate, and shortly thereafter Balfour's private secretary had two interviews with Alverstone. What the men said is not known, but almost immediately Alverstone, sitting next to Lodge and Root on the tribunal while they heard evidence, told them "he must and will decide that the line goes round the heads of the inlets," thus accepting the major American contention. Alverstone added that "he was anxious after doing this to do all he can for the Canadians," but the major hurdle had been crossed.[16]

Two weeks after this conversation, the lawyers droned to a

[15] Roosevelt to Root, Lodge, and Turner, March 25, 1903, Henry Cabot Lodge, ed., *Selections from the Correspondence of Theodore Roosevelt and Henry Cabot Lodge, 1884–1918* (2 vols.; New York, 1925), vol. II, p. 5; Roosevelt to Lodge, June 29, 1903, *ibid.*, p. 37.

[16] Lodge to Constance Lodge Gardner, September 25, 1903, quoted in John A. Garraty, *Henry Cabot Lodge* (New York, 1953), p. 251.

halt. Thereafter, discussion centered on the width of the coastal strip which would separate Canada from her cherished outlet to the sea. At first, though Balfour told Lodge he had impressed upon the Chief Justice the necessity of a quick settlement, Alverstone tried to drive a hard bargain. When deadlock threatened, Choate remonstrated to Lansdowne, and two days later the judge became remarkably more mellow. The Americans offered concessions, chiefly islands, at the extreme southerly end of the line, and Alverstone receded elsewhere. On October 20, 1903, the commission handed down a decision which made the American victory official. Only at the mouth of the Stikine River, far away from the Klondike but conceivably useful as a port of entry, did the boundary touch open water, and at that point the commissioners merely reaffirmed a temporary line established in 1878.

There were screams of protest in England, and for years this episode provided the chief talking point for those who maintained that the Americans consistently bullied England. Most criticism, however, came from a small number of extreme conservatives, and the Liberal Party resisted the temptation to pillory the government for its weakness. The ministry, long reconciled to the inevitable and desiring only that the dispute should disappear, made no objections to Roosevelt's pressure tactics. When Parliament assembled in February 1904, the King's speech expressed pleasure that "the misunderstandings, in which ancient Boundary Treaties, made in ignorance of geographical facts, are so fertile, have in this case been finally removed from the field of controversy." [17] In the ensuing debates in the two Houses, some sympathy for Canada was expressed, but virtually all speakers congratulated the government on eliminating a source of controversy at such small cost.

Canadians were not so philosophical. Their two representatives refused to sign the award. Their newspapers denounced the affair as further evidence that London always sacrificed Canada on the altar of American friendship, and a few frenzied voices

[17] *Parliamentary Debates*, Fourth Series, vol. CXXIX, p. 2.

suggested secession from the British Empire. When Hay proposed to name one of the peaks astride the boundary after Sir Michael Herbert, in honor of his services in negotiating the convention which set up the commission, the Canadians refused. Although they never forgot this British betrayal they gradually became reconciled to the decision. In 1908 they granted the villain of the piece, Lord Alverstone, the honor of naming a mountain after him.

Whether so intended or not, this was a wise reflection of reality. Had the Alaskan affair dragged on, Anglo-American friendship and Canadian-American friendship would have been grievously harmed. Settlement by compromise was politically impossible, as McKinley and Hay found out on two occasions when they sought one, only to have the resulting public uproar force them to retreat. Criticism of Hay's *modus vivendi*, senatorial reluctance to approve the Hay-Herbert convention, and fairly steady public criticism of England all showed that Anglophobia was still a potent force, and the President, too, could have been converted into a foe of England. As it was, this settlement and others involving the isthmus of Panama and Venezuela permitted him to write in 1905, "I regard all danger of any trouble between the United States and Great Britain as over, I think forever." The President never claimed he had a master plan to settle all disputes, and if he subconsciously sought this end he certainly used strong tactics to obtain it. Nevertheless, when Roosevelt left the White House in 1909, London's *Fortnightly Review* rightly commented, in one of many retrospective articles which then appeared, "Under his auspices pretty nearly every issue of any moment or contentiousness has been wiped off the Anglo-American slate." [18] In their way these settlements, particularly the 1903 award, were fully as important as the sentimental effusions of 1898.

The whole affair was characteristic Roosevelt, a combina-

[18] Roosevelt to Strachey, September 11, 1905, quoted in Amy Strachey, *St. Loe Strachey: His Life and His Paper* (London, 1930), p. 182; Sydney Brooks, "President Roosevelt's Record," *Fortnightly Review* (London), vol. XCI (1909), p. 667.

tion of self-righteousness, the big stick, and a certain amount of posturing, all tied up in a bundle of immense energy. Despite the regrettable appointments to the commission and Roosevelt's willingness to risk a serious clash over a mountainous wilderness, there is much to be said in his behalf. Hay, although he conceded nothing and secured a very favorable *modus vivendi* in 1899, failed to gain a settlement, and his tactics had demonstrably failed by 1902. Something had to be done, either directly or through London, to shake good sense into Ottawa. Moreover, Britain was more than half willing to be frightened by Roosevelt, for it permitted her to insist that the Canadians must seek a way out, and even Laurier admitted in 1902 that, convinced the game was not worth the candle, he only sought to escape with minimum loss of face. The appointments to the commission, cynical and suggesting the unattractive purpose of rubbing Canadian noses in the dirt, probably cost the dominion no loss of territory. Roosevelt would never have appointed anyone, even a Supreme Court justice, who did not promise to uphold the basic American claim. He and his agents might, had he been less self-righteous, have accepted a narrower coastal strip for the United States. Because of domestic politics and because they scorned Canada's claim as illegitimate, they could not have compromised on the central issue. Nor would a few thousand square miles of territory have mollified Laurier's people. The dominion wanted valuable ports, not land which has remained almost worthless. For their loss, Canadians could look to England, not Washington.

The isthmian issue, which lowered over the Alaskan controversy until Lord Salisbury and his colleagues cut the two asunder in January 1900, just as clearly reflected Britain's determination to leave the United States a freer hand in the New World. By the Clayton-Bulwer Treaty of 1850, Great Britain and the United States had pledged neither to fortify nor even to build an isthmian canal except in cooperation. Many Americans at the time, and a greater number later on, believed this provision undermined the Monroe Doctrine by admitting an English presence in the area. Moreover, as American ambitions to continental dominion revived, the treaty served as a barrier to forceful approaches to those powers, notably Colombia and Nicaragua, which controlled the prime canal routes. Finally, although Britain showed little interest in the project, Americans came to feel that economic and strategic well-being required the breaching of the isthmus. In 1898 the voyage of U.S.S. *Oregon*, ordered from San Francisco via the Straits of Magellan to reinforce the Caribbean squadron, a voyage which lasted more than two months, dramatized the need for a canal; without one, Mahan's sacred doctrine of a united battle fleet could not be maintained. America could neither wait for England nor agree to share the task with her. Such thoughts led to great pressure upon the British government.

McKinley's annual message of December 1898 called for "some definite action . . . at this session" to initiate a solely American canal and did not even deign to mention obligations under the Clayton-Bulwer Treaty. This omission, and the hue-and-cry in Congress for full speed ahead, raised the specter of an open violation of the old treaty, although Hay assured Pauncefote none was planned. To make this clear, the Secretary of State instructed Henry White to discuss revision of the Clayton-Bulwer treaty with Lord Salisbury. Inviting himself to Hatfield House for a weekend, since Salisbury came to town only about once a week during Parliament's Christmas recess, the chargé explained his mission. Although the Premier had already thought of trading isthmian concessions for a quid pro quo in Alaska, he said nothing along these lines, merely commenting that ships of all nations should be free to use the canal and pay the same tolls. He promised that Pauncefote would be sent instructions to negotiate.

Because Salisbury acted with unwonted speed and Hay, after only minor changes, quickly converted a Pauncefote draft into a final instrument, a treaty was completed by the middle of January 1899. Pauncefote, drawing on his experience at the Paris conference on Suez in 1885, modeled the treaty after the one controlling use of that canal, and he incorporated restrictions on the United States which meant that this treaty fell short of total abrogation of the Clayton-Bulwer agreement. Hay accepted these terms because he was so glad to see teeth drawn from the controversy before Congress stampeded ahead, considered trifling the Suez-modeled restrictions on American freedom of action, and felt grateful for England's willingness—as it seemed in January 1899—to back away from a juridically impeccable position without asking a quid pro quo. Pauncefote erred by not making a grand gesture of abnegation which would have solidified America's wartime friendship, Hay even more seriously by failing to anticipate the sentiments of many of his own countrymen. Had he drafted the treaty himself, or even asked if Pauncefote would have agreed to a direct, unencumbered cancelation of the old treaty, the result would surely have been markedly different. Each of the three important restrictions on American freedom—a ban on fortifications, neutralization of the canal in time of war, an invitation to other powers to become parties to the agreement—gave an international tone to what Americans were determined should be a national enterprise. Pauncefote might well have seen this, and Hay certainly should have.

For more than a year the storm bred by Hay and Pauncefote lay over the horizon because the Ambassador's superiors declined to endorse his treaty. They saw little reason for haste, and Canadians importuned them to withhold approval until the Americans agreed to true arbitration of the Alaskan boundary. Salisbury wrote Pauncefote, "The Cabinet to whom I submitted question of the Clayton-Bulwer Treaty, felt that the force of the U.S. navy would in war be doubled by the project. They are adverse to obstructing what may be of value to commerce, but they fear that if they yield a point so entirely to the advantage of the United States without some diminution at least of the causes which might bring the two countries into conflict"—Salisbury meant Alaska—"there would be serious dissatisfaction here." [19]

[19] Salisbury to Pauncefote, February 2, 1899, quoted in J. A. S. Grenville, "Great Britain and the Isthmian Canal, 1898–1901," *American Historical Review* (Washington), vol. LXI (1955–1956), p. 59.

A subordinate told Henry White that Britain intended to give in in the long run but refused to be hustled in the face of American obstreperousness on other issues. No matter; the decision for delay threw the issue back into the boiling cauldron of American domestic politics. The ministry temporarily avoided trouble with Canada but exposed itself to far greater dangers with the United States, and all to no purpose, since no one in authority, save perhaps the Colonial Secretary for a brief period, expected the Americans to concede in the north to obtain gains in the Caribbean.

When Congress reconvened in the fall of 1900, noisy speeches began. A bill introduced in December called for immediate steps to construct a canal without waiting for British permission, and most observers, Hay and Pauncefote among them, gave it a very good chance of passage. Pauncefote urged Salisbury to throw over Canadian interests "of a purely local character" rather than invite a serious clash with the United States, and, through Choate, Hay warned the British that an attempt to veto American construction of the canal would shatter international relations. "The worst of all for international relations," he added, "is that the veto would not be effective." [20] Congress, in other words, would go ahead anyway, driving the administration along the same path.

As in 1895, a careful rather than a careless examination of realities led Salisbury and his colleagues to back away from the brink. The messages from Hay and Pauncefote produced new instructions to the Ambassador, and on February 5, 1900, he called at the State Department to sign the now venerable document. Neither side thought to consider revisions, and an agreement which might just possibly have been accepted if signed thirteen months earlier, when American opinion was far less excited, immediately ran into serious opposition.

The *New York Times* considered the anti-treaty campaign

---

[20] Pauncefote to Salisbury, January 19, 1900, quoted in Campbell, *Anglo-American Understanding*, p. 190; Hay to Choate, January 15, 1900, quoted in Campbell, *Great Britain and the United States*, p. 51.

"a National disgrace" employing specious arguments and "the familiar ranting of the lowest demagogues in our politics." Still, it became very strong. Tammany Hall and then the Democratic national convention joined in; candidate Bryan threatened to press ahead without British concurrence if he became President. And the spirit spread into Republican ranks as well. After discussion with friends and advisers, including an assistant secretary of state who saw nothing disloyal in undercutting his superior, Governor Roosevelt of New York issued a statement calling for amendments "so as to provide that the canal, when built, shall be wholly under the control of the United States, alike in peace and war. This seems to me vital, from the standpoint of our sea power, no less than from the standpoint of the Monroe Doctrine." (*"Et tu!"* complained Hay. "Cannot you leave a few things to the President and the Senate, who are charged with them by the Constitution?" [21])

In any election year one third of the Senate tends to have elephant ears, and since 1900 was also a Presidential year the pachyderms stirred particularly uneasily. They may not have heard voices of a majority of the American people, certainly not a majority of those usually considered most influential. They did hear enough to realize there were votes to be lost, fewer to be won, by supporting the treaty. Approval, wrote Andrew Carnegie, who wished it were otherwise, would be "political suicide for the forthcoming campaign." [22] Yet fear of prejudiced voters was only one reason for Senate opposition to the treaty, and resistance, strong before the election, remained just as strong when that body reconvened.

The treaty's critics, who had no scruples about appealing to jingoism and Anglophobia, also had respectable arguing points. They complained that the treaty left alive the Clayton-Bulwer agreement and its restrictions upon American rights, particularly

[21] *New York Times*, March 12, 1900; Roosevelt statement, February 12, 1900, Morison, ed., *Letters of Roosevelt*, vol. II, pp. 1186n–1187n; Hay to [Roosevelt], quoted in Thayer, *Hay*, vol. II, p. 225.

[22] Quoted in W. Stull Holt, *Treaties Defeated by the Senate* (Baltimore, 1933), p. 186.

the right to acquire territory in Central America. They argued that it cast a shadow over the revered policy of President Monroe. "We should . . . deal, by implication, a deadly blow to the Monroe Doctrine," one critic charged, "for, if we recognize today the right of European nations to guarantee jointly the neutralization of an American canal, with what force of logic could we deny hereafter their right to extend their power of political regulation over any part of Latin America?" [23] Defenders of the treaty considered this argument specious, but the very words "Monroe Doctrine" had an almost mystical appeal, and critics worked them hard.

Both sides concentrated their arguments upon provisions of the treaty prohibiting fortification of the canal and guaranteeing its neutrality in wartime. Could America be expected, the Chicago *Times-Herald* asked, to give up a large proportion of "the advantage for which we pay?" Could she leave the waterway defenseless and open to enemy use, a road to attack upon her vulnerable Pacific coast? "Such an agreement," argued the New York *Sun*, an influential opponent of the treaty, "would especially disable us in the event of a war with Great Britain, which is not only the greatest naval power on earth, but possesses in close proximity to the Atlantic entrance of the proposed canal a coign of vantage in British Honduras." [24] Some even charged Britain with a diabolic plot to secure American construction of a waterway most useful to herself.

Although talk of war with Britain showed either a miscalculation of realities or a willingness to pander to Anglophobia, most of the treaty's supporters did not challenge their opponents on these grounds. They defended neutralization and demilitarization in principle. An American military zone, they argued, would serve as a magnet for attack. Only ships, not forts, could defend the canal area, and, this being so, it was all to America's advantage to have the neutrality of the canal assured, and thus a

[23] Mayo W. Hazeltine, "The Proposed Hay-Pauncefote Treaty," *North American Review* (New York), vol. CLXX (1900), p. 365.

[24] *Times-Herald,* quoted in *Literary Digest* (New York), vol. XX (1900), p. 202; *Sun,* quoted in *New York Times,* February 10, 1900.

wartime route from coast to coast free from the danger of inter-
ruption. As the New York *Herald* observed, "Neutralization
. . . will give the United States the right to use the canal in
time of war without imposing upon us the burden of fortifying it
and defending it, and will deprive the enemy of the right to seize
or damage it." The argument for defense by naval power had
much to commend it. The further assertion that the canal's neutrality would deflect an enemy who saw a chance to strike a
damaging blow, perhaps to cut American naval power in two,
showed a naive faith in international agreements, as opponents
quickly pointed out. "If the world were a hundred years nearer
the wished for period of disarmament and perpetual peace,"
scoffed the *Review of Reviews*, "the treaty would be as safe in
practice as it is fine and magnanimous in theory." [25]

Neither internationalization nor neutralization and nonfortification accorded with the obvious desire of the American people, inspirited by recent events at Manila and San Juan Hill, to
have a clear, unimpaired title to a canal in what they considered
"their" hemisphere. No doubt the restrictions were more important as symbols than real restraints. American nationalism might
reasonably have been asked to swallow them if they were essential to agreement with England. Hay and his supporters believed
they were. "There will be no way out," the *New York Times*
expostulated, "save to back out, to tear up the [Clayton-Bulwer]
treaty, to break faith with one of the most powerful nations on
earth, and our best friend among them." [26] In fact, Britain attached little importance to provisions largely the personal production of Pauncefote which gave her almost no benefits except
in the unlikely event of war with the United States. There was a
"way out," an alternative between approval of the treaty as it
stood and open defiance of England.

More by accident than intent, the Senate led the way to
discovery of this third possibility. A report presented to the Sen-

[25] *Herald* (New York), February 9, 1900; *Review of Reviews* (New York),
vol. XXI (1900), p. 281.
[26] *New York Times*, February 8, 1900.

ate by Cushman Davis, chairman of the Foreign Relations Committee, in March 1900 endorsed the treaty but recommended an amendment permitting the United States to send armed forces to the canal area when necessary. The Davis amendment roused a storm of criticism among Hay's defenders, and the Secretary himself later castigated it as "a mere *brutum fulmen*; it leaves intact the provision against fortification of the Canal; it reserves to us in vague terms a right which can never be exercised." [27] In Hay's view, these arguments justified rejection of the amendment; to those on the other side, they only made apparent the need for more far-reaching changes. One day of debate made it clear that even with the Davis amendment the treaty could not gain the support of two thirds of the Senate. The treaty was therefore put aside, and the Senate soon adjourned until after the election. The Secretary of State offered his resignation, but McKinley declined to accept it, which was only just since the President had done almost nothing to support his lieutenant.

Even Bryan's stentorian voice died away after November 6, but this did not ease the treaty's path. No sooner had Congress met than a number of voices, Senators Teller and Morgan and Culberson in the van, called for a simple denunciation of the Clayton-Bulwer Treaty or for legislation without waiting for Britain's by-your-leave. To forestall a direct challenge to England, administration leaders hustled the treaty forward again. According to Lodge, the Secretary of State besought the Foreign Relations Committee to detach the Davis amendment, a tactic which reflects unfavorably on Hay's perspicacity, for even after the full Senate added the amendment by a vote of 65 to 17 the treaty remained in a precarious state. To gather more votes its sponsors accepted two additional amendments, one specifically rescinding the Clayton-Bulwer Treaty and the other scotching the internationalization proposal. Fighting off even more extreme, politically motivated Democratic ploys, the Senate then approved the Hay-Pauncefote treaty—if it still deserved that title

[27] Hay to Choate, December 21, 1900, quoted in Charles C. Tansill, *Canadian-American Relations, 1875–1911* (New Haven, 1943), p. 219n.

—by a vote of 55 to 18 on December 20, 1900. Democrats divided almost evenly, but four fifths of the Republicans gave the rewritten agreement their support.

Observers speculated on Britain's reaction to this performance. "The opinion prevails in the Senate," the *New York Times* reported, "that the treaty will be approved by the British Ministry, even as amended." [28] In any case, the paper continued, senators would not give up amendments to secure British ratification. Senator Morgan professed unconcern at the prospect of war if the United States proceeded unilaterally, a prospect he considered unlikely but possible. To these reports from Washington, the *Times* added its own view, one shared by many who endorsed the original treaty, that the British government might accept the Davis amendment, a partial and obscurely worded revision, but would reject the treaty if further amended. Deeper pessimists including the Secretary of State believed even the Davis amendment ensured British rejection. Such people were correct in the narrow sense, wrong in assuming no substitute settlement possible.

Hay's senatorial critics, for all their bluster about proceeding without a treaty, did not press canal legislation during the three months Congress remained in session. Thus they invited further negotiation, negotiation which Hay considered useless but which he soon found could lead to agreement. The nation accepted Congress' inaction without protest, thus showing that, while suspicion and dislike of England could be mobilized to prevent concessions to that country, the same feelings no longer extended as far as a desire to force a confrontation with her.

A few British newspapers pictured developments in apocalyptic terms, London's *Daily Chronicle* even declaring, "we are back again to-day where we were at the time of the Venezuelan imbroglio." Most commentators, while unwilling to knuckle under to the Senate, were more philosophical, foreseeing that some way out would be found. Lansdowne and Salisbury took much the same view. Both deplored the Senate's interference

[28] *New York Times*, December 18, 1900.

while recognizing that sooner or later England would have to stand aside in the isthmus. They rejected Pauncefote's advice— "It would be wiser to secure the Treaty with amendment, objectionable as it is in principle, than have no treaty at all" [29]—and Hay's disingenuous, half-hearted argument that the amendments really did not change the treaty very much. Withholding an official reply until Congress adjourned, they then had Pauncefote transmit a note demolishing Hay's position and announcing London's unwillingness to ratify the treaty.

"I think Lord Lansdowne's position is both mischievous and ridiculous," wrote Theodore Roosevelt.[30] Yet the new Vice-President and most of those who had campaigned against Hay's treaty favored a new approach to London. The Secretary's supporters were only too willing to postpone a direct conflict. In a quick about-face, they even predicted that new negotiations would succeed. Lansdowne's note justified such a view, for in it he had never stated that an unamended Hay-Pauncefote treaty was the only alternative to continuation of the treaty of 1850, nor had he barred further negotiation. In a negative, graceless way, Lansdowne had invited Hay to reopen discussions.

And so discussions resumed. This time Hay carefully consulted senators in advance, and the draft forwarded to London toward the end of April 1901 reflected their views. Lansdowne quickly approved the new agreement, saying that it was only the form of Senate action he found unacceptable. Pauncefote soon sailed to England, and during the summer he and Lansdowne, Joseph Choate and Henry White thrashed out details, their discussions centering on nonfortification and the canal's neutrality in time of war. With Congress out of session there seemed no particular hurry, and the assassination of William McKinley in September diverted Washington's attention.

At the end of September, Hay reported to the new Presi-

<hr/>

[29] *Daily Chronicle* (London), quoted in *New York Times*, December 14, 1900; Pauncefote to Salisbury, December 9, 1900, quoted in John A. S. Grenville, *Lord Salisbury and Foreign Policy: The Close of the Nineteenth Century* (London, 1964), p. 383.

[30] Roosevelt to Lodge, March 27, 1901, Lodge, ed., *Correspondence of Roosevelt and Lodge*, vol. I, p. 485.

dent, "Our Canal Treaty is past the breakers." [31] Formal signature did not take place until November, after Lord Pauncefote returned to his post. The new Hay-Pauncefote treaty explicitly superseded the Clayton-Bulwer agreement, and it did not invite third parties to adhere. Furthermore, the treaty did not prohibit fortification of the canal, and, while paying lip-service to the idea of neutrality, did not require that the canal remain open to vessels of all nations in time of war. In all respects the Senate had its way, but, at the same time, on nonfortification and neutrality the treaty showed some deference, at least by silence, to Pauncefote's original concept. The Senate overwhelmingly approved the treaty in December, although until the end Hay had some fears and Roosevelt felt it prudent to mobilize weapons of persuasion.

Only half a dozen senators and a handful of journals opposed the treaty, primarily because they wanted Britain's surrender made even more explicit. Lacking the ammunition which had been at hand when the first, carelessly drawn treaty came before the country, they found it impossible to make much headway. Many Americans sighed with relief at the escape from controversy, even going so far as to picture it as a victory for both countries. "There is no 'backdown,' as there is no sweeping victory, on either side," the *Nation* declared. Most commentators paid tribute to the British cabinet, especially to Lord Lansdowne. "After fifty years," a Philadelphia paper said, "thanks to the wisdom, the friendliness, and the candor of the British Government, the two English-speaking nations see eye to eye on this momentous issue." [32] Hay received little praise, and although he later claimed the treaty as a personal triumph, he was hardly responsible for it. To all intents and purposes the Senate wrote the treaty at the behest of nationalistic sentiment in the United States.

Because this was so, an outburst of protest in Britain might

[31] Hay to Roosevelt, September 30, 1901, quoted in Dwight C. Minor, *The Fight for the Panama Route: The Story of the Spooner Act and the Hay-Herrán Treaty* (New York, 1940), p. 117.

[32] *Nation* (New York), vol. LXXIII (1901), p. 448; Philadelphia *Press*, quoted in *Literary Digest*, vol. XXIII (1901), p. 759.

have occurred. However, although the *Saturday Review*, playing its usual role of Cassandra, did object to "giving up everything and getting nothing except the hope of American friendship," [33] most commentators considered the elimination of controversy well worth the concessions made. Britain surrendered rights she no longer valued highly and was unlikely to be able to maintain except at the unthinkable cost of a very serious clash. Moreover, all could argue, with Lansdowne, that the difference between the two countries had been one of form rather than substance. To accept senatorial fiat was one thing, to negotiate in traditional—and relatively leisurely—fashion with American diplomats quite another.

Even broader convictions underlay approval of the Hay-Pauncefote Treaty and toleration, a short time later, of American belligerence on the Alaskan question. Englishmen in government and out agreed there must never be a war between the English-speaking peoples, and if this were so it was foolish to try to curb American power. Indeed, Britain might make the chances of future conflict even more impossible by conciliating rather than challenging the United States. Springing from this was a further conviction that, because in most ways the two nations sought the same ends, "accretion of strength to the United States," as Alexander Campbell puts it, "could only benefit Britain." [34] Only a strong America could properly share burdens of leadership imposed upon the English-speaking peoples, could discipline weak states and restrain predatory ones.

Obviously America was best fitted to play this role in the Western Hemisphere. A desire for help and an awareness that Britain's world responsibilities were outstripping her resources both counseled Albion to encourage the United States to step forward on the American continents. "The United States should hold the iron keys of the gate of the two oceans, and should have the power to close it against her enemies," commented a London journal. "That we should suffer in the end by conceding that

---

[33] *Saturday Review* (London), vol. XCII (1901), p. 707.
[34] Campbell, *Great Britain and the United States*, p. 82.

ambition is unthinkable. . . . We ought not to be found in America's way where our interests are secondary and hers are supreme." The British government, acting upon this principle, signed the second Hay-Pauncefote Treaty, and another British commentator wrote, "With the canal question disposed of one may now look forward with renewed hope to an amicable and equitable settlement of the long-drawn-out Canadian controversy. If that is eliminated from the field of diplomatic discussion the last source of friction will be removed, and the Ambassadors in Washington and London ought to be able to look forward to a long period of dignified ease." [35] Things never worked out quite that well, but the two settlements did wipe away the most important conflicts. By settling these issues as Washington desired, by refusing to allow the Canadians to exploit the one to improve their chances in the other, and by withdrawing major naval units from trans-Atlantic waters, the British government showed that it accepted, even welcomed, American hegemony in the New World.

[35] *Fortnightly Review*, vol. LXXVI (1901), p. 570; A. Maurice Low in *National Review*, vol. XXXVII (1901–1902), p. 428.

CHAPTER EIGHT

America's Hemisphere: The Caribbean

BRITISH WITHDRAWAL from the Western Hemisphere gained added dimensions in the Caribbean. There America most often exercised her new power, determined to expand her economic stake and especially to assure the security of routes to the isthmian canal. During Theodore Roosevelt's first term the United States saw, or thought she saw, the shadow of Germany across her path. On the other hand Britain welcomed or at worst accepted American ambitions. Having speeded the way toward a canal, she watched with sympathetic interest the drama which made the canal a reality. She also accepted new American interpretations of the Monroe Doctrine and the policies surrounding them. With one or two exceptions, she did not even challenge the dollar diplomacy initiated by President Taft and Secretary of State Knox, nor did she resist Woodrow Wilson's intervention in Mexican affairs, which, though differently motivated, similarly menaced British investments and trade. While, despite American fears of Germany, no European state seriously thought of resisting the growth of Washington's sphere of influence, none gained the good will that Britain gained. She best concealed what jealousy she felt, and she alone sacrificed an important, well-established political role.

The British spirit is illustrated in her attitude toward isthmian affairs. By the Hay-Pauncefote Treaty she stood aside, but

Roosevelt soon ran into difficulties in negotiations with Colombia, whose territory included Panama. London spurned Colombian feelers for diplomatic assistance and, after the Colombian Senate rejected a treaty forced on the chargé in Washington by Secretary Hay, British commentators more or less anticipated, and welcomed, what was to follow. When Panama rebelled, was quickly recognized by the United States, and signed a treaty establishing the canal zone, England viewed the developments with complacency and even satisfaction. Colombia, it was alleged, had brought all the difficulties upon herself. One or two editorialists said that Roosevelt had pressed the Latin-American republic hard, but most considered his conduct above criticism. They praised his decisiveness in taking advantage of the Panamanian revolution but denied he had played any part in its coming. Finally, Englishmen maintained that the whole affair was a welcome step toward American discipline of the hemisphere and the construction of a canal which would benefit England and the entire world.

In a series of other episodes which, unlike the Panama affair, directly involved British interests, both the government and the English people showed how far they were prepared to go to maintain American friendship. In the first of these, in the winter of 1902–1903, the British government began with a serious misstep but then agilely retreated. As in 1895, a controversy with Venezuela caused the trouble. Cipriano Castro, who seized power in that troubled land in 1899, refused to pay foreign obligations incurred by his predecessors. London, whose constituents were most seriously affected, and Berlin decided to force the dictator to behave. Joseph Chamberlain warned that common action with Germany would be unpopular in England, and Sir Michael Herbert, the new ambassador at Washington, wrote, "I wish we were going to punish Venezuela without the aid of Germany, for I am not sure that joint action will be very palatable here." [1] Why the cabinet—especially Lord Lansdowne, who dominated proceedings—decided to risk disapproval at home

[1] Herbert to Lansdowne, November —, 1902, quoted in Charles S. Campbell, *Anglo-American Understanding, 1898–1903* (Baltimore, 1957), p. 276.

and in the United States is unclear; none of the reasons later given by Lansdowne and Balfour, his superior, are convincing. Probably the cabinet missed the restraining hand of Salisbury, retired since July, and on the American side had not yet learned to accept Herbert's counsel. Perhaps Lansdowne, who deplored the growing split with Germany, grasped at a chance to initiate a rapprochement.

The best defense of his decision is that no one expected punishment of Castro to trouble the President. Roosevelt's performance in 1895 and opposition to the first Hay-Pauncefote treaty showed Britons he was, in the *Spectator's* phrase, "an upholder of the Monroe doctrine in its fullest and most complete form," but there was no reason to believe the doctrine barred efforts to punish delinquent American states. In his first annual message in December 1901, Roosevelt stated, "We do not guarantee any State against punishment . . . provided that punishment does not take the form of the acquisition of territory by any non-American power," a view Hay repeated to German and English representatives. Lord Cranborne, Salisbury's son, explained to the House of Commons that American authorities "recognize that the insistence of England that the Venezuelan Government should meet its engagements and respect the rights of British subjects is in no way an infraction of the Monroe doctrine." [2] What Cranborne and his superiors failed to realize was that the United States wanted reassurances no long-term occupation would follow—Germany gave such assurances in advance, Britain only after the crisis developed—and that any operation involving Germany would provoke lively suspicion.

Germany and England delivered an ultimatum to Castro on December 7, 1902. This rejected, they sank or seized Venezuelan gunboats, blockaded harbors, put troops ashore at one port and bombarded another. At first the United States seemed untroubled; Yankee diplomats took over responsibility for British interests and fought for the release of Englishmen tossed into

[2] *Spectator* (London), vol. LXXXVII (1901), p. 377; *Parliamentary Debates,* Fourth Series, vol. CXVI, p. 1263.

jail by Castro. The wind quickly changed. Newspapers deplored the use of force and the landing of European troops. Herbert reported increasing uneasiness in Washington, although he added that most observers criticized Britain only for going hand in glove with Germany. At the same time, perhaps even a bit earlier, criticism erupted in the London press and in Parliament. Speakers from both sides of the House of Commons attacked the cabinet. Arthur Lee summed up their argument, saying, "United States opinion would never have allowed Germany to have undertaken independent action against a South American State, and Germany, knowing this, had astutely cajoled us into a partnership, and thus was able to use us as a buffer between her and American public opinion." [3]

The government beat a hasty retreat, as much from fear of Parliament as because of what Lansdowne described as "signs that in the United States a storm of public opinion was rising against which the Government there would be helpless." With cabinet approval, the Prime Minister announced that England would not occupy Venezuelan territory, a statement bound to give comfort to Castro, and both Germany and Great Britain soon accepted in principle a Venezuelan proposal for arbitration supported with rising vigor by the Department of State. "The Administration has been most friendly throughout," Herbert reported, "and, if the dispute be referred without delay to arbitration . . . it will be almost safe to affirm that the friendly relations between Great Britain and the United States, instead of being impaired, have, if anything, been strengthened by the Venezuela incident." [4]

Herbert's hopes were quickly dashed, for it proved difficult to fix the details of arbitration. Britain and Germany, joined now by Italy, haggled with Herbert Bowen, the American minister at Caracas selected by Castro to negotiate with the Europeans for

[3] *Ibid.*, p. 1286.

[4] Lansdowne, quoted in Howard K. Beale, *Theodore Roosevelt and the Rise of America to World Power* (Baltimore, 1956), p. 415; Herbert to Lansdowne, December 29, 1902, George P. Gooch and Harold Temperley, eds., *British Documents on the Origin of the War, 1898–1914* (11 vols.; London, 1926–1938), vol. II, p. 164.

him. The Germans insisted, and the British stood reluctantly by
their pledge to act in concert, that claimants from their countries
must receive preferential treatment when Venezuela paid her
debts. The situation further deteriorated in the middle of January when a German vessel twice opened fire on a fort near Mara-
caibo. The concentration of more that fifty American warships in
the Caribbean, signs of official unease, and strident talk in the
newspapers and halls of Congress all warned London that America might clash with Germany and thus with Germany's collabo-
rator, Great Britain. "Our good relations with this country will
be seriously impaired if this Alliance with Germany continues
much longer," Herbert reported early in February. "The time
has almost come, in American opinion, for us to make the choice
between the friendship of the United States and that of Germany." [5] He pled with his government to throw creditors to the
wolfish Castro rather than surrender American good will.

And so Downing Street retreated once again, hastening to
reach a settlement before Parliament reassembled in the middle
of the month. Herbert's gloomy report caused Lord Lansdowne
to tell the German ambassador how deeply concerned he was;
Lansdowne stopped just short of a threat to abandon the pledge
of cooperation with Germany. On February 13 the disputants
signed a protocol referring the dispute and the question of preferential treatment to the Hague tribunal. Balfour told an audience at Liverpool, "We know that . . . [American] public
opinion is naturally sensitive upon what is known as the Monroe
Doctrine. But the Monroe Doctrine has no enemies in this country that I know of." [6] Within a few weeks the ruffled waters were
smooth again.

The Venezuelan affair did no permanent damage to relations at the governmental level. Herbert consistently reported
that public opinion and Congress, not the administration, were
the sources of difficulty. This became the standard British view,
agitation being explained away as a cynical political maneuver. "I

[5] Herbert to Lansdowne, February 7, 1903, *ibid.*, p. 172.
[6] *Times* (London), February 14, 1903.

believe we may expect all reasonable moral support from President Roosevelt," a ministerialist reassured the House of Commons in December, at the same time warning against the danger of a public outcry in defense of the sacred Monroe Doctrine. When the crisis had eased, the Foreign Secretary declared, "During the whole course of these negotiations not one single word was said or written by the United States Government which was not thoughtful and friendly and considerate toward this country," although, Lansdowne added, ". . . a section of public opinion in the United States, not, perhaps, sufficiently informed as to the facts of the case, . . . at one time took a different and somewhat excited view of the question." [7]

This distinction between the President and the public is reasonable, since Theodore Roosevelt roused himself only after the uproar in the United States developed. Moreover, by suggesting the febrility of the criticism, the distinction permitted Englishmen to downplay its importance, with the result that Germany received far more blame than the United States for the difficulties through which England passed. Actually, there were better reasons to minimize the importance of American protest as far as England was concerned. This protest was, first and foremost, a complaint against what was or might become a violation of the Monroe Doctrine, and Britain quickly made it clear she accepted that policy. Furthermore, Germany attracted far more criticism than her coadjutor. Hostility toward England showed its force during the Alaskan and isthmian controversies, when, except for Canada, no other nation provided a target. This time Germany served as a lightning rod, for a whole series of rumors had convinced the American people and even their President that Berlin was determined to establish a foothold in the Caribbean. While undoubtedly present, Anglophobia had become, at least for the moment, a less important mainspring of opinion than dislike of Germany.

Instantaneous protest in Parliament, supported by Conser-

[7] C. E. Schwann and Lansdowne, *Parliamentary Debates*, Fourth Series, vol. CXVI, p. 1252; vol. CXVIII, p. 1068.

vative back-benchers as well as Liberals, and the steady drumfire in the press convinced Americans that Venezuelan policy was a ministerial faux pas which did not reflect public sentiment or even the government's true intentions. "Why the Government should run contrary to the feeling in their own country and take the very great risk of arousing bitter feelings here is something hard to understand," Senator Lodge wrote.[8] Once made aware of American feeling, Cranborne, Lansdowne, and Balfour announced that England did not intend to challenge the Monroe Doctrine, and the British, particularly Sir Michael Herbert, fostered the belief, more accurate for the February crisis than for the one in December, that they had driven Germany to compromise. Americans, irritated by what they considered the dishonest German effort at about the same time to denigrate Pauncefote's role in 1898, found it easy to accept Britain's version of events. Roosevelt and the American people discounted British participation in the affair as an inept, only half-meant step taken in response to Germany's lead.

So it was that in July, when the Liberals last sought to score points against the ministry for its Venezuelan policy, Lord Cranborne could blandly reply, "The criticism which was directed against us in respect of our Venezuelan policy, that it estranged the United States, has turned out to be absolutely untrue. I say that our relations with the United States were never more friendly than they are at the present moment." [9] The British had had very good fortune, an opportunity to throw the onus on Germany. Although Cranborne was correct in this instance, the whole episode warned Downing Street not to run similar risks in the future.

One evening after the crisis had eased, Sir Michael Herbert dined at the White House. When his host observed that the American people would never permit the forceful collection of debts from Latin American states, the Ambassador replied "that

---

[8] Lodge to White, February 3, 1903, quoted in Beale, *Roosevelt and the Rise of America*, p. 426.
[9] *Parliamentary Debates*, Fourth Series, vol. CXXVI, p. 119.

I supposed in that case he would be ready to police the whole American Continent and prevent the general repudiation which would most likely follow any declaration of such a policy." This half-jocular remark pointed to a real problem. If, under the new interpretation of the Monroe Doctrine, Latin American states could not be punished by an outsider, might not many follow Cipriano Castro's example—and get away with it, as he had not? Britain could live with the expanded doctrine, for she had—a few grumbling reactionaries aside—conceded hemispheric leadership to the United States. She did believe the new claim carried with it new responsibilities. During Parliamentary discussion of Venezuela, a ministerial spokesman made the point quite explicit: "If the United States could see their way to the adoption of some effective course by which these almost periodical difficulties arising between the great Powers and some of the States of South America could be prevented, I think I may say it would meet with a cordial concurrence in this country." [10]

Roosevelt made no move for more than a year, preferring as usual to await a specific problem rather than to lay down principles in advance. Revolutions in Santo Domingo ruined that country's finances, and the various competitors often ignored their predecessors' pledges to repay European and American creditors out of customs revenue. For a long time the President refused to act. Then the Hague tribunal declared that investors from those powers which had coerced Castro deserved priority of payment; this decision invited the use of force, which Roosevelt, in the name of the Monroe Doctrine, had pronounced intolerable. After judicious preparation of the ground, particularly in a speech by Secretary of War Root, the Roosevelt Corollary to the Monroe Doctrine—a broad claim of police power in the hemisphere—was announced in the President's annual message of 1904. Root summed it up in blunt language, saying, "what we will not permit the great Powers of Europe to do, we will not permit

---

[10] Herbert to Lansdowne, March 26, 1903, quoted in Dexter Perkins, *The Monroe Doctrine, 1867–1907* (Baltimore, 1937), p. 364; Captain Greville, *Parliamentary Debates*, Fourth Series, vol. CXVIII, p. 63.

any American republic to make it necessary for the great Powers of Europe to do." [11] There soon followed, in February 1905, a protocol which provided for the administration of Santo Domingo's customs by an American citizen. This arrangement went into effect in April, and in due course Santo Domingo's foreign creditors recovered a substantial portion of their investment.

Unlike other powers, some of whom had not yet learned to accept American leadership in the Western Hemisphere gracefully, Britain reacted favorably to the Roosevelt Corollary. She cared little for the sensibilities of Latin Americans threatened by Roosevelt's big stick and was glad to see the United States bear part of the burden of disciplining backward, untrustworthy peoples. Moreover, British investors benefited from the new policy. Those with claims against Santo Domingo, having pressed so strongly for American action that one historian describes them as "in a measure responsible for the intervention . . . and the promulgation of the 'Corollary,'" benefited directly. In addition, the new American position stimulated Latin American securities generally, driving prices up as much as one hundred percent in 1905. One of the British journalists who cast a balance on Roosevelt's administration when he left office wrote, "He has enforced a new and much less one-sided view of the Monroe Doctrine, a view equally acceptable to the non-aggressive Powers of Europe and to all such South American States as pay their debts, keep their word, and act with decency." [12] As protector and policeman of the Western Hemisphere, Theodore Roosevelt served British interests and won British sympathies.

Taft and his secretary of state, Philander C. Knox, changed the emphasis of American policy, using their power not only to discipline Latin Americans but also to discriminate in favor of investors from the United States. Their dollar diplomacy aroused broader English criticism than any other American action since 1895, and for almost the only time backward-looking critics like

---

[11] Quoted in Perkins, *Monroe Doctrine*, p. 429.
[12] J. Fred Rippy, "The British Bondholders and the Roosevelt Corollary of the Monroe Doctrine," *Political Science Quarterly* (New York), vol. XLIX (1934), p. 198; Sydney Brooks, "President Roosevelt's Record," *Fortnightly Review* (London), vol. XCI (1909), p. 668.

the *Saturday Review* found numerous allies. British capitalists complained, and so did sturdy nationalists. Even some of America's best friends revised their views of her Latin American policy. A. Maurice Low objected that the Monroe Doctrine had become an instrument of commercial enterprise. "While in all other parts of the world . . . Americans are given the same privileges as other nationals, . . . in the American sphere of influence . . . discrimination exists," he objected. "Year after year greater obstacles are thrown in the way of the foreigner in Latin America." [13] Most complaints were directed against the misuse of American supremacy rather than the supremacy itself, however, and the protests were sporadic and carping rather than a rising crescendo of calls for positive counteraction.

Twice, the British government intervened in Central America in a way which challenged dollar diplomacy. Instead of undermining American friendship, the outcome of the two interventions showed how far the understanding between the two countries had gone. In 1909 London sent Lionel Carden, an experienced hand at that sort of thing, to Honduras to arrange the refunding of obligations to British bond-holders amounting, nominally at least, to some $120 million. When Washington erupted against the scheme, the British at first urged President Dávila to go ahead but then, thinking better of a challenge to the United States, withdrew from the field. Secretary Knox was left free to negotiate a settlement in 1911 which promised British creditors only about $3 million and placed Honduran finances under American control. Nor did Downing Street act when Knox's settlement failed of ratification, civil war broke out in Honduras, and American troops were landed to establish order. "We are pursuing a policy of drift, which is no policy at all," the *Saturday Review* complained at an early stage of the controversy, "while the Government of the United States is pushing its influence and encouraging its traders in every direction," in South America and Mexico as well as Central America. [14] Once

[13] *National Review* (London), vol. LXII (1914), p. 823.
[14] "The Importance of Spanish America," *Saturday Review* (London), vol. CX (1910), p. 69.

again, this time in an area of British economic predominance, a British ministry decided not to contest the field with the Americans.

In Guatemala, the British government stuck to its guns and the Americans showed a new spirit of toleration. There, too, British interests held most of the national debt, against which coffee revenues were pledged. After the local dictator, Manuel Estrada Cabrera, repudiated this pledge, London subjected him to pressure. Secretary Knox objected and sought to arrange a takeover of the Guatemalan debt by American interests, a maneuver frustrated by British opposition. Knox huffily informed the British government early in 1913 that he hoped it would "examine the question from a much broader point of view [and] . . . give friendlier consideration to the predominant interests of the United States in the Caribbean republics." [15] Britain refused to be deterred, perhaps because the Secretary spoke for a lame-duck administration. Backed by a warship, the ubiquitous Carden showed up in Guatemala in May, demanded restoration of the coffee revenues within five days, and won his way with Estrada Cabrera—and thereby a knighthood from his own government.

Carden's action, the only sustained challenge to America in the Caribbean from 1895 to 1914, failed to arouse the new Wilson administration, which could have forced England to reverse her course. Nor did the American press, lynx-eyed defender of the Monroe Doctrine, behave as it had behaved in 1895 and 1902. Estrada Cabrera was a faithless man, playing off the English-speaking powers against one another, and Americans considered England's grievances real. Years of success had convinced them that Britain accepted the principles of Mr. Monroe, that she could be trusted as no other power could be. The sense of ease added a further dimension to Anglo-American relations.

Moreover, unrest in Mexico took a new turn in the spring of 1913, overshadowing Guatemala and other foreign concerns. Mexico was, after all, far more important to the United States—

---

[15] Knox to Irwin G. Laughlin, January 7, 1913, *Foreign Relations*, 1913 (Washington, 1920), p. 558.

economically, politically, and strategically—than any nation in the hemisphere except Canada. More than fifty thousand Americans lived and worked in Mexico. Investment topped one billion dollars, with heavy concentrations in railroads, mining, ranching, and petroleum. The Waters-Pierce Oil Company, closely connected with Standard Oil, dominated the Mexican market, thanks to a monopoly on imports granted by the dictator, Porfirio Díaz, and to Edward L. Doheny's decision, after he brought in Mexican oil, not to engage in marketing there. For oilmen and others, the attitude and stability of the Mexican government was of paramount importance.

Toward the end of Díaz' regime the dictator sought to reduce his country's dependence upon American capital. He granted favorable terms to European investors, and by 1910 British interests, including shares in American or Mexican firms, approximated those of the United States. The chief figure was Weetman Pearson, or Lord Cowdray, as he became after contributing generously to the Liberal Party. Pearson enjoyed close relations with the dictator, whom he cultivated by such devices as naming the best dredge owned by his engineering firm after Díaz' wife. After Díaz granted him permission to drill on public lands, Pearson threw his energies into oil, and in 1910, just as the Mexican revolution began, he brought in his first great strike. Unlike Doheny, Cowdray decided to challenge Waters-Pierce, just as he had challenged American engineering and railroad interests in the past. When British and American policy toward Mexico diverged, Americans inside and outside the government leaped to the conclusion that Cowdray interests were responsible, while Englishmen thought they descried the sinister influence of Standard Oil.

During the first phase of the revolution—marked by the ouster of Díaz (he took refuge with a Cowdray lieutenant at Veracruz on his way to exile), Francisco Madero's installation as president, and finally the downfall of Madero early in 1913— there was little difficulty between London and Washington. Rumors of a connection between Madero and Standard Oil occasionally troubled British journalists, particularly when it seemed that Taft might intervene to support the new President. (In fact, Cowdray quickly established good relations with Díaz' successor and stood to lose little if Madero solidified his position.) The British government, however, remained faithful to the policy of leaving the role of policeman to the United States. "A conflagration in a neighbour's house," the ambassador at Washington wrote, "has sometimes justified interference which in normal circumstances would be burglary." [16] Some British journalists actively urged the United States to intervene, stressing the familiar argument that the Monroe Doctrine conferred responsibilities as well as privileges.

Victoriano Huerta ousted and killed Madero, establishing himself as provisional president, just before Woodrow Wilson's inauguration in 1913. Huerta's coup had the approval in advance of Ambassador Stronge, the English representative, and of Henry Lane Wilson, his American counterpart, a former Maderista soured by the President's apparent combination of ineptitude and radicalism. The British government, followed by other European powers, recognized Huerta's regime without even seeking to discover the attitude of the new American administration. This careless step, taken because Huerta seemed the only alternative to chaos, produced serious difficulties.

At first President Wilson was deceptively calm, simply announcing that his administration would withhold recognition until more facts were in. When Huerta refused to announce plans for the election of a successor, as Wilson desired, the latter came to believe that he dared to do so because he had been recognized by European governments, particularly England. Sniffing the air, the new President and others smelled petroleum. "The general opinion in the Cabinet," Secretary of the Navy Daniels wrote in his diary after a meeting at the White House, "was that the chief cause of this whole situation in Mex-

---

[16] Bryce to Grey, April 20, 1911, quoted in Peter A. R. Calvert, "The Mexican Revolution, 1910–1914: The Diplomacy of Anglo-American Conflict" (Cambridge University dissertation, 1964), p. 65.

ico was a contest between English and American Oil Companies to see which would control; that these people were ready to foment trouble and it was largely due to the English Company that England was willing to recognize Mexico before we did." When the Admiralty announced signature of an oil contract with Cowdray's firm, American suspicions redoubled. John Lind, one of Wilson's personal agents in Mexico, reported, "the control and monopoly of the oil fields and oil business in Mexico is not only the aim of the Lord Cowdray interests but also of the English government. England's Mexican policy . . . has been shaped . . . with this sole aim in view." [17] Even Henry Cabot Lodge, no friend of Wilson and a critic of his anti-Huerta policy, chided the oil-oriented policy of Britain in a letter to Spring Rice, the old crony who had just become ambassador to Washington.

The President recalled Ambassador Wilson, still a supporter of Huerta, and had the Department of State announce that since Huerta refused to arrange a presidential election the United States would not recognize his provisional government. Secretary of State Bryan explained to Spring Rice that "the President was convinced that if Huerta was definitely recognized the example to all South American Republics would be most deplorable, besides being directly opposed to principles enunciated by the President on his taking office." [18] In Wilson's mind Britain had become a major obstacle to the furtherance of democratic processes in the New World. Less firmly, because many Americans doubted that the ballot box could then easily be exported to Mexico, voices of complaint arose in the newspapers and the halls of Congress.

In fact, the British government had no desire to fight Wilson in Mexico. To Lodge, Spring Rice explained that Britain only desired peace in that country, a condition all powers except

---

[17] E. David Cronon, ed., *The Cabinet Diaries of Josephus Daniels,* 1913–1921 (Lincoln, Neb., 1963), p. 43; Lind to Bryan, October 25, 1913, quoted in Arthur S. Link, *Wilson: The New Freedom* (Princeton, 1956), p. 372.
[18] Spring Rice to Grey, August 17, 1913, quoted in Calvert, "Mexican Revolution," p. 223.

the United States thought most likely under a Huerta regime. However, he added, because "Britain recognizes the dominant position of the U.S. in Mexico," she would not oppose the President's policy. Before Washington openly broke with Huerta, Sir Edward Grey gently urged the United States to accept the fact of his rule, but he never pressed his view as strongly as other powers. When Wilson sent Lind to Mexico to try to secure a free election and Huerta's withdrawal from power, Grey complied with Wilson's request that the powers urge Huerta to receive Lind—failure to do so, said Grey, "would in our opinion be a grave mistake and put Mexico in the wrong"—and Stronge did unofficially introduce Lind to the dictator. (In Berlin, the young American chargé, Joseph Grew, found the Wilhelmstrasse more inclined to argue. "It is unfortunately clear," he reported, "that the views of the German government are diametrically opposed to those of the government of the United States.")[19] Moreover, the British government, like all foreign powers, aided Wilson's effort to bankrupt the Huerta regime by discouraging loans to him. None of these actions mollified Wilson, although in retrospect they seem significant.

Grey acted as he did although he, and almost everyone in England, considered the President's policy quixotic or worse. Of the major journals of opinion, only the *Economist* supported Wilson's decision to break with Huerta, and even that journal argued that "watchful waiting"—the President's phrase—would not bring Huerta down. Many believed Wilson's policy, however noble in motive, served the interest of sinister American capitalists he opposed at home, capitalists who had inspired the Madero revolt and now desired to see his heirs regain power. This feeling infected even the Prime Minister, H. H. Asquith, and Grey admitted that Huerta's fall might hurt British investors. "I do not dispute," he wrote, "the inconvenience and untoward results of

[19] Spring Rice to Lodge, August 2, 1913, quoted in Stephen Gwynn, *The Letters and Friendships of Sir Cecil Spring Rice* (2 vols.; Cambridge, Eng., 1929), vol. II, p. 191; Spring Rice to Bryan, August 11, 1913, quoted in Ray Stannard Baker, *Woodrow Wilson: Life and Letters* (8 vols.; Garden City, 1927–1939), vol. IV, p. 269; Grew to Bryan, August 16, 1913, quoted in *ibid.*, p. 269.

United States policy, but . . . His Majesty's Government cannot with any prospect of success embark upon an active counterpolicy to that of the United States, or constitute themselves the champions of Mexico or any of these republics against the United States." [20]

Wise as this maxim was, Sir Edward had violated it by recognizing Huerta as provisional president, and he proceeded to compound that error by appointing Sir Lionel Carden to succeed Stronge. Carden had a bad reputation in the United States because of his activities in Nicaragua and others in Cuba, where as British minister he opposed American interests so vigorously that Secretary Knox asked London, unsuccessfully, to recall him. As one American historian has observed, "If the British Government had ransacked its diplomatic force to find the one man who would have been most objectionable to the United States, it could have made no better selection." Moreover, Carden's reputation was deserved. A month after his arrival in Mexico City he horrified the German ambassador, an unusually tactful representative of Berlin, by saying, "He has always found them [the Americans] people of bad faith, unbelievable crooks, swindlers. . . . Sir Lionel thinks that now he has run the United States to earth in Mexico, 'now there is a chance of exploding that most foolish of all theories: the Monroe Doctrine.' " [21] In only slightly less flamboyant language, Carden had acquainted Grey with his views before leaving England, and nothing can excuse the Foreign Secretary for the unnecessary risk he ran in sending Sir Lionel to Mexico.

The new envoy arrived in Mexico City on October 11, the day after Huerta arrested Maderista members of the Chamber of Deputies and assumed dictatorial powers, but Carden did not feel this event required him to seek guidance from London. Although Grey had repeatedly assured Washington that Britain

---

[20] Grey to Carden, October 17, 1913, quoted in Calvert, "Mexican Revolution," p. 246.

[21] Burton J. Hendrick, *The Life and Letters of Walter H. Page* (3 vols.; Garden City, 1922–1925), vol. I, p. 197; Paul von Hintze to Bethmann-Hollweg, November 11, 1913, quoted in Calvert, "Mexican Revolution," p. 289.

recognized Huerta only as a temporary authority until elections took place, Carden proceeded to the presidential palace and, in the most ostentatious manner, presented his credentials. Interviewed by American reporters, he derided the election scheme, to which Wilson was devoted, as "ridiculous." "Mexico, he said," according to the *New York Times* correspondent, "needed punitive and remedial methods—a strong man and statesman of no mean ability." [22]

The President, taken aback by Huerta's coup when he thought his own policy on the verge of success, understandably linked Carden (and, by extension, Cowdray) with Huerta's decision to defy him. He composed a fiery memorandum from which he ordered the Department of State to prepare a circular to foreign powers. In this paper he claimed paramountcy in Mexico for the United States, asserted that only foreign support kept Huerta going, and pledged to bring about his overthrow. The circular, he ordered, should be "As strong and direct as the courtesies and proprieties of pacific diplomacy permit," and the copy to England should include an addendum pointing to her special responsibility: "The bottom was about to drop out [on Huerta] when Sir Lionel Carden appeared on the scene and took charge of his rehabilitation." [23] A draft of the proposed circular was leaked to the press, hitting London like a thunderbolt.

Wilson underlined his anger by two further steps. He had Ambassador Page complain to Grey, a task the envoy performed with zest since he shared Wilson's feelings about Carden and Cowdray. "Our conversations about Mexico," the Foreign Secretary wrote in his memoirs, "were not always very sympathetic." The President himself delivered a major speech on Latin American policy at Mobile, Alabama, in October. Assuring Latinos that America desired to work with them as friendly equals, he went on to prophesy that in time they would escape the stranglehold of foreign concessionaires (read Cowdray), working often in

[22] *New York Times,* October 22, 1913.
[23] Wilson memorandum, n.d., quoted in Link, *Wilson: The New Freedom,* p. 367.

league with local autocrats (read Huerta), and promised to aid
the struggle for emancipation. That the Mobile address aimed at
the Mexican situation was obvious to England, where it aroused
deep concern. The *Saturday Review* complained, "the ideal
forms a very convenient cloak for uncompromising realism. . . .
Unconsciously, no doubt, he [Wilson] is becoming the tool of
a gang of his own plutocrats who are anxious to see a change in
Mexican economic conditions." [24] When Wilson blamed British
policy upon Cowdray, it was only just, if ironic, that Englishmen
saw John D. Rockefeller and Edward L. Doheny lurking behind
his policy.

Whatever Grey thought of this line of reasoning, he remained convinced that his country must accept a secondary role
in Mexico, and he worked to seal off the controversy. His task
was made somewhat easier by the fact that, thanks to strenuous
criticism by the counselor of the Department of State, John Bas-
sett Moore, the note drafted at Wilson's direction and leaked to
the press had never been sent, thus making it unnecessary for
Grey to send a formal answer which could hardly have avoided a
direct challenge. First Grey procured from Carden a statement
that the *New York Times* had misquoted him. He extorted from
Cowdray a public statement, really a financial accounting, showing how little he had been connected with Huerta, and when this
failed to quiet American complaints Cowdray called upon Page
four successive days to assure the Ambassador of his good will.
Speaking at the Guildhall, the Prime Minister announced, to
cheers, that Britain would neither intervene in Mexico nor do
anything else to frustrate American policy; he even maintained,
with a straight face, that there had been no acrimony between
the two governments. The *Times*, in what was probably an inspired editorial the next day, repeated Asquith's arguments and
concluded, "there will be no desire on the part of any onlooker
here to cavil about any steps which President Wilson . . . may

[24] Viscount Grey of Fallodon, *Twenty-Five Years, 1892–1916* (2 vols.; London, 1925), vol. II, p. 99; *Saturday Review*, vol. CXVI (1913), p. 548. (The order of the sentences in the latter quotation has been reversed.)

think necessary." [25] Finally, on November 14, poor Sir Lionel, at London's direction, accompanied other diplomats who called upon Huerta to urge him to resign.

While these incidents were taking place, Grey's personal secretary, Sir William Tyrell, was en route to Washington. His visit, although originally planned simply to provide a stand-in for Spring Rice, who was ill, permitted a tidy conclusion to the controversy. Grey's campaign apparently had convinced the President that British policy was not what he had recently suspected it to be, for he brushed aside Tyrell's attempt to explain Carden's attitude, saying it was "of historical interest only." Wilson did not explain in detail his plans toward Mexico (if he had any), simply saying he intended to "teach the South Americans to elect good men." [26] The Briton replied that he could see little difference between Huerta and his rivals, Venustiano Carranza and Pancho Villa, but he did assure Wilson that Britain would support American policy and even use her influence at Berlin and Paris to win their cooperation. After the interview broke up, Tyrell told Wilson's friend Colonel House how pleased he had been with it.

It was symbolic of the new situation that only a few days later, when Carranzistas threatened to destroy Cowdray's oil fields at Tuxpam unless paid $100,000, the local American consul, backed up by a warship, intervened to block the move. Moreover, to ease the British ministry's domestic position, Wilson promised Tyrell to try to promote a Mexican government which would recognize the sanctity of foreign investments. "I hope," he continued, "Sir Edward Grey will feel free to convey the contents of this letter to those British and Canadian investors for whom he, naturally, feels a sympathetic attitude." In return, London recalled Carden, the symbol of discord, early in 1914. Page became exultant. "When your policy was first flung at 'em," he wrote Wilson, "they show^d at best a friendly incredu-

[25] *Times*, November 11, 1913.
[26] Tyrell to Grey, November 14, 1913, quoted in Calvert, "Mexican Revolution," pp. 302–303.

lity: What, set up a moral standard for government in Mexico? Everybody's mind then was fixed merely on the restoring of order —the safety of investments. . . . Well, they've followed a long way. . . . They've done all we ask[d] and more; and, more wonderful yet, they've come to understand what we are driving at, and have given one of their financial Lords a tip that has cost him a long-shot more than his Peerage cost in the beginning. As this poor world goes, all this seems to me rather handsomely done." [27]

Page exaggerated. Cowdray hardly took "a tip"; despite the revolutionary upheaval in Mexico, he carried out his Admiralty contract, vital to Britain after the outbreak of war with Germany. Nor had London reversed policy as decisively as Page believed. As Peter A. R. Calvert, the closest student of the whole affair, observes, "the Government of the United States deluded itself into believing that the British Government was pursuing a policy hostile to its own in Mexico, and, having done so, deluded itself out again." [28] Governments, however, often act upon misinformation and misconception; quarrels are no less real for that. Only the wisdom of Counselor Moore and the rapid series of reassurances extended by Grey prevented serious trouble over Mexico. If it is true that Sir Lionel Carden acted on his own (and thus demonstrated the foolishness of appointing him), it is also true that neither Wilson nor Huerta could know this. Carden's open support strengthened Huerta's resistance to Washington; the Ambassador's muffling and then his removal were matters of substance, not mere symbolism.

Despite Page's reports to the contrary, the British had undergone no change of heart. Permitting Huerta to hold power they still would have preferred, forceful intervention they were prepared to accept, but the policy of "watchful waiting" still seemed to them the worst of all worlds. Sometimes British papers gave Wilson credit for the nobility of his intentions, but

[27] Wilson to Tyrell, November 23, 1913, quoted in Link, *Wilson: The New Freedom*, pp. 376–377; Page to Wilson, January 8, 1914, quoted in Calvert, "Mexican Revolution," pp. 283–284.
[28] *Ibid.*, p. 284.

almost all urged him to make his policy effective by vigorous action. As for the government, it shared the same opinions but refrained from giving advice. "There is nothing to do with this hardened saint," Spring Rice sighed in February 1914.[29] To avoid alienating the United States, England accepted a policy in which she heartily disbelieved.

The few remaining months before Sarajevo showed how far London was prepared to go. In February, while the rebel chieftain looked on, Villa's forces killed an English mining engineer, and even the *Times* joined the call for vengeance raised by less restrained journals as well as Conservative speakers in Parliament. Grey refused to be moved. In April, when American troops landed at Veracruz to prevent the delivery of arms consigned to Huerta (and carried in a German vessel, the *Ypiranga*), British papers applauded the use of force. The *Saturday Review*, formerly a supporter of Huerta but now reconciled to a different solution, declared, "now American troops have landed they cannot return until a stable and satisfactory Government has been established in Mexico. If that intention is avowed the States can feel certain that their action will be watched with sympathy and approval by the other Great Powers." The Royal Navy, like the Kriegsmarine, helped to evacuate American citizens, and the British representative in Mexico City aided Bryan's efforts to bring about neutralization of the oil fields. Moreover, to make it crystal clear that Great Britain had no intention of taking advantage of American difficulties, she agreed that "the status quo should be preserved . . . and that persons or corporations, Mexican and foreign should be prevented from taking advantage of the disturbed condition which prevailed in the oil fields." [30] This understanding was later extended to mining properties as well. Finally, when Wilson disappointed advocates of vigor like the *Saturday Review* by accepting a proposal by Argentina, Brazil, and Chile

[29] Spring Rice to Tyrell, February 7, 1914, quoted in Gwynn, *Spring Rice*, vol. II, p. 202.

[30] *Saturday Review*, vol. LXVII (1914), p. 526; memorandum, British embassy to Department of State, May 25, 1914, *Foreign Relations, 1914* (Washington, 1922), p. 705.

to mediate the conflict, Britain joined Germany and France in pressing Huerta to agree. Thus when war broke out in Europe that summer the Mexican situation was very much what it had been a year earlier, in a state of instability Britain deplored but tolerated so as to avoid difficulty with the United States.

In the spring of 1911, in a secret speech, Sir Edward Grey outlined British foreign policy for the Committee of Imperial Defence and visiting dominion delegates. "The greatest civilised Power in the world, outside Europe, is the United States . . . ," he declared. "The policy of the United States has been formulated under the name of the Monroe Doctrine. We have not the least idea, and, indeed, we should be very foolish if we had, of attempting to acquire fresh territory on the American Continent." Moreover, Grey continued, "In South America it is an instruction to all our Diplomatists that they are to regard their work there as not entailing upon them taking a hand in the politics of South America or acquiring political influence, . . . so we shall not come across the United States as regards our policy in South America." [31]

Despite American misunderstandings partially the fruit, in turn, of inept British diplomacy, the Mexican affair really demonstrated that England was determined not to "come across" the policy of the United States. From the Hay-Pauncefote treaties to the Washington visit of Sir William Tyrell, both Conservative and Liberal governments demonstrated that, for them, the affection of Canada and the weight of British influence in Latin America counted less than the friendship of the United States. Diplomats of the old school, like Sir Lionel Carden, were muffled. Ultraconservatives and devoted supporters of the empire were ignored, primarily because, in urging resistance to the United States, they spoke for a tiny minority in British opinion. As a result, the American stance also changed. Statesmen came to believe, with Roosevelt, that all sources of contro-

[31] May 26, 1911, George P. Gooch and Harold Temperley, eds., *British Documents on the Origin of the War, 1898–1914* (11 vols.; London, 1926–1938), vol. VI, p. 786.

versy had been liquidated, and this belief survived Wilson's outbursts over Mexico. More slowly, British policy in the Western Hemisphere undermined hostile sentiment, with the result that the corrosive suspicion which helped defeat the first Hay-Pauncefote treaty and complicated settlement of the Alaskan boundary lost force. English statesmen deserved high marks for their accomplishments.

CHAPTER NINE

The Anglo-Americans
and Japan

The United States and Japan burst out of isolation at almost the same time, and in the Far East they seemed at first to have the same ends in view. Thus when, after the Americans declined overtures for cooperation, Britain turned to Japan, an alliance between the two island empires did not seem to threaten Anglo-American friendship. Many observers even considered the United States a silent partner in that alliance. Later, particularly after the Russo-Japanese war, American and Japanese purposes came into conflict. From 1905 to 1914 British diplomacy faced a difficult challenge, to maintain the alliance without harming relations with the United States. Britain's success was an important factor in the great rapprochement.

Although Britain also had political ends in view, in the Far East the roots of her policy and America's were predominantly commercial. Britain's position in China lived in the past, America's in a hope of the future. At the end of the nineteenth century, Britain controlled only one third of foreign investment in China, but she dominated that country's trade. She accounted for nearly two thirds of China's foreign commerce and her ships carried eighty-five percent of it. Americans had trivial investments in China—less than $20 million—and enjoyed less than ten percent of her trade. This trade contributed marginally to

American economic health and never reached the size of commerce with Japan, about which much less concern was shown,
but capitalists, traders, and statesmen dreamed of a gigantic market. "America's overriding ambition in the Pacific [was]," as
Thomas McCormick has observed, "the penetration and, ultimately, the domination of the fabled China market." The
United States never gained more than a sixth of China's trade, a
peak reached in 1905, but hope died hard. "In that far-off hemisphere lie the great markets of the future," an Illinois congressman proclaimed in 1904.[1] Many Americans, agreeing with him,
believed it the duty of the Department of State to assist businessmen seeking to build up trade with the Far East.

The veteran and the hopeful parvenu both favored, as they
had for more than half a century, that form of most-favored-
nation treatment of commerce called the Open Door. At the
close of the century the Open Door came under a novel form
of attack. The powers began to seek spheres of influence in
China, areas in which Peking granted them investment privileges
and political concessions. In 1895 European powers balked
Japan when she sought to turn her easy victory in the Sino-Jap-
anese war to the fullest advantage, but the island nation clearly
saw her destiny in Korea and Manchuria, nominally under Peking's direction. The Russians, too, pressed in that direction, and
the Germans had their ambitions to fulfill. In the spheres investment opportunities were by definition unequal, and moreover it
was at least highly likely that the controlling power would use its
position to hinder the trade of others.

Britain, well established in China, deplored developments
which might chip away at her position there. The Americans,
only rarely tempted to seek spheres for themselves, confident of
success in a fair fight between businessmen, looked upon the
predators with distaste. They even conferred special virtue upon
themselves for their abstemiousness; said the New York Times,

[1] Thomas McCormick, "Insular Imperialism and the Open Door: The China
Market and the Spanish-American War," Pacific Historical Review (Glendale,
Calif.), vol. XXXII (1963), p. 155; Foss, in Congressional Record, 58th Con-
gress, 2nd Session, p. 2066.

"the principle of equal opportunity, the principle of the open door, is the principle of civilization, and . . . the advocate of it . . . is a benefactor of mankind."[2] Except that Britain had always to view Asian developments in the light of her European needs, a matter most Americans found it hard to understand, the two nations seemed destined to move hand in hand in the Far East.

During the winter of 1897–1898 Russia sought concessions in Manchuria, causing some talk of Anglo-American collaboration. (A German move into Shantung roused much less concern.) Cushman Davis, chairman of the Senate Foreign Relations Committee, declared that if American commercial rights were threatened the United States would have to abandon isolation and perhaps cooperate with England. Senator Lodge wrote to Henry White, his friend in London, "If I had my way I should be glad to have the United States say to England that we would stand by her in her declaration that the ports of China must be opened to all nations equally or to none." Encouraged by American concern, Joseph Chamberlain proposed to Balfour, in charge at the Foreign Office in Salisbury's absence, that he "approach the United States officially, and . . . ask an immediate reply from them to the question—Will you stand in with us in our Chinese policy?"[3] Chamberlain, who was prepared to seek aid from Germany as well and even to drive the Russians from Port Arthur by force, was not surprised that his colleagues agreed only to approach the United States.

Sir Julian Pauncefote therefore asked authorities at Washington if they were prepared to cooperate with Great Britain. The inquiry came at a bad time, when the administration was wrestling with the Cuban problem. Moreover, it preceded the full flourishing of the dream of the China market which followed Dewey's victory at Manila. Timing was not the only problem.

[2] *New York Times*, April 7, 1905.

[3] Lodge to White, January 31, 1898, quoted in John A. S. Grenville and George B. Young, *Politics, Strategy, and American Diplomacy: Studies in Foreign Policy, 1873–1917* (New Haven, 1966), p. 289; Chamberlain to Balfour, February 3, 1898, quoted in Blanche E. C. Dugdale, *Arthur James Balfour* (2 vols.; New York, 1937), vol. I, p. 185.

McKinley was hardly the man to throw over a hallowed tradition like isolationism, whatever loose talk there might be about cooperation, and the nation would have been highly critical of any President who did so. So the Chief Executive and Assistant Secretary Day both told Pauncefote that while the United States agreed that no nation should gain special privileges in China, they saw no present threat to that principle. On Pauncefote's report, a Foreign Office official minuted, "There is not much solid comfort in this." [4]

More or less as consolation for the failure to save Port Arthur from the Russians, Britain took Weihaiwei for herself. She saw nothing inconsistent between this action and renewed suggestions, in December 1898 and January 1899, of joint action to protect China. These efforts, so feebly pressed as to suggest London had little hope for them, failed to move McKinley.

Thus, although two British subjects contributed to the chain of events which produced Hay's first Open Door note in September 1899, Her Majesty's Government played no part. Lord Charles Beresford, a stormy petrel who dreamed of glory as the reogranizer and strengthener of China, paid a visit to the United States in the winter of 1898–1899, a visit described as "one long after-dinner speech in favor of the open door," [5] and upon his return home wrote a book, *The Break-Up of China*, which aimed, partly with American readers in view, to stimulate action against the Russian threat. Despite suspicions to the contrary, Beresford's visit was his own idea, although British secret-service funds helped pay the expenses of the trip to China which preceded it. Even more clearly, Alfred E. Hippisley, an English employee of the Chinese Imperial Customs Service who played a critical though secret role, had no connection with the British government. Hippisley, visiting his wife's parents while on his way home on leave, simply used his opportunity to urge action in

[4] Minute on Pauncefote to Foreign Office, March 17, 1898, quoted in R. G. Neale, *Great Britain and United States Expansion: 1898–1900* (East Lansing, 1966), p. 118.

[5] A. Whitney Griswold, *The Far Eastern Policy of the United States* (New York, 1938), p. 48.

China's interest. He did so through William W. Rockhill, an advisor of Hay who had served in China and there introduced Hippisley to the Baltimore girl who became his wife.

Throughout July and August 1899, Hippisley corresponded with Rockhill, and Rockhill with Hay, who was on vacation in New Hampshire. Two considerations predominated: the threat posed by spheres of influence and the danger of exposing McKinley's administration to criticism as England's errand boy. Contrary to the British government's current position, Hippisley urged Rockhill to accept spheres of influence as inevitable and merely to insist upon equal treatment of commerce within them; in the end Rockhill and Hay came around to this view. Hippisley's most difficult problem was persuading the Americans to act at all. "The senseless prejudices in certain sections of the 'Senate and people,'" Hay wrote, "compel us to move with great caution." Hippisley argued that unilateral action would disarm critics, and he even predicted that, far from aiding the Democrats in 1900, "the announcement . . . that the U.S. had secured China's independence and so served the cause of peace & civilization would be a trump card for the Admin. and crush all the anti-imperialism agitation of Bryan, Croker & Co." [6] Again the Americans came to agree.

The note, sent to the first addressees on September 6 and to others a few weeks later, asked the recipients to promise equal opportunity for all in their spheres. Hay's note, which received great praise when published with the replies in March 1900, accomplished next to nothing. Not only did it recognize rather than challenge spheres of influence, but it also made clear that the United States would do nothing, certainly not cooperate with another power, to enforce the American request. For officials in England, Hay's action was a confirmation of earlier disappointments.

Thus, although the British public applauded, Lord Salisbury responded much more coolly. First he suggested that Kowloon,

[6] Hay to Rockhill, August 7, 1899, quoted in *ibid.*, p. 67; Hippisley to Rockhill, August 21, 1899, quoted in *ibid.*, p. 71.

an English colony, and Weihaiwei, leased territory, ought not to be considered spheres of influence within which commercial equality should be expected. Then he compromised, dropping the claim about Weihaiwei except to make his acceptance conditional upon that of all other powers with similar positions in China.

In the end the Prime Minister put a good face on things. When Henry White, afraid he might argue that the even more qualified and conditional replies of other countries excused Britain from her pledge, asked his opinion of them, Salisbury blandly replied that "they seemed to cover the ground exactly." He complimented Hay on "a work of great importance and utility to the world and especially to our respective countries." [7] Since 1895 the Prime Minister had learned to treat the Americans in a tactful fashion.

How little he relied upon the Americans and their diplomacy-by-manifesto soon became apparent. A few months later the Boxer uprising, an anti-foreign crusade, swept northern China. The legations at Peking, defended by a motley force of soldiers and civilian volunteers, came under siege at the end of June. Westerners feared their people had all been killed, and the London *Times* printed the obituary of Sir Claude MacDonald, British minister and commander of the defense. Secretary of State Hay dramatically released contrary information, and in August an international force raised the siege. Foreign troops remained until China signed an agreement including an indemnity and an apology in September 1901.

From the beginning there were, from the British and American points of view, two dangers: that the Boxers would massacre foreigners and that outside powers would take advantage of their troops' presence to demand concessions from China in the guise of compensation for losses of life and property. Prompt arrival of an American military force to aid the anti-Boxer campaign (and its continued presence to give meaning to Washing-

---

[7] White to Hay, n.d., quoted in Allan Nevins, *Henry White: Thirty Years of American Diplomacy* (New York, 1930), p. 167.

ton's diplomacy) seemed desirable to London. Secretary of State Hay took the same view. However, 1900 was an election year, and President McKinley moved very cautiously. At first he sought to avoid the use of force, and the London *Times* complained that his government seemed "inclined to sit on the fence as long as it can, . . . [rather] than to act with vigour and promptitude." [8] Ultimately an American contingent reached China, where it played a part in the march to Peking. Against Hay's wishes, the President withdrew it as quickly as possible, before the election. Thus American diplomacy had little weight behind it during the long negotiations which followed. From the British viewpoint, American troops arrived too late and left too soon.

Nor could England draw much consolation from the alternative course selected by McKinley and Hay. In response to stirrings, particularly by Russia, they fell back upon another note. This one, dispatched on July 3, 1900, informed the powers that the United States supported Chinese territorial integrity and would deplore the creation of new spheres of influence. Like its predecessor, the second Open Door note brought Hay acclaim. His friend Henry Adams later wrote that Hay "put Europe aside and set the Washington Government at the head of civilization. . . . History," Adams proclaimed, "broke in halves." British praise, though less extreme, was considerable. The note deserved "general approbation and welcome in this country . . . ," the *Times* said. "The reason is simple. In China the main interests of the United States and Great Britain are at present identical." A. Maurice Low, always dreaming of an Anglo-American league, believed the Americans had learned that "civilization is now witnessing a conflict between the Slav and the Saxon, a conflict in which the United States cannot be a silent spectator, but must perforce . . . become an active participant." [9]

Although the new note extended the scope of the Open

[8] *Times* (London), June 9, 1900.

[9] Henry Adams, *The Education of Henry Adams* (Modern Library ed.; New York, 1931), p. 392; *Times*, July 11, 1900; Low, in *National Review* (London), vol. XXXV (1900), p. 811.

Door from commercial privileges to spheres of influence, once again Washington threatened no action against those who challenged its wishes. Hay did not even seek pledges of forbearance, and only Britain deigned to reply to his circular. The Secretary knew he had done little to prevent extortion from China. He wrote to his aide Alvey A. Adee, "If it were not for our domestic politics we could, and should, join with England, . . . and make our ideas prevail. But in the present morbid state of the public mind toward England that is not to be thought of." [10]

In the next few years the administrations of McKinley and his successor, Roosevelt, showed great concern over events in the Far East. In a small way, by adding its voice to those urging the Russians to quit Manchuria, Washington supported an Anglo-Japanese campaign which forced cancellation of a half-completed agreement between Peking and St. Petersburg, and in April 1902 extorted from Russia a promise to withdraw forces sent to Manchuria during the rebellion. On the whole, at least until the Russo-Japanese War, the Americans did not develop a real policy (except, a British cabinet member complained, the policy of "looking out for a profit from other people's failures"), and the naval forces which might have given strength to their wishes were largely withdrawn to face the presumed German threat in the Caribbean. In 1903 Sir Michael Herbert hoped the Americans "might become educated up to a more vigorous policy . . . in the next two or three years." [11] Until that happy time Britain would have to look elsewhere for support.

Britain first tried Germany. By an agreement in October 1900, both powers pledged to support equal commercial opportunity and Chinese territorial integrity. This agreement, the last negotiated by Salisbury before he handed over the Foreign Office to Lansdowne, soon collapsed, for Berlin refused to agree that it applied to Manchuria, the area where the Russian threat

[10] Hay to Adee, September 14, 1900, quoted in Tyler Dennett, *John Hay: From Poetry to Politics* (New York, 1933), p. 319.

[11] Arnold-Foster to Lansdowne, December 25, 1903, quoted in George Monger, *The End of Isolation: British Foreign Policy, 1900–1907* (London, 1963), p. 151; Herbert to Lansdowne, May 8, 1903, quoted in *ibid.*, p. 131.

weighed most heavily. Nevertheless, British statesmen, including Lansdowne and especially Balfour, were reluctant to give up the search for German friendship. (When Balfour persevered longer than Lansdowne thought wise, the Foreign Secretary employed the disingenuous argument that an alliance with Wilhelm would affront the United States. As his under-secretary put it, the Kaiser's anti-Americanism was alone "sufficient to condemn the policy as far as we are concerned." [12] Yet only a few months earlier Lansdowne had sought agreement with Germany, and the next year he led Britain into cooperation with her against Venezuela.) Wilhelm responded frostily, and after this time, despite the common action against Castro, Anglo-German relations ran downhill. Nor did Lansdowne have more success with Russia, Britain's great rival in Asia and a threat to her positions in Persia, India, and the Far East. The Foreign Secretary's efforts to reach a broad accommodation foundered on the issue of Persia. London was not yet ready for the bold step of an approach to Paris. So Britain turned to Japan, a power which had become increasingly friendly in recent years, which shared her fears of Russian expansion and had, in England's view, played a creditable role during the Boxer uprising and its aftermath.

Lansdowne opened conversations with the Japanese ambassador in the summer of 1901. When these went well he asked the cabinet to approve an offer of alliance. Lord Salisbury, still prime minister and the personification of British isolationism, at first demurred, and Arthur Balfour supported his uncle. However, after Salisbury secured changes in Lansdowne's scheme, the cabinet gave its approval. On January 30, 1902, the Anglo-Japanese alliance came into being. The two parties proclaimed their devotion to the Open Door and the territorial integrity of China. More important, they recognized one another's special interests in China and the predominant position of Japan in Korea. If either party went to war against one opponent, the other pledged its neutrality; if either went to war with more than one enemy, the other promised assistance.

[12] Cranborne memorandum, November 18, 1901, quoted in *ibid.*, p. 66n.

The alliance meant different things to the two signatories. Britain saw it as a prop to the status quo, a way of sharing the burden of defense against Russian ambitions. The Japanese hoped to revise the status quo in their own interest. They valued the alliance because it reduced the danger of war with France as well as Russia if they pressed northward. Lansdowne, who knew the alliance might stimulate Japanese aggression, accepted the risks. Britain was too weak to defend her position without aid, and Japanese advances, if they came, were likely to be in a northerly direction, away from the main theater of British interest. Moreover the alliance destroyed the specter of a Russo-Japanese settlement, a possibility much rumored in 1901, which would have left Britain to face both Oriental powers and France all alone.

Just before the signing of the alliance, a Japanese asked Lansdowne how he thought the Americans would react to it. "I replied," Lansdowne wrote, "that I felt confident that the United States would not disapprove. We had every reason to believe that she desired a maintenance of the status quo in the Far East." Landsdowne's confidence in the Americans, if not his hope the alliance would preserve the status quo, proved justified. Ambassador Choate commented, "the treaty seems to me greatly to forward the policy of the 'open door,' and goes far to secure the independence and integrity of the Chinese and Korean empires." [13] His superiors, Roosevelt and Hay, similarly blinded by fears of Russia, took the same line. No one in Washington or London seems to have considered the possibility that Britain's new obligations might lead her into conflict with the United States if the Americans opposed further Japanese moves.

Editors and commentators took the same easy view of the agreement. "The new dual alliance," a New York paper declared, ". . . will result in the carrying out of an American theory in practice. It must be all the more satisfactory to us when we con-

[13] Lansdowne to MacDonald, January 7, 1902, George P. Gooch and Harold Temperley, eds., *British Documents on the Origin of the War, 1898–1914* (11 vols.; London, 1926–1938), vol. II, p. 110; Choate to Hay, February 12, 1902, *Foreign Relations, 1902* (Washington, 1903), p. 513.

sider that the thing has been done without this country's breaking through the rule to avoid entangling alliances." The selfishness of expecting Japan and England to provide the force, asking
nothing for themselves, while America provided the "theory" escaped this paper and most American commentators. They welcomed the alliance as a barrier to Russia, an adjunct to Secretary
Hay's moral wisdom. Years later Herbert Croly asked, "Is not
the Japanese alliance a dubious device for the partial shifting of
burdens too heavy to bear?" [14] Few asked this question in 1902.

Until the climax of the Russo-Japanese War more than two
years later, the American government remained strongly anti-
Russian. The Russian minister at Tokyo reported, "it is entirely
clear that there exists in fact between America, Britain, and
Japan complete mutual political understanding and cooperation." [15] This report exaggerated, for even Theodore Roosevelt
gave his sympathies far more easily than his cooperation. Horace
N. Allen, the medical missionary turned entrepreneur who had
become American minister at Seoul, visited Oyster Bay to warn
the President that Japanese ambitions in the Far East, particularly Korea, were more threatening than Russia's. Roosevelt
declined to listen, but he limited his opposition to Russia to
gestures he knew would not upset the American desire for non-
involvement.

As early as 1903 the British learned that the alliance might
lead to embarrassment. In April the Russians delayed a promised
stage in their evacuation of Manchuria. The Japanese ardently
sought British support, including a reinforcement of naval units
in the Far East. Their desire to provoke a crisis served London's
interest not at all (Lansdowne was again engaged, vainly as it
turned out, in negotiations with Russia), but Britain did not
want to open herself to charges of betraying the alliance so soon
after its conclusion. Learning that the Americans were also angry

---

[14] New York *Evening Sun*, quoted in Chang-Fu Chang, *The Anglo-Japanese
Alliance* (Baltimore, 1931), p. 242; Herbert Croly, *The Promise of American Life*
(New York, 1909), p. 262.

[15] Rosen, quoted in John A. White, *The Diplomacy of the Russo-Japanese War*
(Princeton, 1964), p. 92.

with Russia, the cabinet leaped at a straw even less substantial than the chaff of 1898. They proposed that Washington take the lead against Russia. In official instructions to Herbert, Lansdowne cabled, "We fully appreciate reasons for which United States Government prefer to act independently, . . . but we are prepared to follow the United States step by step up to any point that may be necessary." [16]

Lest Herbert should fail to understand just how far the cabinet was prepared to go, Lansdowne accompanied these instructions with a private note actually drafted by Joseph Chamberlain, always the apostle of bold departures. Ministers, Herbert learned, would not fight for Manchuria either alone or in league with Japan. (They were not pledged to do so unless a second power came to Russia's aid.) On the other hand, "if . . . the United States government should decide to press their claims even to the extremity of hostile actions H.M.G. would take similar actions, although no previous arrangement or alliance had been made with the United States government." [17] For the only time before 1941, when China's integrity was again at issue, the British government offered to follow the United States into war.

By this fantastic scheme Chamberlain, Lansdowne, and their colleagues hoped to confront Russia with a combination she could not resist or to give themselves an excuse for refusing to back the Japanese in claims Roosevelt disapproved; either development might well save the peace. They woefully misread the situation. Roosevelt made it clear he would not fight for Manchuria. Nor would he consider a combined Anglo-Japanese-American protest to St. Petersburg or the dispatch of naval forces to the Far East, two courses urged by Lodge.

Lansdowne tried to put off the showdown in the Far East, urging upon the Japanese the importance of common action with the United States. He also continued efforts for an accommodation with Russia and, far more successfully, with France.

---

[16] Lansdowne to Herbert, April 28, 1903, Gooch and Temperley, eds., *British Documents*, vol. II, p. 200.

[17] Lansdowne to Herbert, April 28, 1903, quoted in Monger, *End of Isolation*, p. 124.

By the beginning of 1904 he could reasonably anticipate an Anglo-French understanding which would draw some teeth from the Franco-Russian alliance, although the entente which transformed world politics was not concluded until April. At the same time Lansdowne and his colleagues concluded that it would only anger Japan "if we were to stand in her way and deprive her of an opportunity which she is apparently determined to turn to account." [18] Quite cynically, the British gave their blessing to the war which began with a surprise Japanese attack upon the Russians at Port Arthur in February 1904.

At first the Roosevelt administration and Balfour cabinet viewed the war in much the same light. Russia's pre-war minister to Tokyo later wrote, "I personally saw the extent to which . . . the assurances of moral and material support from America was decisive in the counsels of the Japanese government." [19] Washington and London made it clear they hoped for a Japanese victory and would not welcome the entry of a third power on Russia's side. They watched benevolently while English and American bankers jointly loaned more than £50,000,000 to Japan in several installments, and Edward VII later decorated an American banker, Jacob Schiff, for his services to the Anglo-Japanese alliance.

Both powers feared tiny Japan might succumb to the Russian giant, and Japan's role as underdog strengthened Roosevelt's sympathies for her. Lansdowne fretted about Russian victory so decisive as to free her for an attack on China, and he hoped— would foolishness never die?—Roosevelt would join Britain to resist it with force. Eleven months after the war began Lansdowne still worried. He hoped, he wrote Balfour, the United States would "co-operate with us in defending Japan against a blow at her vitals," [20] and he prepared but prudently did not send a letter to the President designed to pave the way. Then, in

[18] Lansdowne to Durand, February 5, 1904, Gooch and Temperley, eds., *British Documents*, vol. II, p. 243.

[19] Rosen, quoted in White, *Russo-Japanese War*, p. 89.

[20] Lansdowne to Balfour, January 18, 1905, quoted in Monger, *End of Isolation*, p. 181.

March 1905, Japanese armies gained a victory at Mukden, and two months later Admiral Togo crushed the Russian fleet at Tsushima. (When three badly battered Russian ships crawled into Manila the Americans interned them.) The specter of Russian victory disappeared.

The new state of things heightened a conflict of views that had already begun to emerge. Britain wanted Japan to destroy Russian power in the Far East, and she deluded herself into believing that Roosevelt shared her views. In fact the President desired a limited Japanese victory, which would, he thought, create a stable balance of power. In July 1904, he wrote, remembering what the powers had done in 1895, "We may be of genuine service, if Japan wins out, in preventing interference to rob her of the fruits of her victory." [21] He later told the British ambassador that Japan should keep Port Arthur and her control of Korea while the Russians withdrew to northern Manchuria and returned the rest of that province to Chinese administration. Lansdowne welcomed these views, which if carried out meant a sharp defeat for Russia, apparently without realizing that Japanese ambitions might grow with victory and that the President might oppose those ambitions.

Roosevelt sought to construct a balance by forcing peace before Russia or Japan gained a complete military victory. The Kaiser helped by putting pressure on his imperial cousin, and his efforts won him effusive thanks even more effusively reported by sycophants. "The President," von Bülow wrote, "is a great admirer of Your Majesty and would like to rule the world hand in hand with Your Majesty, as he certainly conceives himself to be the American pendant of Your Majesty." Roosevelt's unconcealed gratitude, combined early in 1905 with a role in the Moroccan controversy which Downing Street imagined to be pro-German, created alarm in London. The President complained to Lodge, "The heavy witted creatures do not understand that nothing would persuade me to follow the lead of . . . a man

---

[21] Roosevelt to Hay, July 26, 1904, Elting E. Morison, ed., *The Letters of Theodore Roosevelt* (8 vols.; Cambridge, 1951–1954), vol. IV, p. 865.

who is so jumpy, so little capable of continuity of action." [22] Still, the fear existed, a marked contrast to recent views of Roosevelt as potential ally.

While the Kaiser won Roosevelt's good will, London repeatedly turned aside his requests for help. The British were willing to speculate on military events, confident America would not permit a disaster to Japan, and they were unwilling to press an ally to give up dreams of total victory. Roosevelt became irritated. "England has not a man I can deal with," he told his German friend Speck von Sternburg. "I do not think much of Balfour and less of Lansdowne. Chamberlain is quite unreliable and might jump into the Yangtse valley at any moment." [23] Through Spring Rice he slightly more tactfully expressed his views to the Foreign Office, and in the same letter he expressed a wish that his friend would visit Washington so that he might explain himself further and perhaps bring about a change in British policy.

Sir Cecil received this letter while on leave in London. With Lansdowne's unofficial permission, he set off for Washington. To emphasize the personal character of the visit, he stayed with Henry Adams rather than at the British embassy, but the eagle-eyed Sternburg promptly reported his arrival to Berlin. In an interview at the White House, to which Durand, the official ambassador, was punctiliously invited, the two old friends canvassed the Far Eastern situation. What transpired is still the subject of conjecture. Apparently the President stressed his desire to work with England, particularly to secure a peace which would improve Japan's position without leaving her dominant in the Orient. Spring Rice, always bitterly anti-Russian, seems to have emphasized the Russian threat to China and the danger of European intervention on Russia's behalf, two fears which the President no longer gave high priority. Either there was no real meeting of the minds—perhaps because Sir Cecil valued harmony

[22] Bülow to Wilhelm, August 31, 1904, Frederic Whyte, ed., *Letters of Prince von Bülow* (London, 1934), p. 72; Roosevelt to Lodge, May 15, 1905, Henry Cabot Lodge, ed., *Selections from the Correspondence of Theodore Roosevelt and Henry Cabot Lodge, 1884–1918* (2 vols.; New York, 1925), vol. II, p. 123.

[23] Sternburg to Foreign Office, September 27, 1904, quoted in Griswold, *Far Eastern Policy*, p. 106.

above understanding, as usual—or if there was one, London
would not act upon it.

The failure to agree clearly emerges in Spring Rice's report
to the Americans of his reception when he returned to London.
According to this account, the King, Lansdowne, and Chamberlain—Balfour is not mentioned—reacted enthusiastically to
talk of cooperation with the United States. However, Spring
Rice admitted, "Lord Lansdowne was nervous as to outward
manifestations which he was anxious to avoid." This sentence
shows that Britain still refused to join the President's crusade for
a conference, and it makes a mockery of Sir Cecil's assurance
that "we will follow your lead and . . . you will find us ready
and anxious to take any action which you may suggest before-
hand." [24] Britain continued to vacillate, unwilling either to support or to oppose the President.

The man who paid for this evasiveness was Sir Mortimer
Durand. This was unfortunate and even unfair, for no one cherished American friendship more than Durand. "I wish Lord
Salisbury would send me to Washington," he wrote in 1895, during the first Venezuelan crisis. "I know I could get on with these
people, and it would be a grand work to bring England and
America together—the grandest work an Englishman could do
for his country." At a previous post in Tehran Sir Mortimer invited Americans but no other foreigners to the New Year's dinner which capped the legation's social season, and in one of his
novels, *Helen Treveryan, or the Ruling Race*—for Durand was a
literary man as well as a sportsman—he had a character declare,
"I feel as proud of the Stars and Stripes as I do of the Union
Jack." [25] Appointment to succeed Pauncefote eluded him, primarily because Henry White recommended his friend Herbert to
Lansdowne, but in 1903 Durand received the post he cherished.

Since Roosevelt would have preferred Spring Rice, still too

[24] Spring Rice to Hay, March 15, 1905, quoted in Stephen Gwynn, *The Letters and Friendships of Sir Cecil Spring Rice* (2 vols.; Cambridge, 1929), vol. I,
pp. 462–463.
[25] Durand to Mrs. Rivett-Carnac, December —, 1895, quoted in Sir Percy M.
Sykes, *Sir Mortimer Durand* (London, 1926), p. 265; *Helen Treveryan*, quoted in
ibid., p. 265.

junior by Foreign Office standards, Durand arrived with two strikes against him. His first interview with the President went well enough—Roosevelt turned the talk to big-game hunting—but Sir Mortimer, a stuffy man, did not know how to play the role of chorus figure assumed by Spring Rice or that of witty, sometimes bold man of the world played by Sir Michael Herbert. Given a chance to gain Presidential favor during a climbing expedition in Rock Creek, Durand failed the test; at one point the President had to pull his exhausted companion over a crest by his collar. Durand's chief problem, however, was that he did not know how to defend a policy which did not exist. Roosevelt considered him stupid and evasive, and he in his turn, cut off from contact with the President, consistently underestimated the intensity of the Chief Executive's desire for a conference and his resentment at London's lack of support.

Roosevelt began to complain about Durand in the autumn of 1904, and Lansdowne approved Spring Rice's flying visit to Washington partly because the President said he could not communicate through Durand. When Roosevelt increased the pressure for a conference, Durand helped not at all. At Lansdowne's direction, although the President did not know this, he went off to the Berkshires on vacation to avoid involvement in the last stages of the negotiations. The President asked Lodge, in London during the spring, to use any polite opportunity that arose to suggest Durand's replacement by Spring Rice. His relations with Durand never recovered, although he accepted London's explanation that Sir Mortimer could not be replaced at just that time.

Early in June 1905, after intricate negotiations skillfully handled, the President issued prearranged invitations to a peace conference under his sponsorship, and within four days the warring powers formally accepted. The President employed the interval before the plenipotentiaries gathered at the Portsmouth navy yard in attempts, via Berlin and Paris upon St. Petersburg and via London upon Tokyo, to put the belligerents in a conciliatory mood. With Britain he had no success at all. Lansdowne told Ambassador Reid, who had been directed to inquire "whether the English Government really does wish for peace or not," that Britain did want peace but saw no way to further it. Approached again, he stated that he was "indisposed to exert any pressure on Japan about terms of peace." Again the President became angry. "Aha! Now America sees for the first time where the real disturber of the world's peace lies," the Kaiser minuted on a report from Sternburg. But Durand, off in Lenox, reported that all was serene at Washington, and Lansdowne told Balfour, "I doubt whether the President is very deeply concerned that we are obstructing the peace negotiations." [26]

The noble lord ought to have paid more attention to Spring Rice's correspondence with the President. In the middle of June, Roosevelt wrote, "I am bound to say that the Kaiser has behaved admirably and has really helped me. I hope that your people are sincerely desirous of peace and will use their influence at the proper time." When Spring Rice replied with a labored explanation that, while Britain sincerely wanted peace, her sense of honor kept her from urging an ally to moderate her demands, particularly when it was not yet certain what those demands would be, Roosevelt rebuked him for going "needlessly into heroics." [27] He pointed out that France was trying to influence her ally Russia, and made it clear he hoped for the same cooperation from Great Britain.

He received none until the conference had been in session for several weeks. The discussions deadlocked when the Japanese insisted upon a money indemnity and possession of Sakhalin island. Roosevelt persuaded the Czar to give up the southern half of Sakhalin. Disposing of the indemnity proved more difficult. Roosevelt made a new appeal to Britain, writing to Durand that "every true friend of Japan" should urge her to abandon her de-

[26] State Department to Reid, June 15, 1905, quoted in Tyler Dennett, *Roosevelt and the Russo-Japanese War* (Garden City, 1925), p. 211; Lansdowne, quoted in Roosevelt to Reid, July 29, 1905, Morison, ed., *Letters of Roosevelt*, vol. IV, p. 1292; minute on Sternburg to Foreign Office, July 5, 1905, E. T. S. Dugdale, ed., *German Diplomatic Documents, 1871-1914* (4 vols.; London, 1928-1931), vol. III, p. 206; Lansdowne to Balfour, July 9, 1905, quoted in Monger, *End of Isolation*, p. 214n.

[27] Roosevelt to Spring Rice, June 16, 1905, Morison, ed., *Letters of Roosevelt*, vol. IV, p. 1234; Roosevelt to Spring Rice, July 18, 1905, *ibid.*, p. 1283-1284.

mand; to continue the war merely for money, he said, would place the Japanese in a bad light before the world. On the report of Roosevelt's request Lansdowne minuted, "This is a suggestion that we should press the Japanese to make further concessions. Were we to do so our advice would not be taken and would be resented." [28] Instead, he passed Roosevelt's message to the Japanese without comment, a course intended to suggest sympathy with it without embarrassing British relations with her ally. The conferees soon reached agreement. Save that Japan received half of Sakhalin, the terms reflected Roosevelt's wishes at the beginning of the year.

Britain had the good fortune to emerge from this affair with little damage to her relations with America. Only hints of her policy escaped to the outside world, and there was very little comment upon it; furthermore, the American people were slower than the President to see the desirability of limiting Japanese conquests. Roosevelt, having won a great diplomatic victory, was inclined to be generous. "I did not get much direct assistance from the English government," he wrote Reid shortly after his success, "but I did get indirect assistance." He mentioned Lansdowne's transmission of his letter to Durand and the signing of a revised Anglo-Japanese alliance which, he believed, "made Japan feel comparatively safe as to the future." [29] Had the peace negotiations failed, Roosevelt would have taken another tune, a more critical one.

The President could excuse much of the temporary misunderstanding with Great Britain by placing the blame on Durand's shoulders. When in Roosevelt's view Sir Mortimer mishandled negotiations over Morocco, the President wrote, "He seems to have a brain of about eight-guinea-pig-power. Why, under Heaven the English keep him here I do not know! . . . It is useless to have a worthy creature of mutton-suet con-

---

[28] Roosevelt to Durand, August 23, 1905, *ibid.*, p. 1310; Lansdowne minute on Durand to Lansdowne, August 24, 1905, Gooch and Temperley, eds., *British Documents*, vol. IV, p. 105.

[29] Roosevelt to Reid, September 11, 1905, Morison, ed., *Letters of Roosevelt*, vol. V, p. 18.

sistency like the good Sir Mortimer." [30] In the summer of 1906
the latter, again at Lenox, received word from the new Foreign
Secretary, Sir Edward Grey, that because he could not get along
with the President he was to lose his post. Durand returned
briefly to Washington, where he discussed his fate every evening
after dinner with Esme Howard, the young man sent to serve as
chargé after he left. Then he returned to England, finished as a
diplomat at fifty-six.

Grey had made an effort to open an alternative channel of
communication with Roosevelt before dismissing Durand. Had
this worked, he might have left the Ambassador to finish his tour
in gilded idleness. Early in 1906 the Foreign Secretary decided to
send Lord Edward Gleichen, a young cousin of the King, to
Washington as military attaché. Spring Rice, at whose wedding
Gleichen had been best man, endorsed the idea with his typical
cynicism: "The best person to keep touch with the President is
the military attaché, and as Gleichen has been shot in the stom-
ach and the neck, he is quite certain to meet with a favourable
reception. . . . Gleichen would certainly get on there, although
he is rather apt to be scandalised by the unexpected." In Washington the attaché had a long talk with Roosevelt and was
whirled around town in an electric car by the President's vivacious daughter. But he soon failed the rock-climbing test and,
even worse, showed himself the stuffy, conventional man Spring
Rice had hinted he was. Invited to Oyster Bay that summer, he
had a miserable time; Roosevelt sent no one to meet him at the
station, "The luncheon was extremely meagre, and I got up quite
hungry," [31] and he could not follow the President's conversation.
So Gleichen spent most of his time traveling around the United
States on the conventional duties of a military attaché—on one
trip the princeling had the use of James J. Hill's private railroad
car, on another he visited the Wright brothers and was scandal-
ized when they asked £20,000 for an airplane—and returned
home shortly after Durand himself departed.

[30] Roosevelt to Reid, April 28, 1906, *ibid.*, p. 242.
[31] Spring Rice to Grey, n.d., quoted in Gwynn, *Spring Rice*, vol. II, p. 25;
Gleichen to Edward VII, August 31, 1906, quoted in Sir Sidney Lee, *King Edward VII* (2 vols.; London, 1925–1927), vol. II, p. 437.

Roosevelt's policy soon moved in a direction which lessened the danger of an Anglo-American divergence like that which cost Durand his career. As early as 1902 the administration had begun to pull back from the ambitious position taken in the second Open Door note. Unless some third power intervened it was obvious Russo-Japanese rivalry in Korea and Manchuria would end with Peking's authority weakened, and neither the United States nor any other power dreamed of giving China effective support. Accepting the inevitability of spheres of influence, as Hay had done in the first set of notes, the administration concentrated its attention upon equal commercial opportunity in those spheres. Sometimes it acted vigorously and succeeded; sometimes, to the dismay of diplomats in the field, it vacillated; once or twice, it gained assistance from London. Whatever the case, because the new tone made much less likely a clash with Britain's ally over Far Eastern policy, Downing Street welcomed it.

Two understandings with Japan, the Taft-Katsura memorandum and the Root-Takahira agreement, fit into the same pattern. In the summer of 1905 Prime Minister Katsura told Secretary of War Taft, then in Tokyo, that he believed peace in the Far East required "some good understanding or alliance in practice" between his country, England, and the United States. Taft promised close but informal cooperation with the allies, presumably in case the Russians sought revenge for their defeats and the losses the Portsmouth negotiations were soon to impose. Britain knew America well enough to discount such promises, but she welcomed another statement by Taft that the United States recognized the special position Japan had created for herself in Korea. President Roosevelt, cabled a memorandum of the conversation, quickly replied to Taft, "I confirm every word you have said." [32] Thus there was no danger Britain would be caught in the middle in a quarrel between her friend and her ally over Korea.

The Root-Takahira agreement, an exchange of letters be-

[32] Agreed memorandum, July 27, 1905, quoted in Dennett, *Roosevelt and Russo-Japanese War*, pp. 113–114; Roosevelt to Taft, July 29, 1905, Morison, ed., *Letters of Roosevelt*, vol. IV, p. 1293.

tween the Secretary of State and the Japanese Ambassador in
November 1908, was far more ambiguous, for on the one hand it
spoke with respect of the Open Door and on the other recognized the status quo in the Far East which included the Japanese
sphere of influence in Manchuria. When Ambassador Reid told
Sir Edward Grey of the impending exchange, the British diplomat sighed with relief at what he considered the most desirable
of all possible agreements between foreign powers. "As the ally
of Japan we were very pleased with it: because we ourselves were
especially desirous of remaining on good terms with the United
States," he wrote.[33]

American actions, undertaken with little thought of their
effect on Anglo-American relations, found their counterpart in
British policies which did take that factor into consideration.
Early in 1905 London and Tokyo began to discuss revision of
their alliance. They quickly agreed to changes extending the coverage to India, unprotected by the original treaty, and giving
Japan firmer guarantees of gains she obviously was going to make
as a result of the war with Russia. These major problems out of
the way, the negotiators bogged down on two others affecting the
United States. Britain wished to be freed from a promise, made
just after the alliance in 1902, to maintain a naval force in the
Far East equal to that of any outside power. After Tsushima this
could only mean a force equal to the American, so Lansdowne
sought a new standard which would only oblige the Royal Navy
to match the largest European detachment. "We did not consider it at all likely that we should be at war with the United
States," he wrote, "and unless this exception were made Great
Britain and Japan would each be obliged to maintain a superflu-
ous number of ships." [34] The Japanese finally accepted this idea,
although for extraneous reasons it was not included in the new
treaty. The five battleships in Chinese waters sailed home to join
in the concentration of naval power being organized by Admiral
Fisher.

---

[33] Grey to MacDonald, November 27, 1908, Gooch and Temperley, eds., *British Documents*, vol. VIII, p. 462.
[34] Lansdowne to MacDonald, June 10, 1905, *ibid.*, vol. IV, p. 137.

The Japanese sought and the British resisted inclusion of an article specifically recognizing the new Japanese position in Korea. Lansdowne knew Roosevelt welcomed the growth of Japanese influence in the Hermit Kingdom, but he could not be sure the President carried this enthusiasm as far as a willingness to see American treaty rights in Korea trampled upon. Pressed by Ambassador Hayashi, he declined to move. "All we desire," he told his ambassador in Tokyo, "is that we should not be compelled to go to war say with the U[nited] S[tates] in the event of a violation of established Treaty rights by Japan." [35] The Americans themselves finally broke the logjam. Assistant Secretary of State Loomis and Senator Lodge, visiting London at the time, both assured the Foreign Secretary the United States resigned itself to Japanese predominance in Korea. On the very day Roosevelt cabled to Tokyo his approval of the Taft-Katsura memorandum, Lord Lansdowne sent word to the President that Britain would go ahead as the Japanese desired, confident this did not clash with American views.

Two weeks later the new alliance was signed. Durand wrote Roosevelt, "His Majesty's Government felt that by promptly concluding this agreement, and thereby relieving Japan of all apprehension of vindictive action on the part of Russia in the future, they would make it easier for Japan to moderate her demands, and they believe that their action had the result they anticipated." Without going into the question of British motivation, Roosevelt replied that he believed renewal of the alliance was "a powerful factor in inducing Japan to be wise and reasonable." [36]

Roosevelt gained little credit in Japan for his services to the cause of peace. The Japanese people, who did not know that their own government had asked the President to mediate, blamed him for cheating their country of some of the fruits of victory. They were therefore in a nasty mood when, in 1906 and

[35] Lansdowne to MacDonald, July 26, 1905, *ibid.*, p. 154.
[36] Durand to Roosevelt, September 5, 1905, quoted in Dennett, *Roosevelt and Russo-Japanese War*, p. 258n; Roosevelt to Durand, September 8, 1905, quoted in Howard K. Beale, *Theodore Roosevelt and the Rise of America to World Power* (Baltimore, 1956), p. 305.

1907, a quarrel arose between the two countries, growing chiefly out of the treatment accorded Japanese immigrants in California and American efforts to limit immigration from Japan. The sharp estrangement, some thought, would transform the world picture. Kaiser Wilhelm dreamed of a German, Chinese, and American combination in opposition to Japan, Britain, and France.

The dispute troubled Sir Edward Grey. He knew that, as an Admiralty memorandum put it, if war came "the British people would certainly throw the Alliance overboard," [37] and he himself would have done the same. But Grey had almost as little desire to break with Japan as he had to become involved with the United States. The Liberals had misgivings about the alliance negotiated by their predecessors, but they accepted it as a keystone of policy. As a consequence, the new director of diplomacy played a very cautious part, avoiding as best he could criticism from either disputant. Ultimately the pressures were too great (or perhaps Grey overcame his caution), for without ever abandoning hope for a settlement Britain found herself drifting in an American direction. Fortunately the quarrel evaporated before England had to take a stand so open and decisive that it affronted Japan.

At the outset most Englishmen considered the United States clearly in the wrong, particularly California xenophobes. London therefore failed to support Roosevelt's efforts to get Japan to agree to firm limits on emigration to the United States. Then, in September 1907, anti-immigrant riots swept Vancouver, causing more bloodshed than anything that had happened in the United States. This otherwise unfortunate affair worked to Washington's advantage, showing Tokyo that Canada would strain against the alliance and making London less condescending toward and critical of American racism. Elihu Root, one of the few who would have dared, jokingly told Roosevelt he suspected the President's secretary of instigating the trouble in Vancouver. A

---

[37] Admiralty memorandum, February 15, 1906, quoted in Monger, *End of Isolation*, p. 310.

Canadian representative, William L. Mackenzie King, soon visited the President, and they concocted a plan for Mackenzie King to go to London to put the case for immigration restriction. Roosevelt, counting his chickens prematurely, expected the riot and word of Mackenzie King's coming to transform British policy at once, but Grey turned down his first request to intervene at Tokyo. However, the Canadian's visit to London in March and April 1908 brought about a shift in England's stance. No *démarche* went forward, but Grey agreed some check would have to be placed on Oriental immigration.

Britain's reaction to the transfer of the American battle fleet to the Pacific, a movement which became a cruise around the world, followed a pattern similar to that toward the immigration controversy. Grey began with misgivings like those of his ambassador at Tokyo, who believed Roosevelt misunderstood the Japanese: "a menace such as the sending of a fleet leaves them absolutely cold." The fleet's first port of call was Trinidad. At that British colony it received a very cool reception as a result, according to the American consul, of instructions from London. Britain wished to show Japan she did not endorse the American project. The Kaiser, on the other hand, exulted, "I have witnessed with pleasure the departure of the American Fleet. Its cruise around the Pacific knocks all the calculations of the British and the Japanese on the head." [38]

Britain's tone soon changed; the government simply could not maintain an air of aloofness toward the Americans. Australia's prime minister forced London to allow him to extend an invitation to the fleet, and shortly thereafter, seeking to turn the voyage to the use of peace, Britain induced the Japanese themselves to ask for a visit. Roosevelt's acceptance of that invitation in March 1908 largely defused the controversy, although the President told Bryce, the new English ambassador, that he still considered war possible. (Reporting this, Bryce commented,

[38] MacDonald to Grey, March 17, 1908, Gooch and Temperley, eds., *British Documents*, vol. VIII, p. 458; Wilhelm to Bülow, December 30, 1907, Whyte, ed., *Letters of Bülow*, p. 227.

"The world is no doubt full of possibilities. They are even more numerous than facts." [39])

A few months later, as Robert A. Hart tells us in his account of the voyage, the fleet received a tumultuous reception in New Zealand (one Maori chief, wearing a wooden mask modeled after the President, danced up and down shouting "Bully!") and Australia, where the city of Sydney alone spent £50,000 on decorations. Then on to Tokyo for a successful visit during which British diplomats did their best to smooth the path. Proceeding on around the world, the Great White Fleet touched, among other places, at Ceylon, where Lipton's presented a gift of seven tons of tea, provoking the inevitable heavy jokes about the Boston Tea Party, and Gibraltar, where local authorities supplied naval stores for the last lap of the journey when meat bought in France turned out to be spoiled.

The Japanese-American controversy, historians now agree, never seriously threatened to become a war. Neither Roosevelt nor authorities at Tokyo wanted one. To contemporaries, even English statesmen, this was not so apparent. Thus the affair tested British policy and attitudes. Sympathetic to Japanese protests against discrimination, doubtful about the wisdom of the fleet movement, always seeking to avoid jeopardizing the alliance with Japan, the British government nevertheless found itself by the end of the controversy taking a position to which Washington could not object. Moreover, Japanese-American difficulties between 1906 and 1908, warning Britain of dangers in the future, led to negotiations which showed how determined England was to run no risks of conflict with the United States.

As early as 1906 the question was asked in the House of Commons, "Whether there is any provision in the Anglo-Japanese treaty safeguarding His Majesty's dominions from being involved in war with the United States of America on behalf of Japan." [40] While it would have been embarrassing to try to

---

[39] Bryce to Grey, March 19, 1908, Gooch and Temperley, eds., *British Documents*, vol. VIII, p. 459.
[40] Quoted in Chang, *Anglo-Japanese Alliance*, pp. 149n–150n.

revise the alliance while Japan and America quarreled, Grey proceeded to do so, and thus to ensure Britain against involvement in future broils, after the Pacific skies cleared. Thanks to British and Japanese agreements with Russia, the original target of the alliance, the connection of 1902 had lost much of its purpose; the alliance served only to reduce Britain's need for a strong Far Eastern squadron and to provide Japan with a probably unplayable card in controversies with the United States.

London sought to remove even that card from the Japanese hand, and with the aid of Washington she managed to do so. In the summer of 1910 Grey learned that the Taft administration might soon ask him to sign a treaty of general arbitration, an agreement which, as Taft and Knox well knew, would conflict with Britain's pledge to aid Japan in case of war. Grey consulted his allies, who were reluctant to exempt the United States from the operation of their treaty with Britain. The Foreign Secretary pressed hard, urging them to sign an arbitration treaty with the United States or to accept a revision of the alliance exempting the United States by name. "There was such a growing feeling of friendliness between the public in this country and that on the other side of the Atlantic," he argued, "that it was clear we could not undertake any obligation which would involve us in war with the United States." [41] In the end, the Japanese were forced to accept a provision, Article IV of the revised treaty, stating that the alliance did not require a signatory to take action against a third party with which it had a treaty of general arbitration. The effect was the same, or at least it would have been if the Senate had approved the Anglo-American arbitration treaty, signed one month after the new Anglo-Japanese alliance, in August 1911. Ultimately the British were forced to argue, and Japan did not challenge this interpretation, that a "cooling off" treaty signed at Secretary Bryan's urging in 1914 met the requirements of the escape clause.

Britain's desire to revise the alliance was precautionary, not

[41] Grey to Rumbold, July 7, 1911, Gooch and Temperley, eds., *British Documents*, vol. VIII, p. 529.

a sign that she wished the Americans well in the Far East. Her feelings about dollar diplomacy in the Orient were similar to those about the same policy in Latin America, but her official actions were quite different. In the Western Hemisphere she let the Americans have their way. In the Far East, whenever England had to choose between Japanese and American interests, she almost invariably chose the former, although she managed her activities subtly enough to escape recrimination.

In the Far East, dollar diplomacy meant a policy designed to increase American investments, particularly in railroads. Some participants, notably the railroad king Edward H. Harriman, anticipated great rewards from the investments themselves. Most of those involved, including Willard Straight, consul-general at Mukden from 1906 to 1908 and an earnest advocate of the policy throughout the period, expected American railroads to create American markets and perhaps, by broadening the investment base in China, to strengthen that country's political integrity. In particular the policy aimed to break Japan's stranglehold in southern Manchuria, a grip tightened by her control of the South Manchurian Railway, the only line running north from the Yellow Sea. The unimpressive results belied the substantial effort.

Dollar diplomacy gained two ephemeral triumphs, both on battlegrounds in central China rather than Manchuria. Between 1909 and 1911 the Taft administration fought to gain American participation in a multinational project to build a railway from Hankow westward to interior markets. At first Grey roundly refused to admit American interlopers. When he reluctantly accepted their inclusion he worked so hard to reduce the American share that the Department of State sharply criticized him. In England, critics like J. L. Garvin objected to action alienating the United States, particularly when Washington sought to show that "the United States stands inflexibly for the maintenance of the integrity of China proper," a course which deserved British support.[42] Taft and Knox won their way in an agreement signed with the Chinese in May 1911. However, thanks to the

[42] *Fortnightly Review* (London), vol. CXIII (1909), pp. 380–381.

caution of American bankers involved and even more to the impact of the Chinese revolution, the great investment opportunity soon escaped.

The second project suffered a rather similar fate. When the Manchu government sought foreign capital to stabilize Chinese currency, Knox participated enthusiastically in the negotiations. This time Sir Edward Grey made no trouble, and Americans gained their share of the loan arranged in the spring of 1911. The revolution soon destroyed this agreement, and when Yuan Shih-k'ai, who succeeded to the Manchus' power, sought a similar loan the unsettled conditions in China made foreigners wary. American participants sighed with relief when Woodrow Wilson withdrew support from the scheme, arguing that it presupposed unwarranted intervention in Chinese politics.

Toward Manchuria, Conservative and Liberal governments in England both followed an even more negative course. The Balfour ministry helped to frustrate a plan for investment there concocted by Edward H. Harriman, and when the Japanese canceled a tentative agreement with him, British capitalists stepped forward to supply the funds Tokyo lacked. A few years later Grey blocked the creation of an Anglo-American combine to challenge the Japanese railroad. Secretary Knox then suggested that the two governments press for a neutralization of all Manchurian railroads. Grey took refuge in generalities which Knox imprudently declined to interpret as a rebuff. He made public his scheme, only to have Britain join Japan and Russia, the two most interested parties, in turning it down early in 1910. When Japan and Russia sought to take advantage of the revolutionary upheaval to gain further concessions in Manchuria in 1911, Knox again failed to gain British support for his campaign of resistance.

For British policy, the key factor in these events was the Japanese alliance. As Straight's biographer observes, "Great Britain's fear of Germany was making her the accomplice of Japanese imperialism in the Far East just as it was making her the accomplice of Russian imperalism in Persia and French imperialism in North Africa." This course aroused little criticism in the United States because Britain never carried her loyalty to Japan so far as to divert America's lightning to herself, seldom acted against the Open Door in her own interest, and repeatedly professed support for that principle. In 1910, when Knox showed some soreness as a result of the failure of his neutralization scheme, Grey sent the ambassador at Washington a forthright explanation of British policy; however, he told Ambassador Bryce the information was for his eyes only and that the Americans should be told of "our anxiety to maintain the status quo in Manchuria where any change of the kind feared by the United States could not fail to affect our own interests quite as much as theirs in a most detrimental manner." Such tactics were so successful that even Straight only complained against "the cold-footed trimming policy exhibited by the English," not their basic lack of sympathy for American aims. Finally, Britain escaped severe public censure since the Taft-Knox campaign never ignited public enthusiasm, partly because it appeared to be a bankers' cause and partly because Americans were losing the great hopes with which they had greeted the century. Even Theodore Roosevelt considered his successor's campaign impractical. "The open-door policy in China was an excellent thing," he wrote Taft, ". . . but, as has been proved by the whole history of Manchuria, . . . the 'Open Door' policy . . . completely disappears as soon as a powerful nation determines to disregard it." [43] If Americans took this attitude toward the policy announced by Hay years before, they could not easily chastise England for assuming a similar one.

British commentators on dollar diplomacy were far more candid than the Foreign Office. Knox's most ambitious scheme, the projected neutralization of Manchurian railroads, naturally evoked the most comment. The *Saturday Review*, which almost

[43] Herbert Croly, *Willard Straight* (New York, 1925), p. 312; Grey to Bryce, September 22, 1910, quoted in E. W. Edwards, "Great Britain and the Manchurian Railways Question, 1909–1910," *English Historical Review* (London), vol. LXXXI (1966), p. 768; Straight to Huntington Wilson, March 3, 1910, quoted in Croly, *Straight*, p. 323; Roosevelt to Taft, December 22, 1910, Morison, ed., *Letters of Roosevelt*, vol. VII, p. 190.

never had a good word to say about the United States, admitted, "The design of lifting Manchuria out of international politics by syndicating international interests is altogether praiseworthy," but few considered the design a practical one. The *Times* objected to "a plan of which the grandiose simplicity ignores some of the stern politics of the present situation in Manchuria," while various critics objected that America was cloaking selfishness in the language of moral purpose. "Every friend of peace," wrote a contributor to the *Contemporary Review*, "will sincerely regret that an everlasting truce of God—or of trade—was not concluded . . . at the instance of Mr. Philander Knox. . . . But few people were surprised to learn that Japan and Russia turned deaf ears . . . when he asked them to yield their places for his fellow-countrymen, and to give him credit for Christian charity over and above." [44] Making a point American statesmen have always found it difficult to understand, J. L. Garvin contended that the hoped-for commercial advantages were not worth a major investment of American prestige. No more telling criticism could be made of dollar diplomacy or, for that matter, the course of American foreign policy in the Far East since 1898.

As Garvin hinted, American policy had rested on a false base. The Britain of Lord Salisbury, taking American interest at its own valuation, sought cooperation with the United States. The illusion of American power, and of Washington's willingness to use that power, died hard, and even after Britain sought reinsurance through the Japanese alliance, Salisbury's heirs dreamed of an Anglo-American entente. The Russo-Japanese War burst that bubble, and from 1905 onward British and American policy worked very largely at cross-purposes in the Far East. Since Roosevelt kept secret his difficulties with England in 1905 and soon forgave that country, and since Americans did not hold her responsible for the failures of dollar diplomacy, the consequences of disagreement were minor. Americans continued to

---

[44] *Saturday Review* (London), vol. CIX (1910), p. 164; *Times*, January 8, 1910; E. J. Dillon in *Contemporary Review* (London), vol. XCVIII (1910), p. 111.

feel that, on the whole, they and the British were pursuing similar ends, and on the eve of 1914 the two powers really did begin to drift toward similarity of policy. Under Woodrow Wilson the United States abandoned dollar diplomacy, while Britain looked askance at Japanese ambition made more evident when the Chinese revolution began. What might have been a significant conflict of views—what had, indeed, marked policy for the better part of a decade—disappeared. The great rapprochement survived the conflict between American optimism and British realism in the Far East.

CHAPTER TEN

Two Satisfied Nations

I N 1900 THE *Spectator* predicted that, thanks to McKinley's reelection, America would "add almost immeasurably to that mass of force which, needing peace to breed prosperity, makes for the preservation of peace, and steadies the thirst for conquest and enterprise which in several directions now threatens the tranquility of mankind." Like many contemporaries, editor Strachey expected too much. The managers of American diplomacy, even Theodore Roosevelt, showed themselves willing only to observe and to exhort, not to act, unless American interests were directly involved. Learning from events, in 1911 the *Spectator* more accurately assessed the position of the United States. Commenting upon a proposed treaty of arbitration between the English-speaking powers, the journal observed, "The United States is the one Power with which we could enter into an arbitration treaty with perfect confidence. She is neither aggressive nor acquisitive. . . . The United States may be described as a satisfied nation." [1]

Pursuing this same theme a few months later, Strachey observed that America was "the only country besides our own which is content with the *status quo.*" The whiff of imperialism in 1898 failed to intoxicate Americans for long, and the United States quickly became more interested in order than further change. The development of foreign trade—economic imperialism, if you like—depended upon stability elsewhere, not the ex-

[1] *Spectator* (London), vol. LXXXV (1900), p. 649; vol. CVI (1911), p. 388.

tension of American control, and even the Caribbean quasi-imperialism sprang more from a desire to prevent change than to cause it. "In every region of the world we find similarity in our political interests," observed Lewis Einstein, an American diplomat writing pseudonymously. "And the reason is unquestionably because England, with the greatest colonial empire the world has yet witnessed, can seek only to preserve her birthright and not to expand further." [2] Few citizens were either as perceptive or as candid as Einstein. However, a predilection in favor of the status quo colored American attitudes toward Great Britain.

Russia seemed the chief threat to stability around 1900, a great Slav power determined, as Brooks Adams and others alleged, to challenge the Anglo-Saxons for world leadership. This menace ended with the Russo-Japanese War, and Lewis Einstein confidently wrote, "The period of Muscovite aggression is over." [3] Quarrels with Japan sometimes stimulated talk of a "yellow peril," a fear both exploited and fanned by the hunchbacked eccentric Homer Lea, author and military adventurer, in *The Valor of Ignorance*, published in 1909, but most Americans who scanned the foreign scene considered the Japanese a Far Eastern problem only, not a threat to world stability.

In *The Day of the Saxon*, which appeared in 1912, Lea pointed to a different challenger, Germany. Americans never developed the hatred and fear of Germany that grew in England, and they sometimes considered Anglo-German hostility dangerously irrational. However, American statesmen and publicists looked more uneasily upon the Wilhelmian *reich* than any other major power. In a sensationalist tract, *Pan Germanism*, published in 1913, Professor Roland G. Usher alleged that "The Germans aim at nothing less than the domination of Europe and of the world." In *The Promise of American Life*, which appeared four years earlier, Herbert Croly less extravagantly argued that Germany was "the chief menace to the international stability of Europe." [4] Most leading Americans probably agreed with Croly.

[2] *Ibid.*, vol. CVII (1911), p. 272; Lewis Einstein ("A Diplomatist," pseud.), *American Foreign Policy* (Cambridge, 1909), pp. 50–51.
[3] *Ibid.*, p. 43.
[4] Roland G. Usher, *Pan Germanism* (Boston, 1913), p. 1, quoted in Melvin

German militarism, German aggressiveness, German authoritarianism—all by reflection shed a glow upon American relations with Germany's great rival.

Germany retained many friends and admirers in the United States to 1914 and beyond. Her social reforms attracted liberals and some labor leaders. Samuel Gompers' *Labor in Europe and America*, a report on a trip taken by the president of the American Federation of Labor, criticized British conditions and praised those in Germany, and Progressive believers in positive government thought German legislation helped prove their point. Admiration for German culture affected the political views of intellectuals like John W. Burgess and H. L. Mencken, while the anti-German exploitation of Nietzsche's *übermensch* philosophy and the crude militaristic writings of General von Bernhardi did not come until after the World War began. Even the Zabern affair, the brutal use of force by German soldiers in Alsace, which horrified Europe just before the war, left most Americans unmoved. They hoped Germany would evolve toward democracy, and, disregarding the minor role the German constitution allotted to the Reichstag, they welcomed the growth of the Social Democratic Party, which returned more members than any rival in the election of 1912. Such feelings countered the impact of Lea, Usher, Croly, and others who pointed to the German menace.

Nor had Kaiser Wilhelm won the almost universal dislike he later earned. Roosevelt sometimes found him helpful, and he said so, to London's alarm, but the President also eyed the German monarch with wariness. "It always amuses me to find that the English think that I am under the influence of the Kaiser," the President wrote to Lodge when the Senator was in London, where he could presumably set the record straight.[5] Most Americans disliked Wilhelm's bombastic statements and military posturing, although some found them merely laughable. Yet he was

Small, "The American Image of Germany, 1906–1914" (University of Michigan dissertation, 1965), p. 396; Herbert Croly, *The Promise of American Life* (New York, 1909), p. 253.

[5] Roosevelt to Lodge, May 15, 1905, Henry Cabot Lodge, ed., *Selections from the Correspondence of Theodore Roosevelt and Henry Cabot Lodge* (2 vols.; New York, 1925), vol. II, p. 123.

also considered a man who had brought social peace to Germany, fostered patriotism, and yet kept his country at peace. In an autobiography written in 1905, Andrew Dickson White, former ambassador to Germany, compared the Kaiser and the President in a friendly tone, putting them about on a par. In 1913 the American press hailed the twenty-fifth anniversary of Wilhelm's accession.

This praise was possible because Wilhelm's reputation had never been all bad, because many Americans cherished warm feelings about Germany, and because political tensions between the two countries had declined since their peak nearly a decade before. Von Diederichs' actions, the Anglo-German campaign against Venezuela, and rumors of extensive German ambitions in the Caribbean were distant matters. At the end of 1905, Roosevelt wrote to Spring Rice, whose heart can hardly have warmed at the news, that German-American relations were much improved. No longer, said the President, did he fear for the safety of Latin America.

The ground that had been lost could not be entirely regained, certainly not when America's relations with England were so smooth. Tariff "wars" irritated the American government and interested businessmen, who resented autarkic tendencies in Germany at the same time that they supported America's high tariff wall. Between 1910 and 1912 German pressure on Liberia, long considered an American satrapy, troubled the State Department, although probably not many outside it. The commercial rivalry in Latin America became intense, so intense that one commentator, Hiram Bingham, urged his country to throw over the Monroe Doctrine, as it was then interpreted, on the ground that it protected European investors while alienating Latins. "Laughing in her sleeve at the Monroe Doctrine as an antiquated policy, which only makes it easier for her to do a safe business," Bingham complained, "Germany is engaged in the peaceful conquest of Spanish America." [6] Alarmist rumors about

[6] Hiram Bingham, The Monroe Doctrine: An Obsolete Shibboleth (New Haven, 1913), p. 99.

German ambitions in Latin America never completely died, and German-American friction in Haiti on the eve of the war gave them color.

American naval policy aimed at Germany. The retired Admiral Mahan, still influential with those in the service, had a perfect obsession about Germany. His disciple Admiral Dewey, who dominated strategic planning from 1900 until he suffered a stroke in 1914, insisted upon concentrating the battle fleet in Atlantic waters. The last major units left the Far East in 1906, and Dewey and his opposite numbers in the army even recommended an Anglo-American understanding similar to the first Anglo-Japanese alliance, to take effect if some third power came to Germany's side. When the fleet completed its voyage around the world it remained on the east coast, and War Plan Black, completed early in 1914, foresaw a descent upon the Western Hemisphere by a German fleet and three quarters of a million men—and gave the navy only an even chance to intercept it! During the Japanese-American quarrel Grey allowed the Americans to gather that the Royal Navy would never permit a large German fleet to leave European waters, particularly if the Americans sent their ships to the Pacific; *per contra*, it would have been madness for the German Admiralty to risk a trans-Atlantic campaign while the Royal Navy stood athwart its communications. However, the United States Navy, clinging to its decade-long fear of Germany, chose to ignore such factors.

In ceremonial functions, too, the navy revealed American views. Germany received fewer visits from less impressive ships than her rivals. The most elaborate visits followed France's request for an American squadron in 1903. The Germans sought reciprocity. They were at first refused, though no one told them the navy was fully occupied practicing a preventive occupation of the Azores for some future German-American war, but after repeated importunities Berlin won its point. The visit was a formal success, but criticism in the United States forced the administration to issue solemn assurances that, during the Kaiser's tour of the American ships, he had been shown no secret machinery.

The detour to Germany, in its turn, led to British requests for similar treatment, and on the way home the ships stopped at England. At a dinner in London given by the Pilgrims, the tables were shaped and decorated like ships, the Royal Navy and the United States Navy proceeding in column, and the diners were piped to dinner in naval style. The entire visit turned into a love feast honoring Anglo-American friendship.

Germany's two pre-war ambassadors to the United States, Hermann Speck von Sternburg, who died in 1908, and Johann von Bernstorff, did their best to restore real comity, not merely a suspicious truce, between the two nations. Both objected that their efforts were hampered by the German press, which, as Ambassador White had observed earlier, consistently took an unfriendly line, if not with the encouragement of the Wilhelmstrasse at least without its disapproval. Both, but particularly Bernstorff, objected to the clumsiness and arrogance and ignorance of their superiors in Berlin, an ignorance symbolized by General von Moltke's hope that, offered an opportunity to gain Canada, the United States would join a German war against England. "America . . . is for our official circles a *terra incognita*," Bernstorff observed in 1913, and in his memoirs he disgustedly recounted the comment of an *Auswärtigesamt* official who, when asked while dining with the American ambassador if he had ever been to the United States, replied, "No, thank God, never." [7]

Bernstorff also charged that Berlin ignored all opportunities to cultivate the United States. This was an exaggeration. The Kaiser, in particular, sought friendship with President Roosevelt, writing frequently and freely if not always ingenuously to him. Wilhelm also forced the appointment of Sternburg, Roosevelt's old friend, as ambassador, a gesture which helped to ease German-American tensions. Most such gestures failed to achieve their purpose. The most notable fiasco was the visit to the

[7] Bernstorff to Sigfrid Heckscher, December 30, 1913, quoted in Count Bernstorff, *Memoirs* (Eric Sutton, trans.; New York, 1936), p. 124; Kiderlin, quoted in *ibid.*, pp. 105–106.

United States undertaken by the Kaiser's brother, Prince Henry, in 1902. Bülow's lengthy instructions—really a confession of the number of outstanding differences—warned the Prince not to discuss a whole calendar of issues upon which Americans were sensitive, and congressional debates on the cost of his entertainment marred the visitor's reception. At Harvard, where the governing body forced President Eliot to bestow an honorary degree upon the Prince as partial repayment for Wilhelmian gifts to the Germanic Museum, Eliot began his citation by praising German accomplishments—the Reformation, her aid during the American Revolution, her leadership in higher education. Then, abruptly, he turned to Queen Victoria's irenic role during the *Trent* affair of 1861, when England and America seemed on the verge of war. "Ladies and Gentlemen," said President Eliot, "the grandson of that illustrious lady is our guest here today." [8] The Prince and his suite were not amused.

This was Germany's fate. Often respected, positively feared only by a few, she was not allowed to forget that, in the fight for American affections, she could not challenge her great rival. Anglo-Saxonism was against her. Astute British diplomacy, aided by circumstance, was against her, for she neither had items ready at hand to concede, items like the Alaskan boundary and the canal far more important to the United States than to herself, nor, basically, had she made England's decision that American hostility was an unacceptable diplomatic burden.

At the root lay Strachey's observation about the status quo, or rather the implication behind it. Germany and America emerged upon the world scene to find it dominated by an informal balance of power in which Britain played a major role. Lacking Britain's established position, unblessed with America's great resources and immense domestic market, Germany saw her future in change brought about by adroit, aggressive diplomacy strengthened by possession of the world's greatest military force.

[8] Quoted in Jerome D. Greene, " 'First Citizen of the United States:' Recollections of the Days of Charles W. Eliot," *Harvard Alumni Bulletin* (Cambridge), vol. LXVIII (1965–1966), p. 386.

Almost inevitably, Germany and the United States often found themselves in disagreement. Before 1914 none of these differences of view were, perhaps, tremendously important, partly because the United States had not abandoned the idea that she need play no leading part in Old World politics. Still, because they often found Germany taking a position opposed by both England and the United States, these differences helped to further and at the same time reflected the growing Anglo-American rapprochement.

The Hague conferences of 1899 and 1907, the London conference of 1908–1909, and the series of negotiations over arbitration treaties all demonstrate this. At the first Hague conference, viewed with enthusiasm by people the world over but with skepticism in the chancelleries, the Germans foolishly opposed establishment of a panel of arbitrators to whom disputants might turn. The Germans saw this very modest peace-keeping scheme concocted by the top British and American delegates, Sir Julian Pauncefote and Andrew Dickson White, as a threat to the advantage won by their military preparedness. Their ultimate surrender to world opinion—and, as Bülow admitted, the specter of closer Anglo-American ties—came too late to repair the damage. The similarity of British and American interests was also demonstrated in another discussion, one which makes it clear this coincidence of view transcended mere humanitarianism. The two countries' military delegates fought against a proposal to outlaw dum-dum bullets, immensely helpful in fighting backward peoples and rebellious subjects like the Filipinos, but went down to defeat at the hands of twenty-two other nations represented at the conference.

At the second Hague conference eight years later the picture was not so clear. At the outset Sir Edward Grey's failure to interest Roosevelt in any scheme for arms limitation aided the Germans. Like most statesmen of the day, Grey had little faith in disarmament, but some of his colleagues did not share his pessimism and he himself felt it necessary to bow to public expectations. "It will be a poor lame Conference," he wrote the Presi-

dent, "if the Powers all meet there and shirk the question." [9]
Moreover, Grey saw an excellent opportunity to saddle Germany
with blame by getting Roosevelt to put forward proposals Berlin
was bound to reject. The President saved Wilhelm's government from serious embarrassment by declining to take the initiative, partly from lack of hope of success and partly because he
believed the United States, in contrast to European powers, had
too little rather than too much military strength. After only
twenty-five minutes of formal discussion at the Hague the nations merely agreed to consult on disarmament in the future.

Grey, who had promised to support any proposal on armaments put forward by the President, also hoped to create a common front on other issues, notably arbitration and the rights of
neutrals and belligerents in time of war. Roosevelt seemed to be
thinking along the same lines, for when Count Gleichen visited
Oyster Bay in September 1906, the President said to him, "I
want you . . . to tell your Government that I intend to back
them up thoroughly in the Hague Conference. I know Germany
won't expect it, and I am sure she won't like it, . . . but I mean
to back up the British Government all the same." Despite this
breezy assurance and despite, too, Grey's repeated invitation for
pre-conference discussion, coordination proved impossible. The
best the Foreign Secretary could do was to instruct Sir Edward
Fry, the chief British delegate, to keep in especially close touch
with England's two allies, Japan and France, and with the
United States of America. Fortunately for him, differences over
the proper role of the arbitration tribunal were minor, and Berlin's delegates threw away the small chance of gain by taking a
position on arbitration nearly as hostile as in 1899. Germany,
complained James Brown Scott, a quasi-official historian of the
peace conferences, was "seemingly unwilling to trust its interests
to the world at large and it claims and exercises the right to form
its judgment untrammeled by treaty or public opinion. The era

[9] Grey to Roosevelt, February 12, 1907, George P. Gooch and Harold Temperley, eds., *British Documents on the Origin of the War, 1898–1914* (11 vols.;
London, 1926–1938), vol. VIII, p. 203.

of 'blood and iron' is not yet past." [10]

The greatest difficulty between the English-speaking powers arose over neutral and belligerent rights. Although the Liberal government was tempted to abandon extreme parts of British doctrine, it dared not override military experts. On the other hand, for reasons both sentimental and realistic America had, ever since the Model Treaty approved by the Continental Congress in 1776, supported the broadest possible freedom of the seas. The navy proposed to modify this position. The President, however, refused, even in the face of a letter from Mahan which argued, "Great Britain and the British Navy lie right across Germany's trade with the whole world. Exempt it [from danger by forcing England to accept an international agreement], and you remove the strongest hook in the jaw of Germany that the English-speaking people have—a principal gage for peace." [11] Grey's reluctant rigidity and Roosevelt's refusal to budge raised the possibility of trouble.

As Mahan argued, it was clearly to Germany's advantage to restrict the use of British sea power. For that reason, and also because Berlin saw a chance to win American gratitude, German delegates made every effort to establish a common outlook with the Americans. They backed a proposal to exempt private property from seizure and in general, as a British observer noted, though "without any concerted action—as far as we could judge—they found themselves in the same lobby." [12] This irritated unimaginative British diplomats, but there is no evidence that Sir Edward Grey ever expected anything but a reassertion of America's traditional position. Moreover, although British critics failed to notice it, the United States often supported Fry and his colleagues. If American tradition called for limitations upon belligerent rights, it had also called, since the Neutrality Proclama-

[10] Gleichen to Durand, September 2, 1906, *ibid.*, p. 195; James B. Scott, *The Hague Peace Conferences of 1899 and 1907* (2 vols.; Baltimore, 1909), vol. I, p. 128.
[11] Mahan to Roosevelt, n.d. [1906], quoted in Howard K. Beale, *Theodore Roosevelt and the Rise of America to World Power* (Baltimore, 1956), p. 348.
[12] Lord Reay memorandum, n.d. [October 22, 1907?], Gooch and Temperley, eds., *British Documents*, vol. VIII, p. 299.

tion of 1793, for restraint on the part of neutrals. Great Britain found this policy congenial, other powers did not. In their final report the American delegates, headed by Joseph Choate, chose to emphasize not the differences between the two countries, but the times they stood together. Sir Edward Fry, more philosophical than some of his countrymen, also stressed the Americans' basic friendliness. Anglo-American differences at the Hague, the product of tradition rather than a conflict of interest, never came close to fulfilling German hopes.

At the last of the pre-war conferences, held in London between December 1908 and February 1909, the Germans had even less success. During this meeting, devoted to a further exploration of neutral and belligerent rights on the high seas, the Americans sometimes disagreed with their English hosts, as when they sought abolition of the category of conditional contraband, goods which a belligerent might seize as long as he paid a fair price to the owner. In several instances the Asquith ministry, now more firmly in command, overrode naval opinion to abandon extreme or outdated claims for sea power. Although this later led the House of Lords to reject the Declaration of London drafted by the conference, at the time the new approach paid impressive dividends. On most important issues the Americans and British, often with Japanese assistance, opposed suggestions of land powers, particularly Germany, for further restrictions on a belligerent's naval rights. The United States refused, in other words, to lend her support to changes which might upset the delicate balance of world power. In a sense she belatedly adopted Mahan's argument, even at the cost of abandoning her traditional stance. As at the earlier conferences, her sympathies and her assessment of the world situation tended to range her on England's side.

In response to public pressure and to the conferences' failure to build effective arbitral machinery, the American government repeatedly negotiated bilateral arbitration treaties. This effort, and the Hague concept as well, now seems wildly impractical, and even at the time many Americans, Theodore Roosevelt among them, warned against the delusion that nations would surrender vital interests to decision by others, whatever they might by treaty contract to do. Still, the cause of arbitration became very popular, seeming as it did to present an alternative to the use or menace of force, and it became a feature of American policy. Largely to gain American favor, Britain accepted each proposal put forward by the United States. Almost all Englishmen had enthusiastically welcomed the arbitration treaty of 1897, only to have the Senate crush their hopes, so in the new century they were more restrained. The *Spectator* summarized the general view, observing, "War between us is to our mind inconceivable. If arbitration can make the settlement of our differences easier, by all means let us have it; . . . but let us not suppose, as many Englishmen did in 1897, that our friendliness depends upon it." [13]

In this spirit England became one of five countries to sign the Roosevelt-Hay arbitration treaties of 1904, treaties of restricted scope (and thus acceptable to Germany, too) which, however, were emasculated by the Senate and therefore abandoned by the President before ratification. In the same way, England readily signed (but Germany would not) one of the Roosevelt-Root treaties negotiated with twenty-four powers in 1908 and 1909; because they surrendered to senatorial susceptibilities, all but three of these agreements went into effect, including the one with Great Britain. The five-year life of this treaty was extended by agreement in 1914.

President Taft was more deeply committed to arbitration than his predecessor and other Americans in positions of authority. In a talk with Ambassador Bryce in Beverly, Massachusetts, Olney's old stamping ground, in August 1910, Taft spelled out his interest in a broad arbitration treaty between England and the United States. At the time Taft, an Anglophile, planned to negotiate only with England, apparently because he considered potential disputes with that country so unimportant no one could object to arbitrating them.

[13] *Spectator* (London), vol. CVI (1911), p. 46.

Taft's conversation with Bryce bore no immediate fruit. The State Department hardly stirred, and the proposal struck blasé officials at the Foreign Office as one more platonic American gesture. Then the Foreign Secretary himself took up the cudgels. Grey was inspired to do so partly because he wished to arrange an escape valve from the obligations of the alliance with Japan, partly because he thought "The example would spread, and . . . one or more great European Powers would eventually make a similar agreement with us and the United States." This optimism horrified Grey's assistant, Sir Eyre Crowe, who protested, "Vague generalities, especially of the high-sounding kind, are no doubt a passport to American favour, but they are of doubtful value." However, in a statement to the House of Commons the Foreign Secretary invited an American offer. Not to be outdone, Arthur Balfour pledged the Conservative Party to support the proposed treaty. He welcomed Taft's interest as an indication of a "general feeling in the United States that the time has come when those two great countries should, whatever other countries may do, at all events recognize that, so far as they are concerned, peace is the greatest of their interests." [14] Negotiations at Washington soon produced a draft treaty dispatched to London for approval in May 1911.

Then the French insisted that they too be allowed to buy "a passport to American favour," a request the President could scarcely disapprove, although privately he grumbled that the French ambassador, Jusserand, was "the slyest little diplomat in Washington." [15] Next the Germans, overlooking their dislike of arbitration when two rivals seemed about to steal a march, hinted that they too might be interested. To meet these maneuvers and to quiet opposition from German- and Irish-American groups, the President announced that he would make a treaty

[14] Grey to Bryce, March 30, 1911, quoted in H. A. L. Fisher, *James Bryce (Viscount Bryce of Dechmont, O.M.)* (2 vols.; New York, 1927), vol. II, pp. 67–68; Crowe minute, January 29, 1911, Gooch and Temperley, eds., *British Documents*, vol. VIII, p. 550; *Parliamentary Debates*, Fifth Series, vol. XXII, p. 2501.

[15] Diary entry, June 7, 1911, Archie Butt, *Taft and Roosevelt: The Intimate Letters of Archie Butt, Military Aide* (2 vols.; Garden City, 1930), vol. II, p. 672.

with France and negotiate for one with Germany. This done, early in August treaties were signed with England and France which provided for arbitration of all disputes "susceptible of decision by the application of principles of law or equity" and for a joint commission of six to decide, in case of disagreement, whether the treaty was applicable to a particular dispute.

To Bryce's dismay, the treaties quickly ran into opposition. "Few bodies," he wrote, "are less moved by genuine public spirit, few have less width of view and less susceptibility to high ideas or sense of duty to mankind than has the Senate of the United States." [16] Many in the Roosevelt wing of the Republican Party were by no means unwilling to attack Taft, having the campaign of 1912 in view. Before the treaties were signed, the ex-President warned Bryce he would oppose an agreement with England, not because he expected quarrels so important they should not be arbitrated (with the Alaskan boundary out of the way, said he, this was no longer possible) but because he feared the treaty would create a precedent for arrangements with less trustworthy countries. The decision to include France and to talk with Germany reinforced such fears, and Lodge in particular emphasized them in the Senate. In addition to Rooseveltian opposition the treaties encountered the old bugaboo of senatorial prerogatives. Although they provided for senatorial concurrence whenever it was proposed to go to arbitration, legislators objected that, at least by implication, the joint commission deprived them of freedom of action. As a result the two treaties were passed over during 1911 and fiercely amended, so as virtually to destroy the joint commission and also to exempt many categories of dispute, when brought before the new session early in 1912. They were therefore, like the earlier Roosevelt-Hay treaties, pocketed by the President.

The most striking part of the Senate's discussion was the virtual absence of appeals to Anglophobia. A Democrat, Gilbert Hitchcock of Nebraska, delivered two speeches charging that the

---

[16] Bryce to Grey, August 22, 1911, Gooch and Temperley, eds., *British Documents*, vol. VIII, p. 596.

English treaty was a step toward alliance, or at least that it was so viewed in Great Britain, but Hitchcock also argued at length that the two countries' friendship made an arbitration treaty unnecessary. Other senators referred to the charge, whether made by Hitchcock or outside critics, only in order to rebut it or to maintain that the treaties with Britain and France were the first steps in a grand alliance for peace drawing together all nations of the world. Violent change, they hoped, would disappear from the earth.

The Wilson administration, which took office in March 1913, made no effort to revive the two treaties. Instead the Democrats extended the Roosevelt-Root pacts and in addition followed an approach which was the personal property of the new secretary of state. Bryan's treaties pledged the signatories, if diplomacy failed, to refrain from hostilities for one year while a commission prepared a report, purely factual, on the dispute between them; presumably, during this period both sides would think hard about the wisdom of going to war. Even Bryan's chief had little faith in this approach, but ultimately the Secretary signed treaties with thirty nations. Of the major powers, only Germany, again refusing to throw away the advantages of preparedness, and Japan refused to join Bryan's crusade. London reacted coolly to his first approaches, then changed its tune. "The proposal seems to me too theoretical and visionary," complained Sir Arthur Nicolson, the permanent under-secretary, but even he recognized that ". . . we cannot well meet it with a refusal off hand." [17] The Foreign Secretary and other officials favored accepting the American proposal, although Grey considered it an inconsequential contribution to peace. The treaty was finally signed in September 1914, after the World War began, and ratifications were exchanged in November. Britain, like most other powers, considered it a cheap way to buy American good will.

The whole story of arbitration treaties in the pre-war years is a tangled one of unreal hopes, of pride, and of cynicism. For Anglo-American relations the negotiations nevertheless serve as baro-

[17] Nicolson minute, n.d. [January, 1914?], *ibid.*, p. 611.

metric readings. Britain accepted every American proposal, even
the Bryan scheme she understandably considered ridiculous, and
in 1911 she even forced the pace. Of major powers, only France
had a similar record. Although Taft found it necessary to
broaden his approach, in 1911 he dreamed of a treaty with England alone, a risk neither of his two predecessors would even have
considered, and Roosevelt said he would have favored the English treaty if certain it would not create a precedent for agreements with other countries. Negotiations looking to arbitration
treaties did not make the weather, but, like those at the Hague,
they reflected it.

Similar comments might be made about the public campaign which surrounded and stimulated these negotiations.
Many propagandists for peace explicitly called for Anglo-American leadership of the crusade. Thus Norman Angell's *The
Great Illusion* (1910), the most famous tract of the day, contained a peroration on Anglo-American responsibilities to lead
the world toward an irenic paradise. Edwin Mead, one of the
most prolific of a very prolific crew of agitators, waxed so rhapsodic on Anglo-American superiority that one sometimes lost
sight of his professed purpose, which was simply to secure a
treaty between England and the United States as the first step
toward a new world order.

Some of the most sincere believers in arbitration were troubled by their colleagues' emphasis on an understanding between
the English-speaking powers. They were well aware that, with
some justice in the case of such persons as Mead, this exposed
arbitration treaties to attack as a form of negative alliance, protecting Britain's rear while she turned her attention to European
problems, or serving as a buttress to the status quo so advanta-
geous to her. They saw, too, that as long as the movement gave
priority to a treaty with England it could be argued by Irish-Americans and others that arbitration merely served "the purpose of
blinding the American people to the real purpose of Great Britain while she pursues her policy of aggression and spoliation
which," the holder of John Quincy Adams' old seat maintained,

"in time she will endeavor to extend toward this country." [18] Finally, some people believed, an emphasis on Britain's peaceful intentions discouraged negotiations with other and, though they declined to say so, more difficult nations like Germany. President David Starr Jordan of Stanford University, one of Mead's rivals in prolixity, argued in *Unseen Empire* (1912) that Britain, where two dukes and fifty other peers owned shares in the Vickers and Maxim arms combines, was every bit as bellicose as her rivals. Yet even Jordan dismissed the possibility of war with England and France in a short paragraph, but found it necessary to show in several pages of labored analysis that there were no insurmountable obstacles to peace between the United States and Germany. The comparative absence of Anglophobia, whether in Congress or outside, is a striking feature of discussions of arbitration.

Only once did the United States actually go to arbitration with England. This was, however, by far the most important issue the United States submitted to arbitration, involving as it did the most persistent issue in the history of American diplomacy. Ever since 1782 the rights of American fishermen in the waters off and on the coasts of Newfoundland had vexed Anglo-American relations. The joint high commission of 1898 had this item high on its agenda, and in 1902 Secretary Hay negotiated a settlement which, however, failed because the President refused to take up the cudgels when, for political reasons, Senator Lodge and others opposed any concessions. Before the Hay-Bond convention received Senate approval in 1905, it was so substantially amended that Newfoundland not only refused to accept it but also denounced the *modus vivendi* under which fishing operations had been carried on for many years. Lodge therefore proposed to send naval vessels to support what he called the "rights" of American fishermen, only to have Roosevelt reject this suggestion as too provocative. Grey then framed a new *modus vivendi* and forced Newfoundland to accept it, a procedure which pro-

[18] Rep. James F. O'Connell, April 11, 1908, *Congressional Record*, 60th Congress, 1st Session, p. 4649.

voked such heated criticism at the Imperial Conference of 1907
that all mention of it was expunged from the official record. No
one expected this antique issue to lead to war since, basically, it
involved one tiny portion of the British Empire and only one of
the forty-eight states, but a nasty quarrel seemed to impend.

To avoid this, President Roosevelt proposed arbitration via
the Hague machinery. After some months' discussion of the
terms of reference, Ambassador Bryce and Secretary Root
reached agreement in January 1909. (At about the same time
they concluded the Boundary Waters Treaty, which established
a permanent joint commission, ever since the haven of unemployed politicians of the Presidential party in the United States,
to decide disputes involving inland waters.) During the summer
of 1910 the tribunal heard evidence and arguments from both
sides, notably an intricate six-day presentation by ex-Secretary
Root. The tribunal handed down the almost inevitable compromise decision at the end of the year, and even Lodge's constituents accepted it without noisy protest. In 1912 the two nations
agreed to set up a permanent commission to decide such issues of
detail as might arise. Thus there disappeared forever "a controversy," as J. L. Garvin wrote with relief, "which has repeatedly
threatened the peace of the English-speaking world." [19]

Americans, who deeply involved themselves in the campaign for arbitration, played no equivalent role in European politics. The isolationist tradition was too strong, and only a few,
pessimists or realists, considered American interests at issue in
European controversies. Yet attitudes, and occasionally actions,
also demonstrated the emerging community of outlook between
the English and American nations, the belief that Britain and
the United States alike had an interest in discouraging violent
changes in the world equilibrium.

Often, as when they discussed the entente cordiale between
England and France, Americans took a relatively naive view. The
Anglo-French agreement of April 1904, nominally only the settlement of rival colonial claims, actually aimed to draw the two
powers together in the face of a German threat. The American

[19] *Fortnightly Review* (London), vol. XCI (1909), p. 211.

press failed to understand this. "Truly," declared the New York *Globe*, "there is hope for universal peace if statesmen of such ancient foes as France and Great Britain can calmly meet and settle differences so complicated." The New York *World* agreed: "It is a long step in the world's progress through conciliation and arbitration toward universal peace." [20] Only a few editors speculated upon the broad implications of the entente, and then to picture it as drawing France away from her old ally, Russia, still considered a major threat to world stability and a likely victor in the war with Japan which had just begun.

The Moroccan crisis of 1905–1906, Germany's first challenge to the entente, drew Americans a good way from their naiveté. The climax of the Russo-Japanese War and the Portsmouth negotiations, overlapping as they did the first stages of the Moroccan dispute, tended to divert public interest, and the President considered the Asian problem more important. Still, he came to play an increasingly active role, certainly an increasingly anti-German one, and his people followed a similar course, moving from comparative disinterest and "a plague on both your houses" viewpoint to a rather general feeling, when the controversy ended, that Germany had suffered a merited diplomatic defeat.

By the entente cordiale England committed herself to support French interests in Morocco. Paris soon began a campaign to convert the sultanate into a virtual protectorate, a move Germany decided to challenge. Late in March 1905, Kaiser Wilhelm visited Tangier, where he proclaimed German support for the principles of political independence and equality of commercial opportunity. The sultan proposed an international conference, an idea instantly endorsed by Berlin but resisted by the French until July, after the premier had ousted Foreign Minister Delcassé, chief architect of the aggressive policy in Morocco. Throughout these events British officials and the press held loyal to the entente.

Delcassé had challenged the status quo in Morocco; the

[20] New York *Globe* and New York *World*, quoted in *Literary Digest* (New York), vol. XXVIII (1904), p. 547.

Kaiser professed to support the Open Door. As a result, many American observers at first sided with the Germans. "Who can blame them," asked the *New York Times*, "for demanding the open door, a fair field and no favor, in all the unappropriated parts of the earth?" "Germany," said Sydney Brooks, who usually took Britain's part, "occupies an unassailable position both in law and in logic." [21] The influence of such thinking never entirely disappeared, and when Roosevelt came under attack for thrusting himself into Old World politics many who defended him, notably the maverick senator from Colorado, Thomas M. Patterson, did so primarily on the ground that a challenge to American trading interests justified his actions. As time passed, however, the commercial theme became less important. Even at the beginning of the controversy the *Times*, pointing out Germany's imperfect record, suggested that to prove her sincerity she ought to apply the Open Door to her holdings in China.

As challenges flew back and forth, Americans came to see the political as opposed to the economic factors in the situation. They deplored the willingness of both sides to go to the brink over issues of little intrinsic importance. "A tense, suspicious, and timorous state of mind is displayed by nearly all the participants in the controversy . . . ," the *Nation* complained. "The chief stock in trade of the statesmanship of either country seems to be settled suspicion of the other." Above all, American commentators from the President on down saw the German challenge for what it was, an effort to probe the strength of the entente cordiale and if possible drive a wedge between the new friends. Most concluded, and at least by implication welcomed the fact, that this attempt was a failure. A few weeks after the Kaiser's speech, *Collier's* reported, "The German interference in the Moroccan question helped to re-cement the Anglo-French friendship." The title of this article, "Germany Makes Trouble," [22] reflects a view broadly held in the United States.

[21] *New York Times*, April 7, 1905; Sydney Brooks, "The Aims of Germany," *Harper's Weekly* (New York), vol. XLIX (1905), p. 649.
[22] *Nation* (New York), vol. LXXXI (1905), p. 311; "Germany Makes Trouble in Morocco," *Collier's* (New York), vol. XXXV (May 6, 1905), p. 11.

At the beginning of the crisis, while Roosevelt was on tour in the West, the Germans asked him to use his efforts to bring about a conference, particularly by overcoming British resistance. Although he welcomed the idea of a conference, the President moved cautiously. Since John Hay was traveling in Europe in a vain effort to restore his health, Roosevelt approached the British embassy through Secretary of War Taft. He directed Taft, "if Sir Mortimer . . . is in any rational mood and you think the nice but somewhat fat-witted British intellect will stand it," to express concern over the friction between Germany and England and to offer his services as conciliator. By suggesting that France be by-passed this approach served Germany's purpose, whatever may have been the President's motives. Durand therefore responded in the narrowest possible fashion, simply stating that Britain saw no danger of war with Germany. Lord Lansdowne approved this stance, like his subordinate failing to see that Roosevelt expected some signs of British willingness to defuse the controversy. The President talked with Durand, this time explicitly supporting the conference proposal, upon his return from the West. Durand again irritated the President. He seemed more interested in humiliating Germany and avoiding French recrimination than in restoring harmony. Roosevelt even concluded the British "were quite willing to face the possibility of war. . . . I did not think," he later recalled, "this showed much valor on their part, although from their point of view it was sagacious," [23] since the brunt of land fighting would necessarily be borne by France and Germany. Once again, as in the chain of events leading to the treaty of Portsmouth, Britain and America were working at odds.

This time Roosevelt drifted toward the British camp, primarily because he too came to appreciate the danger of an Anglo-French split. His interest in a conference continued, even increased, but his tactics changed. He no longer sought to use Britain as a lever upon France. Instead he told Speck von Stern-

[23] Roosevelt to Taft, April 20, 1905, Morison, ed., *Letters of Roosevelt*, vol. IV, p. 1162; Roosevelt to Reid, April 28, 1906, *ibid.*, vol. V, p. 234.

burg there could be no conference without French concurrence, and he began to urge Paris to agree to one, sweetening the pill by pointing out that realities of international politics made it unlikely a decision would go against France. He himself, he meaningfully confided to Ambassador Jusserand, considered Germany's demands unreasonable. The President's intervention, supplementing domestic developments in France, led Prime Minister Rouvier to agree in principle to a conference. Thereafter, Roosevelt turned his attention to the difficult, often detailed tasks of arranging the timing, membership, and terms of reference. "I want to keep on good terms with Germany, and if possible to prevent a rupture between Germany and France," he wrote. "But my sympathies have at bottom been with France and I suppose will continue so. Still I shall try to hold an even keel." [24] In the end it was the President who made the proposals which resulted in formal agreement, at the end of September, to hold a conference the next January. The Germans, foiled in their effort to split Britain and France, accepted largely because they found themselves diplomatically isolated and could not accept the added burden of American disapproval by fighting further for more favorable terms.

The President and the new secretary of state, Elihu Root, prepared instructions for Henry White, selected to serve as the American delegate to the conference. The formal instructions were bland, clearly designed for future release to Congress, whence already issued some protest against participation in European politics, and to the public. Privately, Root added some spice. "While we are friendly to Germany, and wish to remain so," the Secretary wrote, "we regard as a favorable condition for the peace of the world, and, therefore, for the best interests of the United States, the continued entente cordiale between France and England, and we do not wish to contribute towards any estrangement between those two countries." [25] On the un-

---

[24] Roosevelt to White, August 23, 1905, *ibid.*, vol. IV, p. 1313.
[25] Root to White, November 28, 1905, quoted in Beale, *Roosevelt and the Rise of America*, p. 372.

derlying issue, in other words, the Americans sided with Germany's enemies. Just before the emissaries came together at Algeciras, a Spanish port across the straits from Morocco, Root repeated these sentiments to Durand, at the same time, however, making it clear that the Americans would play their cards close to the chest. Still, having been permitted to glimpse Roosevelt's hand, Britain could face the conference with greater ease.

Henry White and other delegates gathered at the Reina Christina Hotel in Algeciras in January 1906. In the dining room each delegation had its own table, marked with a national flag. On each business day, the delegates pushed back their chairs and proceeded in separate groups to the conference hall half a mile away. For many weeks tension charged the air. White played his role with circumspection; he hardly spoke in formal sessions and at least once withheld his vote to avoid swelling the majority against Germany. He also acted with considerable skill in the search for compromise, shuttling back and forth between suites at the Reina Christina. Agreement on the key issue, control of Morocco's police, did not come until March, and the conference only finally adjourned in April.

White and his chief frequently disagreed with the French, and solution of the police question went further in the direction of Moroccan partition than the President desired. (The British, too, though at different times, considered France unreasonable, and on the whole they probably welcomed White's efforts to get her to moderate her views.) On the major issue—Germany's effort to drive a wedge between France and England by imposing a solution humiliating to France—Roosevelt did not hesitate. He steadfastly opposed Germany's plan for an international gendarmerie, which would have meant the destruction of France's privileged position. Instead, he threw his weight behind a plan for Franco-Spanish control of the police which differed essentially from the French proposal only in that it included mild Italian supervision. When Berlin hesitated he wrote to Kaiser Wilhelm virtually demanding that Germany accept his proposal or face diplomatic isolation. The Wilhelmstrasse perforce gave way, seeking only to salvage control of the police at Casablanca, where alone Germany had substantial interests, for some other power. The President resisted this proposal, warned his friend Sternburg he might recall Henry White and publish his own correspondence with the Kaiser, and finally drove Germany to surrender. After a bit of Rooseveltian sparring with the French, agreement on the police issue was reached on March 27.

Just after the conference adjourned ten days later, the chief British delegate sputtered to Henry White, "The damned Germans have had the audacity to offer us inducements to get us away from France!" [26] This maladroit effort never had much chance of success, but Roosevelt's refusal to support Germany—even though the Kaiser professed to be concerned only to maintain Moroccan integrity, a cause which the President and most Americans supported—certainly eased the strain on the Anglo-French entente. The plan sketched in Root's private letter to White had been followed, to Britain's immense benefit.

Roosevelt did not trumpet his success. Indeed, he did not allow Sir Edward Grey to learn of his decisive role regarding Casablanca until he visited England after leaving the White House, and in 1906 he attempted to convince the Kaiser that, by procuring some semblance of an international presence in Morocco, Germany had won a diplomatic victory. Those on the outside might conclude, like an editorialist in the New York *Tribune*, "There was no suspicion on the part of either Germany or France that Mr. White was seeking to aid the other," but the Germans knew better. Sternburg's successor later remembered the American role at Algeciras as a "fairly trustworthy forecast of all that subsequently happened at the Peace Conference of Versailles." [27]

The intricate Algeciras negotiations hardly lent themselves to confident generalizations. Yet most observers considered the

---

[26] White to Roosevelt, April 8, 1906, quoted in Allan Nevins, *Henry White: Thirty Years of American Diplomacy* (New York, 1930), p. 272.

[27] New York *Tribune*, quoted in *Literary Digest* (New York), vol. XXXII (1906), p. 510; Count Johann von Bernstorff, *My Three Years in America* (New York, 1920), p. 14.

settlement a German defeat. A few Americans praised Wilhelm as a man who valued peace more than victory, and the most earnest advocates of peace maintained that the conference set a hopeful precedent for international settlements. Most commentators agreed that, as the *Nation* expressed it, "the most striking diplomatic result of the conference is the demonstration of the isolation of Berlin." The *Review of Reviews*, admitting as did others that Germany had established a claim to be heard on international questions, noted also that, "instead of endangering the Anglo-French understanding, the Kaiser . . . has shown . . . the world . . . just how close together they have stood." [28] Once concerned about preservation of the local status quo—Moroccan independence and integrity—Americans were now willing to subordinate this question to the larger one, the challenge to stability posed by the German challenge.

Roosevelt's intervention in the Moroccan imbroglio, though cautious and concealed, was his country's deepest participation in European politics. Furthermore, Root's description of the entente cordiale as "a favorable condition for the peace of the world, and, therefore, for the best interests of the United States," was an unusually explicit recognition of the importance of European politics. During a second Moroccan crisis in 1911, for example, neither the government nor the press showed a tithe of the interest shown during the earlier controversy. Most commentators blamed Germany for the crisis, explaining and sometimes excusing her action with the argument that as a late arrival on the world scene she found it necessary to challenge the status quo, but only a tiny handful considered American interests involved—primarily because a German lodgment in Morocco might be a way-station to Latin America—and the Taft administration played no part in negotiations surrounding the crisis.

The death of Edward VII in May 1910, like that of his mother nine years earlier, gave Americans an opportunity to show their feelings. Congress passed a resolution of sympathy praising

[28] *Nation*, vol. LXXXII (1906), p. 276; *Review of Reviews* (New York), vol. XXXII (1906), p. 533.

Edward as a man of peace. Secretary of State Knox told inter-
viewers the King's influence had always been found "on the side
of peace and justice," [29] a sentiment echoed by ex-President Roosevelt in a public statement. Taft asked his predecessor, then
traveling in Europe, to represent the United States at the funeral, a gesture much appreciated in England. Ambassador Reid
feared that, in order to claim a place among monarchs and military men riding horseback in the funeral procession, Roosevelt
would insist upon donning an old Rough Riders uniform he was
rumored to have in his trunk. However, the ex-President behaved
with perfect decorum, accepting a position in the eighth carriage
in line and watching with amusement while other mourners
scrambled for position. Upon Edward's bier the Americans
placed a wreath of magnolia leaves from Washington's grave and
oak leaves from a tree planted there by Prince Edward during a
visit fifty years earlier.

Commentators sometimes praised the King for his contribution to Anglo-American friendship. "His death," one journal
said, "does not tend to dissolve, but to renew, the unwritten pact
of friendship between two nations who have so much in sympathy." In one of the few comments harking back to the racist emphasis of Victoria's day, an Episcopalian clergyman in Boston
declared, "Not as Americans and not as Englishmen, but as
Anglo-Saxons do we gather to worship the God of our fathers.
Today two nations kneel at one bier." [30] However, as if Americans
felt Anglo-American friendship too firmly established to need
discussion, they devoted little attention to it, concentrating instead upon Edward's role in world politics.

Overwhelmingly they agreed that Edward VII had been a
man of peace, largely responsible for the ententes, particularly
the rapprochement with France, which laid to rest ancient quarrels. The *Nation* demurred, pointing out, "this policy of friendships and alliances may . . . actually . . . have accentuated the

[29] Quoted in *New York Times*, May 7, 1910.
[30] *Century* (New York), vol. LXXX (1910), p. 474; *Boston Evening Transcript*, May 30, 1910.

perils of the general European situation," and other commentators admitted the King's prejudice against Germany, which they viewed as a blemish on an otherwise noble record. On the other hand, peace societies competed with one another in the fulsomeness of their praise of the dead King, and editors joined the din. "He accomplished more for the peace of the continent," said the *Boston Evening Transcript*, "than any other single man in modern history." "He found England isolated; he left her the centre of a great chain of understandings, 'ententes,' and alliances," [31] observed the *New York Times*, and the *Times*, like all but the *Nation* and a few others, considered his work to have been a service to peace. Few saw the long-range implications of the polarization of Europe. England's alliances and world peace seemed not only compatible but complementary.

During the pre-war decade, most Americans felt rather than reasoned their way toward a community of outlook. There were exceptions, men who thought or believed they thought in realistic terms, particularly in the circle around Theodore Roosevelt. John Hay talked privately of parallel interests, and he chafed at the restraints—isolationism, Anglophobia—which prevented an alliance. His friend Henry Adams wrote in 1905, "We have got to support France against Germany, and fortify an Atlantic system beyond attack; for if Germany breaks down England or France, she becomes the center of a military world, and we are lost." In private the President expressed the same sentiments, at least to the extent of recognizing that England's fall would confront the United States with a serious challenge from Germany. "Do you know," he wrote to a big-navy friend in England, "I think I have become almost as anxious as you are to have the British fleet kept up to the highest point of efficiency." [32]

Several publicists, Rooseveltians all, raised their voices to deplore America's willingness to base her foreign policy upon out-

---

[31] "England and the Peace of Europe," *Nation*, vol. XC (1910), p. 529; *Boston Transcript*, May 7, 1910; *New York Times*, May 7, 1910.

[32] Adams to Mrs. Cameron, August 27, 1905, Worthington C. Ford, ed., *Letters of Henry Adams, 1892–1918* (Boston, 1938), p. 461; Roosevelt to Lee, August 7, 1908, Morison, ed., *Letters of Roosevelt*, vol. VI, p. 1159.

dated principles and emotional reactions. In *The Promise of American Life*, one of the most widely read and influential political tracts of the day, a clarion call for positive government that helped inspire Roosevelt's New Nationalism, Herbert Croly devoted a few pages to foreign policy. What he had to say was a logical extension of his prescription for domestic affairs. Croly argued in particular that the United States must face the world "with a sound, well-informed, and positive conception of the American national interest rather than a negative and ignorant conception." He hoped his country would be ready to fight for peace, perhaps at the side of England, France, and Italy. "It looks," he wrote, "as if at some future time the power of the United States might well be sufficient, when thrown into the balance, to tip the scales in favor of a comparatively pacific settlement of international complications. Under such conditions a policy of neutrality would be a policy of irresponsibility and unwisdom." [33]

Admiral Mahan sounded the same note in numerous articles, and, most fully, in *The Interest of America in International Conditions*, a book published in 1910. Like Croly, Mahan began by calling for a realistic assessment of interests and then proceeded to argue that such an assessment showed the need for close relations with Great Britain. Both had reason to fear "the greatness and menace of Germany" and, to a lesser extent, the growth of Japanese power in the Far East. "In the horoscope of every nation," the Admiral said, "there usually is one other Power, accordant relations with which are of primary importance. . . . There is strong reason to believe that international considerations should assign to the British Empire this prominent place in the understanding of Americans." [34] The United States should cast off isolationism or cooperate with England.

A much younger friend of Roosevelt, Lewis Einstein, spelled out the analysis in greater detail. In 1909 Einstein, a student of history who wrote four books before he was thirty and a

[33] Croly, *Promise of American Life*, pp. 313, 312.
[34] Alfred T. Mahan, *The Interest of America in International Conditions* (Boston, 1910), pp. 57–58, 114–115.

diplomat who had served, among other places, at Algeciras, brought out a book blandly entitled *American Foreign Policy*. The arguments it contained were far from bland, and the author wisely kept his name off the title page. Einstein argued for active involvement in Europe to prevent its domination by a single power, namely Germany. "Towards England," he argued in a summary sentence, "the clearest dictates of reason impel us to turn." [35] Together the two countries could serve the cause of peace and support the integrity of other nations.

While vacationing in Florence three years later, Einstein sent a long analysis of the Anglo-German rivalry to Francis M. Huntington Wilson, a superior in the State Department. This letter, composed between visits to the Uffizi, the Bargello, and other sights, was an amazing exercise in prophecy. Einstein not only urged Washington to face up to the probability of a European war; he predicted a long, costly conflict at a time when almost everyone else expected the issue, if war came, to be settled in one decisive campaign, and from this proceeded to argue that America would be deeply involved through her credit and her commerce, which Germany was bound to attack. The defeat of Britain, Einstein argued, "would be a defeat for us by the erection of a Power supreme on land and sea," a destruction of the European balance of power upon which American security rested. "It would not be wise statesmanship to remain passive if England should by any series of disasters be crushed." [36] Einstein's arguments impressed Huntington Wilson, who hated Germany, and with Washington's approval the letter, slightly modified, was published in 1913. Once again Einstein discreetly took shelter behind a pseudonym. Less understandably, perhaps through excessive caution, he chose as his outlet an English journal, the *National Review*. The article scarcely caused a stir, and, like Admiral Mahan, Einstein gloomily concluded that his countrymen were incorrigibly blind.

Einstein and other Rooseveltian realists shared one further

[35] Einstein, *American Foreign Policy*, p. 46.
[36] Lewis Einstein, *A Prophecy of the War* (New York, 1918), pp. 46, 45. Theodore Roosevelt wrote the foreword for this republication of Einstein's prewar writings.

concept, a concept not unique with them but a common leitmo-
tif in their writings. All pointed to and deplored the decline of
British power as a result of external challenge but even more as a
consequence of social decadence and loss of purpose. This was
not a new line; Brooks Adams, after all, had emphasized it at the
beginning of the century. Nor was it merely a foreigner's view;
Lord Rosebery publicly wept over England's decay as early as
1905, while in a famous lecture brusquely entitled "Decadence,"
delivered at Oxford in 1908, Balfour levied an assault upon all of
western civilization but particularly his own country. In America,
Croly expressed the concept most brutally, writing that England
"is lacking in purpose. It is lacking in brains. It is lacking in
faith." The root of the problem, he argued, with the hope of convincing Americans to move in New Nationalist directions, lay in
the fact that the English "have erected compromise into an ultimate principle of political action." [37] Roosevelt himself often
expressed similar but less heated views, describing England as
"flabby" and lacking in morale.

Neither Mahan nor Einstein nor Croly called for an alliance
with England, perhaps because they considered it chore enough
to shake the American people out of old habits of thought. The
admiral wanted only a coordination of policies; the diplomat was
not prepared to join England unless German victory seemed im-
minent; the publicist recommended no specific action. There
was, during these years, much less talk of close ties with England
than during the heady days of 1898. In a book written more in
the sentimental spirit of the old days than in that of the new
realists, a Bostonian, Sinclair Kennedy, called for a grand Anglo-
Saxon confederation. William M. Fullerton, a long-time American resident of Paris and former correspondent of the London
Times, concluded a Croly-like analysis of Problems of Power
with an appeal for a vaguely defined "pact for the peace of
the world," [38] uniting Britain, France, and the United States
against Germany and other disturbers of stability. Kennedy and
Fullerton, sometimes joined by the journalist Sydney Brooks,

---

[37] Croly, Promise of American Life, pp. 233–234.
[38] William M. Fullerton, Problems of Power (New York, 1913), p. 315.

were almost alone. Moreover, most Americans read Croly for his ideas on domestic affairs, never heard of Einstein, and found Mahan's views less congenial than his calls for empire in the 1890's. But almost no one took the opposite view, urging America to see that her interests were diametrically opposed to those of England or suggesting that she should bestow her blessings upon anti-British combinations.

Pre-war Englishmen were as cynical, or as realistic, as Lord Salisbury in 1898. They knew Fullertons and Kennedys were a rarity, an impossibly tiny base upon which to build a political connection. Admiral Fisher wrote, "the one absorbing object of my life is the British-American Union, and I am working hard," but even Jackie Fisher, notorious for his lack of tact, knew it was necessary to work *"like a mole!"* When Theodore Roosevelt was leaving the White House in 1909, Arthur J. Balfour prepared for him a long paper on "The Possibility of Anglo-Saxon Confederation," but the actual recommendations of the Conservative leader, himself half a decade out of power, were modest. Moreover Balfour admitted he expected no progress "until some other power rises in the world which makes a rapprochement of England and the U.S.A. a matter of importance from the view of defence," [39] and he knew the Americans did not yet so view the rise of Germany.

Thus when, in a short editorial on "America and the Command of the Sea," Strachey's *Spectator* argued that the United States should and probably would support England against a German challenge, the editorial stimulated violent criticism. British colleagues chastised Strachey for forcing the pace. When the smoke of journalistic battle cleared, a London correspondent assured American readers none but a lunatic fringe in England expected an alliance at the present time. "In some unspecified and incognizable future," he reported, "Englishmen count upon the United States dropping the rôle of a hermit nation and playing a far more active and conspicuous part in international poli-

[39] Fisher to Gerard Fiennes, March 9, 1911, Arthur J. Marder, ed., *Fear God and Dread Nought: The Correspondence of Admiral of the Fleet Lord Fisher of Kilverstone* (3 vols.; London, 1952–1959), vol. II, p. 361; Balfour, quoted in Kenneth Young, *Arthur James Balfour* (London, 1963), p. 278.

tics; and when that time comes they are confident that Americans will find it to their interest to work in co-operation with Great Britain." [40] Until that time Britons were prepared to wait, meanwhile avoiding conflicts which might delay America's emergence from the hermitage. The thoughtful among them deplored talk of an alliance.

British ministries, whether Unionist or Liberal, showed the same acuity, seeking time and again for those "passports to American favour" that evoked Eyre Crowe's sarcasm. In most areas they conceded to American desires, and in the Far East they concealed their disapproval of American policy. "The English never hold their ground against the Americans," the German ambassador to the United States wrote in 1914.[41] This comment was made more in contempt than in envy, for Bernstorff, who wanted Berlin to show greater flexibility, never considered concessions as far-reaching as England's. Nevertheless, London's policy permitted Britain to husband her resources for more important disputes and virtually ensured that the United States would not view those disputes in an anti-British fashion.

Issues of world politics from Algeciras to Sarajevo did not involve the United States, and no one proposed to make them America's business. As observers, most influential American elements found it easy to make up their minds when they sought to identify conservative as opposed to disruptive forces in European politics. Britain represented the status quo more clearly than any other European power including her ally, France. British interests coincided, so it seemed to leading Americans, with those of their own country. The new views spread slowly to the whole country. Those forces which were most horrified by talk of an alliance in 1898, which criticized England during the Boer War and the controversies of Theodore Roosevelt's first term found it much more difficult to gain support. Anglophobia had not died, but it had lessened.

[40] *Spectator*, vol. CII (1909), p. 804; *North American Review* (New York), vol. CXC (1909), p. 128.
[41] Bernstorff to Freiherr von dem Bussche Haddenhausen, January 2, 1914, quoted in Bernstorff, *Memoirs*, p. 122.

CHAPTER ELEVEN

The Liberal Ministry

FROM THE MIDDLE of the Moroccan crisis onward, England had a new ministry. The Unionists became so exhausted and faction-ridden, thanks to Chamberlain's scheme of imperial preference, that Balfour threw in his hand in December 1905. A general election the next month returned four hundred Liberals, including over two hundred new M.P.s, and only one hundred and fifty Unionists; Irish Nationalists and two dozen members of the new Labour Party captured the remaining seats. After sharp conflict made deeper by the reform budget of 1909, the government submitted its record to the electorate. The Liberals lost a hundred seats but maintained themselves in power, aided by some forty Labourites and eighty Irish representatives. A second election, also in 1910, scarcely changed the composition of the House of Commons.

The Liberal government, under Sir Henry Campbell-Bannerman until he resigned in April 1908, two weeks before his death, and thereafter under H. H. Asquith, in no way markedly altered British foreign policy, certainly not toward the United States. It did represent a shift in the political center of gravity— no landed aristocrat held a leading post until the well-descended and also half-American but scarcely wealthy Winston Churchill became president of the Board of Trade in 1908—and it did embark upon social and political reform most Americans found congenial.

Americans, like the British electorate, had been unfavorably

impressed by the Tory government during its last years in power.
Just as in earlier years they failed to give proper credit to William
Pitt and the Earl of Liverpool, so in 1905 American commentators virtually ignored the good work of the Tories headed by
Salisbury and then Balfour. They said little of English attitudes
in 1898, the Hay-Pauncefote treaty or the Alaskan settlement,
although Lord Lansdowne won some praise for his technical
skill. As for his colleagues, especially Arthur Balfour, the press
made clear its feeling that their time of usefulness had passed.
Few realized that the government, whatever its record in world
diplomacy, had on the whole been quick to see the importance of
American friendship and wise in its cultivation.

Neither Campbell-Bannerman nor Asquith ever showed
much interest in the United States. Domestic reform, Ireland,
and European affairs monopolized their attention. Lansdowne's
successor, Sir Edward Grey, a weary, lonely man (his wife died in
a riding accident shortly after he took office) devoted most of his
attention to European concerns. Somehow he managed, as Elie
Halévy has written, "to acquire in a few months an amazing
prestige not only in England but on the Continent, and the can-
dour, honesty, and entire disinterestedness to which everyone
paid tribute invested a policy often ambiguous with the halo of
his personal honour." [1] This was not unimportant for relations
with the United States, for Americans too came to view Grey as
one of the reassuring figures on the European scene.

In addition, Grey somehow found time to cultivate the
United States. He made friends with the successive American
ambassadors who worked with him, Whitelaw Reid and Walter
Hines Page, Reid's replacement after the Democrats came to
power in 1913. Page bestowed upon him an almost unqualified
accolade: "He'd make a good American with the use of very little sandpaper." On substantial matters, notably the arbitration
treaty of 1911 and the Mexican question, Sir Edward deferred to

[1] Elie Halévy, *The Rule of Democracy* (E. I. Watkin, trans.; *A History of the English People in the Nineteenth Century*, vol. VI; rev. ed., New York, 1961), p. 126.

Washington; "he'd yield anything that his party and Parliament would permit," Page maintained.[2] Grey also altered the Anglo-Japanese alliance to lessen the danger of trouble with America, and he preserved a wise silence during discussions of Canadian-American reciprocity.

Even on minor matters Grey was alert. Following an earthquake in Jamaica in January 1907, an American admiral landed marines to protect American citizens against potential Negro violence, not bothering to secure approval from local authorities. Governor Swettenham thereupon wrote a blistering protest, and President Roosevelt called Grey by trans-Atlantic telephone to request a statement deploring the Governor's language. He discovered that Grey had already directed Swettenham to withdraw his protest and ordered the embassy at Washington to extend Britain's apologies. Here, where the American had most seriously misbehaved, Grey did not stand upon ceremony. This type of approach often caused reactionary journals to denounce what one called "obsequious subservience to Washington,"[3] but Grey was untroubled by such criticism.

Shortly before taking office, to reassure those who feared the Liberals might overturn British foreign policy, Grey delivered a major address on the "three cardinal features . . . of British policy, not one of which does the Liberal Party wish to see changed." Numbers two and three were the Japanese alliance and the French entente. "The first," he said, "is the growing friendship and good feeling between ourselves and the United States, a matter of common ground and common congratulation to all parties in this country." The Foreign Secretary never lost sight of this first principle. Speaking to a closed meeting of an imperial conference, he said, "I trust the conclusion of an Arbitration Treaty sooner or later will make it clear to the whole world how very sure, not only we, but the United States, are that there can be no serious cause of trouble between the British Em-

[2] Page to Wilson, October 25, 1913, quoted in Burton J. Hendrick, *The Life and Letters of Walter H. Page* (3 vols.; Garden City, 1922–1925), vol. I, p. 150. The order of the two quoted passages has been reversed.
[3] *Saturday Review* (London), vol. CX (1910), p. 70.

pire and the United States." [4] After war came in 1914 Grey resisted, as long as he remained in office, the pressure of those who gave a much lower priority to American friendship.

Grey it was who brusquely dismissed Sir Mortimer Durand and replaced him with James Bryce. "I suppose," wrote a friend to Spring Rice, who hoped for the job, "the Yanks will be charmed, as what they want is . . . that we . . . send them a celebrity. I think *any* celebrity would suit." Grey chose Bryce largely because of his fame, but it was a special kind of fame, not a vague celebrity, which commended him to the Foreign Secretary. Bryce was well known as a liberal, particularly as a friend of Irish home rule, which most Americans favored. More important, he was universally considered, as a consequence of *The American Commonwealth* and subsequent writings, the most perceptive and among the most friendly foreign observers of the United States. Bryce could not be accused of mere sentimentality, for he mixed criticism, particularly of the misgovernment of cities, with his praise; this candor made the praise even more welcome. Moreover, Bryce had shown himself a firm believer in Anglo-American friendship. The year before his appointment, in an article for an American magazine, he surveyed the changes since his early visits. Among these he noted with pleasure "the warmth of feeling which now exists, and which did not exist in 1870, towards the old Britannic motherland." It was much more, he was sure, than cordiality between governments. "It is in the hearts of the people. *Esto Perpetua.*" [5]

Bryce was the first British ambassador to consider himself an emissary to the entire American nation. Partly for this reason, he declined the well-deserved peerage offered before he left England, preferring to appear in his familiar, more democratic garb.

---

[4] Speeches of October 21, 1905, quoted in George M. Trevelyan, *Grey of Fallodon* (London, 1937), p. 102, and May 26, 1911, quoted in George P. Gooch and Harold Temperley, eds., *British Documents on the Origin of the War, 1898–1914* (11 vols.; London, 1926–1938), vol. VI, p. 786.

[5] Herman Norman to Spring Rice, ——, 1906, quoted in Stephen Gwynn, *The Letters and Friendships of Sir Cecil Spring Rice* (2 vols.; Cambridge, 1929), vol. II, p. 84; James Bryce, "America Revisited: The Changes of a Quarter-Century," *Outlook* (New York), vol. LXXIX (1905), p. 855.

During his five years in the United States he visited every state, giving speech after speech as he went. Only six weeks after his arrival Henry Adams wrote an English friend, "James Bryce is as garrulous as I—almost—and has three speeches a day to make till his chariot tips him out. I've told his wife to stop it, but she pretends she can't. He loves it." Bryce did not always talk politics. "It was an enormous advantage to him," an admiring but sardonic aide observed, "that he could make a speech worth listening to on every conceivable subject from ice caps to deserts, from political Constitutions to astral bodies"—[6] and, one might add, Plato's philosophy and St. Gaudens' sculpture. The circles in which Bryce moved, however widespread geographically, were of course socially limited; the seventy-year-old man had a certain venerable, institutional quality about him; and, surprisingly for a keen observer of American realities, he underestimated the importance of cultivating the press. Still, he was an eloquent, respected symbol of his country.

The President, who would have preferred Spring Rice or Lee but knew neither was possible, warmly welcomed Bryce. However, they never became confidants; Bryce, though president of the British Alpine Club, was too old to follow the rock-climbing road to preference. Mrs. Roosevelt, reflecting her husband's attitude, described Bryce as a "worthy and dull old person." Nor did the Ambassador hit it off particularly well with Roosevelt's successor, although he and Taft, both friends of arbitration, worked together on the treaty of 1911. As a diplomat, Bryce helped to dispose of a number of minor problems and served as a capable reporter to Downing Street. On important matters, notably the Mexican affair and a controversy over tolls to be charged ships using the Panama canal, he showed a sure but not particularly forceful touch. His complaisance brought down upon his head, as it did upon his superior, the wrath of British conservatives. The *Times*, which shared some of this feeling, ad-

[6] Adams to Gaskell, April 15, 1907, Worthington C. Ford, ed., *Letters of Henry Adams, 1892–1918* (Boston, 1938), p. 473n; Esme William Howard, Baron Howard of Penrith, *Theatre of Life* (London, 1936), p. 122.

mitted it was "of little enough account in comparison with the general influence for good which Mr. BRYCE'S reputation and personality have exerted on Anglo-American affairs." [7] Bryce was indeed well suited for service at Washington at this time, just as Sir Julian Pauncefote and Sir Michael Herbert had been in more troubled years.

American commentators welcomed the Liberal regime, and not only because they had lost faith in Balfour and his followers. The new ministry appeared more republican than its predecessor. The central issue in the parliamentary election of 1906, the *Independent* reported, was "the conviction that the Conservatives and the House of Lords stand for class privilege against manhood rights; and, with popular suffrage, the common people begin to learn that they have the right to rule." [8] No American could object to movement in such a direction, although some did fear it might in the long run lead to Labour rather than Liberal domination.

In foreign policy, the area where in American opinion the old government had done best, major changes were not expected. "On the whole," predicted *Harper's*, ". . . Sir Edward Grey will probably follow closely in the footsteps of Lord Lansdowne; and, surely, he could do no better." What was true of world politics was expected to be more specifically true of relations with the United States. "The new administration," the *Review of Reviews* observed, "contains many friends of the United States . . . familiar with our institutions and widely acquainted in this country. . . . It is to be hoped that the Roosevelt administration here and the Liberal ministry in Great Britain may cooperate to promote the world's peace and progress." [9]

President Roosevelt did not dissent from these judgments. Praise for the Liberals quickly began to creep into his letters, and by 1911 he was ready to avow himself pro-Liberal. Only one

[7] Edith Roosevelt to Spring Rice, June 25, 1907, quoted in Howard K. Beale, *Theodore Roosevelt and the Rise of America to World Power* (Baltimore, 1956), p. 134; *Times* (London), November 12, 1912.

[8] *Independent* (New York), vol. LX (1906), p. 178.

[9] *Harper's Weekly* (New York), vol. L (1906), p. 185; *Review of Reviews* (New York), vol. XXXIII (1906), p. 138.

thing troubled the President: the pacifist and anti-imperialist sentiments which found a home in the Liberal Party. He half feared that these influences would lead the Government to a "maudlin extreme" [10] at the second Hague conference and, more generally, that it would cause England to shirk her imperial duty. He need not have worried, for although Campbell-Bannerman was tinged with the sentiments Roosevelt deplored, Liberal Imperialists—Grey, Asquith, and Haldane—dominated the ministry, and Asquith moved into Number 10 in 1908.

Still, Roosevelt's concern was genuine, and he did his best to avert the imaginary danger. When, just before he left office, a flare-up in India kindled anti-imperialist spirit in England, Roosevelt, in answer to several requests from British friends, publicly threw his support behind the *raj*. During his famous post-Presidential safari through Africa—a magnificent expedition, partly supported by a donation of $30,000 from Andrew Carnegie, which employed 260 native bearers and collected hordes of specimens for naturalists—Roosevelt eyed the work of administrators in central Africa and the Sudan. Emerging from the wilderness at Khartoum in March 1910, he praised British control of the Sudan as "really the rule of civilization," [11] and when he reached Cairo he spoke in similar vein. But Roosevelt had also seen and heard things which troubled him; these he planned to point out to his English friends when he reached London.

En route he enjoyed a triumphant progress across Europe. In Berlin the Kaiser invited the ex-President—the first civilian so honored—to ride with him at a review of imperial troops. Roosevelt welcomed the attention but observed ordinary Berliners' coolness toward himself and his country. He urged German leaders to seek an accommodation with England. By agreeing that all the fault was not on one side, that England was sometimes unreasonably suspicious, he let Chancellor Bethmann-Hollweg and the Kaiser delude themselves that basically he was on their side.

[10] Roosevelt to Reid, August 7, 1906, Elting E. Morison, ed., *The Letters of Theodore Roosevelt* (8 vols.; Cambridge, 1951–1954), vol. V, p. 348.
[11] Quoted in William H. Harbaugh, *Power and Responsibility: The Life and Times of Theodore Roosevelt* (New York, 1961), p. 379.

In fact, for some time, perhaps since Morocco, Roosevelt had been moving away from his view that England exaggerated the German menace, although traces of this idea still remained. While he would have welcomed a holiday in the naval race, he considered the British fleet "a great guarantee for the peace of the world" [12] and certainly did not, as the Germans thought, consider England unreasonable to try to maintain her margin of superiority.

The ex-President crossed the Channel in May. *Punch* greeted him with a cartoon showing the lions at the base of Nelson's Column festooned with signs reading, "Not to be shot," a reference to his poor eyesight and the carnage in Africa. Some socialist and extreme conservative journals attacked him, but if Roosevelt read them he welcomed rather than resented their criticism. The *Times*, apostle of the status quo, objected that "Mr. Roosevelt's message . . . consists of half-truths written in large text. . . . He has left it to others to point out that strenuousness is compatible, or may be confounded, with sterile restlessness, and that what is needed, not less than urgent striving, is moderation and just courage." The *Spectator* reasonably replied that earnestness was not necessarily incompatible with moderation. "People here respect Mr. Roosevelt above all things for his plain speaking on moral and political subjects," the magazine said, and its editorial concluded with a hope that, in "one of those plain-spoken addresses such as he has often given his own countrymen," Roosevelt would speak to the English people on "their work here and abroad." [13]

The *Spectator* knew that anything Roosevelt said would not challenge its position, Liberal and imperialistic. The editor, a close friend, may have had more than a general idea of what the American intended to say at a Guildhall banquet ten days later. Roosevelt submitted his manuscript to other English friends, discussed it with Balfour and either read or outlined the speech

[12] Roosevelt to Lee, August 7, 1908, Morison, ed., *Letters of Roosevelt*, vol. VI, p. 1159.
[13] *Punch* (London), vol. CXXXVIII (1910), p. 329; *Times*, May 14, 1910; *Spectator* (London), vol. CIV (1910), pp. 833–834.

to the Foreign Secretary.[14] The *Times* feared Roosevelt would support the ministry's domestic program, in some ways similar to his own progressivism, but its concern was foolish. Even Roosevelt would never have dared to intervene openly in the party battle, just as he would not have been so indiscreet as to take England's part against other major powers. Instead, he planned to rally Britain behind a cause dear to his heart and to urge her to press forward, in this field and by implication in others, with vigor and unanimity.

Thus, when he addressed the dignitaries at the Guildhall, Roosevelt spoke warmly of England's imperial role, particularly in Egypt and the Sudan. It was, Sir Edward Grey recalled, "praise so unstinted and thorough and strong that I listened to it with a glow of satisfaction. It was the finest tribute ever paid by a citizen of one country to the work of another." The imperial burden, the speaker continued, was not a light one. He feared England was becoming less willing to use firm discipline in dealing "with uncivilized peoples, and especially with fanatical peoples." [15] England, he said, should rededicate herself to the imposition of order or else she should quit Egypt.

As Grey had predicted, Roosevelt's speech caused a sensation. Anti-imperialists, including a few important Liberals like John Morley, criticized his major theme. A somewhat larger number, both Conservative and Liberal, considered his admonitions an affront; "no [other] living statesman," objected the *Economist*, ". . . could possibly have thought of seizing an occasion of compliment and hospitality to read such a lecture . . . to a friendly nation and Government." However, when objections were raised in Parliament, with particular reference to Grey's foreknowledge of the visitor's intentions, Sir Edward easily disarmed the critics. From the opposition front bench, Arthur Balfour supported him. Most Britons recognized, even welcomed, the basic friendliness of Roosevelt's speech, and most

---

14 At various times Grey both said that he had and had not read, or had read to him, the entire speech.

15 Viscount Grey of Fallodon, *Twenty-Five Years, 1892–1916* (2 vols.; London, 1925), vol. II, p. 91; Roosevelt, quoted in *Times*, June 1, 1910.

supporters of current policy considered his advice salutary. The warmth of Anglo-American relations excused words which, coming from a German or even a Frenchman, would have been unacceptable. Thus the *Times*, so critical of the traveler a few days earlier, now observed, "Nothing could be more handsome and generous than his tribute to the beneficence of the work we are doing" and then went on to urge that his friendly warning be taken to heart.[16] John Morley was correct when, writing to an American who shared his views, he complained that Roosevelt had strengthened those who, with the benevolent approval of the opposition leaders, sought to hold British policy on a firm course.

Roosevelt's other major appearance in England was the Romanes lecture at Oxford. This talk, entitled "Biological Analogies in History," had been long in preparation, for Roosevelt was invited to Oxford while still in the White House. Lodge read an early draft, as did a naturalist friend who knocked out an analogy between retarded species and backward nations; "I have left out certain passages," this censor observed, "that are likely to bring on war between the United States and the governments referred to." [17] As finally delivered, the Romanes lecture was a vigorous, not very intellectual application of Darwinian ideas to international affairs. The Archbishop of York, one of the listeners, later recalled that the speech contributed little to scientific understanding but convinced the audience Roosevelt was a great man.

The day before leaving England, the only day when both could find time, Roosevelt and Grey went on a bird walk in the New Forest and the valley of the Itchen. For eight hours, until nine in the evening, they tramped together; that night they spent at an inn in Brockenhurst. A common interest in wildlife, congenial political views, and complementary personalities—the one ebullient, the other reserved—quickly did their work. Only Leonard Wood, said Roosevelt, had ever won his friendship as

<hr/>

[16] *Economist* (London), vol. LXX (1910), p. 1232; *Times*, June 1, 1910.
[17] Henry F. Osborn, quoted in Henry F. Pringle, *Theodore Roosevelt* (rev. ed.; New York, 1956), pp. 365–366.

quickly; Grey was the finest man in England, though less decisive than Lloyd George and less brilliant than Balfour. Sir Edward particularly liked Roosevelt's "peculiar faculty . . . of imparting healthy courage and vigour. I have loved him," he reported to his sister-in-law.[18]

Soon Roosevelt sailed for home. He returned only once, in the spring of 1914, when he received almost no public notice. His earlier visit, longest of his European tour, was far more significant, and not only because of the views he expressed. Deference toward him during the obsequies for Edward VII, the generally favorable reaction to the Guildhall speech, the Foreign Secretary's eagerness to serve as personal guide, constant attention by the press—all paid tribute to Roosevelt the man, but also to Roosevelt the American. A few sour voices complained. "Who," asked the *Saturday Review*, "can help being glad that the orgy of Roosevelt-worship is over?" [19] Most Britons, unconsciously or (like Grey) consciously, took satisfaction in a visit which seemed to strengthen Anglo-American ties and surely demonstrated the friendship of the republic's most illustrious citizen.

When Roosevelt urged England to rule her domains with a firm hand he by no means had Ireland in mind. In 1913, at Ambassador Bryce's request, he even wrote a letter endorsing home rule which he permitted the Irish leader Arthur Redmond to read in the House of Commons. In doing so, Roosevelt reflected the long-standing American belief that the Emerald Isle deserved greater freedom. When Gladstone fought vainly for home-rule bills introduced in 1886 and 1893, and again during and just after the first World War, the period of Erin's final struggle for independence, American feeling ran high. In the Liberal era Irish-Americans continued to shrill against British rule, and other Americans supported them, usually in lower key. Still, special factors did mute the issue.

Upon entering office, Campbell-Bannerman somewhat equiv-

[18] Grey to Mrs. Creighton Grey, n.d., quoted in Trevelyan, *Grey of Fallodon*, p. 184.
[19] *Saturday Review*, vol. LIX (1910), p. 743.

ocally pledged his party to home rule, and many Liberals talked of what they intended once they had overcome other challenges. When the elections of 1910 gave Irish M.P.s the balance of power and, the next year, the Parliament Act curbed the House of Lords, pressure for action and chances of success both increased. In April 1912, true to the Liberal promise, Asquith's government introduced the third home-rule bill. From that time until Sarajevo the issue dominated British politics. At least until confronted with possible civil war in Ulster and a mutiny among the officer corps, the ministry fought vigorously for a broad extension of Irish control of Irish destinies.

Except for Hibernian extremists, who wanted complete independence, the American people supported the British government in its fight against the Unionists, the delaying tactics of the House of Lords, and finally the Ulster opposition supported by what Americans considered Britain's most reactionary elements. Some, particularly at the outset, expected home rule to restore intra-imperial peace by satisfying Irish aspirations and even hoped the result would eliminate "one of the disturbing factors in American politics. . . . We shall have," the *Independent* predicted, "a greater Britain and a stronger United States, and an alliance of hearts between the two nations that can never be broken." Almost everyone praised the Liberals for taking a position midway between scuttle-and-run and repression. "It is noteworthy," said the *New York Times*, "that after the hot contest that has raged for so many years the [proposed] outcome should be so moderate, so fair, and so much in the nature of a compromise." [20] Most Americans, certainly most non-Irish Americans, stuck to this view during the political struggle in England. Scarcely meaning to do so, for relations with the United States were a tiny part of their calculations, the Liberals struck a blow at the residuum of American hostility.

The moderate tactics of Arthur Redmond, leader of the Irish Nationalists, contributed to this effect, for Redmond was very popular in the United States. Resisting the temptation to

[20] *Independent*, vol. LXXII (1912), p. 853; *New York Times*, April 7, 1912.

call for immediate independence, Redmond supported home rule. He and his cohorts at Westminister showed real patience, for seven years after 1905 accepting the Liberal argument that reactionaries in England must be defeated before the Irish problem could be faced. During the slow progress of the third home-rule bill Redmondites stood by the government, even when it compromised on the issue of Ulster and, later, when it put off implementation of home rule for the duration of the World War.

A number of Irish-Americans, facing neither political nor personal danger and bearing no responsibility, took a more radical position. Writing in *Forum* early in 1914, James David Kenny denounced the home-rule bill as "a humbug, . . . a lawyer's crooked scheme . . . which withholds from it [Ireland] everything that would give it real power . . . and which, at the same time, reduces it to impotence in the British Parliament by decapitating its representation there." [21] The Clan-na-Gael and other groups called for immediate independence, but not all Irish-Americans took the same uncompromising position. Bourke Cockran supported Redmond, a friend who had once invited him to move to Ireland and stand for the House of Commons. Until the Easter rebellion in 1916, Irish-Americans were divided. Only then did they reunite, and only then did deep concern arise among other citizens of the republic.

Few Americans sympathized with Ulster's resistance to home rule. They refused to believe a predominantly Catholic Ireland would discriminate against Protestantism. They rejected the argument that Ulstermen, like others, had a right to determine their own destiny. Instead they saw the movement, and particularly the Curragh mutiny of 1914, when British officers threatened to resign their commissions unless promised the army would not be used to put down an Ulster rebellion, as part of the continuing battle between aristocracy and democracy. Sometimes Asquith and his colleagues were criticized on tactical

[21] James David Kenny, "The Irish Home Rule Bill: A *Humbug*," *Forum* (New York), vol. LI (1914), pp. 333, 346.

grounds, particularly for indecisiveness in the face of Curragh, but on the whole Americans supported them. Simply because the alternative seemed to be civil war, commentators accepted the final compromise on the six northern countries, but their sympathies always lay with the Asquith government in its contest with Ulster.

Americans also endorsed Liberal domestic reform, particularly after it took the form of a confrontation between the House of Commons and the House of Lords. The ministry, although sometimes frustrated by the lords, passed important social legislation between 1906 and 1911, most notably by implementing, after two years of struggle, the program laid down by Lloyd George in the budget of 1909. Sometimes American conservatives and even progressives, with their special view of the proper kinds of reform, expressed misgivings about aspects of the Liberal program, especially portions of the 1909 budget and its broad revision of taxation as well as the Trade Disputes Act of 1906, which extended the rights of labor unions. A few, like Walter Rauschenbusch, compared British accomplishments unfavorably with Germany's. On the whole, interested Americans, concerned with many of the same problems and inclined in the direction of change, congratulated the Liberals for executing a "noteworthy and estimable reform program." [22] The *Independent*, strongly progressive, even urged the United States to take Liberal reform as its model.

As early as 1907, irritated by obstruction from the upper chamber, the British government began to consider reducing the lords' power, and the budget of 1909 aimed in part to force matters to a climax. After two parliamentary elections and Liberal threats to pack the House of Lords by creating new peers—the only part of the government's approach which met any criticism in the United States—the Parliament Act of 1911 became law, and the power of the House of Lords, particularly with respect to financial legislation, passed into history.

American observers pictured the long, bitter battle as a con-

[22] *Review of Reviews*, vol. XLVIII (1913), p. 23.

test between democracy and hereditary privilege. In *The Promise of American Life*, a bible of the progressive movement written just as the British battle shaped up, Herbert Croly contrasted English weakness with the increasing vigor of her European rivals. The cause, said Croly, was the stultifying influence of aristocracy. The *Review of Reviews* maintained that the issue was simply whether or not Englishmen were willing to remain any longer under the "mental, moral, and social thralldom of the feudal and caste system." [23] Not even the most conservative American was likely to throw his lot against Asquith and Lloyd George when the issue was drawn in such terms, although some—the *Boston Evening Transcript*, for example—permitted themselves nostalgic sighs about the decline of a once noble institution.

When victory finally came, the Liberals won universal praise. A progressive journal considered the event comparable to the Glorious Revolution, the Reform Bill of 1832, and even America's own Declaration of Independence. A midwestern newspaper categorized the act as "A New Charter of Liberties." Many took special satisfaction that England was following a road discovered by the United States, that, as *Harper's* put it, "Public opinion governs Great Britain now, as it does the United States." [24] From whatever angle of vision, American commentators welcomed the Liberal triumph. The apparent democratization of England, the program of social reform, and even the policy toward Ireland won for the ministry a standing in America secured by few if any of its predecessors.

The Britain of the Liberals, vexed by domestic and foreign crises, only occasionally had time to look at American politics. When Roosevelt left office, he was treated, in England as in America, to an outpouring of what might be called premature obituaries. A few conservatives dug into their stock of memories to complain about his methods during the Alaskan boundary disputes, and a larger number objected that his career was, like life as observed by Macbeth, full of sound and fury, signifying noth-

---

[23] *Ibid.*, vol. XLI (1910), p. 7.
[24] *Detroit News*, August 15, 1911; *Harper's Weekly*, vol. LV (1911), p. 5.

ing. To these strictures, the Liberal press and others had easy an-
swers. The President's noisy appeals for righteousness were, they
maintained, full of significance. "Perhaps no higher tribute can
be paid to a public man," declared the *Times*, which despite its
conservatism pulled out all the stops to praise the progressive
President, "than to say that he has purified the moral currency of
his countrymen." Moreover, Roosevelt's eulogists challenged the
allegation that he had actually accomplished little. They mentioned domestic gains but stressed his diplomacy, occasionally
pointing specifically to the fact that "under his auspices pretty
nearly every issue of any moment or contentiousness has been
wiped off the Anglo-American slate." [25]

Everyone agreed that vigor was Roosevelt's chief characteristic. But how differently this spirit had expressed itself, observed
J. L. Garvin, than everyone had expected when he became President, seemingly nothing more than "a bellicose, turbulent
swashbuckler spoiling for a fight." [26] He had matured and, most
important, he had led his country to maturity with him. His
anointed successor, William Howard Taft, was recognized as a
different type, more cautious and less boisterous but, it was believed, an appropriate leader in the second stage of the battle
begun by Roosevelt.

In 1912 attitudes changed. No one expected any of the contestants—Roosevelt, Taft, or Wilson—to transform foreign policy, although the low-tariff plank of the Democratic platform
created some cautious hopes in that direction. On the specific
issue then vexing Anglo-American relations, the weight of
charges on British ships when the Panama Canal was completed,
all candidates seemed equally unyielding. More generally, and
more favorably, it was agreed that most Americans, with the exception of particular racial groups, had learned during Roosevelt's Presidency that antedeluvian prejudices must be modified.
The Democrats had gained respectability Britons formerly con-

---

[25] *Times*, March 4, 1909; Sydney Brooks, "President Roosevelt's Record," *Fortnightly Review* (London), vol. XCI (1909), p. 667.
[26] *Ibid.*, p. 668.

ferred only upon Republicans.

In British as in American eyes, domestic policy and the contenders' personalities dominated the campaign of 1912. After
Taft won renomination at the cost of driving his predecessor
from the party, he was considered so obviously doomed to third
place that he could be ignored. Roosevelt aroused both suspicion
and passion. His few supporters were overwhelmed by the criticism directed at him and the Bull Moose program. His success, it
was predicted, would bring socialism and perhaps "plebiscitary
Caesarism." And few, not even the small group which would
have welcomed a victory for radicalism, gave the candidate
credit for sincerity. The third-party movement was explained as a
mere vehicle of personal ambition. "Mr. Roosevelt is now sigh-
ing again to be in the White House, and, what is more alluring,
in the limelight," a Tory journal said.[27] His preaching, Englishmen felt, was no longer a disinterested plea for righteousness but
rather a cynical pandering to passions he did not share.

Wilson became the favorite candidate of English commentators, as much because of his personal style as his political views.
He had many English friends, probably as many as Roosevelt
and certainly more varied ones. Even Beatrice Webb had been
favorably impressed when she met the young professor in 1898,
and Admiral Fisher, who can scarcely ever have agreed with Mrs.
Webb, had a perfect passion for Wilson, whose election,
incidentally, he predicted two years before the fact. "He is,"
wrote Fisher with less exaggeration than on other occasions, "an
educated Abraham Lincoln, with a Von Moltke brain, and
doesn't care a d——n if he is sure he's right." The candidate appealed because of his academic mien, his personal conservatism
and lack of flamboyance, even his social background (upon
which several writers commented). Wilson, one paper said, "belongs much more to the class of public men we are accustomed
to in England than to the class that has hitherto pretty well dominated American affairs." [28]

27 *Saturday Review*, vol. CXIII (1912), pp. 803, 262.
28 Fisher to Fiennes, March 9, 1911, Arthur J. Marder, ed., *Fear God and*

In a contest essentially between Wilson and Roosevelt, conservatives had little difficulty in making a choice. "And though Dr. Wilson is doubtless a Radical," one observed, "nevertheless his Radicalism is of the constructive sort, that looks before leaping, studying conditions and needs, without haste or fury." [29] Just as Asquith was less abominable than Lloyd George or Churchill, so Wilson was preferable to Roosevelt. On the Liberal side, some expressed doubts Wilson would, or could, carry the Democratic Party very far in the direction of reform. Still, by contrast with Roosevelt's program, which went both farther than and in different directions from Liberal policies, Wilson's New Freedom had powerful appeal. Even Grey abandoned the cause of his bird-watching friend, although he observed a scrupulous silence during the campaign. His agent Bryce quitted Washington, fleeing all the way to Australia to avoid even the faintest chance of involvement.

No one commented on Wilson's close ties with England and with English thought until after the election. Assessing the victor for an English magazine, Professor A. L. P. Dennis of the University of Wisconsin, once Wilson's student at Princeton, pointed out what has become recognized as one of the strongest influences upon the new President. After discussing domestic questions Dennis proceeded, "Mr. Wilson, as President, is also an important if unknown factor in foreign policy. At least four Americans have had in official positions a chance to live in England before they became Presidents. . . . Certainly none of them ever had the chance that Mr. Wilson has had in a private capacity to become acquainted with England. He has often spent his quiet holidays near Grasmere." [30] Since his first visit in 1896 Wilson had repeatedly returned to England, visiting such shrines as the graves of Burke and Bagehot and only once failing to

---

Dread Nought: The Correspondence of Admiral of the Fleet Lord Fisher of Kilverstone (3 vols.; London, 1952–1959), vol. II, p. 362; London *Daily Mail*, quoted in *Literary Digest* (New York), vol. XLV (1912), p. 180.

[29] *Saturday Review*, vol. CXIV (1912), p. 8.

[30] Alfred L. P. Dennis, "Woodrow Wilson," *Contemporary Review* (London), vol. CII (1912), p. 800.

spend time in the Lake District, a special love. By contrast, he made only a single, brief visit to the continent of Europe.

Travel reflected rather than created Wilson's sympathies. "His first real interest in government," reported Professor Dennis, "came to him as a boy by reading in English politics. That study is now part of him, the marrow of his being; and he is the better American for being steeped in the best traditions of English law and history." [31] From his reading Wilson learned to respect orderly change, progress under the law, and responsible republicanism as contrasted to unlicensed democracy on the one hand or tyranny on the other. On the walls of his study at Princeton, alongside portraits of his father and of Daniel Webster, there hung pictures of Burke and Bagehot as well as William E. Gladstone, Wilson's great hero.

Although Wilson believed that "when properly directed, there is no people not fitted for self-government," he felt that as a natural growth the precious plant was virtually confined to British and American soils. Democracy, he once observed, was "the result of the operation of forces permanent in the history of the English race." "The English alone," he maintained, "have approached popular institutions *through habit*," rather than through revolutions of the French or Latin American type which left instability in their wake. As an undergraduate at Princeton, Wilson addressed a commencement upon "Our Kinship with England." As president of his alma mater, introducing John Hay for an honorary degree, he praised Hay for his part in confirming "our happy alliance of sentiment and purpose with Great Britain." [32] He entered the White House with long-established ties of political theory and sentiment.

Until the war came, Wilson paid little attention to European politics. His legislative program, Mexico, and even the Far East seemed much more challenging. Furthermore, during early stages of the Mexican imbroglio Wilson shared the view that sin-

[31] *Ibid.*
[32] Wilson, quoted in Arthur S. Link, *Wilson the Diplomatist* (rev. ed.; Chicago, 1965), p. 14; Wilson, quoted in Harley Notter, *The Origins of the Foreign Policy of Woodrow Wilson* (Baltimore, 1937), pp. 48, 49, 16, 105.

ister British influences made Huerta stubborn. Still, his inclina-
tions were so strongly pro-British that he could be counted upon
to do nothing to delay the great rapprochement.

Oddly, in view of William Jennings Bryan's parochial image, the new Secretary of State had traveled much more widely
than his chief. In 1906, while on a trip around the world, Bryan
visited London and even met Edward VII at the monarch's request. In 1910 he visited the British capital once more, behaving
with such propriety that one reactionary journal used his behav-
ior as a club with which to pound Theodore Roosevelt. Englishmen did not particularly like Bryan—Asquith described him as
"a peculiar product of your country" [33]—but they had lost the
horror of him they had felt in 1896. On Bryan's side, neither
Anglophilia nor Anglophobia played a major role; an interest
in peace and mild suspicion of foreigners generally—these were
the chief attitudes he brought to the Department of State.

Information and opinion flowed to Wilson far more frequently from the new ambassador to London, Walter Hines
Page, an old friend. Sir Edward Grey proposed the toast at the
Pilgrims' now traditional dinner for an arriving ambassador, and
the *Times*, noting that no other diplomat received such a welcome, commented, "it would be against the grain of British instincts if no distinction were to be drawn between the American
and other Ambassadors." [34] Almost immediately Page was entertaining and being entertained by the greats of the political world.
The expense outstripped his income, particularly after he moved
his residence (and the embassy offices) to Grosvenor Square in
1914, but a friend of the President agreed to provide twenty-five
thousand dollars a year so that Page could keep his post.

Like Wilson, Page loved England. However, his reports to
Wilson were by no means simply monotonous defenses of British policy. He bridled at criticism of his government "as a frontier sort of thing without good manners or good faith." He had

[33] Page to House, February 13, 1914, quoted in Burton J. Hendrick, *The Life
and Letters of Walter H. Page* (3 vols.; Garden City, 1922–1925), vol. I, p. 236.
[34] *Times*, June 7, 1913.

qualms about British imperialism. And in a romantic sort of way, he considered England to be on a downhill slope. "The sunlight falls on our New World," he wrote Wilson. "Here we are very gay but—in the shadow." England's economic decline and even the displacement of the aristocracy, an outdated but once noble group, troubled him. "Yet they are all of a vigorous race," he commented. "Else they'd be in real despair permanently. The mills of the gods and of Lloyd George grind slowly." [35] Page's reports thus mingled nostalgia and a touch of national egotism with warm affection. As such, they appealed to Wilson's own sentiments.

Page played a minor role in Colonel Edward M. House's efforts to check the European drift toward war, the one significant trans-Atlantic intervention by the President's closest advisor —indeed by the whole administration—in the fifteen months between Wilson's inauguration and World War I. Like House, Page believed Germany and England were unrealistically, even dangerously frightened of each other. When, after visiting the Kaiser, House came to London, Page supported his efforts to forward stability and peace. Neither House nor Page found anything unsatisfactory in Britain's response; in fact, it warmed them. Although the extent of House's unfavorable reaction to the German mood is sometimes overestimated, on balance the British situation seemed to him better than the German. In any event the House mission was soon overtaken by European catastrophe. After war began both Page and House drifted easily toward the Allied camp.

Despite perplexity and irritation caused by Wilson's Mexican policy, most Britons respected his accomplishments during the pre-war years. The Underwood tariff, passed in October 1913 after a bitter struggle in Congress, evoked the most comment. Some Conservatives alleged that this tariff reduction justified Canada's rejection of reciprocity, since the latter gained many benefits of reciprocity without having to pay anything for them.

[35] Page to Wilson, October 25, 1913, quoted in Hendrick, *Page*, vol. I, p. 145; Page to Wilson, May 21, 1914, quoted in *ibid.*, vol. III, pp. 51, 50.

Most commentators observed that the new tariff left the protective system intact, and several warned against overoptimistic estimates of its effect on British trade. On the other hand, all except tariff reformers of the Chamberlain school welcomed America's drift in the direction of British policy. Englishmen believed the new tariff struck a heavy blow at the special privileges and monopolistic tendencies they deplored, and they gave the President high credit for his skill and tenacity in a fight Roosevelt and Taft had refused to make. The Underwood tariff "has raised him at a single stage from the man of promise to the man of achievement," a London periodical declared.[36]

At one time—say in 1896 or 1900 or perhaps even later—it might have been just to say that Anglo-American friendship depended upon the continued sway of Unionists and Republicans. By 1914 this was clearly no longer the case. Liberals had shown their determination to continue pursuit of what the *Saturday Review*, critical as ever, called "the phantom of American friendship," [37] and their domestic program appealed to Americans caught up in somewhat similar efforts. All three contestants for the Presidency in 1912 had close ties with England. Neither they nor their supporters pandered heavily to Anglophobia, a refreshing contrast to the past, particularly on the Democratic side, and no one considered the outcome vital to continued friendship.

Late in 1910 the Taft administration showed its sympathies, and, even more important, its conviction that the American people would not object to their avowal, by sending the entire Atlantic fleet on a ceremonial visit to England and France. During a convivial banquet at the Guildhall the American commander, Commodore William Sims, injudiciously told his hosts that, should British security ever be threatened, "you may count upon every man, every dollar, every ship, and every drop of blood of your kindred across the seas." [38] Sims' talk created an uproar, and of course he had to be publicly rebuked by Washington. The

---

[36] *Nation* (London), vol. XIV (1913), p. 89.
[37] "America, England, and Japan," *Saturday Review*, vol. CXV (1913), p. 639.
[38] Quoted in *Review of Reviews*, vol. XLIII (1911), p. 154.

visit itself was as far as the American government was prepared to go, but that was far enough. Berlin objected to the snub, and, after trying to fob the Germans off with a visit by a single training ship, the administration sent a small squadron to Germany in 1911. At about the same time the dreadnought *Delaware*, America's most powerful vessel, took part in George V's coronation naval review.

Thus the great rapprochement continued, though the years after 1905 were not marked by the drama which surrounded the Spanish-American War or the series of negotiations early in Theodore Roosevelt's Presidency. On his return to England in 1913 Bryce told the Pilgrims, "the friendship you entertain for the people of the United States is reciprocated by them far more universally and heartily than ever before." The former Ambassador may have forgotten 1898, but otherwise he was correct. Antipathy toward England had steadily eroded during the Liberal years, and even the *Saturday Review* grudgingly admitted that "something of the old bitterness has passed away." When Bryce credited "Nature and history" for the change, he went too far. Progress depended upon Grey's willingness to stand aside in the face of American pressure: Germany's ambassador at Washington frequently commented upon England's "zealous servility" toward the United States.[39] Progress was also furthered by the domestic program of the new ministry and by the election of an American President whose views were congenial to England.

[39] Bryce, quoted in Sinclair Kennedy, *The Pan-Angles; A Consideration of the Federation of the Seven English-Speaking Nations* (New York, 1915), p. 177; *Saturday Review*, vol. CXV (1913), p. 639; Bernstorff to Bethmann-Hollweg, July 21, 1911, E. T. S. Dugdale, ed., *German Diplomatic Documents, 1871–1914* (4 vols.; London, 1930–1931), vol. IV, p. 27.

CHAPTER TWELVE

Strengths and Limits
of Friendship

SUBSCRIBERS TO *Whitaker's Almanac*, a standard English annual, discovered in the edition of 1912 that the arrangement
of data about foreign countries had been changed. The United
States had been moved out of alphabetical order to a special
place just after the empire and ahead of all other foreign powers.
Almost immediately a sharp quarrel arose over Panama Canal
tolls which may have made the editors regret their gesture. Resolution of this dispute, and the growth of a movement to celebrate the centennial of Anglo-American peace, vindicated *Whitaker's* decision, although the rapprochement's limits also became
clear.

The centennial idea was born in American hearts, but a Canadian, William L. Mackenzie King, brought the subject into
public discussion in a speech at the Harvard commencement in
1909. John A. Stewart, a New York businessman and member of
several organizations (including the Pilgrims) devoted to Anglo-
American friendship, raised the matter with Roosevelt before
the latter left office, and Stewart called a meeting at the Republican Club of New York in June 1910, which formed the National Committee for the Celebration of the One-Hundredth
Anniversary of Peace Among the English-Speaking Peoples.
President Taft, pleading the constraints of office, declined the

honorary chairmanship, although he did praise the committee's purpose. Theodore Roosevelt, approached next, accepted after a month's thought. He never played a leading role, partly because he considered the organizers, among them Andrew Carnegie, a stuffily self-important group and partly, no doubt, because he disliked the pacifist overtones the movement soon acquired. On the other hand, the committee won the active support of Senator Elihu Root, formerly Roosevelt's strong right arm, and signed up every state governor and hordes of other celebrities as honorary vice-chairmen.

On the British side, organization did not come until the end of 1911. A committee took form under the chairmanship of Lord Grey, formerly governor-general of Canada, with Lord Weardale the active organizer and English counterpart of Stewart. Weardale proved a good target for whatever opposition the movement aroused. Some labor leaders objected to his connection with Carnegie, "a man who crucified labor at Homestead," although Weardale's only connection was through the peace movement. British suffragettes—particularly "General" Flora Drummond, who smuggled a message out of jail—also attacked the planned centennial, partly because Weardale headed a society opposed to woman suffrage. Among Britain's leaders the movement attracted almost unanimous support. A prestigious mission headed by Weardale traveled to the United States to coordinate plans; the emissaries visited Roosevelt at Sagamore Hill, were entertained by Carnegie at a garden party, were addressed by Secretary of State Bryan, and visited the White House. At a fund-raising affair in London, Prime Minister Asquith declared, "we two great kindred races have come to feel that the shedding of one another's blood in any cause, for any difference, would be a matter diverse not only in degree, but in character to the outburst of war between any two other nations in the world." [1] Until Sarajevo diverted attention, the summer and fall of 1914 in England seemed sure to see an orgy of sentimentality.

[1] Ben Tillett, quoted in *New York Times*, May 2, 1913; Asquith, quoted in *Times* (London), February 4, 1914.

American foes of the centennial far outnumbered English critics. People of German and Irish descent sniffed danger, sometimes even the aroma of alliance. In New York the Clan-na-Gael condemned the "attempt to turn the centenary of McDonough's glorious victory of Plattsburg into part of the so-called Hundred Years of Peace celebration." After all, the society alleged, "during eighty-five years of the ninety-nine . . . England was bitterly and steadfastly hostile to this republic, and availed herself of every opportunity to inflict injury upon it." The president of the German Publication Society pointed out that with Germany "peace has prevailed unbroken since time immemorial and . . . has never been disturbed by a single act of hostility or aggression." [2] Why then should England, the only European power the United States had ever found it necessary to fight, be singled out for special recognition?

These appeals gained some success. In Connecticut, with a group of Irish legislators in the van and Captain Michael J. O'Brien, official historian of the American-Irish Historical Society providing supporting arguments, the legislature rejected a gubernatorial request for funds to support the centennial. Congress avoided action whenever possible, although bills were repeatedly introduced and in 1912 Elihu Root induced the Senate to approve a scheme for an official commission with a budget of $100,000. When a similar proposal finally came before the House of Representatives in June 1914, it ran into heavy opposition. "Why not," asked Congressman James R. Mann of Chicago, "celebrate the day they burned the Capitol Building? Do them honour; do it brown; tell them what great people they were when they marched up to Washington and burned the Capitol Building." [3] Under Wilson's lash the House of Representatives had only recently voted a very real concession to England, equalizing tolls on canal shipping, and the temptation to go the other direction was too strong to resist. Moreover the argument against official involvement in such a celebration was strong. In a very

[2] *New York Times,* November 24, 1913.
[3] *Congressional Record,* 63rd Congress, 2nd Session, p. 11326.

thin house the bill was defeated by fifty-six to one hundred eighty-six.

The critics' position is quite understandable, their suspicions comprehensible. The movement began in part as a self-conscious effort to improve Anglo-American relations. On one occasion Stewart candidly admitted that he saw the centennial as a means "not only for celebrating the signing of the treaty [of Ghent, ending the War of 1812], but [also] for increasing the mutual understanding between the United States and Great Britain." Many supporters looked upon the century since Ghent as a time when, in the words of a labored metaphor concocted by one speaker, "the mighty rivers of Anglo-Saxon life and influence have flowed steadily on and, side by side, never overflowing their banks, but in the very nature of things [mingling] . . . their waters on the great ocean of a common destiny and accomplishment." [4] Despite opponents' fears, almost no one wanted an alliance, but the centennial's original planners obviously hoped to draw the two peoples even more closely together.

To broaden the base of support, from the outset John A. Stewart sought aid from the peace movement. He and his circle usually avoided blatant appeals to Anglo-Saxonism, fearing that pacifists willing to celebrate a century without war might thereby be alienated. However, most of the peace people believed there was some particular virtue in Englishmen and Americans, "that some special fiat of God and nature enjoins enduring peace among those whose blood or language or institutions or traditions . . . go back historically to the snug little island of Britain." They believed the movement had its origins in their countries, and they virtually enshrined the arbitration provisions of the Jay treaty and the *Alabama* claims settlement of 1871 as monuments to the "loftiest of human attributes—the will to adjust frictions of social life by reason." [5] They found it easy to argue that the Anglo-American success might become a model

[4] Stewart, quoted in *New York Times*, December 6, 1913; Congressman William B. Ainey, quoted in *Advocate of Peace* (Boston), vol. LXXV (1913), p. 35.
[5] William A. Dunning, *The British Empire and the United States* (New York, 1914), p. 371.

for all mankind. As a result the peace movement rallied as a single man behind the centennial, and, while they somewhat muted its tone, the peace people proved the most effective agitators in its behalf.

Because the outbreak of European war prevented or, in some minds, made a mockery of celebrations of peace, the movement's substantive accomplishments fell way short of its sponsors' hopes. Many schemes, anyway, had been far too ambitious or fantastic, among them a plan to erect a statue of Queen Victoria in New York's Central Park, which caused Theodore Roosevelt to comment that it would furnish "a steady occupation for the police force in protecting it from celtic enthusiasts whose life ambition it would be to blow it up." [6] Fortunately for "New York's finest," this particular project, like many others, came to nought. At least two histories of the century reached print, one by William A. Dunning and the other by Henry Cabot Lodge, but Lodge's treatment of all but the final years belied his title, *One Hundred Years of Peace*, unless one chose to define "peace" very narrowly. Scores of meetings were held and speeches given, a few of the planned dozens of statues found their way to pedestals, and some other monuments were begun. The fate of the Anglo-American Exposition in London, which opened in May 1914 but closed its doors when Britain mobilized for war, symbolized the larger fate of the movement.

In England—primarily because of the energy of Mrs. Victoria Woodhull Martin, an American who, after a career as spiritualist, feminist, speculator, and charlatan, married a sedate English banker—£8,400 was raised to buy and restore the ancestral seat of the Washington family, Sulgrave Manor, as a "place of pilgrimage for Americans in England and as a fruitful symbol of the kinship of the two peoples." Ambassador Page urged Woodrow Wilson to come to England for the ceremonies, but, despite his warm feelings toward Britain, the President declined. Except for a few minutes Taft spent on Mexican soil, no chief executive

---

[6] Roosevelt to Lee, July 7, 1913, Elting E. Morison, ed., *The Letters of Theodore Roosevelt* (8 vols.; Cambridge, 1951–1954), vol. VII, p. 739.

had ever left the country, and Wilson believed a trip to England "might be the beginning of a practice of visiting foreign countries which would lead Presidents rather far afield." [7]

The centennial movement is instructive as a gauge of opinion, particularly in the United States, for in Britain it had been clear for years that anti-Americanism was losing force. Opposition existed, and Anglophiles found it desirable to modify their approach to secure firm support from the peace factions. The scheme remained very largely the preserve of respectable, established persons. Yet celebration committees were established, usually by executive action but sometimes by legislation, in almost every state in the Union and in eighty-six cities as well, and the Senate agreed to support the movement with federal funds. The legislators, senators, mayors, and governors responsible did not take the easy way out, arguing that celebrations should remain informal and unofficial. Showing either courage and conviction or a shrewd understanding of the decline of anti-British feeling, they gave the celebrations their open support.

Stewart and his allies laid plans for the most ambitious expression of American national sympathies ever contemplated. The war limited their accomplishments, and caution marked their tactics, but the state of American opinion was shown by their success in organizing support and, perhaps most significant, their willingness to undertake the crusade in the first place. No effort was made in 1882 to celebrate the centennial of the peace by which England recognized American independence. Even the tercentenary of Jamestown was celebrated in minor key, largely by naval visits to the site, in 1907. Stewart and his friends correctly judged that the climate had changed.

The outcome of the Panama tolls controversy confirmed this. A law signed by President Taft in 1912, anticipating the opening of the canal by two years, exempted from charges American ships carrying cargoes between the two coasts. It also author-

---

[7] *New York Times*, July 6, 1913; Wilson to Page, n.d. [1913], quoted in Burton J. Hendrick, *The Life and Letters of Walter H. Page* (3 vols.; Garden City, 1922–1925), vol. I, p. 276.

ized the chief executive to fix rates giving preference to other
American ships, wherever bound. Britain believed both provisions violated the Hay-Pauncefote Treaty, which granted all nations the use of the canal on equal terms. However, since Taft
did not use his power to discriminate,[8] the controversy centered
upon the exemption for ships engaged in coastwise trade. Nor
was the issue simply one of law and good faith. The exemption
shifted to other users the share of maintenance costs escaped by
coastwise shippers. In addition, and Grey made much of this,
since most ships carried mixed cargoes—some portions going
from one coast to another, others destined for or coming from
foreign ports by way of the United States—it was almost impossible in practice to decide whether or not a ship was engaged in
coastwise trade.

All shades of opinion in England considered the issue serious, particularly after Taft rejected requests for arbitration during the summer of 1912. The *Saturday Review* railed against
"Yankee perfidy" and even suggested that all maritime powers
withdraw their ambassadors from Washington. Even America's
friends considered her position untenable. "Let us only hope
that the admiration which we extend most warmly to the American people," said the *Times*, "may not be long impaired by the
very different feelings at present inspired in us by the action of
their Government." [9] Although deeply concerned, Sir Edward
Grey withheld a formal protest until after the American election.

All three candidates and all three platforms endorsed preferential treatment of American ships. America, after all, had
borne the costs of construction; surely she had a right to favor
her own ships. Moreover, no one could deny her the right to sub-
sidize her merchant marine as many other nations did; what
difference did it make whether the United States collected tolls
and returned the same amount as a subsidy or whether she sim-

[8] In discussions with the British government, however, the Taft administration
defended the discriminatory principle of the somewhat jesuitical ground that the
Hay-Pauncefote Treaty only pledged the United States not to discriminate between one foreign nation and another foreign nation.

[9] "Panama Perfidy," *Saturday Review* (London), vol. CXIV (1912), p. 258;
Times, September 2, 1912.

ply omitted to collect the tolls in the first place? (Grey admitted the difficulty of meeting this argument.) Thus Knox expressed prevailing opinion when he answered Grey's protest by denying its major premises. He did however state that the United States might go to arbitration after the canal opened and the issue became a real as opposed to an hypothetical one.

Wilson's campaign comments had been casual and uninformed. Even before he became President he shifted his position, in large part because of the impact of an article written for the *American Journal of International Law* by a friend, John H. Latané. Dining with prominent anti-exemptionists headed by Elihu Root, who had just attacked the law on the Senate floor, Wilson promised to work for repeal when politics permitted. But he moved cautiously. When Root's repeal bill was buried in committee, Wilson refused public comment. After becoming President he several times told his cabinet he favored repeal although he regretted that Hay had not protected the right to discriminate, and he sent Colonel House to London to ask Grey to ease his task by keeping silent. He also informed his cabinet, Ambassador Bryce, and Grey's secretary, Sir William Tyrell, who visited Washington in November, that he could not move while tariff and then banking legislation was pending.

In December 1913, on the same day Wilson signed the Federal Reserve Act, Congressman William C. Adamson, a confidant, introduced a bill to repeal exemption. Walter Hines Page urged him to reciprocate British concessions in Mexico, particularly Carden's removal: "It's our turn next, whenever you see your way clear." House told Page this letter turned the trick; Wilson summoned the Senate Foreign Relations Committee to the White House and in a three-hour meeting pressed for action, stressing as had Page the importance of British cooperation in Mexico. He later delivered a special message to Congress, urging those who did not admit that exemption violated the Hay-Pauncefote Treaty to agree to wipe away what others considered American bad faith. The message enchanted Grey; "whether it succeeded or failed in accomplishing the President's object," he wrote, "it was something to the good of public life, for it helped to lift public life to a higher plane and to strengthen its morale." [10] Even more important, the President was at last publicly enlisted, and he threw the full weight of his administration behind repeal.

Most of the press supported Wilson. So did important Republicans, among them Senator Lodge, who had voted against the tolls bill in 1912 in deference to British objections although he believed it did not violate treaty obligations. Democratic leaders including Congressmen Oscar Underwood and Champ Clark and Senator James O'Gorman broke with the President, while many Republicans could not resist the temptation to oppose a "sell-out" to Great Britain. The opposition appealed to American nationalism and more specifically to Anglophobia. They won support from shipping interests, the Hearst press, and Irish-Americans, but suffered a serious blow when Bryan's magazine, *The Commoner*, came out for repeal as an evidence of good faith, for the Secretary of State was rumored to oppose the bill. In an analogous situation the first Hay-Pauncefote Treaty went down to defeat, but by 1914 the situation had changed. The opposition found it difficult to mobilize support.

Following bitter debate, the House of Representatives passed the repeal bill, 247 to 162. Only a few Democrats followed Underwood and Clark. Debate in the Senate was less fierce but prolonged and complex; one day alone produced 186 pages of speeches and documents in the *Congressional Record*. After attaching an amendment asserting the abstract right to levy discriminatory tolls, the Senate passed the bill by a vote of 50 to 35. Despite all obstacles—despite the necessity of reversing national policy and throwing over a plank in the Democratic platform, despite the vulnerability of seeming to make a gratuitous concession to England, despite the obvious opportunity for prejudice to come into play—the bill became law in June.

Walter Hines Page received the news at a Buckingham Pal-

[10] Page to Wilson, January 8, 1914, quoted in Hendrick, *Page*, vol. I, 252; Grey to Spring Rice, March 13, 1914, quoted in *ibid.*, p. 254.

ace ball, and as the word spread many other guests sought him out to offer congratulations. Britain's press rang with plaudits, and officials led by Sir Edward Grey expressed gratification. Bryce wrote Wilson to hail the victory over "the combined forces of monopolists seeking their own gain [the shipping interests] and mischief makers trying to create ill feeling between nations." To this the President replied, "I think that we have reason to be proud of the way in which public opinion of the United States responded to the challenge. . . . I am not so much proud . . . as deeply grateful that the country I love should be set in the right light, in the light of its real principles and opinion." [11]

Ten days before Wilson thus commented on a striking success, Bosnian revolutionaries ambushed the Archduke Franz Ferdinand at Sarajevo. The *attentat* created a political crisis between Austria-Hungary and Serbia, accused by Vienna of sheltering the assassins. Few foresaw that, thanks to interlocking alliances, this foreshadowed a war which would bleed Europe half to death and permanently alter the direction of world politics. Only a little while before, Sir Edward Grey had assured Colonel House his fears of catastrophe were exaggerated. Europe, it seemed, had learned how to keep her crises under control.

Wilson did not mention the Sarajevo incident in his letter to Bryce. Walter Lippmann, discussing socialism with Fabians in England, still hoped to visit the Continent in the fall. American yachts did not interrupt tune-up sails for the forthcoming America's Cup contest against Sir Thomas Lipton's latest *Shamrock*, and the *New York Times* reported that an interest in baseball was sweeping England. Henry White, lazing at the estate of his son-in-law, a German count, heard from his friend Spring Rice, vacationing on the English coast, that the latter expected the quiet state of the world to permit him to extend his leave a further month. Joseph C. Grew, first secretary of the American embassy at Berlin, who had just returned from leave in the United

[11] Bryce to Wilson, June 19, 1914, quoted in Ray Stannard Baker, *Woodrow Wilson: Life and Letters* (8 vols.; Garden City, 1927–1939), vol. IV, p. 419; Wilson to Bryce, July 6, 1914, quoted in Arthur S. Link, *Wilson: The New Freedom* (Princeton, 1956), p. 314.

States, told a friend he was glad to have resumed his normal, peaceful life. The next day Austria declared war on Serbia. Within a week the Continent was ablaze. England entered the fray on August 4, following the German invasion of Belgium just across the Channel.

Until the end most American observers hoped the world cataclysm could be avoided. On August 2, the *New York Times* prayed that war would be isolated in eastern Europe. "The friends of peace have counted upon the highly civilized nations like England, France, with the United States, to discountenance war, to make great wars impossible," the paper commented, shuddering at the prospect of "a frightful backsliding." The next day, as if to prepare its readers for unpleasant developments, the *Times* observed that the peacefully inclined Liberal ministry would go to war only if there was no alternative, and on the morning of England's declaration, before receiving the news, the paper declared that Britain would have to fight to defend Belgium. On August 5, in an editorial entitled "Germany's War," the *Times* came down firmly on England's side:

> in the confusion in which Europe has been plunged the two great representative democracies of England and France have borne themselves with the greatest calm and dignity and sense of international responsibility. Observing in letter and in spirit the neutrality to which the United States is bound, it is still open to us to expect and to wish that the sway of autocracy shall not, in the end, be strengthened.[12]

In the time of excitement, most Americans agreed.

Few wanted to go to war. Henry Cabot Lodge, caught in England when the holocaust began, told reporters upon his return, "If Germany conquers France, England and Russia she will dominate Europe, and will subsequently extend that domination, if she can, to the rest of the world," but the Senator also called for strict American neutrality. In the Sagamore Hill library, Theodore Roosevelt told Herbert Croly, Felix Frankfurter, and

[12] *New York Times*, August 2, 3, 4, 5, 1914.

other young visitors, "You've got to go in! You've got to go in!" but the ex-President soon adopted a more equivocal position.[13] Charles W. Eliot, former president of Harvard, urged Wilson to join England and her comrades in an alliance to punish Germany and Austria-Hungary, but two weeks later Eliot withdrew his suggestion, admitting he had acted precipitately. Until 1917, true war spirit scarcely existed in the United States, and Allied propaganda wisely concentrated on the less difficult task of preserving American favor.

Germany's attack on Belgium dominated American accounts of the crisis. Commentators generally agreed England had no alternative when Germany violated a solemn engagement to observe Belgian neutrality, an agreement to which Britain was a party, and entered an area vital to British security. Moreover, as far as Americans could see, Britain had worked as hard as or harder than any other power to preserve peace in the weeks after Sarajevo. "Her chief interests were on the side of peace," the *Independent* declared, "and until the beginning of hostilities British statesmen labored unceasingly to compose the differences of the powers. . . . With the . . . violation of the neutrality of Belgium in the German advance on France, British interests were directly threatened." [14] Of all European powers, Britain's cause seemed most just, her conduct least provocative.

As Henry May has observed, the cause of Britain and her allies found most support among "the beleaguered defenders of nineteenth-century tradition, and particularly the professional custodians of culture." (Such men as John W. Burgess and Albert J. Beveridge are exceptions to this generalization. So too was Joseph Grew at first, but a barrage of letters from friends and relatives in Boston changed his mind.) Some intellectual rebels and some political radicals endorsed Germany's cause, although right-wing socialists supported Britain. The Irish split. A minority followed Redmond, who rallied behind the cause of his

[13] Lodge, quoted in John A. Garraty, *Henry Cabot Lodge* (New York, 1953), p. 305; Roosevelt, quoted in William H. Harbaugh, *Power and Responsibility: The Life and Times of Theodore Roosevelt* (New York, 1961), p. 467.
[14] *Independent* (New York), vol. LXXIX (1914), p. 202.

Liberal allies; among these was Bourke Cockran, who considered England's war against Germany a "crusade for the regeneration of the world." Far more Irish-Americans saw in the war a heaven-sent opportunity to secure their homeland's independence. "All my sympathies are with Germany," the president of the United Irish League of America wrote Redmond a few months later, "and I believe that nine-tenths of the Americans of Irish blood think as I do." [15] But all these groups spoke against, and felt themselves to be fighting against, the main thrust of American opinion.

As the war moved on and more facts became available, Americans regained some of their balance. Like ex-President Eliot, although more slowly, they came to see that the causes of war were complex, the right not all on one side. Moreover, the isolationist tradition counseled against even the risk of involve-ment; by contrast with 1940 and 1941, few called for aid short of war. American sympathies were involved; fundamental Ameri-can interests did not seem to be. Furthermore, at the outset of the war most who sympathized with England and her friends were confident they would win through to victory. Editors polled by the *Literary Digest* rejoiced that the United States was insu-lated from Europe's madness, and anyone tempted to challenge the editors knew he would also have to reckon with alert, suspi-cious groups, particularly the Irish- and German-Americans. As a result of all these things pro-Allied sentiment did not extend to the support of pro-Allied policy. Like the *New York Times'* edi-torialists, most wanted to cheer for England while remaining safely in the grandstand.

A fortnight after England went to war, President Wilson addressed his countrymen. "The people of the United States," he said, "are drawn from many nations, and chiefly from the na-tions now at war." It would be easy, but dangerous, to mobilize

[15] Henry F. May, *The End of American Innocence: A Study in the First Years of Our Own Time, 1912–1917* (New York, 1959), p. 363; Cockran, quoted in James McGurrin, *Bourke Cockran* (New York, 1948), p. 238; Michael Ryan to Redmond, October 2, 1914, quoted in Charles C. Tansill, *America and the Fight for Irish Freedom, 1866–1922* (New York, 1957), p. 166.

factions against one another. "Such divisions among us would be fatal to our peace of mind and might seriously stand in the way of the proper performance of our duty as the one great Nation . . . holding itself ready to play a part of impartial mediation and speak the counsels of peace." Therefore, the President continued, "The United States must be neutral in fact as well as in name during these days that are to try men's souls. We must be impartial in thought as well as in action." Wilson's speech went beyond Washington's proclamation of neutrality in 1793, which merely called upon citizens, without speaking of their sympathies, "to adopt and pursue a conduct friendly and impartial toward the belligerent powers," and even farther beyond the fireside chat in 1939 in which, while declaring neutrality, Roosevelt added, "Even a neutral cannot be asked to close his mind or his conscience."

Woodrow Wilson's address bespoke his noble hope for peace and the nation's less noble, quite understandable desire for non-involvement. It warned the incautious to hold their tongues, the shrill and active proponents of Germany as well as the far more numerous partisans of England. In urging Americans to be "impartial in thought as well as in action," the speech showed a Wilsonian tendency to strive for the unattainable. Moreover, the President shared the feelings of most of his countrymen. Privately he condemned the invasion of Belgium, considered Germany militaristic, and sympathized with the Allies. He said, the British ambassador reported, "Everything that I love most in the world is at stake." [16] Then, for two years, until Germany unleashed her submarines against American ships, Wilson moved in the direction of neutrality of thought, partly as the result of conscious effort (he refused to discuss the causes of war for fear it would prejudice him) and partly as a result of Allied assaults upon American rights and interests. Still, no one would maintain that he or his people ever became truly "impartial in thought," and no one would deny that his sympathies and those of his peo-

[16] Spring Rice to Grey, September 3, 1914, quoted in George M. Trevelyan, *Grey of Fallodon* (London, 1937), p. 355.

ple helped to explain neutral policies which, however just in terms of traditional international law, worked to the decisive advantage of England and her friends.

Thus Americans reacted—or, perhaps more accurately, divided—in a fashion quite different from 1793, when the last previous great war began and stones were thrown through the windows of the British legation at Philadelphia. They reacted quite differently from the way they would have reacted if the Berlin conference of 1878 had proved the prelude to a general war, or even if a European conflict had begun over the Kaiser's telegram to President Kruger in 1895. Americans were happy—too happy, in the view of some Britons—to remain outside the charnel house, but most of them extended their sympathies to the Anglo-French coalition. Traditional friendship for France partly explained this. Antipathy toward Germany also contributed, but, though suspicion and dislike were present, on the official level relations were better than a decade earlier. In 1909 A. Maurice Low maintained that, "Ten years ago, had there been a . . . war between England and Germany, the sympathy of Americans would have been overwhelmingly in favor of England, now sentiment would be more evenly balanced." [17] Low was both right and wrong. The enthusiastic Anglo-Saxonism which surrounded the Spanish-American War had declined, and fears of German penetration of the hemisphere had abated. But talk of an alliance or even firm cooperation had always been unreal, even in 1898, as men like John Hay well knew. By 1909, and increasingly in the half decade before Gavrilo Princip fired his pistol, the effulgence of 1898 had been replaced by less passionate, more substantial feelings. For the rapprochement to become real, the years after the turn of the century were even more important than those between 1895 and 1900.

Two other observers, Price Collier in 1909, the year of Low's article, and Frederick DeSumichrast in 1914, the testing year, explored the Anglo-American connection more deeply. Collier's book, *England and the English from an American Point of View,*

[17] *National Review* (London), vol. LIII (1909), p. 829.

contained a good deal of criticism of Britain, for some of which the author half apologized, and Collier overemphasized the traditional antipathy between the two peoples. He also observed that on balance England had taken the best road between socialism and democracy. "No intelligent American, no American indeed whose opinion is worth a fig," Collier maintained, "would rejoice to see this nation, which has taught the nations of the world the greatest lesson since Christianity, and that is the lesson of law, and order, and liberty, lose her grip." DeSumichrast warned Englishmen not to expect their cousins to be pale copies of themselves. Still, he observed, there were growing ties of sentiment between the two countries, an increasing conviction the two nations were in the forefront of democracy, even an increasing similarity in their institutions. "As the years go on," DeSumichrast predicted, ". . . the two lands will more and more draw nearer and more and more work for the good of humanity. In their hands lie, to a large extent, the securing of the progress of civilization, of concord, of peace." [18] The two writers, the first an American and the second a Briton who taught at Harvard, expressed feelings that had become common.

For this transformation there were many reasons. Some centered around the *annus mirabilis* of 1898, when Britain seemed more friendly than any other power and the United States embarked upon a course which undermined criticism of British imperialism. "Now that Americans have to meet the same problems and carry the same burden that England has wrestled with and staggered under these many years," Maurice Low observed, "there is a more just appreciation of the responsibilities and obligations of power. You cannot cast a stone at England for her Indian mote when you have your own Philippines beam ever before your eye; Canada seems less incomprehensible when Porto Rico is remembered." [19] The new imperialism was based in large part upon racism and the concept of the white man's burden, but

[18] Price Collier, *England and the English from an American Point of View* (New York, 1909), p. 131; Frederick C. DeSumichrast, *Americans and Britons* (New York, 1914), pp. 325–326.
[19] *National Review*, vol. LII (1908), p. 808.

this was not the only way in which racist views colored American attitudes. Anglo-Saxonism, so much emphasized in 1898, shaded into a less strident advocacy of friendship between the English-speaking peoples. They seemed to have special talents and particularly desirable qualities not possessed by others. Their countries were the garden-places of a troubled world.

Following the Spanish-American War there came about a great cleansing of the slate, the erasure of old and new issues between the two countries. Beginning with obliteration of the Clayton-Bulwer Treaty, the sweep continued through the dramatic events of Roosevelt's first administration and on to such things as arbitration of the Newfoundland fishery dispute, British recognition of American leadership in post-Díaz Mexico, and repeal of the canal toll preferences in 1914. England made the major concessions, adopting a conciliatory policy as part of a broad adjustment to new challenges she faced elsewhere, and after 1903 it was more a matter of keeping the blackboard clean than removing old graffiti. Underlying differences and conceptions in Asia did not disrupt Anglo-American friendship, nor did unfounded British suspicions that on some of those rare occasions when America dabbled in European politics her influence was unfavorable. "The new friendship of the English-speaking peoples," H. C. Allen has observed, "was an indispensable factor in determining the policy of each country and in ensuring that their paths ran on the whole parallel." [20] Only a tiny handful of Americans considered Britain an advanced line of their own defense, but the record of Anglo-American diplomacy and indeed of diplomacy generally demonstrated to the satisfaction of most American observers that the two countries were friends, not the antagonists they so long had been.

British and American politics also furthered the rapprochement. The success of Bryan in 1896 would probably have been a disaster, if only because England would have reacted to it as one. On the other hand, reactionary domination would have strengthened British critics of American materialism. Progressivism, par-

[20] H. C. Allen, *Great Britain and the United States* (New York, 1955), p. 614.

ticularly the domestic policies of Woodrow Wilson and, while he was President, Theodore Roosevelt, undermined this complaint and made it possible for DeSumichrast to maintain that the emphasis on money, money purely for its own sake, was passing. "Americans do love money," he wrote; "they have that in common with the rest of the civilized races of the earth. They also know how to use it wisely and generously. They do not all worship the Golden Calf: they do make the Almighty Dollar their servant." [21] On the English side, Conservatives presided over a major shift in diplomatic policies around the turn of the century, and their reputation for nationalism made them less vulnerable to criticism for conciliating the United States. By 1905 they had exhausted their usefulness, certainly as far as concerns relations with the United States. The Liberals not only maintained the general lines of English policy toward the United States but also quickly established, particularly by their domestic program, a position of respect in the eyes of Americans.

Public feeling sometimes differed from official opinion. In 1898 Englishmen in the streets—or the drawing rooms—indulged their emotions while Downing Street calculated coolly. During the Anglo-German action against Venezuela the government came under public criticism for jeopardizing American friendship. Generally the public, primarily for reasons of sympathy, and the ministry, from calculation, moved in tandem. In America, where public opinion more deeply influenced policy, the picture was very different. During the Alaskan controversy Roosevelt responded to and sometimes went beyond the opinion of his people. Otherwise, public sentiment, or fears of it, almost always served as a restraint on policy-makers. The managers of American diplomacy, from McKinley and Hay through Roosevelt to Taft and Wilson, wished for accommodation with England and contributed much to the new understanding, but not until Wilson fought for repeal of the canal tolls bill did one of them venture a direct challenge to contrary sentiment. By that time, diplomatic settlements, the trend of world events, and the course

21 DeSumichrast, *Americans and Britons*, pp. 217–218.

of British politics had done their work. Wilson's success showed that the people had almost caught up with the diplomats.

Doubts remained, as the war years were soon to show, and to the objections of Anglophobes would always be added the strength of isolationism, a tradition which failed to distinguish between one potential ally and another, which tarred all foreign influences and policies with the same brush of suspicion. Still, the transformation since 1895 had been striking. "The long and inevitable period of irritation and alienation between the two great English-speaking peoples has forever passed," said a leader of the peace movement in 1911, "and the time foretold by Whittier has come,—

> 'When closer strand shall lean to strand,
>   Till meet, beneath saluting flags,
>   The eagle of our mountain-crags,
> The lion of our Motherland!' " [22]

America's traditional enemy, the nation which more than any other had tried to strangle the republic, had become the great power upon which citizens of the United States looked most favorably. Anglo-American relations had changed in a fashion decisive for the world's future.

[22] Edwin D. Mead, *The International Duty of the United States and Great Britain* (*World Peace Foundation Pamphlets*, vol. I, No. 1, pt. 4; Boston, 1911), p. 29.

Note on the Sources

Few periods in world diplomacy have been more extensively studied than the two decades prior to 1914, yet Anglo-American relations remain incompletely explored. This neglect is unfortunate, for it seems clear that, in long-range terms, the growth of understanding and sympathy between the English-speaking peoples was one of the most important international developments of the period. Fortunately, particularly in the few years since the opening of British archives, able scholars have dealt with the first portion of the rapprochement. Alexander E. Campbell, *Great Britain and the United States, 1895–1903* (Glasgow, 1960), and, somewhat more narrowly conceived, Charles S. Campbell, *Anglo-American Understanding, 1898–1903* (Baltimore, 1957), are both excellent, well-informed monographs. John A. S. Grenville, *Lord Salisbury and Foreign Policy: The Close of the Nineteenth Century* (London, 1964), though silent on the Open Door and Alaska boundary questions, probes deeply into other aspects of British policy, and Ernest R. May, *Imperial Democracy: The Emergence of America as a Great Power* (New York, 1961), is helpful on events around the turn of the century. More than any other material examined, these works provide the foundation for the first part of this book.

There are no comparable treatments of the period after 1903. The story is carried to 1906 in Lionel M. Gelber, *The Rise of Anglo-American Friendship* (London, 1938), but this study is necessarily based upon limited sources. H. C. Allen, *Great Britain and the United States* (New York, 1955), by far the best introductory survey, deals only briefly with the pre-war decade. It is therefore necessary to rely upon special studies, none of them concentrating on Anglo-American relations, and upon the correspondence and biographies of contemporary figures. Here, perhaps the most notable are two works which help one to understand a key leader— Howard K. Beale, *Theodore Roosevelt and the Rise of America to World Power* (Baltimore, 1956), a highly detailed, comprehensively researched study, and Elting E. Morison, ed., *The Letters of Theodore Roosevelt* (8 vols.; Cambridge, 1951–1954).

Most of the above works deal with relations between governments.

There is no satisfactory treatment of less formal relations between the two peoples. Bruce M. Russett, *Community and Contention: Britain and America in the Twentieth Century* (Cambridge, 1963), is sometimes suggestive but too prone to substitute data for understanding. Richard H. Heindel, *The American Impact on Great Britain, 1898–1914* (Philadelphia, 1940), is helpful for one side of the story, and the broader study, Cushing Strout, *The American Image of the Old World* (New York, 1963), contains a strong chapter on American views of England at this time. Much, however, remains to be done.

The following bibliography is highly selective. It attempts to single out those works by historians which contribute most, either directly or by implication, to an understanding of Anglo-American relations. Some of the best literature on pre-war diplomacy is therefore omitted, as are all but a few of the relevant contemporary materials. References to the latter will often be found in the footnotes, which give sources of direct quotations.

CHAPTER TWO

The Venezuelan controversy is well traced in Campbell, *Great Britain and the United States*, and May, *Imperial Democracy*. Dexter Perkins, *The Monroe Doctrine, 1867–1907* (Baltimore, 1937), places this episode in the context of the evolution of the great American diplomatic doctrine. Cleveland's unusual stridency still baffles historians. For various explanations, see Allan Nevins, *Grover Cleveland: A Study in Courage* (New York, 1932); John A. S. Grenville and George B. Young, *Politics, Strategy, and American Diplomacy: Studies in Foreign Policy, 1873–1917* (New Haven, 1966), which stresses the role of Scruggs; and Walter La-Feber, *The New Empire: An Interpretation of American Expansion, 1860–1898* (Ithaca, 1963), which argues the importance of commercial motives. On the British side, Grenville, *Salisbury*, based upon broad manuscript research, has much to say.

Among the many works dealing with the American election of 1896, Richard Hofstadter, *The Age of Reform: From Bryan to F.D.R.* (New York, 1955), and J. Rogers Hollingworth, *The Whirligig of Politics: The Democracy of Cleveland and Bryan* (Chicago, 1963), are perhaps most helpful for the purposes of this volume. English views of the candidates and the campaign are conveyed in the account of an English newspaperman, George W. Steevens, *The Land of the Dollar* (Edinburgh, 1897), and a seminar paper prepared at the University of Michigan by Sister John Fisher, I.H.M., "British Impressions of William Jennings Bryan in the Election of 1896."

Nelson M. Blake, "The Olney-Pauncefote Treaty of 1897," *American Historical Review* (Washington), vol. L (1944–1945), pp. 228–243, is standard. Additional material can be found in W. Stull Holt, *Treaties De-*

feated by the Senate (Baltimore, 1933); Henry James, *Richard Olney and His Public Service* (Boston, 1923); and May, *Imperial Democracy*. The history of Bradford's manuscript is told in the introduction to William Bradford, *Of Plymouth Plantation* (Samuel E. Morison, ed.; New York, 1953).

CHAPTER THREE

Previous studies of European reactions to the Spanish-American clash are displaced by May, *Imperial Democracy*, based on broad archival research. For the British position, added material is in Campbell, *Anglo-American Understanding*; Heindel, *American Impact*; and especially R. G. Neale, *Great Britain and United States Expansion, 1898–1900* (East Lansing, 1966), fuller in detail than any other work. Special aspects of wartime relations are treated in Thomas A. Bailey, "Dewey and the Germans at Manila Bay," *American Historical Review*, vol. LXV (1939–1940), pp. 59–81; William R. Braisted, *The United States Navy in the Pacific, 1897–1909* (Austin, 1958); and Norman Penlington, *Canada and Imperialism, 1896–1899* (Toronto, 1965).

The British reaction to America's decision for empire is examined in the works mentioned in the previous paragraph, and also in Geoffrey Seed, "British Reactions to American Imperialism Reflected in Journals of Opinion, 1898–1900," *Political Science Quarterly* (New York), vol. LXXIII (1958), pp. 254–272, an article which, though based on a limited sample, is very valuable, particularly for the light it throws upon imperialistic sentiment in England. Merze Tate, *The United States and the Hawaiian Kingdom: A Political History* (New Haven, 1965), adds a few details.

John R. DosPassos, *The Anglo-Saxon Century* (New York, 1903), conveniently summarizes all sorts of proposals for closer understanding, even alliance. See also Joseph L. Garvin and Julian S. Amery, *The Life of Joseph Chamberlain* (4 vols.; London, 1932–1951), vol. III; and Tyler Dennett's sympathetic biography, *John Hay: From Poetry to Politics* (New York, 1933).

CHAPTER FOUR

The literature on imperialism and the imperialistic spirit is immense and often disputative. While there is no completely satisfactory study of British imperialism, Elie Halévy, *Imperialism and the Rise of Labour* (E. I. Watkin, trans.; *A History of the English People in the Nineteenth Century*, vol. V; rev. ed., New York, 1961), contains much helpful information, as does William L. Langer, *The Diplomacy of Imperialism* (2 vols.; New York, 1935). Foster Rhea Dulles, *The Imperial Years*

(New York, 1956), and May, *Imperial Democracy,* describe American events, and Ernest R. May, "American Imperialism: A Reinterpretation," *Perspectives in American History* (Cambridge), vol. I (1967), stresses American interest in British developments. See also the interesting recent study, Richard Koebner and Helmut R. Schmidt, *Imperialism: The Story and Significance of a Political Word, 1840–1960* (Cambridge, Eng., 1964).

In addition, certain studies, when laid side by side, suggest parallels between the British and American experience. For example, LaFeber, *The New Empire,* and Ronald Robinson and John Gallagher, *Africa and the Victorians: The Climax of Imperialism in the Dark Continent* (New York, 1961), dealing with the United States and England respectively, suggest that in neither country was the imperialism of the period as revolutionary as is usually assumed. Richard Hofstadter, "Manifest Destiny and the Philippines," Daniel Aaron, ed., *America in Crisis* (New York, 1952), describes the connection between domestic unrest and imperialism, an idea also explored in Bernard Semmel, *Imperialism and Social Reform: English Social-Imperial Thought, 1895–1914* (Cambridge, 1960). Albert K. Weinberg, *Manifest Destiny: A Study of Nationalist Expansionism in American History* (Baltimore, 1935), in a sense finds a counterpart in Archibald P. Thornton, *The Imperial Idea and Its Enemies: A Study in British Power* (London, 1959).

Thomas F. Gossett, *Race: The History of an Idea in America* (Dallas, 1963), contains a chapter on the Anglo-Saxonism of this period. One should also examine the subtle discussion in Beale, *Roosevelt,* as well as Richard Hofstadter, *Social Darwinism in American Thought* (rev. ed.; Boston, 1955), and Claude G. Bowers, *Beveridge and the Progressive Era* (Cambridge, 1932). For British views, it is necessary to examine contemporary writings, particularly the usually self-congratulatory discussions of Edmond Demolins, *Anglo-Saxon Superiority: To What It Is Due* (Louis B. Lavigne, trans.; New York, 1898).

Frank Aydelotte, *The American Rhodes Scholarships* (Princeton, 1946), is adequate.

CHAPTER FIVE

Although it fails to generalize about opinion in the United States, John A. Ferguson, *American Diplomacy and the Boer War* (Philadelphia, 1939), contains masses of details upon sympathies and policies. Campbell, *Anglo-American Understanding,* is also helpful. An American ally of Jameson and Rhodes describes his role in *The Autobiography of John Hays Hammond* (2 vols.; New York, 1935). Mrs. George Cornwallis-West, *The Reminiscences of Lady Randolph Churchill* (New York, 1909), recounts the story of the hospital ship.

Beale, *Roosevelt,* is essential to an understanding of Rooseveltian diplomacy. The best biography of the President, although of course far less full than Beale on diplomacy, is William Henry Harbaugh, *Power and Responsibility: The Life and Times of Theodore Roosevelt* (New York, 1961). John Morton Blum, *The Republican Roosevelt* (Cambridge, 1954), a biographical essay, contains many penetrating judgments.

American and foreign diplomats of the period are assessed in Beale, *Roosevelt.* Nelson M. Blake, "Ambassadors at the Court of Theodore Roosevelt," *Mississippi Valley Historical Review* (Menosha, Wis.), vol. XLII (1955–1956), pp. 179–206, catches the spirit and adds a few details. There is no biography of Sir Michael Herbert, and Stephen Gwynn, *The Letters and Friendships of Sir Cecil Spring Rice* (2 vols.; Cambridge, 1929), although very useful for the correspondence it contains, is uncritical. Allan Nevins, *Henry White: Thirty Years of American Diplomacy* (New York, 1930), capably describes the career of a professional diplomat, a well-connected Anglophile, and a blandly enigmatic man, but Edward S. Martin, *The Life of Joseph Hodges Choate* (2 vols.; New York, 1920), is a very bad scissors-and-paste job, while Royal Cortissoz, *The Life of Whitelaw Reid* (2 vols.; New York, 1921), simply shows that wealth, good will, and a talent for after-dinner speaking can make the success of an ambassador in London.

CHAPTER SIX

American economic histories are of surprisingly little help; their major concern lies with domestic developments. A useful compendium is Bureau of the Census, *Historical Statistics of the United States, Colonial Times to 1957* (Washington, 1960), while Russett, *Community and Contention,* has several interesting things to say. On the English side, Elie Halévy's two volumes, *Imperialism and the Rise of Labour* and *The Rule of Democracy* (E. I. Watkin, trans.; *A History of the English People in the Nineteenth Century,* vol. VI; rev. ed., New York, 1961), contribute more than economic histories. However, J. H. Clapham, *An Economic History of Modern Britain,* vol. III (New York, 1938), convincingly if inadvertently demonstrates the greater vigor of American industrial life.

British foreign investments and overseas trade are the subject of many special studies, notably S. B. Saul, *Studies in British Overseas Trade, 1870–1914* (Liverpool, 1960), and A. K. Cairncross, *Home and Foreign Investment, 1870–1913* (Cambridge, Eng., 1953). J. Fred Rippy, *British Investments in Latin America, 1822–1949* (Minneapolis, 1959), and Alan K. Manchester, *British Preëminence in Brazil: Its Rise and Decline* (Chapel Hill, 1933), provide information on trade with South America, and Ross J. S. Hoffman, *Great Britain and the German Trade Rivalry, 1875–1914* (Philadelphia, 1933), occasionally indicates the triangular nature of the competition. On British investments in the United States, see Cleona Lewis, *America's Stake in International Investments* (Washington, 1938). The flow of capital in the other direction is explored in Matthew Simon and David E. Novack, "Some Dimensions of the American Commercial Invasion of Europe, 1871–1914: An Introductory Essay," *Journal of Economic History* (Chicago), vol. XXIV (1964), pp. 591–605, and John H. Dunning, *American Investment in British Manufacturing Industry* (London, 1958). Heindel, *American Impact*, also describes the reaction to the "American invasion."

For the special problem of American economic relations with Canada, the most useful studies are Edwin G. Burrows, "Canadian Reciprocity, 1911" (unpublished honors thesis, University of Michigan, 1964); L. Ethan Ellis, *Reciprocity, 1911: A Study in Canadian-American Relations* (New Haven, 1939); H. L. Keenleyside, *Canada and the United States: Some Aspects of the History of the Republic and the Provinces* (New York, 1929); and Charles C. Tansill, *Canadian-American Relations, 1875–1911* (New Haven, 1943).

In the absence of a detailed history of the movement for imperial preference, one must rely on such works as Garvin and Amery, *Chamberlain*, vol. IV, and Semmel, *Imperialism and Reform*.

It is far easier to establish the acceptability of British literature in the United States than that of American writings in England. Alice Payne Hackett, *Fifty Years of Best Sellers, 1895–1945* (New York, 1945), provides lists which show the popularity of English authors, particularly Sir Gilbert Parker, and their attitudes have been assessed in a seminar paper by Norman McLennan, "American Images of England." Unfortunately, Clarence Gohdes, *American Literature in Nineteenth-Century England* (New York, 1944), has little to say about the century's end, and Amy Cruse, *After the Victorians* (London, 1938), is superficial. In a seminar paper, "American Literature in England, 1895–1907," J. Fraser Cocks III has examined British reviews of American books considered worthy of notice by the *Times Literary Supplement*. One of the American authors most successful in England reminisces about the situation in Gertrude Atherton, "The American Novel in England," *Bookman* (New York), vol. XXX (1909–1910), pp. 633–640.

For the views of American textbooks and scholars, two volumes by Bessie Louise Pierce are still valuable, *Public Opinion and the Teaching of History in the United States* (New York, 1926) and *Civic Attitudes in American School Textbooks* (Chicago, 1930). Supplementary material is provided by Charles Altschul, *The American Revolution in Our School Text-Books* (New York, 1917); Ruth M. Elson, *Guardians of Tradition: American Schoolbooks of the Nineteenth Century* (Lincoln, 1964); Heindel, *American Impact*; and John Higham *et al.*, *History* (Englewood Cliffs, 1965). Very interesting, particularly for its discussion of racism, is Edward N. Saveth, *American Historians and European Immigrants, 1875–1925* (New York, 1948).

Most studies of immigrant stock either begin at or emphasize the period after 1914. An exception is Rowland T. Berthoff's informative study, *British Immigrants in Industrial America, 1790–1950* (Cambridge, 1953). For the Irish, the two most important books are Charles C. Tansill, *America and the Fight for Irish Freedom, 1866–1922* (New York, 1957), and James McGurrin, *Bourke Cockran: A Free Lance in American Politics* (New York, 1948), but both are strongly partisan and superficial. Randolph S. Churchill, *Winston S. Churchill,* vol. I (Cambridge, 1966), touches upon the strange friendship of Cockran and Churchill. On the Germans, John A. Hawgood, *The Tragedy of German America: The Germans in the United States of America during the Nineteenth Century and After* (New York, 1940), is disappointing, and Clifton James Child, *The German-American in Politics, 1914–1917* (Madison, 1939), and Carl Wittke, *German-Americans and the World War* (Columbus, 1936), contain only a few insights. Melvin Small, "The American Image of Germany, 1906–1914" (University of Michigan dissertation, 1965), is a thoughtful and intensive study which fills a void.

The British Left's dislike of the United States is made apparent in D. W. Brogan, *American Aspects* (London, 1964), a collection of penetrating essays, and in more detail in Henry Pelling, *America and the British Left from Bright to Bevan* (London, 1956). For the ultraconservative position, one must have recourse to contemporary writings. The views of British visitors to the United States are commented upon and collected in Allan Nevins, ed., *America Through British Eyes* (New York, 1948).

The Pilgrim Society finds an uncritical historian in Sir Harry Brittain, *Pilgrim Partners* (St. Albans, 1942).

The close contact between British and American reformers is stressed in Arthur Mann, "British Social Thought and American Reformers of the Progressive Era," *Mississippi Valley Historical Review,* vol. XLII (1955–1956), pp. 672–692. Further details are in Aaron I. Abell, *The Urban Impact on American Protestantism, 1865–1900* (London, 1943); Charles H. Hopkins, *The Rise of the Social Gospel in American Protestantism, 1865–1914* (New Haven, 1940); Henry F. May, *Protestant Churches and Industrial America* (New York, 1949); and Georgiana P. McEntee, *The Social Catholic Movement in Great Britain* (New York, 1927).

Hesketh Pearson, *The Pilgrim Daughters* (London, 1961), is entertaining popular history.

CHAPTER SEVEN

British naval policy, necessarily discussed in general studies of diplomacy, finds special treatment in E. L. Woodward, *Great Britain and the German Navy* (Oxford, 1935), and, more helpful for the present study, Arthur J. Marder, *From the Dreadnought to Scapa Flow,* vol. I (London, 1961), and Kenneth Bourne, *Britain and the Balance of Power in North*

America, 1815–1908 (Berkeley and Los Angeles, 1967). Halévy, *The Rule of Democracy*, discusses parliamentary debates on the two-nation standard.

England's withdrawal from the Western Hemisphere, perhaps foreshadowed during the Venezuelan controversy of 1895–1896 and reflected in naval policy, gained speed at the time of the contemporaneous disputes over the Alaskan boundary and the isthmian canal. Beale, *Roosevelt*; Campbell, *Great Britain and the United States*; Campbell, *Anglo-American Understanding*; and Dennett, *Hay*, all deal with these disputes, differing only in detail and emphasis. John A. Garraty, *Henry Cabot Lodge* (New York, 1953), draws on the otherwise almost unused Lodge papers to deepen the story of both episodes. For the Alaskan boundary, see also Tansill, *Canadian-American Relations*, based on Canadian and American archives, and for the Hay-Pauncefote treaties, see also J. A. S. Grenville, "Great Britain and the Isthmian Canal," *American Historical Review*, vol. LXI (1955–1956), pp. 48–69; Grenville, *Salisbury*; and Holt, *Treaties Defeated by the Senate*. Dwight C. Minor, *The Fight for the Panama Route* (New York, 1940), is invaluable for background.

CHAPTER EIGHT

For the Anglo-German blockade of Venezuela and the Roosevelt corollary, Perkins, *Monroe Doctrine, 1867–1907*, is undisplaced thirty years after publication. Although Seward W. Livermore, "Theodore Roosevelt, the American Navy, and the Venezuelan Crisis," *American Historical Review*, vol. LI (1945–1946), and, less cautiously, Beale, *Roosevelt*, challenge Perkins' interpretation of Roosevelt's policy toward Germany, they confirm his account of Anglo-American relations during this affair. The story of the Roosevelt corollary is deepened and also extended past 1907 in Dana G. Munro, *Intervention and Dollar Diplomacy in the Caribbean, 1900–1921* (Princeton, 1964). J. Fred Rippy, "The British Bondholders and the Roosevelt Corollary of the Monroe Doctrine," *Political Science Quarterly*, vol. XLIX (1934), pp. 195–206, shows how Santo Domingo's creditors welcomed the President's actions.

The most balanced treatment of the Mexican imbroglio is in Arthur Link, *Wilson: The New Freedom* (Princeton, 1956). This treatment is supplemented by Peter A. R. Calvert, "The Mexican Revolution, 1910–1914: The Diplomacy of Anglo-American Conflict" (Cambridge University dissertation, 1964), based largely on British archives and very critical of the United States. Burton J. Hendrick, *The Life and Letters of Walter H. Page* (3 vols.; Garden City, 1922–1925), exposes American suspiciousness. John A. Spender, *Weetman Pearson First Viscount Cowdray* (London, 1930), is virtually silent on Mexican and British politics.

CHAPTER NINE

A. Whitney Griswold, *The Far Eastern Policy of the United States* (New York, 1938), is standard but badly in need of revision. For example, Griswold's implication that British influence lay behind the Open Door notes has been disproved, most recently and conclusively in Neale, *Britain and Expansion*. Campbell, *Great Britain and the United States*, and Campbell, *Anglo-American Understanding*, also discuss the English position. Dennett, *Hay*, and Paul A. Varg, *Open Door Diplomat: The Life of W. W. Rockhill* (Urbana, 1952), trace the formulation of the notes. A work which appeared after the present volume was completed, Thomas J. McCormick, *China Market: America's Quest for Informal Empire, 1893–1901* (Chicago, 1967), also sheds light on American aspirations and policy.

Ian H. Nish, *The Anglo-Japanese Alliance: The Diplomacy of Two Island Empires, 1894–1907* (London, 1966), a well-researched and judicious work, displaces Chang-Fu Chang, *The Anglo-Japanese Alliance* (Baltimore, 1931), written before much archival material was available. A stimulating study, George Monger, *The End of Isolation: British Foreign Policy, 1900–1907* (London, 1963), stresses, perhaps too much, the Asian emphasis of British policy. Grenville, *Salisbury*, sheds new light on the Prime Minister's role in construction of the alliance, and Zara S. Steiner, "Great Britain and the Creation of the Anglo-Japanese Alliance," *Journal of Modern History* (Chicago), vol. XXXI (1959), pp. 27–36, is interesting. None of these works gives much attention to American policy or reactions to the alliance.

Roosevelt's role during the Russo-Japanese War is discussed in three early works, Tyler Dennett, *Roosevelt and the Russo-Japanese War* (Garden City, 1925); Griswold, *Far Eastern Policy*; and Gelber, *Rise of Anglo-American Friendship*. Beale, *Roosevelt*, and especially Raymond A. Esthus, *Theodore Roosevelt and Japan* (Seattle, 1966), an exceptionally able study, add both details and insights. Monger, *End of Isolation*, describes Britain's difficulties, and Gwynn, *Spring Rice*, shows how they led that English diplomat down unpleasant paths. John A. White, *The Diplomacy of the Russo-Japanese War* (Princeton, 1964), is comprehensive and detailed.

Durand's downfall is sympathetically treated by a friend, Sir Percy M. Sykes, in *Sir Mortimer Durand* (London, 1926). Esme William Howard, Baron Howard of Penrith, *Theatre of Life* (London, 1936), recalls Howard's conversations with Durand at the time. Major-General Lord Edward Gleichen, *A Guardsman's Memoirs* (London, 1932), is more revealing than it intends.

Japanese-American relations during the latter portion of Roosevelt's administrations are best treated in Esthus, *Roosevelt and Japan*. Thomas

A. Bailey, *Theodore Roosevelt and the Japanese-American Crises* (Stanford, 1934), and, more briefly, Beale, *Roosevelt*, and Griswold, *Far Eastern Policy*, cover much of the same ground. In addition, especially for the Taft-Katsura and Root-Takahira agreements, one should consult Raymond A. Esthus, "The Changing Concept of the Open Door, 1899–1910," *Mississippi Valley Historical Review*, vol. XLVI (1959–1960), pp. 435–454, and Charles E. Neu, "Theodore Roosevelt and American Involvement in the Far East, 1901–1909," *Pacific Historical Review* (Berkeley and Los Angeles), vol. XXXV (1966), pp. 433–449. Robert A. Hart, *The Great White Fleet: Its Voyage Around the World, 1907–1909* (Boston, 1965) is a colorful account, incomplete on the diplomatic side.

For dollar diplomacy in the Orient, Charles Vevier, *The United States and China, 1906–1913: A Study in Finance and Diplomacy* (New Brunswick, 1955), and Herbert Croly, *Willard Straight* (New York, 1925), are basic. Added material is provided by Esthus, *Roosevelt and Japan*; Griswold, *Far Eastern Policy*; Varg, *Rockhill*; and a somewhat emotional account by a witness, John Gilbert Reid, *The Manchu Abdication and the Powers, 1908–1912: An Episode in Pre-War Diplomacy* (Berkeley, 1935). E. W. Edwards, "Great Britain and the Manchurian Railways Question, 1909–1910," *English Historical Review* (London), vol. LXXXI (1966), pp. 740–769, elucidates Grey's difficulties during this episode.

CHAPTER TEN

German-American friction around the turn of the century is mentioned in most histories of the period, but see especially Perkins, *Monroe Doctrine, 1867–1907*. For the later period, there is no substitute for Small, "American Image of Germany." Braisted, *Navy in the Pacific*, and Grenville and Young, *Politics, Strategy, and Diplomacy*, explain American strategic planning. The *Memoirs* of Count Bernstorff (Eric Sutton, trans.; New York, 1936), are quite perceptive.

The literature on the arbitration movement and the Hague conferences, much of it nearly contemporary, is immense, but almost none of it explored the Anglo-American theme. James B. Scott, *The Hague Peace Conferences of 1899 and 1907* (2 vols.; Baltimore, 1909), and Joseph H. Choate, *The Two Hague Conferences* (Princeton, 1913), like other publications of the time, suffer from lack of perspective, while the more scholarly treatments, Merze Tate, *The Disarmament Illusion: The Movement for a Limitation of Armaments to 1907* (New York, 1942), and Calvin D. Davis, *The United States and the First Hague Peace Conference* (Ithaca, 1962), are unsympathetic to the emotional fervor of the movement. Barbara W. Tuchman, *The Proud Tower* (New York, 1966), is sardonic. Philip C. Jessup, *Elihu Root* (2 vols.; New York, 1938); Holt, *Treaties Defeated by the Senate*; and John P. Campbell, "Taft, Roosevelt and the

Arbitration Treaties of 1911," *Journal of American History* (Menosha, Wis.), vol. LIII (1966–1967), pp. 279–298, discuss the fate of bilateral treaties. Tansill, *Canadian-American Relations*, explores the successful use of arbitral machinery.

The American role during the first Moroccan crisis is made clear in Beale, *Roosevelt*, and Nevins, *White*. Dennett, *Roosevelt and the Russo-Japanese War*, and Gelber, *Anglo-American Friendship*, stress the connection between this controversy and the one in the Pacific. Eugene N. Anderson, *The First Moroccan Crisis, 1904–1906* (Chicago, 1930), detailed on the role of European powers, relies upon Dennett to explain that of the United States.

American attitudes toward European politics in the years immediately preceding World War I deserve much more attention than they have received. Robert E. Osgood, *Ideals and Self-Interest in America's Foreign Relations* (Chicago, 1953), a very able work, provides a take-off point. Also helpful are portions of Beale, *Roosevelt*; Norman A. Graebner, ed., *Ideas and Diplomacy: Readings in the Intellectual Tradition of American Foreign Policy* (New York, 1964); and Small, "American Image of Germany." William C. Askew and J. Fred Rippy, "The United States and Europe's Strife, 1908–1913," *Journal of Politics* (Gainesville), vol. IV (1942), pp. 68–79, concentrates on Einstein. Contemporary literature is abundant.

CHAPTER ELEVEN

For the rise of the Liberals, Halévy, *The Rule of Democracy*, is most useful. Roy Jenkins, *Asquith: Portrait of a Man and an Era* (London, 1964), is perceptive; George M. Trevelyan, *Grey of Fallodon* (London, 1937), is sympathetic; and H. A. L. Fisher, *James Bryce (Viscount Bryce of Dechmont, O.M.)* (2 vols.; New York, 1927), is disappointing on Bryce's service in the United States.

In the absence of a scholarly treatment of America's reaction to the home-rule controversy, one is forced to rely upon Tansill, *America and the Fight for Irish Freedom*, a passionate work. McGurrin, *Cockran*, makes clear the factionalism of Irish-Americans.

The multivolume biography of Wilson by Arthur S. Link, still in progress, is the best study of the Democratic President. See also the short volume, Arthur S. Link, *Wilson the Diplomatist* (rev. ed.; Chicago, 1965). William Diamond, *The Economic Thought of Woodrow Wilson* (Baltimore, 1943), shows the President's obligations to English economists, while his debt to British political theorists emerges in Harley Notter, *The Origins of the Foreign Policy of Woodrow Wilson* (Baltimore, 1937), an exhaustive study somewhat broader than its title. There are no satisfactory studies of Bryan during the period after 1908. Hendrick, *Page*, is very revealing for the letters it contains.

Naval visits during the Taft-Wilson period are discussed in Seward W. Livermore, "The American Navy as a Factor in World Politics, 1903–1913," *American Historical Review*, vol. LXIII (1957–1958). The same author's "American Naval Development, 1898–1914" (Harvard University dissertation, 1943), repays study. See also Elting E. Morison, *Admiral Sims and the Modern American Navy* (Boston, 1942).

CHAPTER TWELVE

A seminar paper by Thomas Maddux, "The Movement to Celebrate the Centenary of the Treaty of Ghent, 1908–1915," is invaluable in the absence of printed material other than the Marquess of Crewe, "The Sulgrave Institution and the Anglo-American Society," *Nineteenth Century and After* (London), vol. XCI (1922), pp. 396–397, brief and chatty.

Link, *Wilson: The New Freedom*, explains the President's victory in the fight over canal tolls. Further valuable material is in Ray Stannard Baker, *Woodrow Wilson: Life and Letters* (8 vols.; Garden City, 1927–1939); E. David Cronon, ed., *The Cabinet Diaries of Josephus Daniels, 1913–1921* (Lincoln, Neb., 1963); and Hendrick, *Page*.

Although reactions to the outbreak of war in Europe are best studied by an examination of the contemporary press, both Arthur S. Link, *Wilson: The Struggle for Neutrality* (Princeton, 1960), and Henry F. May, *The End of American Innocence: A Study in the First Years of Our Own Time, 1912–1917* (New York, 1959), contain very shrewd analyses of the depth of American feeling and the divisions in American society. Detail is provided by specialized studies, Edwin Costrell, *How Maine Viewed the War, 1914–1917* (Orono, 1940); John C. Crighton, *Missouri and the World War, 1914–1917: A Study in Public Opinion* (Columbia, 1947); and Cedric C. Cummins, *Indiana Public Opinion and the World War, 1914–1917* (Indianapolis, 1945). For Grew, see Waldo H. Heinrichs, Jr., *American Ambassador: Joseph C. Grew and the Development of the United States Diplomatic Tradition* (Boston, 1966).

Index

Abbott, Lyman, favors Anglo-American alliance, 54–55
Adams, Brooks, 53; and growth of American power, 8–9; *Law of Civilization and Decay*, 69–70; emphasizes markets, 71; fear of Russia, 77, 242; and Boer war, 94; and decline of Britain, 270
Adams, George B., favors Anglo-American alliance, 55
Adams, Henry, 33; attitudes toward Britain, 4–5, 131, 154, 156; and growth of American power, 8; attitudes toward Germany, 11, 40; relations with Hay, 56, 114, 156, 215; pessimism, 89; and Boer war, 92, 94; and Roosevelt, 102; and Spring Rice, 108, 223; praises Open Door policy, 215; on European politics, 267; on Bryce, 277
Adamson, William C., 303
Aguinaldo, Emilio, leads Filipinos against Spain, 45–46; revolt against United States, 50, 86, 93, 248
Alaskan boundary dispute, 106, 110; origins, 162–163; negotiated, 163–168; modus vivendi, 164–166; settlement, 168–171; reactions to, 171–172, 184–185, 287; settlement evaluated, 172–173, 274, 313; and isthmian question, 174, 175
Alford, John, criticizes Pound as American, 131
Algeciras, *see* Moroccan crisis, first
Allen, H. C., on Anglo-American friendship, 312
Allen, Horace N., and Korea, 219
Alliance, Anglo-American, *see* Entente, Anglo-American
Alliances, British, search for, 156–157, 217. *See also* Anglo-Japanese alliance; Entente, Anglo-American; Entente cordiale; Germany, alliance with Britain
Altgeld, John P., 22

Altschul, Charles, on historians' prejudice, 140–141, 155
Alverstone, Richard, Viscount, and Alaskan boundary dispute, 169–172
"American invasion," of British industry, 124–125
American Protective Association, 143
American Revolution, Trevelyan's history of, 139; historical treatment of, 140–141
Ancient Order of Hibernians, and Boer war, 91–92
Angell, Norman, 256
Anglo-American Exposition, 300
Anglo-American League, 54, 115
Anglo-French entente, *see* Entente cordiale
Anglo-German agreement of 1900, 12
Anglo-Japanese alliance, 12, 209, 239; negotiated, 217–218; American views of, 218–221; revised (1905), 227; Grey's views of, 230–232, 275; revised (1911), 234–235; and Taft-Knox treaty, 253; and Liberals, 275
Anglophobia, American, influence of, 4–5, 118, 120, 141, 143–144, 191, 267, 272, 314; and followers of Bryan, 21–22; in election of 1900, 97–98; and diamond jubilee of Queen Victoria, 115–116; Roosevelt evaluates, 154; and Alaskan boundary dispute, 164, 172; and Hay-Pauncefote treaty, 177, 178; and arbitration treaties, 255–257; in election of 1912, 294; and Panama tolls controversy, 304
Anglo-Saxon Review (London), 94
Anglo-Saxonism, *see* English-speaking peoples
Anti-British Alliance Society, 52–53
Anti-imperialism, American, and Britain, 49, 53
Anti-Semitism, 76–77
Arbitration, and Venezuela dispute (1895–1896), 17–19; Olney-Paunce-

BRADFORD PERKINS

Bradford Perkins is Professor of History at the University of Michigan. He has published three books on the history of Anglo-American relations from 1795 to 1823. The subject of this volume formed the basis for the Commonwealth Fund Lectures at University College, London, in 1965.